W9-CUX-100

ONE OF THE FORGOTTEN THINGS

ONE OF THE FORGOTTEN THINGS

Getúlio Vargas and Brazilian Social Control, 1930–1954

R. S. ROSE

Contributions in Latin American Studies, Number 15

GREENWOOD PRESS
Westport, Connecticut • London

Library of Congress Cataloging-in-Publication Data

Rose, R. S., 1943–
    One of the forgotten things : Getúlio Vargas and Brazilian social control, 1930–1954 /
by R. S. Rose.
      p.   cm.— (Contributions in Latin American studies, ISSN 1054–6790 ; no. 15)
    Includes bibliographical references (p.—) and index.
    ISBN 0–313–31358–X (alk. paper)
    1. Vargas, Getúlio, 1883–1954. 2. Brazil—Politics and government—1930–1945. 3.
Brazil—Politics and government—1945–1954. 4. Social control—Brazil—History—20th
century. 5. Political corruption—Brazil—History—20th century. I. Title: One of the forgotten
things. II. Title. III. Series.
F2538.V3 R67 2000
981.06'1—dc21   99–088457

British Library Cataloguing in Publication Data is available.

Library of Congress Catalog Card Number: 99–088457
ISBN: 0–313–31358–X
ISSN: 1054–6790

First published in 2000

Greenwood Press, 88 Post Road West, Westport, CT 06881
An imprint of Greenwood Publishing Group, Inc.
www.greenwood.com

Printed in the United States of America

The paper used in this book complies with the
Permanent Paper Standard issued by the National
Information Standards Organization (Z39.48–1984).

10 9 8 7 6 5 4 3 2 1

In memory of Juanita Vertreese Rose

Contents

A photo essay follows page 76

Preface

This project owes a debt of gratitude to numerous people. First to receive thanks, as always, is Knut Sveri, my teacher from the University of Stockholm. Knut, inspirasjonen din skal aldri glemmes! Then comes Peter Wickman who kept me focused. Leslie Laczko and J. Barry Gurdin gave me the encouragement to keep going when I could not find an academic appointment in the United States.

I will forever be indebted to Nilo Batista for graciously allowing me to be the first civilian researcher to spend 14 months looking through the mountain of documents comprising the DOPS Archives[1] at the Arquivo Público do Estado do Rio de Janeiro. Also deserving thanks are Luís Carlos Prestes and John W.F. Dulles, two truly inspiring, but totally different men. Katie Chase and John W.F. Dulles proofread the manuscript and offered their constructive criticisms. Douglas Corbishley unfailingly provided a friendly interface between aging computer software and the present.

There were a score of others who somehow found time to lend a hand at just the right moment. Among these were Muriel Agnew, Кирилл Михайлович Андерсон, Thomé Amado, Anonymous-3,[2] Paulo Roberto de Araújo, Harold E. Barron, Lars Erik Björlin, Armando Boito Jr., Cecil Borer, Suely Braga, Mike Conniff, Андрей Доронин, Leila Menezes Duarte, Noé Gertel, Kurt Jacobsen, Yelena Gogolieyn, Jacob Gorender, Stanley E. Hilton, Rita J. Jeremy, José Joffily, Karén V. Ketendjian, Jeff Lesser, Robert M. Levine, Maria de Fatima Lima, Solomão Malina, Lícia Carvalho Medeiros, Eliana Furtado de Mendonça, Michael Ormsby, Waldecy Catharina Magalhães Pederia, Jorge J.C. Posse, Anita Leocadia Prestes, Lygia Prestes, Maria do Carmo Ribeiro, Yuri Ribeiro, Jose Luiz Del Roio, Sonia Maria Ronzani, José Homem Correia de Sá, Vladimir

Sacchetta, Gordon Scott, Julio Cesar da Costa Segura, Nelson Werneck Sodré, Luíz Henrique Sombra, Marly de Almeida Gomes Vianna, and William Waack.

Not to be left out are all the people who crossed my path at the Arquivo Histórico do Itamarati, Arquivo Leuenroth, Arquivo Nacional, Arquivo do Palácio da Catete, Arquivo Plínio Salgado, Arquivo Público do Estado do Rio de Janeiro, Arquivo Público Histórico do Rio Claro, Biblioteca da Fundação Getúlio Vargas, Biblioteca Mário de Andrade, Biblioteca Nacional, Fundação Casa Rui Barbosa, Fundação Getúlio Vargas/CPDOC, Instituto Brasileiro de Geografia e Estatística, Instituto Histórico e Geográfico Brasileiro, National Archives, Public Records Office, Российский Центр Хранения и Иэучения Документов Новейщей Истории, and Superior Tribunal Militar.

Finally, a word of appreciation is due to my editors, Heather Staines, Marcia Goldstein, Heather Malloy, and Katie Chase, plus all of their colleagues at the Greenwood Publishing Group, for their help and patience as well as for believing in me and in this venture.

Abbreviations

AFM   Arquivo Filinto Müller (Filinto Müller Archive)

AIB   Ação Integralísta Brasileira (Brazilian Integralist Movement)

AN   Arquivo Nacional (National Archive)

ANL   Aliança Nacional Libertadora (National Liberation Alliance)

APERJ   Arquivo Público do Estado do Rio de Janeiro (Public Archive of the State of Rio de Janeiro)

APS   Arquivo Plínio Salgado (Plínio Salgado Archive)

ARC   Arquivo Público e Histórico do Município do Rio Claro (Public and Historical Archive of the Municipality of Rio Claro)

CPDOC   Centro de Pesquisa e Documentação de História Contemporânea do Brasil (Center for Research and Documentation of Contemporary Brazilian History)

DESPS   Delegacia Especial de Segurança Política e Social (Special Police for Political and Social Security) (the political police in the Federal District from January 10, 1933 to March 28, 1944)

DIP   Departamento de Imprensa e Propaganda (Department of Press and Propaganda)

DOPS   Departamento de Ordem Politica e Social (Department of Politi-
                cal and Social Order) (the political police in the state of Rio de
                Janeiro from 1938 until 1975; also, the generic term applied to
                all forms of the political and social police in various Brazilian
                states from the mid-1920s until 1983)

DPS   Divisão de Polícia Política e Social (Division of Political and
                Social Police) (the political police in the Federal District from
                March 28, 1944 to January 1, 1960)

HAHR   Hispanic American Historical Review

JISWA   Journal of Interamerican Studies and World Affairs

JLAS   Journal of Latin American Studies

LARR   Latin American Research Review

LATI   Linee Aeree Transcontinentali Italiane (Italian Transcontinental
                Airlines)

LBR   Luso-Brazilian Review

НКВД   Народный Коммиссариат Внутренних Дел (People's Com-
(NKVD)   missariat of Internal Affairs) (the Soviet political police from
                1934 to 1946)

OMC   Отдел Международных Связей (Department of International
                Contacts)

PCB   Partido Comunista do Brasil (the original Moscow-oriented
                Brazilian Communist Party, changed its name in 1961 to the
                Partido Comunista Brasileiro; the same acronym is used in the
                text for both organizations)

PPARJ   Political Police Archives, Rio de Janeiro (see the explanatory
                note at the start of the Bibliography)

PRP   The São Paulo, Partido Republicano Paulista (São Paulo Repub-
                lican Party)

PRR   The Rio Grande do Sul, Partido Republicano Rio-Grandense
                (Rio Grande do Sul Republican Party)

РЦХИДНИ   Российский Центр Хранения и Иэучения Документов Новейшей Истории (Modern Russian History, Document Conservation and Research Center)

SD   Sicherheitsdienst (Nazi security service)

SIS   Secret Intelligence Service (the British intelligence service before the creation MI-5 and MI-6)

SOPS   Seção de Ordem Política e Social (Section of Political and Social Order) (the political police in the state of Rio de Janeiro from September 27, 1934 until October 11, 1938)

STM   Superior Tribunal Militar (Superior Military Tribunal)

TSN   Tribunal de Segurança Nacional (Tribunal of National Security) (see also under Segurança in the Selected Glossary)

UKPRO   United Kingdom, Public Records Office

USDS   United States, Department of State

USNA   United States, National Archives

Introduction

Toward the end of August each year, an eerie melodrama is played out in Brazil. The stage is always the same. As the month unfolds, editorials and articles begin to appear in the country's newspapers, over the radio, and on television. The vast majority of these creations pay routine homage to the most controversial figure in Brazilian history. Like an orchestra building to a crescendo as the magical finale approaches, August 24th, we are reminded of this or that exceptional quality of the fallen hero.

In fact, the occasion has nearly become a national holiday. Nowhere is this more apparent than in his hometown, in the state capital, and in the old Federal District of Rio de Janeiro. In all three cities, bronze busts of his likeness were cast and put up before the end of the decade of his death. Porto Alegre included his suicide note etched in the amber metal, bolted to one side of an eight-ton stone. It was unveiled at the exact minute of the first anniversary of his passing.[1] On the requisite date, each monument acts as a magnet drawing in the sheaves to garnish his effigy and enshrine his memory.

In some years it's almost gaudy how speakers bellow his phrases in the halls of legislative bodies, in the mass media, and especially at those forums friendly to him before his death. In Rio, the main bearer of this cross used to be one tabloid, *Última Hora*, a paper whose origins were shrouded in charges that owing to his financial connections it was his unofficial daily. The edition of *Última Hora* that hit the streets on the first anniversary of his passing devoted four pages to the lamentable tragedy. There were comments by historians, journalists, politicians, and sociologists–all exuding his virtues. He was likened to Solomon, Louis XI, and Stalin in one sentence. *Última Hora* concluded by noting that 1,000 candles were lit at 6 P.M. at the base of his statue in Rio's Cinelândia square.[2] Only *Tribuna da Imprensa*, the daily of his last great enemy, king-slayer Carlos Lacerda, held its comments to a minimum.[3]

As the years rolled by, other stories and editorials appeared on August 24th that combined the nation's flair for hyperbole with restricted memory. Brazilians are said to be a people who can always find something good to say about their dead. The deceased champion was thus characterized as a "major political genius,"[4] "one of the most important men of our country,"[5] and "a solitary giant,"[6] who left "an indelible mark on the history of our evolution."[7] He was a "simple, humane, good man"[8] who "did not cultivate ill will, nor did he allow one to harbor hatred or revenge in their hearts."[9] "The blood of the great leader was not shed in vain,"[10] since "he fought against the ruination of Brazil."[11] "His period of office was marked by the predominance of ethics in the social [legislative] sphere."[12]

Most of these accolades ignore what was perpetrated on his authority by the police and representatives of the security apparatus during his governments up to 1945; governments that perfected savagery while he was in power. These policies, in turn, were deterministically inherited from administrations prior to his as normal ways of conducting the affairs of the elite vis-à-vis the multitude. This former head of South America's largest country was thus a victim only of his heritage but not of his own devices. He was innocent solely in this one respect. He was guilty of allowing inhumane methods of social control to be perfected and applied in unheard-of, indeed unthought-of, ways. Yet his defenders would prefer us to believe that "the one who censured was Lourival Fontes, the one who tortured was Filinto Müller, the one who instituted fascism was Francisco Campos, the one responsible for the *coup* was Eurico Dutra, and the one who supported Hitler was Góis Monteiro."[13]

These vindicators would urge us to conclude that he was untainted of all of these things. They would rather have us see their protagonist not as an evasive tropical dictator, but as the "Father of the Poor" or the builder of Brazil's first steel mill at Volta Redonda.[14] Each disciple somehow ignores the evidence of his fixation on staying in power come what may. When despite everything and he was about to lose his vaunted prize a second and final time, these sponsors would have us forget that he even used his death to obscure his legacy.

Yes, the 24th of August is almost a day of national mourning in Brazil.[15] For many, this one instant is a time of *saudades* (of longingness) to some idealized moment when he was in control and things were supposed to have been better. These dreamers dream of what for them was the renowned charity, the Christian spirit, and the profound humanism of the great architect of modern Brazil.[16]

1

THE ROAD TO POWER

It was autumn in the Southern Hemisphere when his cries first pierced the air. Getúlio Dornelles Vargas had come to life on a *fazenda*, or landed estate, some eighteen and a half miles outside São Borja in remote Rio Grande do Sul on April 19, 1882.[1] Just across the Uruguay River from Argentina, the part of Brazil into which he was born was not all that dissimilar from the frontier environment of the country's Northeast. There were of course the obvious differences: the larger number of poorer and racially mixed *sertanejos* up North versus the customarily richer and whiter Europeans in the South. There were also the parched *sertão* and cash crops of the Northeast as opposed to the lush grazing lands and cattle in the southern states. All of this was fought over. Up North some of the brawling was among the wealthy themselves together with their associated enforcers. In Rio Grande do Sul men with power not only battled each other, assisted by their own brand of killers called *peões*,[2] but the Argentines and Uruguayans were frequently involved in the bloodbaths right along with everyone else.

The parents of Getúlio Vargas were no different. They had their hired gunmen for protection and other duties. Together with what has been described as ample wealth,[3] Getúlio's father and mother, General Manuel do Nascimento Vargas[4] and Cândida Dornelles Vargas, produced four additional sons. Preceding Getúlio, who if he was not the runt of the litter was close to it, were Viriato and Protásio. Next came Getúlio, then Spartaco, and finally baby Benjamin. The only daughter died in infancy.[5]

Because Manuel had been a hero in the Paraguayan War (1864-1870), the Vargas home was often filled with stories of the splendor of combat, and the young boys developed a lively interest in their father's retelling of his wartime exploits. This fascination with things military took root not merely in Getúlio, but also found fertile soil in the minds of Viriato and Protásio. It was consequently a proud day when Manuel Vargas sent teenage Protásio and Viriato to Brazil's best engineering college four states away in Ouro Preto, Minas Gerais. The two youths later convinced their parents that the regional *ginásio* would be perfect for Getúlio. After graduation from the high school, he too would enroll in the college.[6]

At first everything went smoothly in Ouro Preto. But it was not long before the reunited brothers found themselves involved in the bizarre assassination of another student, an eighteen-year-old *paulista* (a person from the state of São Paulo), on June 7, 1897.[7] The most recounted version of the victim's meager crime was that he stopped a fight between the Vargas' and another pupil at a local pool hall. The following evening Carlos de Almeida Prado Junior was ambushed in a deluge of bullets from the three young men, aided and abetted by Fernando Kaufmann, Baltasar Patrício de Bem, and Benjamin Torres Jr.[8] The ghastly affair naturally caused an uproar in Ouro Preto. Protásio and Kaufmann were the only ones ever caught. Viriato was injured but got away and hid out for nearly two months in the drugstore of Benjamin Torres. Once things died down, Viriato ducked out of town. There were enough witnesses, however, to entangle the entire Vargas trio. Each of Manuel's boys at Ouro Preto, apprehended or not, were among those placed under indictment for the crime.[9]

WHILE UP NORTH . . .

By way of comparison, on July 7, 1897, exactly one month after the Minas Gerais killing, Virgulino Ferreira da Silva, or "Lampião," was born up in the desolate interior of Pernambuco. While Lampião and two of his brothers would one day be branded as rural outlaws by an angry neighbor for trespassing on his property, their family was poor. Getúlio and two of his brothers had committed one of the most loathsome acts imaginable, but their family came from the ranks of the elite. Yet the careers of the two men did have one important if not sickening parallel. The 1,000 murders that would be attributed to Lampião and his group would pale in comparison to coming events once the smiling hangman[10] from Rio Grande do Sul took national power.

BACK IN MINAS GERAIS

General Manuel Vargas, with all of his military bearing, arrived in Ouro Preto and immediately went to see Protásio in jail. It had been a long and tiring journey, and he was in no mood to waste time. After all the greetings and excuses had been given, the elder Vargas left the confines and got to the real reason for the trip from São Borja. His motives were really quite straight-forward. He was going to fix the case against his boys.

General Vargas was a man of influence, power, and connections. He had retained a close friend and rising star of *gaúcho* (or Rio Grande do Sul) politics, *Coronel*-Senator Pinheiro Machado[11] to help defend the immature criminals if need be. His three sons were definitely not going to rot in some stinking prison.

"Besides," the general must have thought, "This is 1897, and such privileges have always been an accepted custom of the well-to-do."

A number of examples that made it all the way into the English language leads one to suspect that the head of the Vargas clan was right. In 1810, Henry Koster noted that a "murderer escapes who has the good fortune to be under the protection of a powerful patron,"[12] or *patrão*. Three decades later, in 1842 in the province of Alagoas, Daniel Kidder confirmed that if charged with an infraction, "those who have some powerful man on their side are sure to be fully absolved."[13] In the 1850s, another commentator observed that when someone of influence wants a murder committed he either does

the deed himself, or has it perpetrated by one of his slaves who is ready to lend himself for the purpose in consideration of a mere trifle. The discovery of the crime need cause the assassin no anxiety, provided he is rich: for in this country, I was assured, everything can be arranged or achieved with money. I saw several men in Rio [de] Janeiro who had, according to report, committed, either themselves or by means of others, not one, but several murders, and yet they not only enjoyed perfect liberty, but were received in every society.[14]

By 1884 little had changed. A final individual duly noted in that year, only thirteen years before the episode in Ouro Preto, that "the punishment of a criminal who has any influence whatever is becoming one of the forgotten things."[15]

So it would be on this occasion too. The matter was resolved in a single meeting at the home of the local judge, Augusto de Lima.[16] Once sizing Lima up, old man Vargas produced a message from the positivist dictator and governor of Rio Grande do Sul, Júlio de Castilhos,[17] and handed it to His Honor. The note demanded in no uncertain terms that the charges against the Vargas brothers be dropped. And this is precisely what Augusto de Lima did. Both Protásio and Viriato were declared innocent. Getúlio was found to be under the culpable age of fourteen, and therefore not responsible for his actions. Secretly, Lima believed that Getúlio was fourteen years, one month, and nineteen days old when he had a hand in his first murder. The malleable magistrate was one year under the mark. No matter, the truth could be stretched. His honor was in the power profession. He knew what real power meant, even when it came as a veiled threat from several states away.[18]

GETÚLIO GOES HOME

Arriving at the family *fazenda* in São Borja, Getúlio was still intent on a military career. He thus joined the 6th Infantry Battalion, stationed in his hometown, as a private in 1898. This was done to ease his way into the officer training course at the Escola Preparatória e de Tática in Rio Pardo, some seventy-five miles west of Porto Alegre. A good trooper, Getúlio Vargas was soon made a sergeant second class in his company by its commander, Carlos

Frederico de Mesquita,[19] then a lieutenant-colonel and bound for tarnished fame.[20] The War Ministry also got in the act by accepting Vargas to the Rio Pardo school provided that he wait a full twelve months. The delay was stated to be for lack of space.[21]

Subsequent to Getúlio's entering the military academy, he evidently made at least normal progress for about two years. As time passed, however, a student rebellion simmered to the surface and several cadets were dismissed from the institution. Although his family later claimed[22] he had nothing to do with it, Getúlio was implicated, demoted back to the rank of private, kicked out of Rio Pardo on May 15, 1902, and sent packing to Porto Alegre. There, with the 25th Infantry Battalion, he served out the rest of his tour. The 25th was eventually sent east to the Corumbá area in a flare-up over the international boundary with Bolivia.[23]

In the field, Getúlio made up his mind that the army was not for him. Even though his sergeant's stripes were returned at Corumbá, the middle Vargas decided that he was going to study jurisprudence in Porto Alegre.[24] After his hitch in the army was over, in 1904, his father opened his purse once again and Getúlio began the study of law in the gaúcho capital. Three years later the young lawyer graduated.[25]

Circumstances now began to assume forms that were more to Getúlio's liking. Fresh out of law school, he was given the job of Porto Alegre's district attorney, which he accepted only too gladly after turning down an offer to become the chief of police. Both positions were made available from a longtime ally of his father, state Governor Antônio Augusto Borges de Medeiros, who had replaced Júlio de Castilhos. Medeiros wanted someone he could trust to watch over things. This worked for awhile, but Getúlio soon quit and returned to São Borja to practice law. In 1909, Manuel Vargas arranged for his rising star to be "elected" to the state legislature, and the family prodigy faithfully served in this capacity until his father had a falling out in 1913 with Medeiros' Republican Party (known as the Partido Republicano Rio-Grandense or PRR).[26] Getúlio returned again to São Borja; a move which, in 1915, allowed him to take care of some unfinished business.

The old friend of his brother Viriato, and partner in crime, Benjamin Torres Jr., had become something of a nuisance. Following the murder of Carlos Prado, General Vargas, through his influence with Pinheiro Machado,[27] peddled the young man a public post to help him complete his medical studies. Obtaining his degree, he was assisted once more,[28] this time to settle in São Borja and set up practice. In the face of all of this help, Dr. Torres made the lethal error of involving himself with Vargas' political rivals. The added accusation that he dishonored a bevy of local maidens may be true or may have been thrown in as camouflage. As an author friendly to the Vargas family suggests, on their own home turf and in the face of all the Vargas power and connections, Torres would have been naive indeed to be so blatant.[29] When remembering that he could be counted among the six criminals at Ouro Preto,[30] one wonders if it was not really what he knew—and might be trying to do with it—that was his undoing. Once it was decided that the namesake of Benjamin Torres must go, Getúlio Vargas apparently had a major role in planning the murder and in despatching the *peão* to carry it out.[31]

After everything was over there was no trial this time either. Getúlio simply continued working as a lawyer in São Borja until his family made peace with Medeiros' forces in 1916. Vargas then returned to the state legislature, where he became the busy majority leader and budget commission secretary.[32] Even though his time was limited, owing to these important posts, there is some evidence to suggest that together with another man, Getúlio found a moment to knock off a couple of Rio Grande do Sul Indians in the first weeks of 1920.[33] Whether it was for sport, part of some new plot, or the result of a grievance, the reasons for these murders—the last ones to come to light before national politics—remain unclear.

Getúlio for his part was indifferent to the incident. He was more interested in cultivating the good wishes of the PRR. No one really cared anyway about Indians. What was of concern within the Republican movement centered on the fifth consecutive term of Borges de Medeiros for state governor. The *gaúcho* elections in November 1922 were designed to settle this issue. At least this was the plan. On election day, the democratic process witnessed a different scenario, if only in the number of votes thought to be fraudulently cast. Getúlio, who headed the election commission, nonetheless ignored the final tally, and declared his boss, the governor, duly elected once again.[34]

The losing side wasted little time in claiming the elections were rigged and another *gaúcho* conflict soon erupted. The hostilities dragged on until the end of the following year, causing Medeiros to fear that federal troops would be sent in to put his house in order. When the fighting at last stopped, the cagey governor (he was sometimes referred to as "Old *Chimango*" and "the Grasslands' Pope"[35]), was careful to show his gratitude. Among those to know his benevolence was his faithful PRR comrade in arms, Getúlio Vargas. The loyal Getúlio was made a federal assemblyman.

Taking office, Vargas was immediately dispatched to the nation's capital, where his main task was to impede any military intervention by government forces into Rio Grande do Sul.[36] In this he succeeded along with his other activities, which included serving as an insignificant member of the finance committee in the Chamber of Deputies. Getúlio also came out against the military uprising in São Paulo in 1924.[37]

Before the national elections of 1926, which brought Washington Luís to the presidential palace at Catete, Borges de Medeiros agreed to a truce in Rio Grande do Sul. But there was a catch. He was not to run again in the next gubernatorial contest. As a concession to the *gaúchos*, Washington Luís appointed Getúlio Vargas as the incoming finance minister in his new cabinet. In late 1927, however, fresh elections were scheduled for Rio Grande do Sul, and Vargas was selected by Medeiros to be his temporary replacement.[38] The Grasslands' Pope evidently believed that he could continue to dominate the always condescending Getúlio. Sitting alone in his office at the Piratini Palace (the executive mansion in Porto Alegre), Medeiros clearly did not know with whom he was dealing. Vargas had come to understand the advantages of duplicity; a trait that would remain with him the rest of his political life. He would soon have a chance to show what he had learned. As there were no other contestants, the aspiring Vargas was voted into office in early 1928.

Getúlio spent the first half of his term as governor initiating several reforms that played directly into the pockets of the state's elites and upper-middle class. Nothing of substance was done for the great bulk of ordinary working men and women. This was not the goal of the son of Manuel and Cândida, and it is debatable if it ever was. On the contrary, while the chief administrator of Rio Grande do Sul he was noted, at least among the leftists, for breaking up strikes and for multiple deportations.[39]

The picture [then] of Getúlio Vargas up to 1930 is almost complete. Few changes or surprises were seen in the next twenty-four years that were not revealed in this formative period.   Vargas was conditioned and trained to practically every level of political experience in Brazil. Pragmatic and unromantic concerning the political process, Vargas appeared to hold few illusions about the body politic in Brazil. He had been groomed in a political atmosphere that understood the use of power.[40]

The circumstances that propelled the temporary governor to center stage were part of the fight between Washington Luís and the man in charge in Minas Gerais, Antônio Carlos. The obstacle between the two men was the selection of Washington Luís' successor–the government's candidate in the 1930 presidential elections. For some time the country had been informally bound to the selection policy of *Café com Leite* ("Coffee with Milk," or coffee from the groves of São Paulo and milk from the cows of Minas), wherein the governors from São Paulo and Minas Gerais took turns at the national helm. Also known by the title of "Little Trepov,"[41] Washington Luís made the error of attempting to snub the presidential aspirations of Antônio Carlos. Since Washington Luís had been the governor of São Paulo before coming to office, Antônio Carlos felt that by virtue of the gentleman's agreement, he was next in line for the presidency. Little Trepov, however, did not trust Antônio Carlos.[42] Slowly, so as to mask his true intentions, Washington Luís broke with tradition and moved toward open preference for his fellow *paulista*, Governor Júlio Prestes. Realizing that he was not going to be Brazil's next head of state, Antônio Carlos reacted with an attempt to block Júlio Prestes. He did this by cleverly conspiring with Rio Grande do Sul to offer the governor there as a compromise candidate to the nation.

The ever-plotting Getúlio, however, was apprehensive. Reaffirming his loyalty to Washington Luís, he despatched his own second in command, Vice-Governor João Neves, to delicately see what could be arranged in the federal legislature. Though he was reported to have been told not to agree to anything,[43] Neves soon came to an accord with the brother of Antônio Carlos. The understanding provided that Minas Gerais would support the candidacy of

Borges de Medeiros or Getúlio Vargas should Washington Luís fail to nominate Antônio Carlos as his successor.

When told of these developments, Old *Chimango* withdrew, deciding that Vargas was more attuned to national desires.[44] Washington Luís, on the other hand, could not have been more flabbergasted, especially since a coy Getúlio declared his innocence at what had happened. Meanwhile, the native of São Borja let his camp scurry about for a running mate. They settled on João Pessoa Cavalcanti de Albuquerque, current governor of the state of Paraíba, and favorite nephew on his mother's side of ex-President Epitácio Pessoa.[45]

As the race unfolded, those siding with Washington Luís and Júlio Prestes were pitted against what came to be called the Liberal Alliance of the states of Rio Grande do Sul, Minas Gerais, and Paraíba. The campaign featured rounds of unending political violence and passionate if not largely frothy rhetoric. It all came down to March 1, 1930, when an electorate of predominantly white adult males totaling 5.7 percent of the population was allowed to cast their ballots. Getúlio won impressively in Rio Grande do Sul, 287,321 to 789, but he lost nationally, 744,674 to 1,097,379.[46]

Though the results probably did not surprise many people, even before the votes were being counted Getúlio was instructing some aides to seek a way out of his being a candidate. He then told others to push forward with his candidacy. The first group came to a meeting of the minds with the president. What they agreed to seems peculiar until one remembers who did the empowering. The emissaries concluded that if Vargas was defeated at the polls no harm or retribution would be taken against the state of Rio Grande do Sul or anyone who supported their candidate.[47]

THE SPARK

Then, on July 26th, almost five months after all of the electioral hoopla, João Pessoa was shot to death as he sat sipping tea one state away in Recife in the Glória Confectionery Shop. The murder was in retaliation for Pessoa's order to his state police, directing them to ransack the apartment used as a secret love nest by political rival João Duarte Dantas. The authorities were supposed to be looking for contraband arms bound for a Washington Luís-backed insurrection in the state's interior; but they uncovered numerous personal letters and Dantas' diary, which was chockful of intimate passages and suggestive sonnets. They likewise came upon photographs of the adversary and his paramour in compromising positions. It was when hints of this political treasure trove began being printed in Pessoa's Republican Party state newspaper, *A União*, that Dantas went gunning for Pessoa. The erotic material was not published but was said to be at the station house for those strong enough to view it.

The offended lover did not get very far. As he walked out of the pastry store, Pessoa's chauffeur fired a revolver in his direction, knocking him to the ground with a grazing head wound. Picked up, Dantas was hustled off to jail where he recovered long enough to have his throat cut. This was carried out by the guards or others loyal at least to Pessoa, on October 6th, shortly after the mounting revolution's success was assured in Pernambuco. The death of João Duarte Dantas was registered as a "suicide." In a revealing coincidence, however, his brother-in-law, who was thrown into jail with him, his mother, and his female companion also "killed themselves." His father was simply liquidated.[48]

Owing to the inevitable rumors that Washington Luís was responsible for Dantas' deed, Pessoa's murder prompted near riotous scenes in several parts of the country The police were called out in mass in Bahia. Down in São Paulo they brutally attacked a protest by law students at the city's university.[49] On the streets of Rio de Janeiro, Federal Congressman João Suassuna, the governor of Paraíba just prior to Pessoa, and now another of his political adversaries, was killed under cloudy circumstances, accused of collusion in the death of Vargas' vice president.[50] While Getúlio might have found some other way to realize his political ambitions, it was the murder of his running mate that ignited the embers of the Revolution of 1930.

CLOSING IN ON THE PRIZE

Events were now moving quickly, manipulated by the eager hand of Oswaldo Aranha, one of Getúlio's principal advisors. Vargas had given in to Aranha and let the likewise on-again off-again plans for a revolt become the main avenue in his attempts to gain the presidency. Aranha thus represented a second option for Getúlio that stretched back to preelection days. In September 1929, Aranha contacted Luís Carlos Prestes, a fugitive in Buenos Aires, and arranged for the first of two secret meetings near Porto Alegre between himself, Vargas, and the former leader of the celebrated *Coluna* Prestes. From October 29, 1924, until February 3, 1927, the *Coluna* had fought its way over more than 15,500 miles of the Brazilian interior, trying to stir up penniless peasants against then sitting president Artur Bernardes. They never lost a battle and were often referred to as the *Coluna Invicta* or "Undefeated Column." Their only setback was that in running out of ammunition, they were forced into exile.

Now, standing before Getúlio and Oswaldo, Prestes was presented with 800 *contos de réis* (written 800:000$000 and worth just over $94,560) to gear up for and lead a Liberal Alliance insurrection against Washington Luís. Although he gladly accepted the money, the hero of the true Long March subsequently said that he was uninterested in fighting for Vargas. Years later, Prestes calmly mentioned that Vargas himself had bankrolled not the uprising of 1930, but the one of 1935. Shocked, his questioners demanded to know what he meant. It was simple Prestes said. He saved the eight hundred *contos de réis* Vargas gave him to help finance a real proletarian revolution. Actually Prestes turned $20,000 over to Lieutenant Orlando Leite Ribeiro to take to Europe to buy arms. The weapons and the money never reached nor were ever returned to Prestes. A significant portion of the remaining funds went to finance Prestes' network in Brazil.[51]

Described as impetuous and impatient, Aranha was not to be dissuaded. If Luís Carlos Prestes would not fall in line, someone else would. Oswaldo finally reached an agreement with an overweight lieutenant colonel and former combatant against the *Coluna Invicta*. The hand-picked officer went on to earn one critic's sobriquet of "Gás Morteiro" or "Deadly Fumes." Pedro Aurélio de Góis Monteiro would lead the military side of the struggle. Among his forces were numerous rebels called *tenentes*, or "lieutenants," from the 1922 and 1924 uprisings against Bernardes.[52] Some of these men had fought with Prestes but were now disillusioned with his turn to the left.

Aranha was also secretly at work contacting foreign arms manufactures. He had already talked a reluctant Borges de Medeiros into the conspiracy. Borges was only the chairman of the PRR, but he was still one of the most important cards in Getúlio's hand. Old *Chimango*'s significance was obvious. When Borges opted to join the plotters he brought with him the loyalty of his army-strength state police, the Brigada Militar. In the interim, Aranha expertly milked Pessoa's death to the point where the dead governor had fast become a national martyr.[53] Everything was thus in place. The first troops could move.

2

HEAD OF THE PROVISIONAL GOVERNMENT

The Revolution of 1930 began in a coordinated attack in Rio Grande do Sul and Minas Gerais on October 3, 1930.[1] Up in Paraíba things were delayed. Juarez Távora, the *tenente* in charge of the conspiracy in Brazil's Northeast, thought the opening shots were to ring out on October 4th.[2] But it mattered little because Washington Luís was totally unprepared for the number of his soldiers who deserted to the other side. He was equally ill-equipped for the wave of public sympathy that began sweeping Getúlio Vargas toward Catete.

First Rio do Sul fell, then the neighboring states of Santa Catarina and Paraná. Paraíba was secured after a single day's fighting. On the 7th, the state capitals of Rio Grande do Norte and Pernambuco joined the Vargas crusade. They were followed by Ceará. It seemed that everywhere troops were marching toward Rio. As the noose tightened, a clique of military officers near the capital acted independently. Calling themselves the Junta Pacificadora (or loosely, the "Pacification Group"), they deposed Washington Luís on October 24, 1930, without consulting Getúlio. These efforts were but a stopgap, however, as the Junta itself was forced aside under the threat of being buried by the approaching Vargas onslaught.[3]

TAKING CHARGE

Crossing into São Paulo, Getúlio realized that the *tenentes* and other insurgents in the army had insured the success of his *gaúcho*-led movement.[4] He thus reasoned that they would demand too much influence in any new administration as their reward. To neutralize this prospect, on taking control of the federal government he named two of their members to important posts. Perhaps he thought he could play one individual and his supporters off against the other. Elderly, but still respected by the *tenentes*, General Isidoro Dias

Lopes led one bloc. The general was appointed military commander of São Paulo. The other faction was headed by the chameleonic[5] *tenente*, João Alberto. Alberto was placed in the new *interventor* seat in São Paulo. Semi-independent state governors and presidents, with the exception of Minas Gerais–their compensation for supporting the revolution–were done away with. Vargas created *interventors* instead. The idea was that the holder of each position would be directly answerable to the country's chief executive and not to the fancies of local elites be they rural or urban.[6] It mattered little to Getúlio that João Alberto was a viewed by powerful·*paulistas* as a meddling outsider and communist; a mistake that would come back to haunt him the following year.

In another seeming overture to the 1922 and 1924 rebels, Vargas decided, eight days after his November 3rd move into Catete Palace, that by decree he would suspend the constitution. As chief of the Provisional Government he also discontinued all rights guaranteed by the document and closed Congress. Power was to be in his hands alone. As for abiding by the law, Vargas is known to have said at least once during his career, "The law? Who cares about the law?"[7]

Such sentiments were already shared by the men riding Getúlio's coattails to the Brazilian capital. Many of these individuals were given or would carve out little fiefdoms of authority. One such personality was João Batista Luzardo, who was to become the chief of the Polícia Civil in the Federal District. A police corps usually assigned detective roles (the name came from the fact that they wore civilian clothes), the head of the Polícia Civil was a crucial job in Vargas' plans to keep his revolution from going too far. So once Luzardo took up his new office, it was not long before he announced plans to reorganize Rio's police department. A commission was established to study just how this should be done; but its recommendations became the subject of political intrigues and were never put into effect. The proposals were partly a disguise anyway to try to dismiss several of Washington Luís' appointees from the force. There was nothing new in this style of leftover removal, as it was standard policy whenever a fresh *patrão* took control the police.

A new face that Chief Luzardo managed to advance was another *gaúcho*, Joaquim Pedro Salgado Filho. He was placed in charge of the *carioca* (people or things from the Federal District) political police. Since 1922 they had been called the 4ª Delegacia Auxiliar (police from the 4th Auxiliary Department). Composed of several branches, the 4ª Delegacia's Seção de Ordem Política e Social (SOPS, the Section of Political and Social Order) had its name corrupted by the public, who since the mid-1920s called it the "Delegacia" instead of the "Seção." This was a meaningful distinction because plebeians tacked the acronym DOPS onto the entire political-police apparatus in different states despite the intervening years, areas of responsibility, or new names. One of these alterations occurred in 1933 in the Federal District when the 4ª Delegacia Auxiliar was replaced by the Delegacia Especial de Segurança Política e Social (the Special Police for Political and Social Security), or DESPS.

Unlike the group he commanded, Salgado Filho did not need a face-lift. Out to make a name for himself, he augmented past 4ª Delegacia policies by giving the order to pick up any pesky labor leader, and by issuing a blanket prohibition against all strikes. He did his job so well, and Getúlio was evidently so pleased, that Salgado Filho was later accorded another administrative position as befitting his successful efforts: that of Brazil's second minister of labor.

Luzardo next selected one of his former schoolmates to lead a new police unit in the scientific assault on crime. Leonídio Riveiro was installed as the head of the Laboratory of Criminal Anthropology and set about classifying lawbreakers according to the criminal-by-body-type theories of Cesare Lombroso. The personnel under Riveiro's direction were triumphant in this exercise in nonsense, and were awarded the Lombroso Prize in 1933 for their work unmasking the physical characteristics of prospective black and homosexual offenders.[8]

LABOR

In January 1931, when communists tried to hold a hunger march for impoverished *cariocas*, Luzardo ordered out the Polícia Civil and Polícia Militar. Independent from each other, the latter functioned as the principal police entity in uniform. Both detained anyone caught disturbing "Hunger March" flyers on charges of instigating disorder. It was enough to be seen just reading one of the handouts. An arrest or at the very least some type of harassment was sure to follow. Besides his boss and minister of justice, Oswaldo Aranha, the new head of the Polícia Civil was in continuous contact with the chief of the Provisional Government, Getúlio Vargas. And Vargas supported all of the steps taken by Luzardo.[9] These measures included lining the Praça da Bandeira (Flag Square), where the protest was to be held, along with a number of other key points in the capital, with scores of policemen. In fact, Luzardo called in so many constables that he could confidently declare, "Anyone who sticks his head outside, does so because he wants to commit suicide!"[10]

The total number of arrests was not small and the apprehensions were not limited to Rio de Janeiro. The press even insinuated that there was an *agent provocateur* angle behind the rally after the seizure of three foreigners. When the Federal District's police claimed that they had also uncovered communist plans to include the states of São Paulo and Pernambuco in the protests, Luzardo contacted the new *paulistano* (referring to the city of São Paulo) chief of police, Miguel Costa. Costa was an efficient officer. Units of his Força Pública (the Polícia Militar in some states) were dispatched to apprehend suspicious-looking subversives both in the state capital and in its port city down at Santos. The docks in Santos were sealed off and placed under the barrels of entrenched machine gunners.[11] Though many were soon released,[12] the government was anxiously coming to realize the potential danger of the situation. This was underscored at the end of the month when another demonstration, a peaceful one, made up of some 15,000 workers, marched to Catete to be met by Vargas and his initial labor minister, *gaúcho* Lindolfo Collor.

The Ministry of Labor had been one of Vargas' inventions to appease the urban working man. But it was really not his intention that it should actually do very much.[13] Perhaps that's why Collor was chosen for the job. He was supposed to have been a man so blinded by ambition and the pursuit of wealth that he once cheated his own father-in-law out of a large sum of money.[14] Minister Collor, however, surprised everyone by conducting

his own social revolution with a flood of labor laws. He established a government-supported union structure, a series of labor courts and employer-employee conciliation commissions, a set of government social security institutes, a collective bargaining process, and a minimum wage system. Collor's reforms had such an emotional impact on the laboring class that when he toured northern Brazil in November 1931, he encountered tumultuous receptions at every stop. Observing Collor's triumphal junket, the perspicacious Vargas began to contemplate labor as an untapped source of political power. Yet Collor's and later Vargas' reforms applied *only* to [some sections of] urban labor. The revolution never reached the rural workers, including those belonging to Vargas and his fellow Gaúcho ranchers (italics added).[15]

This restricted application was no understatement. Vargas pundits would later claim that he was "The Father of the Poor." But the ones who really benefited were members of selected professions in the cities. If considered from the more inclusive dichotomy of rural or urban residence, the emptiness of the claim is glaringly evident. By five-year increments until 1954, the percentage of Vargas era urban population was:[16]

1930[a]	1935[a]	1940	1945[a]	1950	1954[a]
27.0	29.0	31.2	33.7	36.2	39.6

a=estimate

Peasants remained virtual chattels of the *fazendeiros* (or estate owners), and have done so right up until the present time. Except for a late bid from Vargas, which João Goulart put into law in an improved form when he became Brazil's leader, all Brazilian presidents have essentially disregarded rural workers or only toyed with the notion of helping them. As an example of other elites' regard for agricultural help, we only need examine one of the original demands of Francisco Julião's Ligas Camponesas or Peasant Leagues. Founded on January 1, 1955, some four months after Vargas' final exit from the political scene, one of the things the Ligas attempted to win was the right of rural workers to be buried in their own coffins. This goal was in reaction to established policy, which allowed local overseers to utilize a reusable, false-bottomed casket that unceremoniously dumped each corpse into its grave following the entombment ceremony.[17]

No, it was not the agricultural laborer that Vargas would cultivate. Rural potentates were generally left to run their own properties and their own employees as they saw fit. Getúlio would make some concessions to the emerging urban middle class,[18] and eventually even a number of minimal reforms to the urban proletariat. All of these modifications, on the other hand, were to have nothing to do with the political left. Vargas had decided to come out against communism even before he was sworn in as the new head of state.[19]

PUTTING HIS HOUSE IN ORDER

Some six weeks after the Rio "Hunger March," the Brazilian government asked the United States for help in fighting bolshevism. The American State Department directed this request to the police department in the city of New York. New York's finest sent a team of agents to Brazil with the goal of organizing a section of the Brazilian police in this effort.[20] Whether the American instructors had anything to do with it or not is unclear, but one month later, in April 1931, there was a massive arrest of communists followed by a bomb exploding inside of police headquarters in Rio de Janeiro. It is not known if the police or the leftists set off this blast.[21] Luzardo (Vargas) conveniently used the incident as a pretext to forbid any kind of 1st of May demonstrations. This put a damper on the event but did not end it. When May Day arrived, there were still several small clashes between the authorities and workers in Rio and Recife.[22]

If communist thinking was repulsive to the nation's new leader, he was certainly not a party of one. With the downfall of Washington Luís, some of the *tenentes* formed the 3rd of October Club to promote their own interpretation of just what would be a better Brazil. At the same time there seemed to be a near breakdown in authority owing to the events that brought Vargas to power, and the sorting out of new centers of strength within the regime. Turning his attention in this direction, Getúlio was at once embroiled in a political balancing act. He had to tread carefully since the *tenentes* were one of the country's most influential voices.[23] They were not, however, the only voice; a multitude of men in uniform attempted or actually succeeded in taking what passed as the law into their own hands in other parts of the country.[24] Still, the 3rd of October Club was different. Its members were ostensibly more interested in national goals than overt displays of territorial power grabbing. They were not interested in an immediate return to democratic government on the grounds that this would only bring back the politicians of the old order. As they saw their role, the 3rd of October Club's mission was to reshape the political mind of the country through a protracted dictatorship led by a controlled Vargas.[25]

But Getúlio outflanked everyone by slowly moving the 3rd of October Club to one side. He then pretended to listen to their opponents, the Constitutionalists, who were interested in a faster return to representative government and a liberal constitution. The main concentrations of this second position were centered in Vargas' Rio Grande do Sul and in São Paulo. Aggravating the debate in Brazil's most productive state, *Interventor* João Alberto had succeeded in irritating the regional ruling class. These were elites who had never really forgiven Vargas or his *tenente* allies for making fiascoes of the twin *paulista* presidencies of Washington Luís and Júlio Prestes.

Now the São Paulo establishment was having to stand by and watch João Alberto's efforts at promoting bourgeois-autocratic reforms in their sacrosanct spheres of influence. Not only did this interloper hand out too many plush jobs to his military cronies; but he had the audacity to have the political police shadow state politicians considered unfriendly to Rio de Janeiro. He went on to decreased the urban workweek to forty hours while increasing the minimum wage by 5 percent, break up an array of bankrupt *fazendas*, and organize São Paulo's assorted unemployed into a quasimilitary, pro-Vargas mishmash called the Legião Revolucionária (Revolutionary Legion).[26] Finally, he took the seemingly unprecedented steps of momentarily legalizing the PCB (Partido Comunista do Brasil), or Brazilian Communist Party, and in allowing the formation of the Friends of Russia Society. Whether this leftist indulgence was done for expeditious reasons, or as a method of securing names for the political police, or both, remains obscure.[27]

In any case, most of João Alberto's changes and the reactions to them were superficial. The actual core of the *paulista* resentment was the depressed coffee industry. In the 1931 marketing year, the price of coffee had sunk to 8.4 cents per pound on the New York exchange. This was the lowest price in nearly a decade.[28] While courting the São Paulo coffee barons just prior to and then during the 1930 Revolution, Getúlio was on their side or at worst posed no economic threat to them.[29] But after coming to power, and in the name of patriotism, he turned on these individuals to protect Brazil's most valuable cash crop. Since the São Paulo-run Coffee Institute had made such a shambles of things by encouraging ever larger coffee harvests in a depressed world economy, Vargas appointed troubleshooter João Alberto to head the organization. Huge stockpiles of coffee were soon being burned to force prices up. Furthermore, a hefty export tax was imposed–so it was said–to help defray lost profits to the growers. This feature was formulated to comfort elite nerves. Yet it was only a bluff as the coffee producers never received a thing.[30]

It is doubtful whether João Alberto or anyone else could have contained the displeasure of the vain old order in São Paulo for long. The opulent were starting to lose money under Vargas, and future prospects did not seem promising. It was at about this point that a manifesto began circulating, accusing João Alberto of communist connections. The declaration did not use the word coffee a single time.[31] It stated openly and simply that the only cure for the evils plaguing "occupied" São Paulo was for João Alberto to be replaced by a *paulista* followed by a rapid reconstitutionalization of the country. In other words, what the local elites were after was a return to the system of the division of power wherein they controlled everything that moved in São Paulo.

João Alberto and Getúlio found all this wistful posturing dangerous for the country if not for them personally. Some kind of bilateral action seemed to be coming closer with each passing day. From time to time Vargas did mention that there would be elections; but his thinking was really going in a different direction. In the privacy of Catete, he approved of another show of strength. São Paulo's Força Pública was ordered to ransack the homes of persons thought to be guarding the manifesto for distribution. This produced a number of arrests; and among those apprehended were eighteen members of the Partido Democrático, or Democratic Party, the political right arm of the state's upper classes.[32]

João Alberto resigned on July 24, 1931. He eventually took over for Luzardo as the new head of the Federal District's Polícia Civil.[33] The ex-chief had stood idly by, presumably on directives from Vargas, while a Rio newspaper critical of the administration was plundered. A face-saving device was hence in order. It allowed Vargas the opportunity of moving João Alberto to Rio de Janeiro. To the *paulista* dignitaries of power, however, the change came as too little, too late.

In early January 1932 the Partido Democrático decided that it could no longer support the Provisional Government. It was joined in this conviction the following month by the São Paulo Defense League, and by part of the PRP, Partido Republicano Paulista, or São Paulo Republican Party. That May, the three formed an alliance with similar groups opposing Vargas in Rio Grande do Sul and Minas Gerais. Together they called themselves the Frente Única or United Front. If this were not enough, the state's Força Pública had revolted some months earlier over being made to do the dirty work of the national government, and at being led by *tenente* Miguel Costa. Catete then reacted with a preview of things to come. The lawmen's uprising was dealt with briskly, resulting in the arrests of more than 200 policemen and the transfers of numerous army officers to other parts of the country.[34] Isodoro Dias Lopes went on the block as well. He was fired as the leader of federal troops in São Paulo.

Now a general, Góis Monteiro was given Isodoro's command and immediately passed it on to a subordinate, Colonel Manuel Rabelo Mendes. Rabelo was a loyal choice. Upon taking up his new duties, he quietly began increasing the number of men under arms loyal to the government. In the meantime, Isodoro switched sides and was made chief of the São Paulo Constitutionalist forces. He took the additional step of securing the help of another Vargas outcast, pint-sized General Bertoldo Klinger. Klinger's most recent posting was with the short-lived Junta Pacificadora as chief of the Polícia Civil. In his new role he would lead the *paulista* forces in any coming hostilities with the national administration.

At the same time, instrumental *gaúchos*, such as Lindolfo Collor, who quit his post as minister of labor; Maurício Cardoso, who took over for Aranha at the Justice Ministry before resigning; along with João Neves and Baptista Luzardo, all returned home to join with those opposing the Vargas dictatorship. Cantankerous old Borges de Medeiros was waiting for them with open arms in Porto Alegre. He too had become dissatisfied with his former pupil.[35]

Getúlio wanted an understanding and not a conflict with Borges. So he sent Oswaldo Aranha on an unsuccessful mission to Rio Grande do Sul to try and work something out. On his way back to the capital, Aranha stopped off in the heart of São Paulo where angry throngs cried out such things as, "Death to Vargas!" and "Death to Aranha!"[36] In all there were two days of protests and a night of bloody rioting. Sufficiently impressed, once he was safely back in Rio de Janeiro, Aranha began to suggest that Getúlio take a softer approach to the *paulista* problem. This tactic, however, was only for São Paulo. In the Federal District the government acted differently to prevent any loosening of the Vargas grip.

THE SPECIAL POLICE

Evermore in need of an offensive police unit, Getúlio had João Alberto organize a new, openly impetuous group for just this end. An arm of the Polícia Civil, the unit was called the Polícia Especial, or Special Police. Known more colloquially as the "Tomato Heads," because of their khaki uniforms and red caps, their exact composition is still debated. It has been said that they were composed of 500 professional fighters and wrestlers chosen from the ranks of the military. Others include a number of soccer players and strong-backed rowers. Official sources state that the Tomato Heads were permitted to have a complement numbering no more than 234 men. This same figure was evidently retained through 1937, but reduced to 221 in 1938, and finally to 214 in 1939. How close these limits were to reality at any one time is also unknown. Whatever their former professions, physical attributes, or actual numbers, there is no denying that these police bruisers were despised by a good portion of the *carioca* public. This distaste was perhaps increased by the fact that, owing to their low pay, some of the Heads doubled as pimps.

The Polícia Especial were led up by Lieutenant Euzébio de Queiroz Filho. A sadistic homosexual, he allowed some young applicants to join so that he could sexually exploit them. Euzébio and his men had their headquarters high up on now-removed Santo Antônio Hill. Like the "Heads" themselves, the sprawling facility was feared by ordinary people as something out of the Inquisition. This was certainly true for those suspects who reached the place. More than one never made it that far because they were "taken care of" without delay. The Tomato Heads would later be compared to CENIMAR, Centro de Informações da Marinha (the Naval Information Center), one of the most fiendish torturing arms of the 1964-1985 military dictatorship. There is also the observation that the style of policing used by the Polícia Especial served as a model for the various groups of Polícia de Choque, or Shock Police, in our own times.[37]

REVOLT IN SÃO PAULO

It was against this backdrop, on July 9, 1932, that the *paulistas* decided to have their civil war. As before all clashes on a grand scale there was an enormous amount of pomp and bombast awash among grains of truth. The stated goal was to "reconstitutionalize" the country or, if this could not be accomplished, to secede and form a new sovereign nation. It was amazing what was about to take place. The São Paulo coffee elite and their allies were creating a civil war to return Brazil to the Constitution of 1891 so that they could again rule over the largest revenue-making item in the Brazilian economy. In essence they were out to exchange the Vargas dictatorship for an archaic one of their own. Brazil was going in circles.

Getúlio, however, was rarely one to be caught sleeping. After he had talked his *interventor* in Rio Grande do Sul, José Antônio Flôres da Cunha, into standing with the national government, any insurrection in the *gaúcho* state was all but over. To insure compliance, Flôres turned his state into a tightly controlled camp. Full media censorship, spot road checks, scrutiny of ship and rail passengers, and the ever-present arrests, all became an intensified part of the daily routine. The main focus of this activity was an attempt to neutralize those in positions of responsibility within the Frente Única.[38]

Meanwhile in the crucial center of the country, Minas Gerais backed down, leaving the *paulistas* to go it alone.[39] This isolation of São Paulo also had an internal dimension as it was soon apparent that its attraction was largely limited to members of the upper and middle classes. Workers pretty much avoided becoming involved. This was not necessarily because they had some kind of preference for Getúlio Vargas. Rather, it was the view of many people with lower earnings in São Paulo that support for the rebels was tantamount to support for the *paulista* Republican Party. The PR was the party that had equated the "social question" (read: the fair treatment and compensation of workers) "as a question for the police" during the term of Washington Luís.[40]

It was a short if not glamorous little war. Most of the flair was on the home front, where citizens favoring the rebellion were fed a continuous barrage of flowery propaganda as they opened up their wallets and threw much of their jewelry to the almighty God of local nationalism. Yet once all of the flags, speeches, and contributions were peeled away, the bald fact was that the state of São Paulo was just not prepared for hostilities that could drag on for more than a few months. After an initial advance turned into a stalemate, federal forces began to get the upper hand if only through attrition. Getúlio then had his miniature air force fly over the city on a bombing run. This so disturbed the *paulistano* business community, they were aghast that Vargas would devastate Brazil's commercial heartland,[41] that Klinger was given orders to surrender. São Paulo's self-proclaimed independence lasted just eighty-four days.[42]

Vargas realized early that it would be good tactics to offer the olive branch to the defeated elite when and where this could be done. No matter which group of jail keepers controlled it, coffee was still Brazil's most important commodity and São Paulo still grew most of it. Getúlio thus took almost predictable steps in putting on a mollifying face. His opening move came even before a truce had been signed. "Rio," Vargas said, "would send wheat to help feed war-tired *paulistas*." Next, Valdomiro Lima, São Paulo's new military commander, declared on instructions from Rio de Janeiro that "all resentments are forgotten."[43] The administration likewise promised to make good on war bonds floated by the rebels, a move which no doubt brought tears of joy to the *paulista* investment community. The real crowning touch, however, were the national elections Getúlio had been promising to hold all along. They were still going ahead as planned. Vargas thus maneuvered himself into the position of the actual constitutionalist, portraying those still against him as nothing more than self-centered separatists.[44]   The chief of the Provisional Government was a master at such deceptions.   Part of his talent was an ability to shift the responsibility of events onto others. In a speech that September, he let it be known that federal authorities "did not consider the people of São Paulo guilty. They were only the major victims. At a specified time, those in fact responsible will be obliged to meet an inflexible judge, capable of dictating and executing a sentence upon them."[45]

While there already were a few federal concentration camps, such as the one at Ponta Grossa in Paraná,[46] most of the prisoners of war taken by the government's side were transported to Rio de Janeiro during the conflict. This included sympathizers, apprehended spies, and those picked up for suspicion. Arriving in the nation's capital, the batches of captives were divided into two lots: those to be questioned further or watched more carefully, and those to be shipped straightaway to one of several island prisons. Those chosen for special questioning, along with anyone Getúlio wanted to keep an especially close eye on, often ended up in the holds of the *Pedro I*. Together with her sister ship, the *Pedro I* was one of the two largest vessels in the commercial fleet run by Lloyd Brasileiro.   Originally she was named the *Wyreema*, an English-built freighter that had been sold to Lloyd in 1926. But due to her deep draft and a prodigal appetite for coal she had not been on active duty. The events of 1932 pressed the *Pedro I* back into service again, this time as a military prison moored in Guanabara Bay just off the Glória shore and south of the center of town.[47] Once her massive bulk was towed into position, security was maintained on board by another big object: a cruel, obese policeman named Paula Pinto. Pinto had at his command the assistance of a "considerable detachment of the federal militia and a squad of agents specialized in discovering conspiracies."[48]

Those deemed to be not worthy of such close scrutiny, together with the usual cargo of destitutes and ordinary lawbreakers, were ultimately all boated down to the Dois Rios (Two Rivers) Correctional Colony on Ilha Grande. The island itself is situated not far from the coast at the western tip of the state of Rio de Janeiro. Initially it was a leper colony, and then a center for the quarantining of passengers off of disease-ridden ships. With the Vargas regime, iron-fisted control of the island was passed to Lieutenant Vitório Caneppa and his right-hand man from the capital, police Inspector Francisco Anselmo das Chagas. To maintain the kind of order Caneppa relished, Inspector Chagas had several Rio policemen with him. Some like the notorious "26," whose real name was Manoel da Costa Lima, worked as functionaries or guards. Others were dis-guised as prisoners. Their job was to report on plans of escape, mutinies, and probably anything else that might have been of use to Caneppa. The prisoners could not help but know about the infamy preceding Francisco Chagas and Twenty-Six. Besides their police duties, they had been police torturers in Rio during the government of Artur Bernardes. They were also two of the four defendants charged in the scandalous murder of Conrado Niemeyer in 1925.[49]

Despite the fact that overcrowding on Ilha Grande was consistently high, the fear that people like Chagas and Costa Lima must have caused helped keep prisoners docile. When they stepped out of line, the first rung on the warden's ladder of inmate control was bathing. It was prohibited for anyone causing the smallest problem. Since there was no other way to cleanse the clinging sweat from oneself, this usually produced the desired change after a few days in the muggy heat. There was likewise the aspect of physical separation as all correspondence from the mainland and all newspapers were banned. Prisoners were told about events from the outside only by the prison staff or the newly arrived.[50]

Those who tried to flee were chased by dogs and pursuing sentries noted for firing their weapons liberally into the bush. If they were brought back still breathing, and for other intractable prisoners, Dois Rios had three subterranean cubicles for solitary confinement not far from the sentry's quarters. Each was filthy, humid, and lacked fresh air and light.[51] There was also another singular cell so remote that its occupants virtually rotted to death no matter how loud they shrieked, swore, or begged.[52]

At Dois Rios, the vanquished doubtlessly came to feel that they were "packages consigned to death."[53] Some were killed for no apparent reason by the guards; some were executed during or after bungled breakouts. Those who escaped as far as the beach were now-and-again found putrefying in small boats anchored along the shore. For the athletic, trying to swim the roughly two and a half miles to the mainland, their wakes routinely turned blood red as sharks cruised in the waters off the coast.[54]

Amnesty for less than half of the reported 6,000 inmates on Ilha Grande, and on the smaller "Island of the Flowers" (Ilha das Flores) in Guanabara Bay, came shortly after hostilities officially ended on October 2, 1932. The rest of the wartime captives were slowly released in the following months.[55] All, that is, except those aboard the *Pedro I*. They were taken to Ilha Grande on October 23rd,[56] where many were eventually among the hundreds the government decided to deport to Europe, especially to Salazar's Portugal. No small number of those expelled had little or nothing to do with the Constitutionalist uprising.[57]

WINDS FROM THE RIGHT

In the aftermath of the 1932 civil war, Vargas busied himself with electoral reforms. One of his main priorities continued to be the communists. Declared illegal again, the country's only forbidden political party was not invited to the coming elections. As an added safeguard, agreements of mutual cooperation were signed with the police in Argentina and Uruguay to exchange intelligence and otherwise help one another in a common battle against Moscow.[58] At home, this meant that the government's pursuit of leftists, their families, friends, and meetings took on an accelerated dimension. As for the extreme right, or Integralists as they were called, their activities almost seemed to be encouraged. By way of illustration, a single police report for the state of Rio de Janeiro lists the ensuing 1933 breakdown[59] for the stalking of political groups:

	Niterói	Interior
Socialist meetings attended	65	-
Extremist meetings attended	-	1
Extremist rallies attended	8	-
Extremist rallies attended	1	-

The Integralists were one of two larger groups coming into existence at this time who were interested in dramatic solutions to Brazil's problems. Integralism (Ação Integralísta Brasileira, AIB, or the Brazilian Integralist Movement), owed its origins to the fascism of Benito Mussolini and the world economic depression of the 1930s. It was led by Plínio Salgado, a brooding, mustached writer from a remote corner of the state of São Paulo. Salgado had been just another lost intellectual until he visited Europe in 1930, where he had the luck to meet *Il Duce* himself. Plínio came away from the encounter markedly starstruck and soon decided that "the Fascist concept of existence will be the light of a new age."[60]

Returning to Brazil the day after the opening salvos of the Revolution of 1930, Salgado organized the AIB out of a *paulista* study group on October 7, 1932.[61] And what an organization it was. Almost from the beginning there were internal squabbles between the two faces of *integralismo*. On one side there were those headed by Salgado, the *Chefe Nacional* (or national chief), and Miguel Reale, the head of the Departamento Nacional de Doutrina (propaganda ministry). This faction was influenced by the Italians, and to a degree by the ideas of Portuguese fascism. The adherents on the other side opted for German Nazism. The main proponent of the second group was the noted anti-Semitic, Gustavo Barroso.

Barroso, whose mother had been born in the Fatherland, was a founder and director of Brazil's National Historical Museum. He was even elected to the hallowed Brazilian Academy of Letters as its youngest member ever in 1923. Barroso regularly wore his Integralist uniform, including pith helmet, to Academy meetings. He had an unstable personality and was prone to violence. These attributes were put to the test in a hard campaign, which he won, to become the Academy's president. He thereupon set out to turn the esteemed repository of Brazilian culture into a center for Integralist erudition.[62]

Gustavo was afflicted with painful bouts of erysipelas. This contagious and recurring skin ailment periodically sidelined him from party and other official functions. But they did not keep the man who used to say "You have to be bad to live" from writing.[63] Rendered with English titles, a sampling of Barroso's Integralist period output include: *The Paulista Synagogue; Brazil, Colony of the Bankers; Communism, Christianity and Corporativism; The Secret History of Brazil; Judaism, Masonry and Communism; Integralism and Catholicism; Integralism from North to South;* "The Kike Killer"; *What Every Integralist Should Know; The Fourth Empire;* and *Roosevelt Is a Jew.*[64] In 1937 he translated into Portuguese, and was a strong propagandist for, *The Protocols of the Elders of Zion.* It is not clear if Barroso knew or even cared that *The*

Protocols were originally forged by the czar's secret police and first published in 1903.

Despite the fact that his mother was German, Gustavo could not speak her language well enough to communicate with his friends in Berlin in anything but French. He nevertheless visited the Reich in 1940 and wrote several articles that were translated before being published in the German press. As early as May 1934, he wrote the Berlin newspaper *Reichswart* to say that he "was in frank agreement with your views on the classification of Jews."[65]

Jews and communists had come to be equated as one in the same in the minds of many Brazilians on the political right.[66] While Barroso was not the first to come to this spurious conclusion, he was one of most rabid.[67] Neither was Barroso the only author whose hate literature became a part of the AIB's repertoire of "evidence" against the Star of David.[68] Barroso was not even very original. He merely mouthed long-held convictions that Jews had *sangue infecto*, or "infected blood."[69] Such beliefs had laid dormant in Portuguese-speaking cultures until becoming a major European force in the 1930s.

Comparable with what was taking place elsewhere, a eugenic interpretation to this racial concern likewise developed in Brazil. Lighting the way was the Sociedade Brasileira Eugénica de São Paulo (the São Paulo Eugenics Society). Founded back in 1918 by a Brazilian of German extraction, Renato Kehl, the group disbanded two years later. Parts of it, including Kehl, resurfaced in 1922 in Rio de Janeiro as the Sociedade de Higiene Mental (Brazilian Society for Mental Hygiene). The curious mix between eugenics and psychiatry was popular in several Latin American countries of the period. Both were claimed to be effective tools to reduce if not eliminate insanity and crime. By 1929, the Sociedade de Higiene Mental was promulgating opinions in its own journal, the *Arquivos Brasileiros de Higiene Mental.* From 1931 on, this publication devoted more and more space to racial questions neatly dovetailed into matters of "social hygiene." Reading its pages one learns, for example, that Italian and German Brazilians are not prone to alcoholism; while the drinking habits of blacks, mixed-race individuals, Asians, and Jews are a disgrace. The conclusion was that such sots should not be allowed into Brazil. Likewise, there was the parallel social-Darwinist urging to sterilize the insane, criminals, beggars, and vagabonds. The AIB loved such stuff; as they did in 1934 when the editor of the *Arquivos* proposed to: (1) start eugenic courts, so that it could be established just who may have children; (2) reform wages along eugenic grounds (whites were to earn more than all other races); and (3) promote the multiplication of the white race through the creation of a human-stud system of genetically superior persons. This last suggestion would have no doubt resulted in a Brazilian variant of the German *Lebensborn* program.[70]

As contradictory as it may seem, there were a limited number of black and Asian AIB members.[71] This was apparently done for propaganda purposes in a country long noted for racial mixing.[72] We might expect that these people would have been sacrificed had the Integralists emerged differently from the events of the 1930s. In any case, such situational exceptions were never granted to Jews or Freemasons. One only needed to consult the pages of the AIB's principal newspaper, *A Ofensiva*, often with lead articles and columns by Salgado, Reale, and Barroso, to draw this conclusion. Similarly, the advocates of communism, socialism, liberalism, democracy, *laissez-faire* capitalism, spiritualism, secular education, sex education, movies, popular music, and equal rights for women–including the vote–were all the automatic enemies of these builders of a new Brazil. With the field of candidates thus reduced, almost anyone else who professed the sanctity of the family, Christianity–especially Catholicism[73]–those who proclaimed unwavering Brazilian nationalism, and those who believed in the primacy of the "leadership principle"[74] could become strutting Integralists.

Perhaps it was the marching and parades. Perhaps it was the uniforms. It may have even been the dogma for some because Brazilians joined from all walks of life. By 1936, the AIB was claiming[75] its membership consisted of:

Persons under 16 years of age	10%
Professionals	23
Students	15
Industrialists, businessmen, and agricultural landowners	2
Members of the armed forces	4
Rural and urban workers	46

The AIB borrowed the Nazis' love of ceremony, although they were nowhere near as good at it as their Teutonic brethren. Members wore green shirts and dark ties with white or black slacks and black shoes. This was topped off Hitler style with the Greek letter sigma, or Σ, arm band which stood for unity. The Integralists tried to intimidate their way to power through too many marches–for a time there was a goose-stepping militia led by Gustavo Barroso–and too many Fascist salutes accompanied by frenzied shouts of *Anauê!* Salgado was to be greeted by all members with three cries of *Anauê*. Other party big shots with two *Anauês*, while the ordinary rank and file acknowledged each other through but a single *Anauê*. Each was to be barked out together with a stiff-armed salute. In all the excitement, however, no one was allowed to touch the sacrosanct body of the *Chefe Nacional*.[76] As befitting the befuddled visions of the man, Plínio himself had dug the word *Anauê* out of the Tupí Indian language. It means "Hail." The only thing left out, once he decided it would be part of the organization's salutation, was "Salgado!"

During the high-water mark of integralism, also in 1936, there were some 3,000 AIB centers flung across the country with 1 million dues-paying members. In a letter to Vargas in 1938, Salgado claimed that AIB ranks had jumped to 1,500,000.[77] As they grew, the movement kept abreast of Fascist developments in other parts of the world. Melo Mourão, the former chief of the AIB Office of Foreign Relations, later commented that through his hands, passed all the political intelligence of other like-minded parties in Europe and America. In the name of integralism I corresponded with the French Fascists for years. I received personal letters from Leon Degrelle, head of the rexism in Belgium. Others came from executed Dutch *Führer* [Anton] Mussert, and from the chief of the National Socialist Party of Chile, Jorge Gonzalez. I welcomed emissaries from Fascist Italy, from the Portuguese movement led by Rolão Preto, from the Syrian Fascist Party, from the Mexican Gold Shirts, from the Guard of Iron of Rumania, and even from Fascist organizations in Egypt. I kept contacts with the leaders of Russian fascism; who with their headquarters in Harbin, had tried a revolt by aircraft in 1937 that ended in blood and silence behind the Iron Curtain. I was also sent presents from Sir Oswald Mosley, chief of British fascism. He mailed me books with enthusiastic dedications.[78]

Foreign events, in doctored form, were woven into one of the AIB's five daily, or 120 weekly, nationwide newspapers. There were forty books of dogma, numerous athletic facilities, out-patient clinics, social programs, primary schools, high schools, colleges, and trade schools. Finally, in the true spirit of National Socialism, there were several dispensaries giving away free milk to the children of AIB members. This was how it looked on paper anyway, as many of the figures and services were grossly over exaggerated by Salgado himself.[79] Much of the money that came in to support these activities went straight into AIB coffers and stayed there.

Aside from members' dues and initiation fees, the *Chefe Nacional* made clear in his directives what would be donated from the party faithful: all valuable metals, precious stones, and works of art.[80] These offerings, together with "taxes," 1$000 Sigma coupons,[81] and other gimmicks were augmented by no less than two further sources of economic support. Under the table the Italian government furnished a minimum of $75,000.[82] There were never substantiated allegations as well that the Nazis bought up all the bonds at an Integralist fund raiser, through a German bank in Brazil, for 6,000 *contos de réis* (then worth $383,386.20).[83] What has been documented shows that Third Reich money was made accessible to the AIB via German firms in Brazil, and to local Nazi *Bunds* in Paraná, Santa Catarina, and Rio Grande do Sul. Besides accumulating secret files on 125 prominent individuals, pro-Nazi and soon-to-be-picked chief of the Federal District's Polícia Civil, Filinto Strubling Müller was reported to have had close connections with the finance outfit Südamerika through which a good deal of this money passed.[84]

It could well have been that Filinto received funds directly from German spies operating in Brazil. Nowhere was this more likely than in the backwater known as Müller's home state, Mato Grosso. The Müller family had virtual free run of the place for years. In May 1941, the U.S. military attaché remarked that Mato Grosso was "the worst hotbed of nazism in Brazil–probably with Mueller's [Müller's] cooperation."[85] These assertions by the American officer gain credence when one remembers that the state capital, Cuiabá, had an Italian mayor. There was also at least one German citizen working in the state government. But more important, Júlio Müller, one of Filinto's brothers and Mato

Grosso's *interventor* from 1937 to 1945, kept company with suspect Germans in addition to having large amounts of arms and munitions stashed at his *fazenda*. He acquired the weapons from the state's Força Pública.[86] Unless Júlio had another estate somewhere in Mato Grosso, his *fazenda* was the one derisively named *Abolição*, or "Abolition." It was not a property where the end of slavery was celebrated; but rather, one where prisoners were nearly worked to death. "All laborers who put up a fuss about their [low] wages were arrested and sent there. They were then forced to toil without pay. From 4 A.M., until sunset each received only a small piece of meat under the system of the billy club."[87]

Police Chief Müller had another brother, Fenelon. For six months in 1935, Fenelon too had been Mato Grosso's *interventor*.[88] In whatever capacity, the entire Müller clan was to be taken seriously. One of the cousins even owned "a Rosary made from the ears of prisoners."[89]

The AIB meant business too. Covertly they plotted to kill members of the military and commit acts of sabotage, while out in the open they played up to the Brazilian armed forces, extolling the soldierly arts and the gory glory of combat. Military allies were actively sought and conversions in the next few years were considerable, particularly by the Polícia Militar, at some army installations,[90] and most noticeably in the navy.

The fleet was really a special case owing to the fact that within the armed forces it was the most rabid Integralist cauldron. This is underlined by the discovery that up to at least 1936 there was a secret AIB hit-team in the navy that poisoned the opposition and anyone who did not want to join the ranks of Sigma righteousness. The group was made up of Lieutenant Marcelino J. das Chagas, three-identified sergeants (Waldemiro Silveira de Andrade, Salvador Bispo Corrêa, Conrado A. Fahide), a nameless sergeant, and a steward known only as "Henrique." Andrade was stationed in the office of Naval Personnel. He is said to have sifted through records to help pick out targets. Chagas was a pharmacist and provided the chemicals. Fahide and Henrique distributed them. Corrêa was connected to stewards who placed the substances in the victims' coffee. Finally, the nameless sergeant saw to it that poisoned food was sent to the homes of adversaries on selected military bases.[91]

Once the hour of national awakening arrived, all Green-shirted men and women (the women were called Green Blouses[92]) were to rise up and deliver the nation to its destiny. The AIB maintained a secret police plus Green shock and assault troops to help win this objective.[93] In addition, the Integralist National Council had a section, curiously called the Information Service, which was composed of five subsections. Four of these units were responsible for the buildup of portfolios on enemies. There was a division for Jews, one for communists, another for liberal democrats, and one for Freemasons. What would have happened to all these foes of integralism had the AIB won control of the government is not difficult to imagine.[94]

Somewhere along the way the AIB assembled definitive lists of people to be executed after taking power. One such inventory for Bahia still exists. Besides all the other undesirables on the AIB's day of reckoning, the following state representatives were to be shot: Nestor Duarte, Oscar Nollat, Maria Luiza Bittencourt, and Aliomar Baleeiro. Also to be slain were Edson Carneiro, Carmen Lins Coelho, and Aydano Couto Ferraz, plus "various students."[95]

THE PROGRESSIVES

It went without saying that progressives of every stripe found the AIB nauseating, and even referred to them as *galinhas verdes*, or "Green Chickens." This colorful label originated from the fact that when confronted with superior numbers, it was not uncommon for AIB activists to hurriedly take off their green shirts and run for cover.[96] But when size was with them, or when they thought they had a chance, they stood and fought. Probably the first notable clash between the two bodies occurred on June 11, 1934. There were numerous battles thereafter, some being provoked by the various shades of red and green adherents in the accompanying state's security forces. The confrontation at the Praça de Sé in São Paulo on October 7, 1934, was a good example. On that occasion, a Sunday afternoon AIB rally was to be held immediately after a demonstration put on by leftists in the same location. The Fascists had hoped for 10,000 participants but only 500 showed up. Diverse green-shirt sympathizers were stopped from entering the Praça by the followers of the earlier gathering. Machine-gun-toting police then began to clean the area of demonstrators. Assisting the authorities were the 1st, 2nd, and 6th army Infantry Battalions, sections of the fire department, a mounted regiment, units of the civil guard, and a number of investigators from the social section of *paulistano* political police; the last also armed with machine guns. Suddenly, officers of the law opened fire on the progressives. Soldiers then began shooting at members of the AIB and at their own police colleagues. When it was all over there were at least four dead (two from the political police, one Integralist, and one student). Thirty-odd people were wounded.[97]

Before heads cracked in São Paulo, those opposed to fascism in Brazil organized themselves into a united front, the Aliança Nacional Libertadora or National Liberation Alliance, which became the second major political group of this era. The ANL had its roots partly in the anarchist and socialist movements that permeated Brazil's major cities at the turn of the century. It likewise found inspiration in the communism advocated by the USSR if only through the beliefs and growing connections of some of its members. The ANL, though, was not a communist organization; not at first anyway. Its makeup encompassed all types of left-of-center thinkers, including persons simply opposed to the fascism and racism of the AIB, along with a handful of radicals, some *tenentes*, and many enemies of Getúlio Vargas.

The link with the Soviet Union originated out of the 7th International Congress in Moscow of the Communist International, or Comintern,[98] in July and August 1935. These were meetings where Georgi Dimitrov, a Bulgarian member of the executive committee acting as Stalin's spokesman, held sway over the assembly on one important point. Dimitrov convinced the delegates that anyone willing to fight against fascism should be accepted into a broad popular front of people determined to stop this pestilent adversary.[99] On a deeper level, however, there was an additional and more salient goal that was not immediately apparent to outsiders. For it had already been planned in Moscow that the united fronts' common efforts would inevitably result in a radicalization process. In Brazil's case, this endeavor would go one step further in the battle to win the hearts and minds of the Brazilian masses.

"PRESIDENT"

Rio's first public meeting of the ANL took place in a smoky theater east of the downtown business district on Saturday, March 30, 1935. The weekend date was chosen in order to get as many people as possible to attend. It turned into a memorable event not only because of the size of the gathering; but because of a young political novice named Carlos Lacerda. The already controversial Lacerda galvanized over 2,000 persons packed into the auditorium by proposing an absent Luís Carlos Prestes as the ANL's honorary president.[1] His nomination was enthusiastically approved as was a five-plank program. Even though this agenda was later augmented by Prestes, the initial document came at a time well enough into the Vargas administration to show how little the man from Rio Grande do Sul had really done for the country. The five points called for:[2]

1. "The Suspension of All Foreign-Based Imperialist Debts."

In millions of dollars, Brazil owed its foreign creditors the following amounts, including interest, calculated at mid-year:[3]

1928	1929	1930	1931	1932	1933	1934	1935
$1,247	1,227	1,298	1,347	967	1,139	1,337	1,285

2. "The Immediate Nationalization of Foreign-Based Imperialist Enterprises."

The 1930s were to witness a slow decline of British investments in Brazil followed by an over 50 percent reduction in the 1940s. The English were losing this market to the rapidly ascending Americans. Note that the ensuing figures do not reflect this change. For 1930, the estimated foreign investment in Brazil in millions of dollars was:

Great Britain	$1,396.3
United States	557.0
other European countries	203.0
France	200.0
Canada	100.0
Germany	97.0
Argentina	50.0
Japan	25.0
Total	$2,628.3[4]

3. "The Ceding and Division of Large Agricultural Estates to the People Who Work Them, While Protecting the Small and Middle-Sized Proprietor."

Karl Loewenstein has pointed out that as late as 1944, after fourteen years with Vargas in control,

the wealthy class of Brazil [still] derives its income from agricultural sources. There are . . . huge *latifundia* [*sic*], not unlike semifeudal duchies in size and administration; particularly in the less open spaces of the vast country the owner of the *fazenda* is a political as well as a social and economic power. But the coffee and cotton aristocracy invested their profits in industry, and the men successful in business–the Crespi, Mattarazzo, Guinle, Simonsen–control today large tracts of land managed on a rationalized basis like industrial enterprises. The old landed nobility and the new aristocracy of entrepreneurs have merged. In spite of the battering which landed wealth took in a predominantly one-crop economy, the landowners still form a disproportionately large group in the governing class; and they see to it that the regime abstains from taxing away the foundations of their power as has happened in Britain. They are part and parcel of the regime; Vargas has nothing to fear from them.[5]

No, Getúlio had nothing to fear from the *fazendeiros*. He was one of them.[6] His class, or in terms of actual size in 1920, 1.8 percent of the population, owned 72.4 percent of all agricultural land. Twenty years later, in 1940, these lopsided proportions had improved only slightly with 3.3 percent of Brazil's citizens in possession of 64.4 percent of its arable land.[7]

As for workers on the sections of these properties used for some productive end, 71 percent of the national population lived in rural environments in 1935.[8] Neither then nor at any other time during Getúlio's terms of office were individuals who worked in agriculture organized into unions. The average wage for adult male rural workers–women and children were paid less–was the equivalent of 19.5 cents per day as late as October 1937.[9] Loewenstein continues, mentioning that the way these people were forced to live was so primitive that a visitor from abroad,

with the glamour of the sophisticated residential sections of the big cities on the seashore still before his eyes, is prone to saddle the governing class of the present no less than of the past regimes with the gross neglect of the masses of a fine and decent people In rural districts shoes are commonly not available for the families of the agricultural laborer: clothes are of the cheapest cotton: dirt floors in the roughly made houses. nonexistent sanitary commodities, the scantiest and poorest furniture (if it is more than some pots and pans, wooden dishes, and a few pieces of miserable bedding).[10]

Virtual vassals of the rural power brokers, members of this overlooked majority would now and again tire of their dire working and living conditions and migrate to the larger coastal communities.   Yet without any useful professions, they were only destined to swell the number of constantly growing deplorable *favelas* (shantytowns). Our writer from the mid-1940s concludes by observing that:

any casual visitor who. strolling away from the marble hotels. casinos. glittering show windows and race courses. chances into the appalling quarters of the poor on the hills in Rio de Janeiro or in the slums of São Paulo. will encounter such misery that not even the tropical sun can romanticize it for him. let alone for the people who have to live in tin-can shacks and mud hovels.[11]

4. "The Right to Full Liberties."

Brazil's appointment with poverty was made in colonial times. Economic hardship possessed the slave and devoured the immigrant. By 1935 the country continued to be a dismal place in which to live for most people. The rural *povão* (or peasantry) was particularly susceptible, in addition to falling prey to all the accompanying problems–such as disease. Once in a while, some of the more lethal sicknesses even found their way into urban areas. There were virtually no government social services for the poor. As the provincial destitute trickled into the cities, one of the things this produced was a corresponding drop in entrepreneurial concern for urban-worker welfare. Such was but an outgrowth of the corresponding increase in cheap labor desperate to find and keep a job. As for those members of the less-fortunate group with darker hues of skin, they were looked on as "almost animals that the municipalities allow to pass through their streets only to work for the white."[12] Wages were unusually low, and the rich paid no income or inheritance taxes. Joining a union could, and often did, bring immediate dismissal without compensation.

To protect themselves, the upper classes allocated as much as one-half of the country's budget to the War Ministry and only one-twentieth to the Ministry of Education, Public Health and Culture. Sending one's children to what was made available to public schools, once health and culture took their portions, was tenuous at best. Teacher preparation was next to nothing; since about 65 percent of the country's primary school instructors received a total education of less than four years. In terms of enrollment, an education was looked upon as something for the elite as the succeeding national percentages[13] plainly illustrate:

	7-10 Age Group Enrolled in Primary School	11-12 Age Group Enrolled in Secondary School	18-21 Age Group Enrolled in Higher Education
1930	39.0	1.7	.063
1940	46.0	3.5	.058

Illiteracy, and a malleable populace, were the natural products of this ongoing educational charade. By sex and race for the year 1940, the percentage of Brazilians ten years of age and older who could *not* read or write[14] was:

	Males	Females	Both Sexes
Black	75.1	83.0	79.1
Brown	66.3	75.2	70.8
White	42.1	52.6	47.3
Yellow	26.0	44.4	34.4

In all, it should have come as no surprise to Getúlio or any of his associates that the ANL grew in membership with a speed that was without precedent in the history of Brazilian political parties. Between the date of its founding and the end of May 1935, the ANL claimed an affiliation of several hundred-thousand members. In May alone, 3,000 joined the Aliança Nacional Libertadora each day. Although another estimate of its total size is considerably lower, between 70,000 and 100,000,[15]

much of what success the ANL enjoyed among the urban working class derived from . . . the movement's efforts to unmask official claims regarding advances under Vargas' ambitious but largely ineffective social and working-class legislative program. The ANL advocated a true eight-hour work day, minimum salary scales, two month's severance pay, unemployment insurance, improved facilities for public health, lower consumption taxes for necessities, and equal salary for equal work, all conditions guaranteed for the most part by the 1934 and [coming] 1937 constitutions, but largely abused or ignored.[16]

5. "The Organization of a Government Solely Oriented to the Interests of the Brazilian People in Which All Brazilians Can Participate."

Nominally the country was governed under the Constitution of 1934, which was not too dissimilar from the charter that became law in 1891. The newer document allowed for the formation of political parties; but women were still denied the vote, in a *de facto* sense, as were illiterates, and enlisted men.[17] There was likewise an omen of what was just over the horizon, despite a feint at reducing the powers of the president, since the new constitution permitted a slight corporatist composition to the Chamber of Deputies. True, there were changes at the top and an increasing role for the middle class; but behind the scenes the nation's elites continued to coerce the long arm of the law to maintain a government of themselves, by themselves, and for themselves.

To accomplish the adherence necessary for this structural regeneration to prosper, the police were employed as never before to break up all kinds of suspect (i.e., threatening) activities. Particularly vulnerable were occurrences that involved worker's organizations, meetings, rallies, and protests. Anyone who objected was introduced to the truncheon. Laborers and organizers were arrested, tortured, deported, and, in some cases, unobtrusively killed. Others were murdered openly in cold blood like Tobias Warchavski.

BLAME IT ON THE REDS . . .

Warchavski was a seventeen-year-old member of the Union of Young Communists and the Aliança Nacional Libertadora. Toward the end of 1934, the ANL requested permission from the police to hold a rally in the Praça da Harmonia, not far from the city center, in the Rio suburb of Saúde. Authorization was first granted, then denied at the final moment. This last-minute maneuver was calculated to allow the authorities total leeway in dealing with the 200 to 300 persons already filling the square. The first individual to address the crowd was to be Tobias Warchavski. When the meeting's organizing committee received orders from the police that the demonstration had been abruptly declared illegal, Warchavski was already preparing to pull himself up on the base of a street light, so as to be higher than his listeners, and begin speaking. Seeing this, one of those responsible for the rally gave Carlos Lacerda an order to go tell Warchavski not to start his speech. Lacerda was more a man of words than one of actions. He understood what he was supposed to do, but he proceeded to disappear into the crowd without delivering the warning.

As Warchavski climbed to a position where he could be seen, he was about to open his mouth when a salvo of bullets cut him down. The shots came from inside the gates of the 15th Polícia Militar Battalion on western edge of the *praça*. Instantaneously, the crowd panicked and ran for cover. When it was safe, the police came out of their compound and strolled over to Warchavski's lifeless corpse. Determining that he was dead, they moved the body across the square to one corner of Rua Harmonia (now renamed Rua Pedro Ernesto). Those who slowly returned to see what had happened could actually walk right up and touch the dead youth. The following morning, however, October 19, 1934, Tobias' body was gone. A few days later it was "discovered" by the police on the side of the road up in the peaks behind Gávea, near a breathtaking panorama called "The Chinese View." The authorities said the communists liquidated Warchavski because he had been a traitor.[18]

POLICE THUGS AND THE RISE OF FILINTO MÜLLER

Back in Getúlio's home state, Flôres da Cunha did not ease up after the *Constitutionalista* Civil War. Workers who tried to stay out of the clash found the *gaúcho* police forces turned against them. One only had to be suspected of harboring left-of-center ideas to be picked up. More than once, such persons were charged with being "thieves" in order to justify their arrests. Many were taken to the celebrated police station of Sant Ana in Porto Alegre where they were tossed into cubicles lacking water, beds, blankets, lights, and sanitary fixtures. All the cells had to offer was cold concrete. Next came the pounding around of suspects until they confessed; a process that sometimes continued even after they had told everything. But this type of torture did not apply to military captives. They were shot. Others were carted away to Cachoeirinha, Rio Grande do Sul's own version of Dois Rios. Treatment at Cachoeirinha was so bad that prisoners were known to leave needing psychiatric help. This mental assistance was, naturally, not forthcoming. Instead, mental cases were stripped down to their shorts—winter or summer—and had their heads shaved. They were then dumped on the other side of the border with Uruguay or Argentina without any money. Excluded from much of this were the political prisoners in outlying districts. Far from the help and concern that urban areas could provide, they were summarily sentenced to the timeless yoke of forced labor.[19]

The *paulista* multitudes saw no better. Workers in metropolitan São Paulo championing labor's banner after the war were hunted down and taken to the *geladeira* ("ice box" literally; but in reality a large common cell) at the Gabinete de Investigação (Office of Investigation) on Rua dos Gusmões in Santa Efigênia. Referred to by everyone as the "GI," its overcrowded cells were said to be nothing more than black, windowless boxes. The food GI interns were given was rotten as was the medical attention. Problem-causing prisoners were placed in a special reprimand confine with a brick floor, zinc-lined walls, and an imposing iron door measuring just over 3'3" square. Inmates were jostled into this unit completely nude so that buckets of cold water, periodically tossed on them during the night, could have the maximum effect. When one's nerves provoked it, or when required to do so naturally, defecation had to be done in a toiletless corner.

The GI, however, had one saving grace: it was not the Sacomã Jail. Generally considered to be worse, the Sacomã facility had been preceded by one in Cambuci on Rua Barão de Jaguara as the most feared dungeon in São Paulo. The older edifice contained a multitude of standing-room-only cells measuring two extended palms wide by three across. After Cambuci was demolished, Sacomã was as far down the list as one could go. Located in the southern part of the city, it is reported to have been a place where several variations of whips tore into the backs of inmates. There were also the *palmatorias* (holed, wooden paddles, or ferules), the thumbscrews, and even instruments to cut off body parts one at a time. And, as in Rio Grande do Sul, slave labor was made a part of the picture for some detainees taken to a place decorously named the Island of the Pigs.[20]

In 1934 an English diplomat who had resided in Brazil for twenty-five years commented on what it was like to go through life with such ghastly prospects hanging over one's head:

Little things like a magistrate's warrant for arrest are quite obsolete in up-to-date republican Brazil. The police are not exactly beyond or above the law. They are a law unto themselves, and the imperialism of their methods is felt in the commonest episodes of everyday life. The police is accuser, judge, and "lord high executioner" as well. There is no appeal. So accustomed have Brazilians become to being "bossed" and ordered about that they accept such a state of affairs as quite normal and meekly resign themselves to it—until they periodically revolt against it by backing a revolution which, whatever its upshot, leaves them more under police control than before.[21]

In the country's capital the police had become more vile than ever under one of Vargas' new "bosses." Now formally installed, Polícia Civil Chief Filinto Müller was the most renowned outcast of the *Coluna* Prestes. He was also a hater of organized labor, leftists, nonwhites, and Jews.[22] Shortly before the ANL was formed, one Rio daily commented on the methods of the police under Müller's command with the ensuing poignant observation:

We are returning to what appears to be the days of Bernardes, when prisoners were thrown through the windows of the public building on the Rua da Relação [the Polícia Central, or the Central Police Station, known habitually as "the Central"], when the *"geladeiras"* functioned day and night, when Clevelandias existed, crowded with poor devils, and the "bombs" prepared by the police themselves exploded all over the place to justify the most incredible violence; crimes that were even more hideous.

Have we actually returned to practicing these same atrocities?

Everything indicates that we have.[23]

How true these words would prove to be. Filinto Müller personally saw to their fruition. His dark career began years before as a student when he got away with cheating without being expelled from Rio's Realengo Military Academy. Later, in 1925, Müller was kicked out of the *Coluna Invicta* by Prestes himself while the rebels were in the Iguaçu Waterfall area of Argentina, Brazil, and Paraguay. Encamped on the Brazilian side of the Paraná River, Filinto wrote a letter to his superiors stating he wanted to visit his family, then exiled in Paraguay. He promised to rejoin the Column after it wound its way into Mato Grosso. But his real plan was to desert on turning coward at a 2½-mile crossing of the Paraná. The mighty tributary was just too turbulent for Müller's liking. Convincing a number of soldiers under his command in a second letter that they should go with him—both messages were soon turned over to Prestes—Filinto fled into Argentina. Before leaving, though, he helped himself to 100:000$000 (or $10,526.32) of the *Coluna*'s money.

Making his way to Buenos Aires, Müller fell into a succession of jobs: car washer, taxi driver, and real-estate agent, among others. Returning to Brazil in 1927, he was apprehended and sentenced to two-years' imprisonment. Filinto conspired in a minor way in the 1930 movement that brought Vargas to power and ended up on the staff of Getúlio's first minister of war, General José Fernandes Leite de Castro. In 1931 he became secretary to João Alberto in São

Paulo. Moving to Rio with João Alberto in July of that year, he was made an inspector of the Guarda Civil (civil guards), a subsection of the Polícia Civil. In January 1933, Filinto was picked to head DESPS, Vargas' restructured and renamed Federal District political police. Two months later, and on the recommendation of João Alberto who he was replacing, Müller was anointed chief of the Polícia Civil. This final assignment carried *de facto* cabinet status. Filinto, in addition, was the only member of the government's top echelon to have free access to the leader of the country.[24]

A reporter later asked Luís Carlos Prestes if it was true that he once said: "Don't leave money near João Alberto nor a chamber pot next to Filinto Müller." Adroitly, Prestes answered that he had "never said that about João Alberto."[25] Indeed, Filinto always seemed to have his fingers in several pies at one time.[26] In 1939 he was given 3,500,000 *cruzeiros* (then over $200,000) for his efforts to "capture" a number of workers. After the scuttling of the German pocket battleship *Admiral Graf Spee* on December 17th of that same year, the chief of Rio's police was reputed to have furnished some of the scuttled ship's crew with Brazilian passports, no doubt at a tidy profit.

Müller lived in a veritable mansion at this point in his career. Located in the upper-class suburb of Ipanema near the Clube dos Caiçaras, was such a dwelling really feasible on the chief's official earnings? Many of Müller's subordinates tried to imitate the lavish lifestyle of their boss. Almost all of them became important businessmen who owned stores, apartments, and *fazendas*. The most prudent ones had the wisdom to open up bank accounts in Argentina, Uruguay, the United States, and Europe. Filinto, soon to be made a major, is also said to have channeled secret government money to the construction of expensive houses that he either rented or sold. This wheeling and dealing raised so many eyebrows in the corridors of government that by January 1940 a number of insiders, including Benjamin Vargas and Luiz Aranha, the brother of Oswaldo, counseled Getúlio to fire Müller. The figure in Catete, however, did nothing.[27]

Vargas was occupied with something else. He was feeling more and more that it was time to act against the ANL. Getúlio wanted to close the organization because he was afraid of its rapid growth; just as he feared the massive popularity of its honorary president. He would soon have his chance to deal with both issues through Brazil's first Lei de Segurança Nacional, or National Security Law. Often called the "Lei Monstro" ("Monster Law") by its opponents, the statute defined what constituted the crimes of political and social order against the state. Vargas eagerly signed the bill into effect on April 4, 1935.[28]

ENTER THE CONSPIRATORS OF THE LEFT

One week later Luís Carlos Prestes returned to Brazil via Santa Catarina accompanied by his companion Olga Benário. After entering Bolivia with part of the *Coluna* in 1927, Prestes moved to Argentina where he was converted to communism. Either because certain Argentine generals sold themselves to the interests of the United States, or due to a request for his extradition by Washington Luís, Prestes was briefly arrested in Buenos Aires immediately prior to the outbreak of the Revolution of 1930. Released on the condition that he leave the country, he moved to Montevideo where his life was economically difficult. In 1931, communist agent Arthur Ernst Ewert convinced Moscow that Prestes should be smuggled to the USSR to study the building of socialism at first hand. Prestes agreed and even sent his mother and sisters to the Soviet Union via a different route. For safety's sake the women traveled separately from Prestes to Germany. The family was reunited in Hamburg, and continued to the USSR together. Prestes' trip to the promised land, though, did not come cheap. The legendary warrior agreed to turn over $20,000 of the cash given him by Vargas to lead the military side of the Revolution of 1930. The funds, which Prestes delivered personally, were to be used by the Comintern to help fund the activities of radicals in South America, especially those in Brazil. It was the price the new convert paid to be accepted into the communist fold.[29] The money doubtlessly helped change Moscow's view of the man, who was seen by some, in particular some of his homegrown critics, as too self-serving.

By 1934, after a little over three years in the Soviet Union, the Comintern secretly decided to send their new adherent and a team of other revolutionaries to Brazil. They were instructed to organize and promote a national uprising through the impoverished peasants of the Northeast. The theorizers in Moscow, chiefly Bulgarian Georgi Dimitrov and Soviet Dimitri Manuilski, classified Brazil as semicolonial and ripe for insurrection from the countryside with support in the cities by the ANL.[30] Prestes was to return to the land of his birth as the husband of Olga Benário, whose real job was to be his bodyguard.

Olga left behind her legal husband, B.P. Nikitin, to travel with the famed Brazilian. Nikitin and Olga had been married about a year when she was given her new assignment.[31] A fugitive from her native Munich, she was in Moscow and wanted by German authorities for breaking an earlier lover, Otto Braun, out of prison. Born into a middle-class Jewish family, Olga rebelled and became a communist at fifteen.[32] Growing into adulthood, she could speak four languages fluently. A markswoman, Olga also knew how to fly a plane and use a parachute. She had already been on short missions to England and France. Back in Moscow, she would ultimately work for General Jan Karlovich Berzin, chief of the IV Department of the Red Army, or military intelligence.

At the direction of Manuilski, Olga was placed in personal charge of Prestes' safety and, as they left the Soviet Union, she could almost always be found near his side armed with an automatic pistol. Their trip began at midnight on December 29, 1934. Once out of the USSR, they secretly traveled through parts of Scandinavia and Western Europe as Antonio Vilar and Maria Bergner Vilar. The couple's false passport stated that he was a Portuguese businessman accompanied by his wife. They booked passage on a steamer to New York, and by Pan Am Clipper on a many stopped-flight leaving Miami for Santiago de Chile on March 31, 1935. On April 9th, they continued with Panagra Airways from Santiago to Buenos Aries, obtained Brazilian visas, and flew to Montevideo on the 13th. There they changed to the French airline Latécoère.

Latécoère ran a once-a-month mail seaplane up the Brazilian coast and on to France. As there was not enough mail to fill the plane, two seats were made available to passengers. The timing was perfect. On the morning of April 15, 1935, the long journey ended when they lulled the plane's captain into believing that Olga had relatives living in the north of Paraná. The craft was scheduled to make a short stop anyway. *Senhor* and *Senhora* Vilar told the crew that they did not want to continue to their ticketed destination of Praia Grande on the coast of São Paulo. She and her husband wanted to visit her relatives. The pilot agreed and the pair stepped out of the seaplane near the beaches of Florianópolis, the Santa Catarina state capital. There were no passports to be shown and no suitcases to be opened. In fact there were no formalities of any kind. The two leftists simply hailed a car to take them into the city. Shortly thereafter, the British informed the Brazilian government that Luís Carlos Prestes was back in the country and traveling under the name of Vilar.[33]

Preceding Prestes and Olga, on March 6, 1935, Arthur Ernst Ewert, or as he was known on his fake American passport, Harry Berger, arrived in Brazil from Buenos Aires. Called "Sabo" by her friends, his wife, Auguste Elise Ewert, reached Brazil five days later. She too was using false American documents.[34] From 1928 to 1930, Harry Berger had been a communist member of the German Reichstag. He had been in Mexico on the Comintern's behalf, and in 1931 participated in a meeting of the South American leaders of the Communist International in Montevideo. There he met Prestes and added his voice to those wanting him in the movement. Ewert next appeared as one of the organizers of the failed communist revolution in China in 1933-1934. Given another chance, he left for Brazil via Buenos Aires toward the end of 1934. Once in place in Rio de Janeiro, he successfully helped the Brazilian communists organize the ANL.

Among the tourists disembarking in Rio from the ship *Western World* on April 11th, and using the alias of Luciano Busteros, was the head of the Argentine Communist Party, Rodolfo José Ghioldi. Ghioldi was accompanied by his wife, Carmen de Alfaya Ghioldi.[35] Arriving on November 5, 1935, was an Italian communist, Amleto Locatelli, also know as "Bruno." He was to function as a military trainer in the Northeast. Slowly building a radio transmitter, a dangerous job because the parts had to be purchased separately to avoid suspicion, was the group's only American. Already sickly when he entered Brazil on July 15th, Victor Allen Barron was the son of American communist Harrison George. His mother had divorced George, remarried, and legally changed her two sons' last name to that of her new husband.

Four of the remaining members of the incoming inner circle traveled under names the rest of the group believed were genuine. There was the supposed monetary advisor, Leon Jules Vallée and his wife Alphonsine, both of whom passed themselves off as Belgians. Actually Leon was to be the Brazilian head of ОМС (Отдел Международных Связей), or the Department of International Contacts, and responsible for all finances and communication from and with Moscow. A Russian who spoke excellent French, his true name was Pavel Vladimirovich Stuchevski.   He was a member of the НКВД (Народный Коммиссариат Внутренних Дел), the People's Commissariat of Internal Affairs, or ominous NKVD, the Soviet political police.   Alphonsine, also a Russian, and also from the IV Department, was really Sofia Semionova Stuchevskaya.   She had phlebitis in her right leg which caused her to limp slightly. Sofia's job was to encode and decode telegrams given to trusted third parties to be sent to Europe.

Working for Pavel were two runners who shuffled the coded messages between Rio, São Paulo, and Buenos Aires. There was Marcus Jungmann (a.k.a. Meyer Jungmann, "Arias," and "Ramon"), an Argentine of Polish extraction, and a second individual, probably a female, known only as "Carmen."

Finally there were the Grubers (actually Johann Heinrich Amandus de Graaf and Helena Erma Krüger), whose false names everyone in the small band of leftists believed were real. Both claimed to be Austrians. She called herself Erna Gruber and said she was a typist and driver. Her reputed husband was an authority on explosives and sabotage. He went by the name Franz Paul Gruber. When the couple was alone she called him "Johnny." In return, he referred to her during these endearing moments as "Lena" or "Lee."[36]

All of these individuals were dedicated revolutionaries determined to overthrow Vargas and bring a Soviet-style government to Brazil. All of them that is except one. For, unknown to the rest of group, and even to his own common-law wife, Johann de Graaf was a double agent working for England's Secret Intelligence Service (or SIS). When requested, Britain's spy apparatus provided selected bits of information to Brazil's Foreign Ministry, the Itamarati. This body, in turn, informed Filinto Müller.[37]

END OF THE ANL

Once reaching Rio de Janeiro–two foreign agents tipped off the Brazilian police that Prestes had now traveled to the capital[38]–the plotters sat about altering the thrust of the ANL.   Their orders were to turn it into a radical-political forum, take power, and once firmly in control move toward socialism. On May 13th, the forty-seventh anniversary of the abolition of Brazilian slavery, the ANL announced that Luís Carlos Prestes would issue an important statement on July 5th. This was the same portentous day as the start of the 1922 and 1924 *tenente*-led uprisings. But just as the earlier revolts had gone off prematurely due to bad planning, so too was Moscow about to make a crucial blunder. The seeds had already been sown by the Brazilian communists exiled in Moscow. This key group had vastly overrated their capabilities and the true situation back home.   By 1934, the Moscow-Brazilians had convinced their Comintern superiors that Vargas could easily be toppled.   Unwilling to listen to voices saying the time was not ripe, the leaders of world socialism were at fault for insisting on the inclusion of the cumulating line in Prestes' remarks; words that would seal the fate of the ANL. The Comintern duplicated Bolshevik sloganeering from 1917 too closely to understand that there is no set way to start a revolution. Ewert, Ghioldi, and Prestes were against Moscow's directive. But after several delays and excuses they were ordered to give in.[39]

As he began to read his July *manifesto*, Prestes declared that the ANL was continuing the fight that began in 1922 on the sands of Copacabana. "The Brazilian people," he said

are united, more by the suffering, by the misery, and by humiliation in which they vegetate, than by an impossible national unity under the semi-colonial and semi-feudal conditions of today's Brazil! . . . Where are the promises of 1930? What a difference there is between what they said and vowed . . . and the terrible reality now vivid these five years with Getúlio.[40]

Known as the "Cavalheiro da Esperança," or "Knight of Hope," Prestes went on to analyze how Vargas had betrayed the people's trust by handing the country over to commercial interests in England, the United States, Italy, Germany, and Japan. All were eager to divide Brazil into their own spheres of economic influence. In his view, the only way to save the nation was to create "a popular revolutionary, anti-imperialistic government . . . [which would] end the monstrous inequality that domination by the *fazendeiros* and the imperialists have imposed on the country."[41]

It was a mastery, he continued, that hid behind the banner of a nonexistent liberal democracy; but which the people knew only through "the bloody dictatorships of Epitacio, Bernardes, Washington Luís, and Getúlio Vargas. . . . The moment [thus] demands of all honest people a clear and defined position for or against fascism, for or against imperialism! An opinion between these poles is not possible nor justifiable."[42]

Prestes then called on every Brazilian who was against these evils, regardless of their political views, to support the revised program of the ANL. The new agenda called for:

1. The cancellation of all foreign debts.

2. The termination of all imperialistic treaties.

3. The nationalization of the most important public services and those imperialistic enterprises that fail to subordinate themselves to the laws of the popular revolutionary government.

4. An eight-hour workday. Equal pay for equal work and a minimum wage.

5. A fight against conditions of slavery and feudalism at the work place.

6. The distribution without indemnification of lands and water rights from the imperialists, the most reactionary large estate owners, and the Church–to the poor, farm workers, and other laborers.

7. The return of lands taken by violence from the Indians.

8. The increase of popular liberties. The elimination of differences and privileges based on race, color, or nationality. Complete religious liberty and the separation of church and state.

9. The rejection of all imperialist wars, and the alliance with similar movements in other Latin American countries, and with all oppressed classes and peoples.[43]

He then continued by calling on discontented soldiers all over Brazil, true democrats, agricultural workers, and common citizens to organize themselves. In block letters his words grabbed at them: "DOWN WITH FASCISM!" "DOWN WITH THE HATED VARGAS REGIME!" "FOR A POPULAR REVOLUTIONARY GOVERNMENT!" Concluding, Prestes proceeded to include the mistake from Moscow. The Soviets thought it would ignite the first socialist uprising in the Americas. It only helped to put it out: "ALL POWER TO THE ANL!"[44]

Getúlio found the excuse he had been waiting for. Polícia Civil Chief Filinto Müller promptly declared that Soviet communists controlled the ANL, and that Moscow had plans to promote revolutions through it in Brazil and by way of affiliated "neo-movements" in Argentina and Uruguay. He submitted his analysis to the minister of justice, Vicente Ráo. The minister then drafted a decree outlawing the ANL under the terms of the hardly three-month-old National Security Law.[45] Vargas put his name to the measure on July 11, 1935; but it was not made public until the 15th in order to give the police time to raid the offices of the ANL. There were several arrests, no less than one kidnapping, and an unexplained murder in the process.[46]

NOVEMBER 1935

Closing the Aliança Nacional Libertadora only forced it underground, although with a vastly reduced membership. It likewise marked the start of a period of increased police violence against anyone politically left of center that would explode into a full-scale onslaught later in the year. The final attack sprang from hastily starting the scheduled uprising too early in Rio Grande do Norte and Pernambuco.[47]

Events in the Northeast had become a powder keg. Regional political issues, strikes, and discontent among noncoms in the army stationed in Natal all combined to produce a tinderbox. It was questionable if the revolutionaries ever could have kept a lid on everything until the agreed-upon date of action. Vargas was aware of the tense situation, and was informed of the plans for the coming rebellion, at least in Pernambuco, through the efforts of Johnny de Graaf. Moscow, too, knew by the end of July 1935 that the English were being kept abreast of their intentions.[48] The fact that the coup was touched off prematurely indicates that Getúlio may well have been a step ahead of his opponents. One narrative states that this resulted from intelligence agents and a forged, coded telegram to the chief of the Polícia Militar in Natal, Aloísio Moura. Chief Moura is said to have had close connections with the insurrection's regional leadership. The cable ordered what was essentially an untimely start to the revolt for the evening of the 23rd of November.[49]

Another version maintains that the drama began differently. According to this account, the line between military dissatisfaction, leftist activity, and open banditry was often tenuous among enlisted men in the Northeast. So, when the commander of the 21st Gunnery Battalion in Natal expelled a group of soldiers from his unit for having held up and robbed a streetcar the week before, the discipline proved to be more than the accused's friends back in the barracks could take. Led by Sergeant Raimundo Francisco de Lima, the irate soldiers placed the watch officer under arrest "in the name of Luís Carlos Prestes" and started everything.[50]

As rebellions go in Brazil, this one was another quick affair. The whole misadventure never became a serious threat to the national administration. After the shooting began up North, Vargas telephoned Johann de Graaf's Secret Intelligence Service handler, Alfred Hutt. Hutt was the general assistant superintendent of Light, Rio's Canadian-owned electric company, and the SIS's chief agent in the Brazilian capital. Getúlio wanted to know if there was any likelihood of a communist victory. Hutt immediately contacted de Graaf for his opinion. De Graaf told his supervisor to tell Vargas in no uncertain terms, "Not a chance!"[51] The observation proved prophetic. The leftists had been unprepared and largely caught off guard. Their uprising was rapidly contained in Natal and Recife. In Rio de Janeiro, the main fight was put up by the 3rd Infantry Regiment stationed out on Praia Vermelha. Most of the other units failed at their assigned tasks throughout the city and by November 27th it was all over.[52] The Comintern's social revolution, which would come to be known in Brazilian history as the *Intentona Comunista*, ended in a preempted four-day failure.[53]

REACTION

At the same time the outcome could not have been rosier for Getúlio Dornelles Vargas. He asked Congress for and was given a one-month state of siege. This was expanded to an internal state of war, lasting ninety days at a time, and renewed continuously until June two years later.[54] These directives allowed the police and other subelites[55] of the administration to operate under the freedom of martial law in their search for communists and communist sympathizers.[56] The persons chosen to fulfill these enforcement roles, in what became a red-scare pogrom, came from the furthest corners of reactionary society. The Integralists naturally supplied men and information as did some well-connected private citizens.

Likewise, from early 1936 on, there were the National Commissions to Suppress Communism, the first of which was led by Federal Congressman Adalberto Correia.[57] Among its various activities the Commission put together a list of suspected leftists and leftist supporters in several parts of the country. The following is one of their very first tallies of progressive enemies in selected Brazilian states:[58]

Alagoas	53
Amazonas	5
Bahia	
suspects	109
communists	27
Ceará	9[a]
Pará	14
Piauí	51
Rio de Janeiro	
suspects	210
communists	116
Rio Grande do Norte	402
São Paulo	121[b]
Sergipe	
arrested leftists	28

a=probable
b=Files were begun for all 121 employees at São Paulo's Light & Power as their names arrived at SOPS. Fourteen of these employees already had their names in the police archives.

All of the progovernment patriots joined hands with the 5,000 or so policemen under the command of Getúlio's alter ego, Filinto Müller, to look for a red under every rock.[59] Vargas used the occasion for two goals. The first was to deal with the leftists and their supporters. The second involved the selective removal of obstacles to his own grab at more power that was still two years away. The short-lived rebellion provided the needed justification for this more important objective. Thereafter, anyone who refused or vacillated to become a team player might find himself labeled a communist. And communists were officially designated as public enemies number one more so than at any time in the past.

The wave of terror that originated in the last weeks of 1935 was the largest of its kind in the country's history. It began in the capital on November 27th as soon as a surrender was arranged. Without delay, some of the "officers in the revolutionary forces . . . [were] taken by the police out into the woods behind Rio [Tijuca] and shot."[60] Roadblocks were placed on the highways leading from major metropolitan centers and anyone who wanted out was checked. After just the first four months of the operation the authorities had

made 3,250 investigative detentions, 441 residential searches (a euphemism utilized to designate the invasion of homes, generally at night, without judicial mandate) and had imprisoned a little more than three-thousand [3,250] persons, of whom 901 were civilians and 2,146 military personnel. And all of this was only in the official jurisdiction of Filinto, that is, the city of Rio de Janeiro.[61]

As for the nation taken as a whole, by mid-1937 estimates of the total number of detained persons varied from 7,000 to 35,000.[62] The actual figure is perhaps unimportant. What is significant is that Vargas was not going to give any quarter to leftist sentiment. To this end, all kinds of callousness became justified to maintain order by way of example.

SAFE SCAPEGOATS

In the Northeast, the Caldeirão affair was but one of these episodes. It was explained to the world as a religious or quasicommunistic movement made up of leftist fugitives from the events in Natal and Recife.[63] What really transpired was another matter, and actually began with a black *Beato*[64] named José Lourenço and a young zebu bull. Lourenço was given the animal as a present from *Padre* Cícero Romão Batista of Juazeiro do Norte in Ceará. Considered a living saint in the Northeast, Cícero ministered to the spiritual needs of those living in and around Juazeiro until passing away in 1934. Part of the time, the venerated *Padre* was forced to conduct his services in an unofficial capacity as he had been defrocked out of jealously.

The young bull became a favorite with locals who started calling him *Boi Santo*, or the Saintly Bull. People were soon presenting the docile creature with garlands of flowers and special food, and even came to wear little vials of its urine around their necks as good luck charms. Affectionately known as "Mansinho" or "Little Tame One," the zebu was nonetheless butchered in 1926 on directives from Federal Congressman and *Coronel* Floro Bartolomeu, *Padre* Cícero's protector. Floro decided to act after he came to believe in the rumors and allegations that the bull was fast becoming both a totemic and fetishistic object.

Thrown in jail in Juazeiro, Lourenço was made to eat the flesh of the dead animal. Following his release, he moved to Caldeirão and over the next few years the community became a self-sufficient, almost idyllic place to live. Everyone worked, even Lourenço. All 5,000 inhabitants were devotees of *Padre* Cícero. They did not need the outside world for very much; and this one fact was enough to spread fear among those who believed in the sanctity of capitalism over collectivism. Others say that since the title to Caldeirão's property was given to the Salazarirans following Cícero's death, the religious order was irritated with Lourenço because he failed to pay them any rent.

Soon the police were called in to defend the lowest common denominator. They gave residents a deadline to leave but before the final day arrived, returned to burn part of the village to the ground. This provoked a division at Caldeirão. Lourenço headed a band of some thirty nonviolent families who moved away in compliance with the authorities orders. The second group, numbering about 100 families, advocated armed resistance. They were led by Severino Tavares, and moved through several locations in the interior until being accosted by a police patrol in May 1937. The outcome resulted in four causalities for the authorities.

When details of these fatalities reached Rio de Janeiro, everything started to come apart. Commands were dispatched to crush the rebellious *sertanejos*.

Vargas authorized his minister of war, General Eurico Gaspar Dutra, to exterminate the belligerent Caldeirão faction. By then, they had put down roots near the village of Pau de Colher in neighboring Bahia. Two army battalions, a company of men from the Polícia Militar, and reserve troops from Pernambucano, all converged on the little community in January 1938. Airplanes were flown over Pau de Colher only for tactical support and not on bombing or machine-gun runs. Certainly they could have been fitted out for the latter types of sorties had the fighting gone against the government. Such draconian alternatives were not necessary because the outcome proved only too predictable. Upwards of 400 rural laborers, including Severino Tavares, were slaughtered in a lopsided conflict. José Lourenço lived in fear the rest of his life; but in the end died of natural causes in 1946 at seventy-four years of age.[65]

OTHER PERSECUTIONS AND THE ARREST OF THE EWERTS

It was also in the post-*Intentona* climate that the deportations of foreigners possessing "Central or Eastern European sounding names"[66] became more conspicuous. Occurring mainly in urban areas, seizures of non-Brazilians began to take on anti-Semitic overtones not only due to the expulsions, but because it was a convenient means of fleecing wealthier Jews. One way this was done was to pick up innocent followers of the Star of David for the express purpose of getting their families to bribe them out of jail. Some Jewish leaders felt the hand of Müller, if ever so suggestive, behind it all.[67]

From a critical standpoint, three of the more prominent "Hebrews" that Filinto was out to get were soon to be captured. Harry Berger and his wife, Sabo, made up two-thirds of this meager but important group. Yet despite their best efforts, the police were having trouble making the connection to the German couple they had only heard about. By December 1935 a decision was finally made to have their police liaison ask the SIS for help. Once approval was given, the English instructed de Graaf to provided the address. He gave it to Hutt, who passed it onto the British Embassy, who told the Itamarati.[68]

The Ewerts were arrested at 2 P.M., the day after Christmas. Olga, Locatelli, and an innocent-acting Franz Gruber separately witnessed the commotion at Rua Paulo Redfern 33 in Ipanema as Müller's Polícia Civil picked up the Ewerts from their rented house.[69] Among the arresting party was a pale blond who took personal charge of Berger. After placing Harry in a paddy wagon and securing his hands to a metal bar behind his head, a machine gun was shoved against his chest. Then the fair-skinned individual calmly proceeded to pull a nutcracker from one pocket and break open a few hazelnuts. Suddenly, he took firm hold of the left hand of the prisoner and placed the device on Berger's thumb. With unexpected naturalness, he crushed the bone into what must have been several pieces. Harry Berger broke into a cold sweat but infuriated his captors by failing to utter a sound. Startled at this self-control, the blond put his head to Berger's and was overheard growling in perfect German, "Kommunist Sohn von einer Hure!" ("Communist son-of-a-bitch!") Even the Gestapo was working with Filinto Müller.[70]

The Geheime Staatspolizei had a secret verbal agreement with the Brazilian political police, which came into force sometime after November 1935, to battle bolshevism and other dogmas considered dangerous to their mutual regimes. This collaboration was later confirmed in a confidential communication from Richard Heydrich to Herman Göring dated August 22, 1938. The Brazilians likewise received information on suspected communists, together with antileftist publications, from the Anti-Comintern Bureau in Berlin. Brazil's ambassador to Germany, Muniz de Aragão, used the Bureau so much that he tried to get Rio de Janeiro's permission for an annual Brazilian contribution of £150. Müller's suggestion that the Gestapo formally send specialists to Brazil was also rejected by Catete. Instead, DESPS Chief Affonso Henrique Miranda Corrêia went to Germany in March 1937 to study the *Reich*'s efforts in dealing with communism. There for nearly a year, he personally met Heinrich Himmler. When the DESPS leader returned, his bags were full of photographs and files of information on Comintern agents. The United States similarly assisted the Brazilian police and probably knew of the Gestapo connection. American Ambassador Hugh Gibson is said to have had especially close contacts with Miranda Corrêia.as well as with Captain Francisco Julien. Both had been invited to the United States but Julien was the only one who went, visiting the FBI Academy in Washington D.C., in addition to the Chicago and New York City police departments.[71]

ANGUISH AND THE EWERTS

Sabo and Arthur were taken to the Special Police headquarters on Rio's Santo Antônio Hill and acrimoniously grilled on the whereabouts of their still-at-large comrades. They had already incriminated themselves and the movement by leaving a huge amount of evidence at their residence in Ipanema. A safe bomb designed by de Graaf not to go off provided much of this windfall. But Ewert was also notoriously lax about leaving things out in the open. His only play once taken to the Central was thus to keep quiet. Sphinx-like, the Bergers did just this. They sat like ice through all the questions, pokings and proddings, refusing to cooperate. Well enough, but the Brazilians and Germans were not ready to give up their search so easy, especially for Prestes.

The two communists were stripped naked and forced to stand for seventy-two hours. Neither was allowed to sleep completely for eight days. Nothing was provided to eat or drink. At the start of the fourth night they were marched out to the garage and submitted to one grim ordeal after another. From that moment, torture became an on-again off-again barrage, usually in the wee-morning hours, that ended months later. Somewhere during this madness, Arthur was chained nude to the bars of his cell with his arms and feet spread eagled. Then a nearly twenty-inch wire was forced up into his bladder through his penis and slowly heated. Later, he was shocked when other cables connected to generators were twisted around his sexual organs or crammed into his anus.

The German's head and testicles were squeezed in an apparatus allegedly designed by Müller himself. A number of Ewert's ribs were broken. Still without clothes, he was taken by firing squad to a grave his wife had been compelled to dig. After waiting at the edge of this pit for endless minutes, without the command to fire being given, he was led back to his cell. On another occasion he was again marched out, made to stand waiting for the bullets to crash into his chest, and then executed by a detachment of men who shot blanks. Pins were pushed under his fingernails and his buttocks were blowtorched. Other parts of his body were seared with cigars and cigarettes some 200 times. When he almost nodded off one night, the jailers became so incensed that a typewriter was tied to his head. To keep from breaking his neck, he then had to stand as straight as a board until daybreak. During another interrogation, Ewert nearly died after being intensely beaten on the head. Fearful that he would go to his grave before revealing what they wanted to know, the police hurriedly called in a physician to save him.

Berger's main torturers were Antonio Emílio Romano,[72] chief of the Political Section at DESPS, and Miranda Corrêia. When all else failed, other Brazilians, some Germans, and White Russians tried to get Ewert to talk. One of the questioners was the American State Department's special agent, Theodore Xanthaky. Initially, Xanthaky used the pretext of the false U.S. passports as his reason for a private questioning of the Bergers. After being transcribed and sent to Washington, these conversations naturally found their way back to the Brazilian government. Present for some of the other interrogations were Müller, the German ambassador, and representatives of the SIS.

The shock therapy and burning tobacco were likewise applied to Auguste Ewert, who had one ear badly scorched as a result. Different from her husband, she was buried alive and then dug up still breathing. Elise was also yanked about by her hair and bosom in Harry's presence. Repeatedly whipped by a Gestapo agent, her breasts were slit and crushed. When not being raped again and again by her captors, billy clubs alternating with burning cigarettes were shoved into her anus and vagina. Sleep too was used against her, sometimes allowed, sometimes denied, for weeks on end. Drinking water became a privilege, heightened due to an eventual diet made up entirely of salted fish.

The methods used on the Ewerts provide a rare glimpse into the macabre world of what we might call tactics of a second level. If questioning occupies the first and sole ethical method of interaction with suspects, the second tier comprises third-degree techniques only heard about in whispers or in open comments by the foolhardy. By 1936, Brazilian subelites were among the world's experts in this murky, subsidiary area of interrogation. In the face of all of the coercive expertise, however, the Bergers remained silent and with incredible determination refused to divulge anything of substance. Their idealism kept them going, battered, but alive nonetheless.[73]

Held incommunicado until the press caught wind of the story on January 5th, the first accounting of the couple in the by-then Nazi owned *A Noite* said that Harry was a Slav. The next day they reported that he had "a nose characteristic of the sons of Israel."[74] The comments in *O Globo* approached the level of frenzy usually found in the German media. Also on the 6th, topped by front page banner headlines, *O Globo* picked up the story and screamed, "SON OF ISRAEL AND AGENT OF MOSCOW!" Under three large pictures of the Bergers, the caption started, "The Famous Jew." As if she was forgotten about, no reference was made to Sabo's Jewishness until the following day. Looking just at *O Globo*, there were numerous occasions in the editions of January 6th and 7th where *O Globo* used the word Jew or a variation of it when referring to this case.[75]

All of the hysteria about the Ewerts' religion came from a ruse. The police, the press, and the public fell for the deception. Their reaction provided a weather vane of anti-Semitism endemic in the country by the mid-1930s. Ewert was not a Jew; nor was his wife. On being taken to the Central, and still using the name Harry Berger, Ewert was asked for the names of his parents, which he furnished. Not a procedure specifically aimed at communists, Brazilian official-dom has insisted on knowing one's parentage for generations. Confronted with this formality, everyone in attendance must have sucked wind when Berger stated that his father's name was Israel Berger. The senior Ewert's real name was actually Franz Ewert.[76] His son, Arthur, slapped Brazil in the face with its own prejudice and hardly anyone realized it.

PAVEL AND SOPHIA AS SUSPECTS

On December 28th, Pavel telegramed the USSR via Paris about the Ewerts' arrest along with the compromising documents recovered by the police at their residence. He also informed his superiors that Prestes was in a very dangerous predicament and that Barron had been sent to Buenos Aires to establish direct connections with Moscow. Six days later, on January 3, 1936, the Stuchevskis were also picked up. Someone had apparently turned them in. It is doubtful that the Bergers said anything, as they were keeping a stony silence. The most-often-named candidate was Ewert's maid, Deolinda Dias, who had seen Pavel and Sofia numerous times at her employer's Ipanema home. Sofia's game leg, so it was said, made her identification easier. An engineer, a businessman, and two of the telegraph clerks Pavel used were other possibilities. Each was brought in, questioned, but soon released. The actual informant, however, was probably Johnny de Graaf.

Searching through Stuchevski's apartment, the police seized 6,000 Argentine pesos (roughly $1,700) inside a suitcase. They missed some 12,000 florins ($7,800) hidden in both a false-bottom bag and a small world globe. Sofia's code book was confiscated because of the word "Communism" written in the volume's dedication; but the police were unaware that they held the key to decipher Moscow's telegrams in their hands. Truly, DESPS did not realize the importance of the suspects they had caught.

Driven to the Polícia Central, the NKVD agent and his wife artfully dodged most of the questions put to them at the dungeon on Rua da Relação. Vallée used the cover story of having come to Brazil that April with a sick wife in need a better climate. He claimed that since all his money was in Argentine pesos, he obviously had not planned on staying long. The Brazilian political police, however, were not the total fools their Russian counterpart thought them to be. By January 11th, Miranda Corrêia got the idea that if the Vallées were let go perhaps they would lead the police to bigger things and maybe even to Prestes himself. Just before midnight this theory was put to the test. The couple was freed by Müller's secretary, Carlos Brantes, but told to report back every Monday and Friday. They immediately took a taxi to their Copacabana apartment, trailed the entire way.

MORE ARRESTS

Better known as "Miranda," Antônio Bonfim and his twenty-one-year-old illiterate companion, Elza Fernandes, were detained, because of de Graaf, on January 13, 1936. Miranda had been Brazil's communist leader before the advent of Prestes. He clearly disliked his replacement. Although it is not clear at what point during the first days of his incarceration he began to reveal things to the police, once Bonfim opened his mouth, he gave the authorities a wealth of information. Prodding him to cooperate, torture was used often enough to require the removal later of one of his kidneys. Antônio swore that he was abused for four days and nights by the Polícia Especial. Then he said he was taken to the Social Section of DESPS, or S-2, where he was fed once every twenty-four hours and made to stay on his feet. His claimed his clothes were taken away and he had to constantly keep moving, walking about in a room above the courtyard. The only pause came when the guards beat him, which usually happened a few times each day and periodically at night. When he screamed, they choked him until he passed out. On three or four occasions they took him to be executed, only to use blanks. Temporary Police Chief Miranda Corrêia and the head of S-2, Serafim Braga, sometimes left their offices to watch these oppressive data-gathering sessions with Miranda.

Elza Fernandes claimed that she had her hair pulled by Emílio Romano. He also hit her with a rubber hose twice on the back, twice on the soles of her feet, and six times on the nape of her neck. She indicated that she was surprised not to have her breasts pulled or what would have been the "Mustard Plug"[77] forced into her. But she did mention that the police threatened to take her up the road to the Chinese View, to drown her by shoving a sponge laced with alcohol into her nose, that Serafim Braga would thrust a pen into her back, and that every half hour or so they ordered her to tell them what they wanted to know so as not to be shot. Her captors did manage to fire off a few blanks in her direction as a warning. Bonfim later wrote to one of Elza's brothers informing him that neither he nor Elza had given up Rodolfo Ghioldi to the police as some newspapers insinuated.[78]

The following year Julien, in fact, mentioned that Ghioldi was recognized by accident by one of his men. Carmen and Rodolfo were immediately put under surveillance and picked up in the early morning of January 23rd,[79] while trying to flee to São Paulo by train. Once in police custody, and despite their being comrades-in-arms, Ghioldi reacted very differently than did Harry Berger. Having lived next to Brazil most of his life, the Argentine knew about the kind of inhumanity awaiting him should he fail to cooperate. Thus, without having had so much as a finger laid on him, he promptly identified a photograph of Leon Jules Vallée. No matter that he did not know their real names, he furnished the authorities enough information to confirm their suspicions about Pavel Stuchevski and Sofia Stuchevskaya. Moreover, between Bonfim and Ghioldi, the mayor of Rio, Pedro Ernesto, was tied into the plot. Ghioldi supplied the police with Prestes' address on Rua Nossa Senhora de Copacabana. Finally, he offered up a gem by mentioning that the leader of the rebellion was married. Besides a description of the young woman, he even identified a photo of the American radio expert, Victor Allen Barron, and he did the same favor for Marcus Jungmann.[80]

ESCAPE OF THE TWO RUSSIANS

Soon after returning to their apartment, Pavel and Sofia began leaving the building at four o'clock each afternoon to walk along the same route in Copacabana. This was done to tire their followers and to pass by the preset rendezvous points with those members of the plot still at large. If one failed to show up, the other party might keep coming to the same bench or restaurant day after day. Stuchevski and his wife evidently wanted to give a signal to Barron, now back in Rio, and to Jungmann. By not acknowledging them, or by flashing some type of gesture, it was hoped they would perceive the danger, say nothing, and realize that it was time to clear out. The two were subjected to this cold-shoulder tactic by Pavel and Sofia as they passed each other a few times during the course of the week. Apparently, the two young men did not understand and kept returning..

On Friday, January 24th, Pavel reported in as usual at the Polícia Central. He was met by a terse inspector Francisco Julien who told him that he and his wife were henceforth prohibited from leaving the country, that they would have to stay in Rio, obtain a lawyer, and that their passports were being confiscated.[81] Julien was the link between DESPS and the SIS.[82] Perhaps it was this ironic fact that produced Julien's gruff attitude. Whatever it was, it tipped the Russian off that the police were ready to pounce. The next afternoon, at 4 P.M., the Vallées left their apartment for their customary walk. The usual DESPS detectives lurked behind, in and out of the doorways. Suddenly, Pavel and Sofia broke the routine by bolting onto a bus. Several minutes later they got off outside a cafe and went in. Next, they walked to a movie but left before the film was half over.

This was followed by another restaurant, bus ride, taxi, and a final bus. When they were sure that they were not being tailed, they walked to one of the mapped-out meeting places and found Jungmann, who told them that Barron was waiting with a car in another part of town. The two Russians then took a taxi and bus, and reencountered Jungmann at the designated spot. After the American drove up, he took the trio to Pavel's own emergency safe house at Rua Honório 279 in Méier.

It was exactly to this hideaway that Barron had already delivered Prestes and Olga. Once the Ewerts were captured, Olga hurried to the house she and Prestes rented, not far away, on Rua Barão da Torre. The two then hastily departed by taxi for Stuchevski's Copacabana apartment. Like the Ewerts, they left behind a large number of ensnaring documents; documents that were not destroyed because of another dud bomb installed by Johann de Graaf.

Aware that both couples could not live in his flat for long without causing suspicion, Pavel provided Olga and the rebellion's leader his own safe house in Méier. Now face to face again, the foursome discussed what to do next. New passports were on their way from Buenos Aires for Rodolfo, Carmen de Alfaya Ghioldi, as well as for Olga and Prestes. The other Carmen was bringing them from Argentina. She was to turn the documents over to Jungmann at one of the street encounters. But when Carmen reached Rio something had happened to Marcus Jungmann. Arais was nowhere to be found during the ensuing five weeks as Carmen unwaveringly waited at the designated locations to meet her contact.

Moscow gave orders for Prestes to leave the country immediately for France; but he refused to abandon the Honório house before the arrival of the new passports. As the days rolled by, another secure house that Stuchevski succeeded in arranging for Brazil's most wanted couple was never put to use. Pavel and Sofia finally left the Méier address alone on February 18, 1936. They pleaded with Prestes and Olga to leave too but to no avail.[83]

"SUICIDE"

Once the American Embassy gave its oblique go-ahead,[84] twenty-seven-year-old Victor Allen Barron was tortured by the men under Filinto's command. All were vying with one another to be the first to discover Prestes' whereabouts. Barron had been picked up on January 28th and beaten for twenty-four hours with rubber hoses. The police intermittently touched burning tobacco to his flesh and squeezed his testicles with Müller's invention. Besides many of the delicacies inflicted on Arthur Ewert, the American was fitted with an electric helmet that produced shocks in his ears. The authorities even had a physician helping them. He was able to pick out areas known only to practitioners of the healing arts, where pain could be inflicted with more precision. He also administered a series of injections, or somehow introduced a substance into Barron's body, aimed at producing a more cooperative prisoner.

Unlike Arthur Ewert, an already frail Barron died as a result of the abuse he suffered while in police hands.[85] Jungmann, as well, was picked up shortly after the American and tortured to death by police frantic for information. A third person, the identity of whom is unknown, died for the same reasons. The bodies of Jungmann and the mysterious third person quickly disappeared.[86] The fact that no DESPS *prontuário*, or police record, on Jungmann exists, underlines the probability that he was not processed through their formal bureaucracy. Most likely, Müller's assistants killed him while trying to obtain a lead on Prestes.

But for some reason Barron was different. Perhaps it was because he was an American and the American Embassy was involved. How to cover up the killing of this particular foreigner thus presented a momentary dilemma. Then someone at the Central Police Station remembered how former colleagues dealt with the cases of Luís "Lulu" Barbosa, Conrado Niemeyer, a maritime union leader named Aloisio Rodrigues de Souza, and the more recent incident with Salomão Zelcer.[87] The world was told that yet one more prisoner had evaded his guards and committed suicide by jumping from the second floor of the Central Police Station. This time, it was into the interior patio, a distance of 5.55 meters plus ninety-seven centimeters from the top of the railing (nearly twenty-one feet, five inches). Barron, the authorities proclaimed, revealed that he had taken Prestes and Olga to Méier, and then killed himself out of guilt on learning of their capture.[88]

TRAITORS

It is interesting to note, however, that part of the police's statement fits a newly uncovered passage from the political police archives in Rio de Janeiro. Inferring from that excerpt (given below), what could have happened was that Barron mentioned he took Prestes and Olga to Méier without giving his interrogators a street or an address. But then, Marcus Jungmann could have said the same thing. Ghioldi did not know where Prestes, Barron, or Jungmann were staying. Once Rodolfo fingered the picture of the American and the Argentine, it was only a matter of time before one or both were picked up. The relevant pages in Ghioldi's formerly closed DESPS file could not be clearer on his own connection to the scenario. Rodolfo and his wife were

tratado . . . com cavalherismo e generosidade que caracterisam a alma brasileira. GHIOLDI prontificou-se logo a colaborar com as autoridades na captura de LUIZ CARLOS PRESTES, tendo, para isso, saído diversas vezes pela cidade acompanhado de agentes da Polícia carioca. Foi graças a essa colaboração que a Polícia conseguiu deter um elemento ligado a PRESTES que, interrogado, denunciou o esconderijo do Chefe Comunista onde foi êle, efetivamente prêso.[89]

• • • • •

treated with kindness and generosity, attributes that characterize the Brazilian soul. Ghioldi soon offered to help the authorities in the capture of Luís Carlos Prestes. To do this he left [the Central] various times and traveled through the city accompanied by *carioca* police. It was due to his assistance that the police succeeded in apprehending an individual linked to Prestes. During questioning this person revealed the whereabouts of the communist chief's hiding place and Prestes was effectively captured.

Meanwhile, following the foreign intelligence tip that Prestes had prevailed in getting to Rio, the police made up a short list of persons in the former Federal District who were close enough to the Cavalheiro da Esperança so as to warrant round-the-clock attention. There were only three names on the list: André Trifino Correia, Astrojildo Pereira Duarte Silva, and Graciliano Ramos. After the authorities determined that Prestes was in Méier, they began to look more closely at everyone in the suburb. This policy ultimately bore fruit. While riding their motorcycles in the area, three policemen thought they spotted Astrojildo walking in the opposite direction. By the time they were sure, and could turn their machines around, Astrojildo had turned up a street and disappeared. A house-by-house police search began immediately.[90]

As for Ghioldi, Müller wanted to milk him for more information or protect him, or both, so the Barron cover story may well have been partially or even entirely invented. Conceivably the American was killed just to make it all believable. But what about the reported nervous admission by the police chief at a hastily called press conference the day the American died? It may well have been just that, nervousness. Müller was telling the truth when he informed the media that Harrison George's son died *before* giving his people Prestes' address. Too much was read into the remark. Filinto meant "exact address" and not "general address." Müller's uncustomary behavior had only a cursory connection to the destiny of the young American. His excitement was a product of the details he had really come to announce.

END OF THE CHASE

The search of Méier came to a conclusion at 7:45 A.M., on March 5, 1936. The tropical rains briefly let up on a dreary overcast morning when a noticeably pregnant Olga and The Knight of Hope, the most wanted of the revolutionary figures, were finally apprehended. There is the observation that Vargas, in all likelihood, gave Müller orders not to bring in Prestes alive. Thus it was that in the first crucial moments following their capture, Olga probably saved Prestes' life by jumping between him and José Torres Galvão of the Polícia Especial. Galvão's group, and another led by Ernani de Andrade, had surrounded the little house in Méier. Galvão, who had been in direct contact with Filinto on a squad-car radio just moments before, entered the structure and barked at Prestes that he was under arrest. Without a weapon to defend himself, and with Olga as his only shield, Prestes gave up with a simple, "Está certo" or "All right." The couple were taken to the Polícia Central and separated for the last time in their brief life together. They would never see each other again.[91]

FIGHTING OVER THE SPOILS

Four months and two days later, Ernani de Andrade coolly pumped six bullets into José Torres Galvão at Polícia Especial headquarters. This tragicomedy arose from Galvão's apparent dishonesty in acquiring the entire 50:000$000 (or just over $2,900) reward offered by the English through the Light Electric Company for the capture of Prestes.[92] The day after the big arrest, Galvão went alone to Light and claimed the prize. He then took a vacation in Bahia with the money. On returning to Rio, Ernani confronted him about what he thought should be his half of the spoils. Galvão replied that he had spent everything up in the Northeast and, that as far as he was concerned, it was tough luck for Ernani. Just in case, he then started a rumor that Ernani was stealing Polícia Especial rifle parts and selling them to the communists. The story was, of course, concocted to protect Galvão. As it circulated, Ernani was brought before his superiors and disciplined for damaging a Tomato Head machine gun. Deductions to cover the marred weapon ended up being taken out of his salary. One day at work, Ernani passed Galvão sitting with two others, Octavio Jayme of the Guarda Civil, and Lino Gonçalves Ribeiro of the Polícia Especial. As he walked by, words were exchanged, then insults, then Ernani pulled his service revolver and emptied it into an unarmed Galvão. Lino was shot through the left hand.

Seized immediately, Ernani was moved in the next few hours to the Polícia Central office of Emílio Romano for questioning. In the meantime Filinto Müller was called away from his lunch at the Taberna Azul Restaurant and went to Santo Antônio Hill to decide with Euzébio Queiroz what to do. Soon they were joined by Serafim Braga in a meeting that lasted until just before midnight. Back in Romano's office, Ernani began to be whacked around. The beating grew worse and within twenty-four hours of the murder of Galvão, Ernani too was dead. His body, like that of Victor Allen Barron's, found its was over the veranda of the second floor at the Central Police Station and crashed into a bloody clump on the pavement of the inner courtyard. The police said it was one more suicide.[93]

PRESTES IN CUSTODY

Rather than give the leftists a martyr, the authorities tried to rattle Luís Carlos Prestes in other ways. First they brought in some captured revolutionary sailors and began hitting them one at a time in his presence. Then the communist leader was informed that he was going to be shot in the back so it would look like he was trying to escape. Men were constantly stationed outside of his Polícia Especial cell for this express purpose should there be any kind of attack against the confine. Transferred to the Casa de Correção, his correspondence and reading material were occasionally denied by the new warden and now member of the AIB, Vitório Caneppa. A Vargas crony, Caneppa so abhorred Prestes' books that when punishing him, he regularly packed the volumes into boxes of codfish.   Following a few months' fermentation they were unusable.   Other reading materials and information on the situation outside were smuggled into Prestes on rolled up wads of paper. Prestes stored these notices under his mattress. Every couple of weeks the guards would enter and remove the accumulated heap of correspondence.

Beaten only once while at the Correção, Prestes saw his guards begin to wear Σ lapel pins after the proclamation of the *Estado Novo*.[94] At one point a number of hookers shared the cell next to him.   They jabbered and screamed about their Johns and profession day and night.   Prestes' ex-officio lawyer, Sobral Pinto (Prestes and Berger did not want him but he was appointed in their behalf anyway), felt this was a tactic done to rattle his client. Finally, Pinto complained that as of February 22, 1943, Prestes had been kept in total isolation for nearly seven years.

For a time, Harry Berger also was imprisoned at the Casa de Correção. Slowly losing his mind due to the torture, Berger howled at night not only as a result of his mental condition; but also because Caneppa kept the guards from giving him any pain-killing medicine. Every time Prestes protested about Berger's treatment, Caneppa would lock him up for months on end, stop his letters, or collect his books for the fish procedure.[95]

REPRESSION

Although Prestes and Olga suffered few physical abuses after they were taken in, many persons were not as fortunate. Of course, Vargas and Müller steadfastly denied everything. But try as they might, the tales of police atrocities began to make the rounds anew.   Returning to the capital from Petrópolis on May 11, 1936, the president had occasion to refer to the whispers with these grandiose words:

I can assure you . . . all of the detained are treated with kindness, a position that contrasts with the violent methods that they proclaim and systematically practice.   This magnanimous behavior is not an expression of weakness.   On the contrary, it is an attribute belonging to the strong who never degrade themselves in a fight due to their ability to maintain with equal integrity the boldness and the sympathy of humane justice.[96]

Müller followed his boss' remarks nearly one month later with a formal letter of denial to the press:

Against actual communists, yes, the police carry on a tenacious campaign. But they do not have to use illegal means to support their actions. Rather, within the law, the Policía Civil in the Federal District are working with all of their energy without descending to violent means so pleasing to those who, in the name of the spirit of humanity, now express sentiments that they do not possess themselves.[97]

Both statements were bald-face lies and each man knew it. Until 1941, Brazil would be subjected to a subelite savagery that surpassed even the harsh times of Artur Bernardes.[98] Following the November uprising of 1935, the police of Getúlio Vargas

murdered in the streets, invaded homes at all hours, invented stories, forged documents, planned conspiracies, and tortured both witnesses and the accused. They instituted, in the best model of fascism, allegations as the norm of conduct, the process of denouncing for any reason. They removed from the people their freedom to write, to speak, to meet with others, to criticize, to protest, to reason, to converse, and to dissent. It was the longest night of terror that this country ever knew.[99]

The steamroller that got under way in Brazil the last weeks of 1935 was really something to behold. At a minimum, countless people lost their jobs. As for the maximum, in Rio, bodies began to be found in the forested areas outside the city. Other persons, like Marcus Jungmann and his unknown associate, simply vanished.

Up north in Recife, some ANL members, denounced leftists, and the usual no-goods, were rounded up and shot by the forces of Pernambuco's secretary of security and Polícia Civil chief, Malvino Reis Neto. He was assisted by Major Higino Belarmino. Most suspects—at one point there were some 600 men and a disputed number of women—were herded into the confines of the city jail. There, cells that were originally built to hold two prisoners were crammed full with fifty. No space was left over. Every morning some of the captives, exhausted from the constant pressure of being squeezed together and from not being fed, were taken away and beaten by torturers like Etelvino Lins, Frederico Mindelo, Vander Koche, "Chico Pinote" (Francisco de Assis Lima), and Manuel da Farinha. Just who would receive this special treatment came on orders from the lockup's Integralist administrator, or someone else higher up. Even Malvino Reis got into the act. He personally tortured several prisoners and most notably, one Gregório Bezerra.

From humble origins, Bezerra had learned to read in the army, an institution he joined in 1925. The following year, he was made a sergeant and clandestinely became a member of the Communist Party. By 1935, Bezerra had risen to such a point in the PCB that he was picked to become Pernambuco's chief of the Popular Revolutionary Government. In the fighting that November, he killed two loyalist soldiers, Lieutenant Aguinaldo de Almeida and Sergeant José Alexandre Vieira, at the Reserve Officer Training Center in Recife. He did not escape unscathed, however, suffering a wound to his thigh. Taken to a clinic, Gregório was seized on the operating table and brutally tortured by the police. Part of this mistreatment took place in the Beberibe woods where he was whipped over and over again, because Malvino Reis wanted him to confess that he killed his superior, Lieutenant Xavier Sampaio. Later, in August 1936, Bezerra's brother, José Lourenço, the father of five small children, was so badly manhandled by Etelvino Lins and Frederico Mindelo that he died in captivity. The police said it was a another suicide.

Promoted to general, when Manuel Rabelo Mendes visited the dismal facilities for political prisoners in Recife, he ordered a number of on-the-spot improvements. Yet the only change that actually took place, once the general left, was an increase in the number of cadavers discovered in Recife's outskirts. The faces of the corpses were always smashed in so as to make identification virtually impossible.[100]

Down the coast in the Federal District things were not much different. Besides the soldiers who were shot immediately once they surrendered,[101] there were many more who were seized as the weeks turned into months. The majority were released; but not before being questioned and perhaps tortured. They could consider themselves lucky because a portion of the picked up soldiers were not only questioned and roughed up, but executed later. This last job stretched through most of 1936 and usually took place up at the Chinese View. These summary executions, like the Tobias Warchavski case, were invariably laid at the door of the communists.[102]

In the navy, one of the hotbeds of Green Shirt activity, Captain Lúcio Martins Meira was appointed to find out which sailors in the capital had been part of the revolt. A faithful Integralist, Meira saw this as the AIB's chance to cleanse the navy of all enemies, real or otherwise. Deciding just which seamen should be purged was not difficult. Anyone who disagreed with the bombast of the AIB, anyone who failed to read *A Ofensiva*, and anyone who was not a dues-paying member of Salgado's pack of fascists was suspect.

In their mad rush after dangerous elements, Meira and his subordinates imprisoned hundreds of ordinary seamen and enlisted officers. Many were sent to Ilha das Cobras and eventually handed over to the Polícia Especial to be tortured. This frequently meant being thrashed about with the ubiquitous rubber hose, or having hair pulled out by the roots, or both. No less than one sailor was made to lap-up the blood of a colleague who had been struck repeatedly in the face.[103] There was also a variation on face smashing wherein a gunny sack was slipped over the victim's head first. And whenever they could be found or were on hand, the Polícia Especial were likewise said to enjoy witnessing the effects caused by scorpions, centipedes, and other venomous creatures. Meira arrived at the headquarters of Euzébio de Queiroz Filho's Tomato Heads each evening at eight o'clock to supervise the carnage. Sometimes helping Meira, but never becoming involved himself, was a brute known only as Mattos.[104]

It should prove illustrative here to consider what happened to just one seaman, Francisco de Oliveira Melo. Melo was in the navy in 1936 when the AIB started a campaign to recruit more members. Because he refused to join, he was taken before his commanders and warned that everyone in the navy was a Green Shirt. He was told that those who did not want to sign up, did so because they belonged to the Communist Party. Melo replied that he had never been a communist, only a sailor in the Brazilian navy. He was thereupon turned over to the police and beaten from 10 P.M. until 2 A.M. in the presence of Captain

Meira. The following day he was mauled once more and informed by Meira, "I know you're not a communist; but you're anti-Integralist." "No!" cried Melo, "I'm not against the Integralists. I am only a sailor. I'm not involved in politics of any kind!" Ignoring this explanation, Meira tried to get him to report on those who were communists down in the ranks. When Melo refused, he was beaten again. Several days passed during which time Meira attempted again to convert the seaman. Still unwilling, Meira coldly advised Melo that he was to be tried by the TSN[105] as a Bolshevik. After a brief stay in the Casa de Detenção, the hapless sailor was let go; but picked up again by agents from DESPS and notified that he had been sentenced to five years and eight months imprisonment.[106]

Informants

Known as *dedo-duros*, or "finger pointers" (i.e. stool pigeons), Protogenes Guimarães, Nilo de Souza Pinto, Jeronymo Cardoso, Agenor de Oliveira, Messias José Telles, and a man known only as "Pergentino," all tattled on their fellow sailors for money, jobs within the government, or better naval assignments.[107]

Later, following the failure of Prestes to take power, Filinto Müller began a Judas program of his own. Squealers were paid 50$000[108] for each "communist" they turned in to the authorities. Some betrayers were police agents who had infiltrated leftist ranks. Here one could find Humberto de Campos Paiva, Carlos Pascal, and Romualdo Marinho.[109] Others were party members, sometimes important party members, like Adalto Alves dos Santos. Adalto was the Director of Publications and later Chief of International Contacts for the PCB. He provided information to Cecil Borer of the Polícia Especial, Quadro Movel, and later of the political police, from 1940 to 1965.[110] José da Mota, or "Tupã" as he was referred to by intimates (his nickname means "Thunder" in Tupí), was another valuable tool in the police arsenal. Previously part of the Partido Comunista do Brasil, Tupã had compiled a long list of member's names before the PCB expelled him. Once Müller set everything up, whenever Tupã needed money, he turned in one or more of his former comrades to Serafim Soares Braga and received his bounty.

Serafim, who was Portuguese, is rumored to have once been a crook in Rio's Lapa district. But times had changed in his favor after he was promoted to lead the Social Section at DESPS. It was a job that brought the likes of Braga and Tupã into harmonious contact. So grateful were the men in blue for the help of this one informant—over 2,000 persons (including more than 800 "heads of households") are said to have gone to prison on his account alone—that an additional perk was given him at no charge. Located in the northern suburb of the capital called Ricardo de Albuquerque, when Thunder moved into his beautiful free home he understood why he had become a snitch.

Denouncements were not limited to police infiltrators, political enemies, party turncoats, or to citizens like Tupã. There were also those in the business community who quickly took the cue and fired at will employees who were nearing ten years of service. Once a person had been on the job for a decade they were entitled to a permanent position. The dismissed workers were accused of holding suspect political sympathies and simply shown the door. Vargas' war against communism allowed employers to terminate leftists without even so much as severance pay.[111]

In the Nation's Capital

In most instances, those who fell into police hands in Rio de Janeiro were taken to one of four old standbys to await what was called a trial. First on the list was often the Central Police Station. Conditions there had not improved since the building was erected in 1910.[112] Rio's police, as did their colleagues up in Recife, liked to cram people together, many times forcing eighty to a hundred individuals into small, cramped cells measuring 16'5" square apiece. The Central's *geladeira* was still in use and it too was often filled to overflowing. There was no water, no sanitary facilities, and no blankets. Sleeping literally had to be done in the standing position since everyone was pressed up against one another like sardines. Rancid-smelling food was slopped into the prisoner's tins once a day. Bathing and a change of clothes was unknown. Individual cages were opened only when the occupants were transferred into the Central's squalid Depósitorio dos Prisioneros (Depository of Prisoners) in the basement, when they were to be tortured, or when it was too late for medical attention.

The brawn for the rough-stuff routine in the 1930s and 1940s came from several sources within the military and police apparatus. It was provided by the likes of Alvaro Gurgel de Alencar Filho, Clodomir Collaço Véras, Afonso Rodrigues da Costa, Felisberto Batista Teixeira, Newton Costa, Benedito José da Costa, Riograndino Kruel, Severino Monteiro da Silva, Cecil de Macedo Borer, Orlando Caetano da Silva, and Walter Segadas Viana. Segadas was an attention-grabbing figure who had eyes that were different colors (one was light brown, the other light green). He was a particularly vicious individual. So too was the insatiable Emílio Romano. Even Serafim Braga stepped in on occasion to slap around an always restrained suspect.

Some men like "Buck Jones" used an alias while in front of their victims. Taking his *nom de tortura* from the Hollywood western figure, the Brazilian Buck Jones was no hero of the plains. He was originally a soldier from Pernambuco who found himself imprisoned on Fernando de Noronha for reported leftist activities. Released and transferred to Rio Grande do Sul, his army career was at an end. So he joined the police force. A light-skinned mulatto, Buck Jones was 5'10" tall with a huge scar, *à la Al Capone*, on the left side of his face. The disfigurement was a gift from "Moleque IV," a small-time mugger who tried to slice Jones' throat during an arrest. In Rio, Buck was said to be capable of anything; that is, any kind of torture or dirty work imaginable. One of his *fortés* was patrolling the streets as a taxi driver. During the 1930s, Rio's taxi drivers were known far and wide for being politically left of center.

Whatever tidbits of information Jones overheard from the conversations of his passengers, or from the discussions of his fellow drivers, went straight back to his superiors at the Polícia Central.

Other inquisitioners, such as "Tira" (or "Cop") Vasconcelos, and Mattos were never known by anything other than incomplete names. When not helping Captain Meira weed out suspects from the navy, Mattos was a presidential guard at Catete. It is said that he had been trained in the finer methods of torture in Germany by the Gestapo. The Germans themselves regularly participated for awhile, aiding the Brazilian guardians of the law in one interrogation session after another, all in the name of fleeting justice.[113]

Besides the fists, boots, *palmatorias*, and rubber hoses–applied to the soles of one's feet on up–Vargas' police had become truly ingenious in the macabre science of information extraction and enforced cooperation. The process began when anyone entering the Central, designated for the treatment, was separated from the rest of the prisoners. This was done to keep victims psychologically isolated as torture sessions frequently went on for several weeks. It was likewise standard policy so as to keep outsiders and other suspects, who might turn into witnesses in the future, from seeing the victim's wounds. By 1940, much of the dirty work was taking place in a special closed cubicle on the fourth floor called the "*quadrado*" (or "Square") to further guard against just such concerns.

Before the *quadrado* came into use there were already well-established torture techniques designed for each gender. In addition to being stripped and sexually molested–sometimes before the imploring eyes of their husbands or children or both–females may have had a *bucha de mostarda*, or "Mustard Plug" (a sponge soaked in mustard), shoved into their vaginas. Hemorrhaging and death were not uncommon in these situations. The Polícia Central at one time even had a "Beauty Parlor" for the ladies where hair was not primped and pruned but ripped from the entire body with pliers.

For both sexes there was a saber that the police slid into a victim's anus. When this was not used, there were plenty of other equally as grisly options open to the men in uniform. Each was designed to produce knowledge from pain. One was simply but permanently to gouge out an eye. A more sophisticated choice was to handcuff a prisoner with his hands behind his back. Then a *máscara de couro* ("Leather Mask") was buckled around his head, allowing in just enough air to keep him from passing out. Punches and kicks to the detainee's nude body completed this sadistic process. More than one individual was reported to have become mentally incapacitated from the combined effects.

A recipe that had been around in various forms since the days of slavery was the *pau-de-arara* ("Parrot's Perch"). Captives to be strung up in the *pau-de-arara* are forced to sit on the floor. They then have their wrists bound together with bent knees protruding between their arms. An iron pole is then slid through the gap just under the bent knees and on top of the individual's arms. So constrained, the iron pole is lifted off the ground and placed in some kind of secure position, such as between two stacks of tires. With the wailing torturee, suspended like a piece of beef on a spit, the victim is raped, beaten, burned with cigarettes, drowned, or shocked.

Another lesson in cooperation was called *adelfis* (from the botany term for a flower's stamen). The procedure entailed tying the subject in an outstretched posture between two rows of cells or onto the bars of an individual cell. The Central's pain crew accompanied these activities with periodic gulps of *cachaça* (sugarcane brandy). By the time they began singing and mixing *sambas* with their whoops and drinking, everything was about ready. On reaching the right frenzy, someone would grab the victim's hand while another slowly began tapping a bamboo or steel pin under a fingernail. If this didn't bring forth a quick confession, another finger was targeted, then another, and then the toenails. Occasionally, the slivers were even pushed down into the gums of the teeth. *Adelfis* sessions always took place at night when most of the Central's functionaries, not a part of the torture, had gone for the day. Then, at unsuspecting times before daybreak, the neighbors on surrounding streets would be jolted from their slumbers by shrill voices. Next came the moans of mutilation so often crudely muffled under an abruptly blaring radio or a continuously revved up motorcycle in the Central's garage.

The *tortura chinesa*, or "Chinese Torture," consisted of several events all at once: the simultaneous crushing of testicles, pins or spikes being pushed under the nails, and burning the suspect's flesh with cigarettes or cigars. Or subjects could land bound and blindfolded in the *cadeira americana* ("American Chair") only to be thrown suddenly against a wall by the powerful spring in the chair's seat. There was even supposed to have been an "American Room," without windows, where prisoners were made to take off their clothes. Different investigators then entered and with truncheons began turning people into raw meat. To drown out the sounds, the radio or the motorcycle were once again made a part of the melody.

One last item completed the composition. The police at the station on Rua da Relação were particularly fond of fire. Alongside of the constant searing from tobacco products, Müller's torturers relished the blowtorch. They also liked to circulate freely through the rooms where confined persons were being interrogated. Arriving unannounced, they would deliberately blurt out in front of their colleagues, "Is this the guy to be liquidated today?" It was no jest. If all the terrorizing failed to produce the desired results, and many times even when it did, stubborn prisoners, as well as those selected to lessen the overcrowding, were taken from the Central in the early morning hours to desolate areas of Rio and drilled full of holes.[114]

The guards at Rio's Casa de Detenção also were known for their propensity to beat captives and for dragging people into their own special room to be tortured. Such perverted episodes were diabolically called *sessões espritas*, or "Spirit Sessions," by the prison's staff. After a hunger strike by prisoners in 1933, when Warden Aloisio Neiva was in charge, some of the political holdouts were penalized by being hauled over to Filinto & Company at the Central for a different kind of talking to. All were bloodied and battered. A few were then transferred to a mental institution. Most ended up being thrown in the holds of ships and ferried out to Dois Rios.[115] Following the protest the administration made certain to separate common criminals from those who were there for idealistic reasons. Later, the Detenção itself was modified to accept over 2,000 political detainees. The *pavilhão dos primários*, or the area for ordinary criminals, was evacuated in 1935 to make room for the new arrivals.[116] There was also a female section to the institution; but it was appropriated and turned into the *seção militar*, or Military Section, with the influx of so many captured men. Women were then confined to two small cells where they cared for what were often sick children, many times fathered by some unknown torturer and born in prison.[117]

There were numerous acts of homosexuality, promiscuity, and deviant behavior[118] in the otherwise unaltered physical surroundings of the individual cells. Besides being dark and full of cockroaches, sometimes as many as fifty or sixty prisoners occupied the ordinary cubicles that were no larger than 16'5" square. Most confines were a mere 5'3" in height, making it impossible for many detainees to stand up straight.[119] Guards had to be bribed for all kinds of things, including being let out to go to the exercise yard. It was cold in the winter and boiling hot during the long, sticky summer. Problems with the pipes lay behind the absence of water in the sinks of some cells. In such circumstances, prisoners had to quench their thirst from the toilets, that is, when the toilets were not backed up. When they were obstructed, they were emptied once every eight days.

There was virtually no medical help; and what food there was found its way to each cell, heaped onto dirty metal pans. Utensils were not a part of the eating blueprint. Sleeping was done in shifts in enclosures that were actually designed to hold a maximum of four to five prisoners. When one's turn to rest finally did come, there was the added problem that the floor was stone cold and occasionally damp. The walls too were often saturated with moisture; elements that combined to produce a number of cases of tuberculosis and pneumonia, often going untreated. One of the things that had to be coaxed from the guards were the filthy, thin-straw mats made available on an intermittent basis. Graciliano Ramos described his first night in the Detenção laying on the floor, blessed with one of the flimsy mats, contemplating his fellow prisoners spread out before him. "It was as if I had found myself in a common grave, the only survivor among the cadavers."[120]

Richer detainees, in a mirror image of Brazilian society, were often able to buy their way out of a good deal of this agony. The Detenção did have its more amicable *apartamentos*, or lodgings where persons with cash were housed. The privileged few had their favorite foods and liquors brought to them by the guards. For the rest, it was a brown liquid the jailers called coffee plus a speck of bread in the mornings topped off with a semisolid mass of sometimes putrid, uneatable rice and beans in the evenings.[121]

Things were not that different nearby on Rua Frei Caneca where the Casa de Correção stood basically unchanged since it was first erected in 1835.

Normally an all-male setup, women began to be sent there when the institution for them in Bangu, in the northern suburbs, became too full. And different from the Detenção, the Correção put its prisoners' idle hands to work in one of several money-earning operations. There was a shoe factory, book bindery, carpentry shed, and a tailor's shop. Other choices included the laundry, a garage, and a tin-smiths. Of more immediate need to the inmates, there was an infirmary, pharmacy, and a small school which doubled as a chapel. The preponderance of cells at the Correção were found in the five levels of beat-up enclosures, totaling 216 in all, called the *galeria*. The size of the *galeria*'s cubicles measured nearly 8'8" in width by 5'5" in length. Each was just over 9'10" in height. They were dark and humid, with no direct light, and had low-clearance doors. There was no running water. Toilets were installed in 1933; but proved useless due to low water pressure. All defecation was done in a can that was placed in front of one's cell each morning, right next to the container with drinking water. Any mix-ups were the prisoners' responsibility.

If it could be imagined, there was an even a darker side to the Correção. Since its earliest days guards were known to intermittently torture prisoners behind its foreboding walls. But by the 1930s, such events came to be largely confined to the *seção de explosivos*, or the Explosives Section. The idea for a room specifically used for torture probably came to the Correção with Alvaro Gurgel de Alencar Filho. Referred to as "The Epileptic" or "The Barbarian" by those in custody, Alencar Filho hopped back and forth, plying his trade on the political detainees at the Central and those at the Correção. Prisoners were handed over to him to be tortured in more than just the usual way at the various police stations.[122]

As captured "communists" arrived almost daily, full use was made of all possible jail and prison space. What overflow there was came to an ordered halt at dockside, ready to be transported out to the *Pedro I*. Returned to prison duty yet one more time, the old tub barely had a chance to leave Guanabara Bay following the fighting in 1932. Now, as more and more politicals came on board, each was jostled down into the ship's hold and left to deal with the overcrowding, the heat, and the offensive odors.[123]

Misery in São Paulo

The earliest *paulista* political detention center was at one time located on Rua Liberdade. Being on this street produced the facility's paradoxical name, the "Political Prison of Liberty." But because the Liberty suffered from being too small, it was eventually moved to Rua Paraíso 28, where its official designation became the "Political Prison of Paradise." The new unit, under the direction of Plínio de Sousa Morais, was a converted residence and usually reserved for dissidents from the better-off classes or for those who needed what was claimed to be medical attention. Cramped as well, this meant that the bulk of the detainees from the events of November 1935 went to another institution: an abandoned textile mill named Maria Zélia.

Situated five miles away at Avenida Celso Garcia 471 in the suburb of Belém (now part of Belenzinho), the former factory was next to a bend in the River Tietê. It was from the Tietê, the city's principal tributary and main sewage system, that the Maria Zélia got its untreated drinking water. This oversight, or intention, provoked unrelenting rumors that the prisoners at Maria Zélia were slowly being poisoned. Even if the staff knew it was the reason, the bad water was probably looked upon as something the political prisoners deserved. The fact that inmates were sick to varying degrees was likely seen as an ally in keeping the institution pacified and under control.

The head of the political police in São Paulo, Egas Botelho, answered the skeptics by informing journalists that the prisoners at Maria Zélia were receiving "all the compassion possible, and even dental assistance."[124]   None of the reporters bothered to confirm the chief's claim. In actuality, there was but one physician along with a layman dentist to attend to the needs of some 400 inmates. The doctor showed up once a week for half an hour. He prescribed bogus drugs that were filled only at retail prices by two pharmacies: the "Guanabara" in Vila Mariana and the "Montenegro" in Belém. Both the physician and the pharmacies made a lot of money in this deal which saw the wrong drugs, or ineffective ones, assist the bad water in doing its work.

When Adrião de Almeida Monteiro was transferred from Campinas to head the prison guards at Maria Zélia, things got worse. Monteiro was characterized by the prisoners at the transformed factory as ruthless and full of hate. This opinion came in part from the fact that the authorities were constantly sending fake letters to selected political offenders stating that a wife or a girlfriend was seen at a movie or in a restaurant with a handsome stranger. The lie was repeated over and over again each time with the couple in a different location. The food too became a part of the psychological torture. Prisoners repeatedly found their beans rotten and their meal topped off with a gob of spit from the guards.

Physically, Maria Zélia was a cavernous structure. It measured just over 131' by 328 feet. Inside were eight big pens constructed entirely of wood. Owing to prisoner complaints, the doors to these compounds were temporarily opened in January 1936. From that month on, each of the inner enclosures was called Pavilion A, B, C, D, E, F, G, or H. Among the usual assortment of jail keepers, Maria Zélia had police infiltrators masquerading as inmates. One of these was Generoso Gáudio Anastácio who turned in many a man behind bars. Other guards, like Lindolfo Carlos de Carvalho, were motivated by the same utopian ideals that had imprisoned nearly everyone else. He provided the political prisoners with the identity of the newest implanted police informant, and kept them informed on the tactics of his superiors.

Later that January, Monteiro ordered all inmates locked in their cells. In retaliation the leftists started breaking up the timber confines. Monteiro then backed off; but one month later issued a order informing all prisoners who wanted visiting privileges to refrain from singing in their cells. Even though the singing ended, Monteiro decided to suspend visitor's day, April 30, 1936, anyway. He then changed his mind, allowing the visits, then he reversed himself a final time back to his original position. Each change of heart caused an uproar in the cell blocks. Once again the wooden stalls took the brunt of prisoner reaction. The guards were called in and after an hour of fighting an uneasy peace was restored. There were no fatalities; but two of the large pavilions lay in ruins.

The scene shifted dramatically that August when inmate Manoel Medeiros sought treatment for a ruptured diaphragm brought on by the coughing from tuberculosis. He had been to Maria Zélia's doctor one evening but nothing was done. On hearing this, another prisoner, Aldino Schiavi,[125] who also happened to be a physician, examined Medeiros. It was after midnight when Dr. Schiavi concluded that an immediate operation would be necessary to save Medeiros' life. As word of these events spread from prisoner to prisoner, the mood inside Maria Zélia grew ugly. Sensing that he could lose control of the situation, Chief Guard Monteiro announced that Medeiros had been operated on that morning and that Aldino Schiavi was being transferred.

This was the last straw. With Dr. Schiavi gone the prisoners felt there would be no one to give them honest medical advice. They decided to hide Schiavi and refuse to give him up. The outcome was a standoff in Pavilion H that lasted into a second night. Just as the guards threatened to use violence to achieve the transfer, it was announced that Medeiros had died. A general riot ensued in which the combined police force, headed by Egas Botelho, used machine guns, tear gas, and even mustard gas to force the prisoners to surrender. Part of Maria Zélia burned to the ground without the fire department being called.

Once the authorities regained order, Adrião Monteiro made a list of nineteen prisoners he personally disliked, and whom he claimed were responsible. These men were ordered to leave Pavilion H. With no alternative, the designated prisoners walked out only to be pounced on by the guards. They were clubbed with rifle butts. The next stop was political police on Rua Visconde do Rio Branco (now Avenida Campos Elíseos) where the trouncing continued. In the meantime, Dr. Schiavi was found and moved, despite the fact that he had just undergone stomach surgery himself. More beatings with rubber hoses took place the next morning when the *paulistano* Polícia Especial were called in. Not only did they subdue the prisoners, but they also took delight in destroying the cubicles and robbing anything of value.[126]

Escape attempts were not treated lightly. In April of the following year, news of a breakout at Paraíso set a number of prisoners to plotting at Maria Zélia. Cutting a hole in the concrete wall next to the main door of their pavilion, twenty-six prisoners tried to break out. It has been suggested that government plants may have alerted the guards. Nonetheless, two men, José Aparecido da Fonseca and Francisco Ferraz de Oliveira, managed to get away. The remaining twenty-four were captured after taking refuge in a Maria Zélia bathroom. Each recaptured man was forced to lie on the ground in the surrounding courtyard. As the guards inspected their quarry, one prisoner was shot in the foot. A few of the others were made to eat bits of soil and cement. Everyone was next hurried into one of three groups to be battered and poked at by the turnkeys. The last bunch falling into line came under the unblinking glare of Sergeant Gregório Kovalenko. A Brazilian of White-Russian heritage, Kovalenko did not care for socialists. He and his men shot three prisoners in their group to death. Kovalenko smashed in the skull of a fourth man, Naurício Maciel Mendes, before the headlights from arriving ambulances startled him into stopping. Seventeen guards were charged with various crimes in the aftermath. Kovalenko, Francisco Dulisk, and Etelvino Domingues Paes were all found guilty. Kovalenko was given a seven-year sentence but never did any time.[127]

Similar displays of excess took place down at São Paulo's port city, in the Santos city jail. Out of the mainstream of attention, guards at that lockup simply ignored the possible consequences of their behavior. Each female leftist was normally thrown in with the prostitutes even if unoccupied cells were available. The jailers snickered at this just as they did when they escorted all male arrivals to Cell No. 3, which was Santos' niche for sadistic inmates. The guards regularly tortured political prisoners who were let out, sometimes to death.[128]

Segurança

From one end of the country to the other, the haggard souls who were left might be hauled before the puppet court that Getúlio had empowered out of the National Security Law.[129] The National Security Tribunal, or more informally the TSN or the Segurança, started hearing cases on September 11, 1936, at the Alberto Barth School in the then quiet Rio suburb of Flamengo. Located on Avenida Oswaldo Cruz, the single building that comprised a grammar school was specifically appropriated to serve as the seat of the TSN. To this day there is still no marker or plaque anywhere in the structure or on its facade to commemorate the kangaroo justice that took place within its walls.

The sole function of the Segurança was to adjudicate political offenses against the Vargas regime.[130] In this regard, one writer has stated that it resembled "the People's Court (Volksgerichtshof) of the Third Reich or the Special Tribunal for the Defense of the State [Tribunale Speciale per la Difesa dello Stato] in Fascist Italy."[131] It was a summary affair that many of the political prisoners refused to recognize. They had good reason. The court could change the indictment(s) against a defendant in the middle of the proceedings. All offenders who were brought to trial were presumed guilty à la Code Napoléon until proven innocent. Lawyers had three hopeless days to prepare a defense; and after May 16, 1938, up to fifteen minutes to present the entirety of their cases. They were afforded the luxury of no more than two witnesses. Each witness could speak for a maximum of five minutes. The whole process became one of speed,[132] as the sentences might indicate. Most convictions were not for revolutionary activity but for belonging at one time or another to an antifascist group like the ANL. Prison terms typically averaged between four and six years at hard labor.[133]

Hard labor for nearly every sentenced male, and for numerous other detained persons whom the government simply saw fit to freight there without trial, usually meant the country's principal island concentration camp: Ilha Grande. One journalist who was included in a group of condemned men being moved from Rio's Casa de Correção to Ilha Grande on May 22, 1936, described the trip from the Correção to the harbor as a march where the Polícia Militar guarded everyone. Talking was not permitted. Prisoners were smelly and dirty, almost cadaver-like from the lack of food. Unshaven, pale, crawling with parasites, injured from being tortured; they moved dejectedly down to the water's edge in filthy old clothes with bits of uneaten bread hanging from their pockets.[134]

Meeting each steamer as it reached the island was the stern, balding figure of Vitório Caneppa. He was still in charge of things at Ilha Grande's Dois Rios Correctional Colony, which had been renamed an "agricultural" penitentiary.[135] Lieutenant Caneppa was fond of giving each batch of newcomers his first order personally as they were hurried off of the Lloyd Brasileiro ships. "Attention! Cross your arms over your chests and remain silent!" He would shout.[136] Anyone showing the least bit of disrespect, such as by dropping their arms, was likely to be thrashed with a special whip called a *camarão*, or "shrimp." Once both political and common prisoners were standing in the prescribed way, they were marched up to the camp's four main barracks.[137] Before they arrived, guards watered down the sand floor of each compound. The sand was full of biting insects ready to gnaw their way into any warm-blooded object that came to rest above them. Straw mats were sparingly distributed since Caneppa was interested in promoting as much sickness and discomfort as possible.

Also that first day, work details and numbers were assigned to prisoners, the latter to be used henceforth instead of names. Every inmate was forced to assemble at 4 A.M., ready to go to work. The only exceptions were those in the colony's hospital and those being punished with solitary confinement. There were six work gangs to which one could be delegated: *a viga*, prisoners who cut down trees and moved heavy logs; *a olaria*, the brickyard; *a estrada*, working on the roads; *a lenha*, collecting firewood; *a horta*, the agricultural crew; and *serviços diversos*, or diverse services. Prisoners assigned to the brickyard provide a good example of what working conditions were like. They had to walk between 6.2 and 9.3 miles per day, carrying an average of just over sixty-six pounds on their shaven heads. Each man was regularly shoved and screamed at by the guards who sometimes shot into the ground around a convict's feet to get him to move faster.

Prisoners who completed their sentences, but whom Caneppa did not want to release, were transferred to the state of limbo known as the Colônia Livre, or "Free Colony." Colônia Livre inmates could be either political or common, or even several levels of intellectuals. While not formally classified as Colônia Livre material, erudite offenders were nonetheless still considered too dangerous to set free. Graciliano Ramos, arguably Brazil's greatest man of letters, found himself so categorized for part of his stay on the island. Free Colony prisoners did very little work and usually got the lightest chores.

Throughout all of this there apparently was an effort made to separate both types of criminals. When this failed, as in the case of one ordinary lawbreaker who infuriated his jailers by giving a carton of cigarettes to a leftist, the results could prove lethal to those involved. Caneppa, who liked to turn up un-expectedly, might be seen nearby laughing at everything. As for anyone who entertained ideas of getting away, when such inmates were caught, they were thrashed with sticks until all but dead and then thrown into an isolation cell to die without medical attention.

The diet on Ilha Grande was designed for selective emaciation. The only other meal after coffee and bread in the morning consisted of beans and two pieces of lettuce. Following a hard day's work, say in the *viga*, this was not nearly enough nourishment. On the other hand, common criminals enjoyed the additional luxury of meat, rice, and fruit. But woe be it to any political prisoner who so much as picked up a piece of rotten banana from the ground, or even a banana peel. The guards would immediately pounce on such rule breakers. They would also beat inmates for no apparent reason. One of the most vicious at this was Domingo Lopes. Lopes also had a son with the police detachment on Ilha Grande who was known for using his billy club first, and asking questions later.

There was a priest, if one wanted to call him that. He was decidedly more of an authoritarian than a forgiver of sins. The cleric would circulate among the men seated at Sunday service with an open Bible in one hand. Preaching from the Holy Book, he would use his free hand to smack any prisoner who in his opinion was not paying rapt-enough attention.

Not only did captives have to fear the guards, the lack of food, the damp-sand floors, the insects, and the cold; but becoming sick was one event that these men must have dreaded. When prisoners came down with something–there were hundreds of cases of tuberculosis–they were taken to the infirmary of a short, thin, prune-faced dentist, Dr. Hermino Ouropretano Sardinha, who acted as the camp's physician. Sardinha gave nearly everyone coming before him the same mysterious injection. The medication produced an identical reaction each time it was used. At first the patients got better, then they got worse, then they died. All of the condemned who were murdered in this and other ways were buried on the island.

When political prisoners needed dental treatment, Sardinha abruptly removed the problem tooth and any neighboring teeth that got in the way with pliers; but without anesthetic. Progressives who became seriously ill for different reasons, or those who had been physically castigated so badly that their lives were in danger, were left to linger, unattended, until the dentist felt that death was a certainty. They might then be sent to the mainland for what little attention a hospital could provide before passing away.

It was said that the Brazilian agricultural penal establishments served as models for the concentration camps that the Germans were already constructing in the *Reich*. Every now and then European-looking civilian agents would come through the Brazilian prototypes taking pictures of everything. Who these people were and where their photos went can only be imagined.[138]

As the years passed, the number of inmates at Ilha Grande grew to a worrisome level. For this reason, in 1943, there was a suggestion made to move the political prisoners to an agricultural colony in either Goiás or Mato Grosso. By this time they were being housed more often with routine lawbreakers, the chronic unemployed, and various underage offenders. To deal with the growing throng, plans began to be made for the construction of a huge number of new concentration camps. The government's draft proposal called for 1,000 colonies. Although the project was quietly shelved, one wonders if some of the reported 250,000 abandoned children in Rio the year before would not have been among the youthful deportees had the ideas been enacted?[139]

The Survivors

For those who went through the totality of violence and came out alive, more than one bore lifetime scars inflicted at police stations, prisons, or camps. Others were barely touched and released at the discretion of the authorities. Subelites were thus the final deciders of who would receive punishment or leave custody, not the courts. Even so, it would have proved embarrassing to Vargas, Müller, and the other officials to have newly released men complaining about the brutal treatment they had received. This problem was solved in a novel way. Just before being set loose, detained persons, and in particular those who had been tortured, were threatened with "grave consequences" if the facts of their injuries came to the attention of the public. Most ex-prisoners thus refused to talk about their experiences once they left confinement. When these men somberly returned home, more than once they found that Filinto's boys had been there first looking for "evidence." This was the reinforcement. It allowed for possessions to be confiscated at will–usually to furnish the homes of the investigating police–and sometimes for the violation of wives and daughters. Yet the vast majority of these men still refused to complain, knowing full well that the chief of the Polícia Civil would simply say that the parolee was apparently continuing with his revolutionary activities. They would then have him rearrested or fall victim to something even more permanent.[140]

Such were the choices faced by the mayor of Rio de Janeiro, several legislators, a score of lower-order bureaucrats, professionals, workers, students, young idealistic members of the armed forces, and all too numerous members of the public at large. Many lives were ruined if not lost. Comparable fates awaited some of the leaders of the uprising of November 1935.

DESTINY OF THE REVOLUTIONARIES

That Amleto Locatelli took part in the 1935 insurrection was unknown in the West until 1993. He was the last of the leadership to reach Brazil and the first to leave. Amleto caught a ship for Buenos Aires on January 13, 1936. From there he returned to Europe and the USSR, reaching Moscow that June. This also made him the first of the inner circle in Brazil to arrive back at the center of the Soviet power. His accounts of what went wrong proved devastating to the other returning participants and to Dimitri Manuilski, since Manuilski had been the rebellion's main articulator within the confines of the Comintern. But Manuilski knew that Locatelli was gay and used this against him to force a retraction. The formal apology saved Dimitri's skin. The Italian was then gotten rid of with a ticket to Spain to fight on the Republican side against Franco. It is presumed, although not confirmed, that he died there as a result of combat injuries in March of 1937.

Before Locatelli recanted, Moscow ordered Pavel Stuchevski and Sofia Stuchevskaya home from Buenos Aires. The two escaped the collapse in Rio through the help of local party members and sympathizers. Leaving Méier they moved in with a sergeant in the naval medical corps and his wife. But unfortunately, Sofia and the woman did not get along. Part of this was brought on when the passports from Argentina finally arrived only to be unalterable for use by the Stuchevskies. The Russian couple moved again, this time to the home of a Portuguese friend of Eduardo Ribeiro Xavier, or "Abóbora." Abóbora was the PCB's organizational chief. He would also be the first of the peripheral circle to return to Moscow.

A way out of Brazil was found in April when the runner Carmen delivered a genuine Argentine passport, which when doctored allowed Sofia to begin her journey to Buenos Aires as the wife of an Argentine. She and her bogus husband left Rio on first-class train tickets for São Paulo. From São Paulo they took a cab to Santos; but an automobile accident blocked the road and delayed their arrival. They missed the ship to Argentina. Fortunately, there was another steamer heading for Montevideo. In Uruguay, Sofia changed to a new passport so as not to enter Argentina as a national of that country. A prearranged message in the classified section of the press then alerted Pavel that his wife had made it.

The NKVD agent left Rio via the same route some five weeks after his wife. In a glum analysis of the agents sent to carry out the revolution that never was, Stuchevski remarked to a few members of the PCB before departing as follows: "The foreigners screwed you!"[141]

When Pavel Stuchevski and Sofia Stuchevskaya returned to the USSR, almost one year after the events of November 1935, the two were not given a hero's welcome. Moscow's attitude was that they should have returned on their shields. The pair were met with suspicion in the Soviet capital, and the fact that the Stalinist purges were in full swing did not help their case. Sofia was at length accused of harboring a person sought by the NKVD. Pavel made the mistake of living too close to the German commercial liaison. He also gave parties that foreign women attended along with out of favor party functionaries. Both were liquidated toward the end of 1938.

The Grubers were apprehended in their apartment by the Tomato Heads at 8 P.M., on January 5, 1936. Taken to the Central, the police claimed that a

Portuguese teacher he and Helena had in common with the Ewerts turned them in. This individual was produced but contradicted himself. Bright, Franz had learned Portuguese well enough not to need an interpreter. He was told that merely by being a foreigner the authorities were interested in him. They were especially inquisitive about his means of support in lieu of the fact that he had been in Brazil for over a year without working. Johann explained that his abilities as a businessman produced sufficient funds for a long honeymoon. He and his lovely young wife happily were on such a voyage. His money was in the Bank of London. Unconvinced, the police asked the pair's neighbors and a personal reference for their testimonies. No one said anything really damaging and so the Grubers were released the next morning. A week later they were granted an exit visa by Müller himself. On the 21st of January, Johnny and Helena legally walked aboard a passenger liner bound for Buenos Aires.[142]

It was a cold March 5, 1937, just over thirteen months later, when de Graaf completed his voyage and arrived back in Moscow. He too had been ordered home. But oddly, his wife was not with him. Immediately causing eyebrows to raise, Johann sadly informed his debriefers that Helena had committed suicide on the eve of their departure for Europe. The situation was indeed peculiar. All the more so because Johnny had helped the Buenos Aires police investigate the case; but failed to inform the local OMC. He said he used his Franz Gruber passport when dealing with the Argentine authorities in his wife's passing. But by that time he was wanted internationally, and the police of both Argentina and Brazil had an agreement to assist each other fight communism. There was no notice in the *porteño*[143] press of a suicide during the period of Helena's reputed death. Johann also used an English ship to travel back to Europe. This was strictly against long-standing Comintern orders. And even though he was sought by the Gestapo since 1933, he traveled straight to Berlin presumably to see his wife's family.

The strangest, however, was yet to come. As his train rolled to a stop in Moscow's Beloruskaya Station, Johnny had already decided on a bold, three-part defense of his actions. He felt it was a strategy that would keep him both alive and financially secure for some time. Soon after arriving, Johann was telling his Comintern superiors that he had run across an inventor in Argentina who had perfected a smokeless, noiseless, electric cannon. All the inventor wanted was free passage and asylum for himself and his family in the USSR. He would then turn his miracle weapon over to the Soviet Union. As this was sinking in de Graaf came to his *pièce de résistance*. Through his contacts in the Brazilian upper classes, and if the Comintern gave him a free hand along with enough money, he could return to Brazil and arrange for the release of Ewert and Ghioldi. His chances of succeeding, he said, were about 90 percent. Prestes would have to wait until his case could be carefully studied. Finally, Johnny offered to continue the valuable work he had to leave to return to Moscow: preparing South American terrorists, and infiltrating them back into the Argentine army and navy.

De Graaf's main questioner, the much-feared Bulgarian Stela Blagoeva, listened to it all but remained suspicious. She ultimately turned his case over to a nearly inescapable fate: the NKVD. In the midst of the Stalinist purges, this usually was equivalent to a sentence of death. In Johnny's case, however, it was not. He would return to Brazil in 1938, with a second Krüger sister at his side, on another Comintern misadventure.[144]

Subsequent to his arrest Miranda, or Antônio Bonfim, was among the group of prisoners boycotting the *Segurança*. He was nonetheless sentenced to four years and four months on May 7, 1937. Following his release, Miranda fell into complete political obscurity, eventually dying of tuberculosis at Alagoinhas in the interior of Bahia.[145]

Rodolfo Ghioldi likewise was ordered to serve four years and four months of confinement. He spent a large portion of his sentence on the island prison of Fernando de Noronha. After being freed he was scheduled to be deported but asked to visit Rio de Janeiro first. His wish was granted and he was allowed to wander about the capital with but one plainclothesman at his side. Despite police warnings that he was planning to lead a new revolution, all of his impounded belongings, including a large sum of money—probably of Comintern origin—were returned to him before he left for Argentina. He died Buenos Aires, still revered by his countrymen on July 3, 1985.[146] His wife, Carmen de Alfaya Ghioldi, languished for a short time in Vargas' prisons. She was then "given her freedom as a gesture of tolerance in virtue of the collaboration given the authorities by her husband." She was deported on November 2, 1936. Still alive and residing in Buenos Aires at the time of this writing, Carmen became bitter about the events of 1935, and about the failure of the world communist movement. She routinely refuses all requests for interviews and all inquires about writing her biography. In the words of one relative, "Carmen will carry big secrets with her to the grave."[147]

Arthur Ernst Ewert received a term of thirteen years and four months. On entering police custody, Harry Berger weighed a robust 238 pounds. Following many months of what can only be described as grotesque treatment, he had dropped to a shell of his former self at just over 119 pounds. Besides the complete gamut of special effects by Müller and the men under his command, Berger was placed in a closet-like cell under a staircase up at the Santo Antônio Hill stronghold of Euzébio de Queiroz Filho and his Polícia Especial. Ewert's ex-officio lawyer, Sobral Pinto, appealed to the court for more humane surroundings but nothing was done.[148] The commander of the Tomato Heads later laid the government's duplicity on the line:

It is true, the accused, Arthur Ernest Ewert or Harry Berger, can be found in the place described by Dr. Sobral Pinto, which is in the paymaster's cubicle at our police complex. We were forced to use it since we did not have a more appropriate cell. Such was the case because the only confine capable of providing comfort and security was destined for the prisoner Luís Carlos Prestes. In virtue of the fact that the latter is being held incommunicado, it was not possible for us to place them together. We thus made use of the paymaster's enclosure since it offers a degree of security.[149]

In fact, the little office of the paymaster lacked adequate space to stand upright. The constant pounding of feet going up and down the stairs made sufficient noise to aid in the eventual collapse of its once vigorous prisoner. *Two years* later, without ever having been taken out for fresh air or exercise, without ever having had a bath, a hair cut, a shave, or a change of clothes, Berger had lost his sanity. He was transferred in 1942 to a hospital for the criminally insane where the torturing continued. The mental institution made him sleep on a naked-wire bed frame that cut into his skin. As late as 1943, the Americans were still interested in Ewert and even sent a major in the U.S. army to visit him and check on his well-being. But Harry Berger's mind remained broken. He was diagnosed as too sick to be released in the amnesty for ninety-four political prisoners in 1945. It took the Brazilian government until June 26, 1947, to free him. Ewert left Brazil on a Soviet scientific ship, the Александр Крибдорген (*Alexander Krybdorgen*), that was in southern waters to study a solar eclipse. The vessel took him to the former German Democratic Republic, where he died in Eberswalde in 1959 without ever recovering his psychological health.[150]

Berger's wife, Sabo, was deported to Nazi Germany on the ship *La Coruña*. Named after the port city in Northwestern Spain, the seaboard around La Coruña is known as "The Coast of Death." It was an apocalyptic link. Once the craft docked in Hamburg, Sabo was taken to Berlin. She was reported to still be there on April 20, 1937. Little information about her exists after that date. Some say she fell victim to pneumonia in January 1939. Others are convinced she died in the second half of 1939 or that she passed away in 1941 in Ravensbrück of pneumonia and typical Gestapo abuse. There is likewise the report that she succumbed after the fall of Poland due to a weakened body from forced labor and a bout with tuberculosis. Jorge Amado indicated that she died in Germany from the tortures suffered while in Brazil. It has even been suggested that Sabo escaped from the Nazis before the outbreak of World War II and fled to France.[151]

Gregório Bezerra was sentenced to twenty-seven years and six months for the two killings at Pernambuco's Reserve Officer Training Center. He spent the first three and a half years in Recife followed by the same amount of time on Fernando de Noronha. He then passed through Ilha Grande before being shipped to the Casa de Correção in Rio. At the Correção, he shared a cell with Prestes. Released in the general amnesty for political prisoners of 1945, Bezerra set to work organizing the PCB's secret police and Prestes' bodyguards. Captured after the *golpe* (*coup*) of March 31, 1964, he was brutally tortured by the army and dragged through the streets of Recife. Flown into exile in September 1969, along with fourteen comrades in exchange for the kidnapped American ambassador to Brazil, Charles Burke Elbrick, Bezerra lived first in the Soviet Union and then in Cuba before returning to Brazil in 1979. He resigned from the party in 1980, along with Prestes, following a policy dispute. Politically active until the end, he died in São Paulo on October 21, 1983.[152]

Olga Benário was not allowed to visit with the father of her unborn child after the couple was driven from Méier to the Polícia Central by Müller's men. She became the object of various anti-Semitic comments in the press and was moved to the capital's Casa de Detenção to await her fortune. Even in the mid-1930s, no one could be legally deported from Brazil who had children with a Brazilian national. Thus, when Olga became ill during her pregnancy—one can only speculate as to the real cause—she was taken immediately to the Detenção's hospital. Müller was informed and quickly instructed the physician in attendance, Dr. Manuel Campos de Paz, to perform an abortion using the cover that it would be done to save Olga's life. But Olga refused, forcing the circle around Vargas to think up another way to resolve the real issue. The answer came from the lips of Supreme Court Justice Carlos Maximiliano. The magistrate concluded that the government could never be sure who the father of Olga's child was, since no marriage certificate was ever produced as proof of a legal union. To this was added the remonstrations of Clóvis Bevilácqua, the darling of the establishment's legal set, who summarized that pregnant or not, it was in the nation's best interest to deport this woman. The Integralists and the Nazis, for good measure, included their weighty voices for Getúlio to act.

Filinto, who never had the courage to confront his old commander in person after Prestes' arrest, was determined to have his revenge;[153] and Getúlio was just as resolved to send a token of his respect to Adolf Hitler. Knowing full well what this would mean to a communist Jewess, on August 27, 1936, Vargas nonetheless signed the decree expelling Olga to Germany on the same ship, *La Coruña*, as Sabo. While the government deported hundreds of undesirable aliens, including Jews, Olga Benário and Elise Ewert were the initial individuals the administration handed over to the Germans for execution. Their expulsion represented the first extradition between Brazil and Germany under the terms of a mutual anticommunism pact.[154] This kind of deportation to a sure death took place as well *after* the Spanish Civil War. In that instance, DESPS teamed up with the Spanish political police and returned a number of Republicans to Spain where they were given over to and garroted by the forces of Francisco Franco. In 1936, however, symbols of Getúlio's friendship with Franco's Nationalist cause were still limited to secret donations of Brazilian sugar and coffee.[155]

Using Olga and Sabo for political aggrandizing turned scores of people against Vargas. The U.S. military attaché remarked that the heavily controlled "press terms the decision to deport these women instead of punishing them 'a gesture of gallantry.'"[156] Yet Getúlio's necessary final approval motivated journalist David Nasser to mention much later that he favored Lee Harvey Oswald to Getúlio Vargas.[157]

After her arrival in Germany, Olga was transported to Ravensbrück Concentration Camp. There she gave birth to a daughter whom she named Anita Leocadia. The child's middle name was in honor of Prestes' mother. Both before and after delivery, Olga was forced to work in the facility's slave-labor operations. Around Easter in 1942, with her body exhausted and her usefulness to the Nazis at an end, she was taken to Bernburg, a former mental institution, and executed together with countless others in the camp's genocidal gas chamber.[158]

On May 7, 1937, Luís Carlos Prestes was given one of the longest sentences handed out to the dominant personalities of the failed revolution: sixteen years and six months. Later, an additional thirty years were added on charges that while behind bars he had given the go ahead to a plan to murder a suspected communist turncoat. The victim–who probably was not a traitor at all–was Elza Fernandes, the girlfriend of Antônio Bonfim.[159] A worldwide campaign to free Prestes for this, and for the original conviction, failed to budge Vargas. Quite the opposite, anyone signing a letter or postcard urging Prestes' release had their name catalogued together with the 30,000 names of the politically suspect over at DESPS.[160]

Brazil's most renowned communist walked free only following the general amnesty of 1945. He was elected senator for the Partido Comunista Brasileiro when the party was briefly legal from 1945 to 1947.[161] But Prestes' liberty and elected position were mere ruses as he continued to be watched by the political police.[162] Going underground following the *coup d'état* at the end of March 1964, he left the country from early 1971 to October 1979 with his new *companheira*, Maria Ribeiro. On returning, his flight was met by an estimated 10,000 persons at Rio's Galeão Airport. Times had changed, however, just as they had within the PCB. There were serious dogmatic disputes within the party. As a result, Luís Carlos Prestes resigned from the leadership in May 1980. He remained an independent-communist beacon until his death at ninety-two years of age on March 7, 1990.[163]

Photo 1. While on his daily walk, the "Father of the Poor," Getúlio Vargas (in white suit) being confronted by a cripple. Fundação Getúlio Vargas/CPDOC/Arquivo Getúlio Vargas

Photo 2. Coriolano de Góes (left) and Getúlio Vargas. *Correio da Manhã*/Arquivo Nacional

Photo 3. Protásio Vargas and his wife, Getúlio Vargas, General Manuel Vargas, and Benjamin Vargas at the family *fazenda* in São Borja. Agência Nacional/Arquivo Nacional

Photo 4. From left to right: Argentine President, General Agustín Justo (partially hidden), Getúlio Vargas, and Góes Monteiro at a military parade on Brazilian Independence Day, September 7, 1942. DIP/Arquivo Nacional

Photo 5. Euzébio Queiroz Filho. *Correio da Manhã*/Arquivo Nacional

Photo 6. Filinto Müller dressed in his formal major's uniform in June of 1943. *Correio da Manhã*/Arquivo Nacional

Photo 7. Serafim Braga, chief of DESPS' Social Section, probably on June 3, 1935. The soup stain on his lapel is in the original. *Correio da Manhã*/Arquivo Nacional

Photo 8. Vitório Caneppa on August 25, 1945. *Correio da Manhã*/Arquivo Nacional

Photo 9. A birthday party for Filinto Müller at the Polícia Central. Müller can be seen directly behind the floral arrangement. Other identifiable individuals include: Euzébio Queiros Filho (third from the left), Castelo Branco (no relation to the future president—sixth from the left, with hat in hand), Civis Müller (immediately to the right of Filinto's shoulder), Frota Aguiar (the shortest man in the picture, and next to Civis Müller), Cezar Garcez (in glasses, beside Frota Aguiar), and Israel Souto (who substituted for Filinto when the latter was absent—third from the extreme right, with buttons showing on his suit). PPARJ/Arquivo Público do Estado do Rio de Janeiro

Photo 10. Emílio Romano at his desk. PPARJ/Arquivo Público do Estado do Rio de Janeiro

Photo 11. Front row, from left to right: Francisco Julien, Miranda Corrêia, and Serafim Braga welcoming Corrêia on his return from the south of the country on February 28, 1936. PPARJ/Arquivo Público do Estado do Rio de Janeiro

Photo 12. Felisberto Batista Teixeira. *Correio da Manhã*/Arquivo Nacional

Photo 13. Paula Pinto in 1935. PPARJ/Arquivo Público do Estado do Rio de Janeiro

Photo 14. Cecil Borer's 1939 police identity photo. *O Mundo*/Biblioteca Nacional

Photo 15. Clodomir Collaço Véras. *Correio da Manhã*/Arquivo Nacional

Photo 16. Egas Botelho, Superintendent of the political police in São Paulo. PPARJ/Arquivo Público do Estado do Rio de Janeiro

Photo 17. Frederico Mindelo Carneiro Monteiro, Secretary of Public Security in Pernambuco in 1935. PPARJ/Arquivo Público do Estado do Rio de Janeiro

Photo 18. Etelvino Lins in March of 1945. Arquivo Nacional.

Photo 19. Malvino Reis Neto in Rio de Janeiro in the mid-1930s. Fundação Getúlio Vargas/CPDOC/Arquivo Pedro Ernesto

Photo 20. Two Polícia Especial motorized assault squads on patrol. Note the mounted Hotchkiss machine guns. *Correio da Manhã*/Arquivo Nacional

Photo 21. The São Paulo political police gathered for the camera in February of 1937. Four members of note begin in the center with Marques, or "Gomes," dressed in white with hands at his side. Marques was the right-hand man of Chief Inspector Luiz Apolonio, standing behind him in a gray suit. *Paulista* leftists considered Apolonio the very essence of reactionism. To the right of Marques is Captain Bruno, said to have been the left hand of Apolonio. In back of Bruno, also in a gray outfit, is the torturer "Farina." Courtesy of the Herminio Sacchetta family

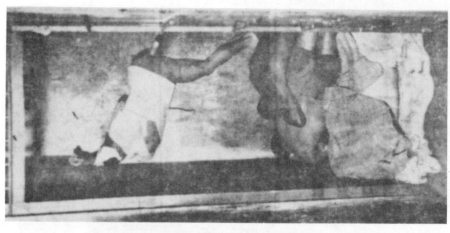

Photos 22 and 23. Two of the photographs accompanying the stories by Edmar Morél on the inhumane conditions in Rio's jails. *Última Hora*/Biblioteca Nacional

4

ESTADO NOVO

Over in Catete Getúlio's star reached the apogee of its drift to the right. He decided that the fascists were probably going to win and that it was time to get in line. On the evening of November 10, 1937, he announced to the nation on the radio that he had taken Brazil without delay into a dictatorial *Estado Novo*, or New State. Lucky for Vargas and his fellow countrymen, he really did not want to step aside and leave anyway, despite promising that presidential elections would be held in 1938. As for the military, they cooperated because they were still blinded by the dread of a communist threat.

The type of government that Getúlio had in mind was already the norm in several European countries. It was time for strong leadership, and those nations with fascist administrations came close to fitting his own ideas quite nicely. To this might be added the fact that among Brazil's traditional rivals in the South, authoritarian regimes were in place and functioning: Uriburu and Justo in Argentina beginning in 1930, and Terra in Uruguay since 1933.[1]

The only thing that was really left for Vargas to determine was the alibi. So what better explanation than another, and more daring, leftist conspiracy? How convenient it must have been then when Captain Olímpio Mourão Filho, a card-carrying Integralist, put together an AIB contingency plan about a hypothetical communist insurrection, and somehow army Chief of Staff Góis Monteiro was handed a copy complete with a fitting Jewish name: the Cohen Plan. Góis and his military colleagues altered the document where necessary and ascribed its authorship to the Comintern. It was the decisive part of the argument. Vargas could say that a majority of the generals and admirals were ready for a hard-line government to neutralize this threat from the nearly extinct Brazilian Bolsheviks.[2] On September 30, 1937, the country awoke to detailed descriptions in the press and over the radio about the fresh Soviet plans for Brazil. Just seven weeks later, Vargas announced to a complaisant nation that because of the selfish ambitions of the other presidential candidates in this hour of red peril, he was enacting forthwith a new body of laws, the Constitution of 1937.

The new law of the land put legal teeth into the *Estado Novo*. When and where necessary it left it up to the president, *l'état c'est moi*, to use and interpret the almighty will of the Brazilian people. To safeguard that covenant, Getúlio declared that the times demanded a national state of emergency. He thereupon gave himself unlimited dictatorial powers, deeming it advisable to close Congress, proclaim all political parties obsolete; extend his own term of office until 1943 or longer, annul civil rights (particularly those involving governmental criticism), promulgate the death penalty, formalize censorship, and require that one of his pictures be conspicuously displayed in each and every place of business.[3]

In respect to institutionalizing censorship, Vargas had given his initial Federal District Polícia Civil chief Batista Luzardo wide powers in this area back in the first days of November 1930.[4] Censorship in several forms merely continued from that point until it was officially recognized with the proclamation of the *Estado Novo*. One subtle refinement, however, was that after November 10, 1937, a good deal more of what passed under the sensitive nose of the government's censors was viewed as leftist propaganda. Three months later, an American weekly remarked on all this as follows:

The charge of communism is used with telling effect in Brazil. I obtained copies of the law requiring every school teacher to devote five minutes each morning to indoctrinating against this "plague." Since many of the teachers do not know what communism is, the results are humorous. Articles in the Brazilian papers in November [1937] criticized the Federal Council of Churches of Christ in America as a "Communistic organization" and declared that the Catholic Association for International Peace had similar aims. "Dangerous Communistic" literature such as "Tarzan" and "Tom Sawyer" is carefully kept from children or [*sic*] adults.[5]

Along with the political issues there were also the racial concerns. Carnival in Rio de Janeiro had long been the target of the anti-African-minded well-to-do. As early as the *Belle Époque* (roughly 1890 until the start of World War I), elites tried to purge those black aspects of the *carioca* carnival that could frighten or offend international entrepreneurs. With the *Estado Novo*, censors began to cut into *samba* lyrics. Their job was to delete the embarrassing "primitive" sides to the music. At the same time, they were to encourage the opinions of the dominant class regarding just what kind of work and patriotic attitudes lower-class nonwhites should have.[6]

As the current chief of the Federal District's Polícia Civil, DESPS was under Müller's command. In November 1935, Filinto had a section of this unit expanded and, by decree, changed it two years later into the Serviço de Divulgação (the Communication Service). Inspired by the Nazis, the reorganized unit's job was to see to it that Vargas' new will became the people's new desire. Through a network of some 1,300 publications, the Serviço de Divulgação contributed articles and commentary to every corner of Brazil. They just as readily gave instructions on the hiring, firing, and control of the massive number of middle-class and lower middle-class governmental employees–employees who were growing by leaps and bounds. Vargas thus created and would continue to expand "a massive patronage system, one that served, in fact, as a state-controlled political apparatus."[7]

As long as the chief executive offered paychecks, these bourgeois workers and their families would remain loyal to him. A political party was, accordingly, unnecessary since by virtue of such an arrangement, Getúlio had become Brazil's all time *coronel*. There was even built into the new constitution a legally proscribed way of dealing with anti-Vargas elements. Article 177 of the document gave the administration the right to remove bureaucrats and military personnel from their appointments "in the interest of public service or for the convenience of the regime."[8]

As for organizing these and any other city wage earners, Getúlio's much touted (urban) worker legislation was constructed so as to emasculate the independent union. This was because the government, in its corporate-like way, directed all unions. Each of these worker confederations, including their leaders, had to be sanctioned by Müller's office or be ready to face the music. Strikes were prohibited. Any kind of legal labor meeting had to have the prearranged blessings of the political police.[9] One American who visited Rio a year later tersely described what was happening:

People cautioned me not to "talk," not to discuss Brazilian politics, not to discuss democratic principles or government, or Russia, or communism, not to discuss public figures like President Roosevelt, not to ask questions, not to take pictures, not to talk with the lower classes who might be disaffected by the inflation and the general political insecurity.[10]

In sum, with his *Estado Novo*, Vargas created a system of checks and balances that was designed to hamper social change. This in its turn was not solely due to Getúlio's whims or mere capitalistic greed on the part of Brazilian elites. The racial component was explicit in upper-class commentary until World War II. Many whites openly felt–and still feel–that one of the functions of Brazil's ruling class was to prevent the largely nonwhite, lower classes from obtaining any positions of real power in the political or labor spheres. Everything was premised on the long-held belief that the darker the worker's skin, the closer he or she was to African, and hence to un-Christian, and therefore to uncivilized origins.

And what about the Jew in Brazil's New State? One of the falsehoods of the postwar period is that Oswaldo Aranha befriended the Jews in 1947 by urging the United Nations to create the nation of Israel. It would be more accurate to say that Aranha was an opportunist, like Vargas, ready to change his spots and go with the flow. Back in 1937, when it looked more rosy for the

Nazis, Oswaldo was Brazil's U.S. ambassador and then its foreign minister. During his tenure in these two positions, while fortunate Jews were escaping from Europe in any way possible, Aranha sent a circular to Brazilian embassies and consulates describing how to pick out Jews through their physical characteristics. There was even a never promulgated law to prohibit any part of this exodus from obtaining visas and eventually landing on Brazilian soil. That this never took place was probably due to the urgings of the United States and Britain. The numbers of Jews let in remained constant throughout this period. In 1939 it was even higher than any of the previous ten years.

There were, of course, a number of Jews who switched religious sides, perhaps only cosmetically, or who bribed their way in. There were likewise those who were denied admittance, some in quite unbelievable circumstances. Two examples of Aranha's reticence in this respect are particularly illuminating. In 1941, Oswaldo *refused* an appeal from Albert Einstein–and another one year later from his own mother–to assist specific European Jews wanting to immigrate to Brazil. These Jews were probably unqualified or poor because in 1938, Aranha established a set of classified provisions to the laws, whereby Jews could enter Brazil if they were members of sought-after professions, or if they were wealthy. This arose after a number of American Jews with money had been turned back; only to return home and raise a ruckus with their elected representatives. During the *Estado Novo* immigrants to Brazil were supposed to have $20,000 in start-up capital. Bribes too, were a standard part of the process and included officials at all levels of the host country. In addition to the Jews, Aranha did not care for and at times did his part to deny entry to communists (even though a younger relative, José Antônio Aranha, was a PCB member). Also making Oswaldo's list of *indesejaveis*, or "undesirable" people, were Masons, Japanese, blacks, and Hindus.[11]

OLD FACES AND NEW FACES IN THE NEW STATE

As the extreme right in Europe and at home applauded many of these measures,[12] Brazil's now stronger than ever strongman was busy planning his next moves. Vargas claimed that with his recent steps toward fascism, Plínio Salgado and his AIB Green Chickens would become more influential and ultimately more inclined to "Hindenburg" him if given the chance.[13] So he decided to put a kind-of an end to *integralismo*. There would be one leader in Brazil and everyone knew who his name was. In his New Year's speech of 1937, "Gegê" (a name given to Getúlio by the multitudes[14]) outlawed all flags other than the national banner, all distinctive songs, salutes, uniforms, and emblems devoted to political organizations. Salgado would be allowed to name the new minister of education only if he cooperated. But he refused and before sulking off to São Paulo begrudgingly turned the AIB into the first of what would be several cultural clubs.

The Integralists continued this splintering process to try to hide their activities, and to attempt to fool that part of the public unknowingly contributing funds to their bank accounts. These citizens might not have been so willing to open their purses had they been aware of the name of the parent, and now illegal, political group. The major AIB offshoots,[15] some infiltrated by DESPS' operatives, included:

Academia Juvenal Galeno
Adelia Foot-Ball Club
Apollo Sport Club
Associação dos Amigos de São José
Cadernos da Hora Presente
Centro Espírita Nossa Senhora do Carmo
Clube Hipico de Vila Guilherme
Colégio Andrade
Cruzada Juvenil da Bôa Imprênsa
Curso Tuiutí
Distinta Atlético Clube
Empresa Metreleco
Excelsior Sociedade Anônima
Revista Brasil Mineral
Sociedade Dramatica Particular Filhos de Talma
Socorro Verde
Vida de Jesus

Vargas had in fact slowly incorporated many of the things the Chickens were promoting into his newest governmental scheme. So it was that pro-Nazis like Francisco Campos, Filinto Müller, and Lourival Fontes assumed ever more important roles. Besides the abhorrent Müller, Campos and Fontes had their own suspect qualities. Francisco Campos plagiarized so much of the fascist Polish constitution into the one he wrote, the Constitution of 1937, that it was commonly referred to as the "*polaca*," or "Polish woman" (slang for a prostitute). Vargas never liked the *polaca*, and preferred to do exactly as he wished without regard to the document. This so irritated "Chico" Campos (Chico is the common nickname for Francisco), that he argued repeatedly with Getúlio about the matter and ended up getting himself fired.[16] Earlier in his career, while Campos was secretary of education, he had another conversation, this one about his political philosophy, with a member of the 1934 Constitutional Assembly. It was a most revealing discussion. Campos told the delegate, "Do not deceive yourself with democracy. The democratic phase has ended. It is now the phase of the strong regimes. Plínio Salgado is on the right track."[17] Chico also had a rather kinky private life. He is said to have often been the patron of no less than two Rio whorehouses where, together with a male friend and several prostitutes, they engaged in bizarre sexual acts.[18]

Lourival Fontes did not have the flair of Francisco Campos. Originally a journalist, Lourival had been around since July 10, 1934, when he was placed in charge of the national censorship apparatus. Through a number of bureaucratic changes the agency remained in Fontes' hands. Two days after Christmas in 1938 everything was reshuffled again, this time coming out as DIP (Departamento de Imprensa e Propaganda), or the Department of Press and Propaganda. Fontes was still its director and would remain so, with more power, until mid-1942. He is described as a man with no personal aspirations. Lourival was no intellectual. He never read books or newspapers. Rather, he was a patronizing yes-man to the president and openly profascist only when Getúlio was so inclined; although he did have an interesting history with the future Green Shirt *Chefe Nacional*.[19]   But, when his boss and leader of the government took a stance with the Allies, the life-long enemies of Fontes immediately became Germany, Italy, and Japan.   At one time he was closely linked to the Italian Embassy and the Casa d'Italia.   In that endeavor Fontes directed or facilitated a portion of fascist propaganda in Brazil.   He probably knew that the Italian Embassy was bribing the editor of *A Tarde* 10:000$000 a month to write articles favorable to Italy and Germany. In his home he proudly kept Italian bric-a-brac, letters, photos, and even a bust of Mussolini. He is said to have been so close to the German ambassador that he was the best man at his wedding.[20]

One of the things correspondents dreaded during these years was being called to DIP headquarters at Tiradentes Palace to account for some kind of affront.   On arriving for their appointment they were invariably made to wait hours on end in an outer office. They were not allowed to leave even to get a drink of water or go to the bathroom. The plan was to humiliate each of them before they were shown into see Lourival or one of his assistants.[21] A foreign correspondent who made it through the long delay observed what it was like to finally have only the odd reasoning of the man running DIP to contend with. On meeting the journalist eyeball to eyeball, Lourival remarked as follows: "I will be obligated to censor your dispatches if you continue to insinuate that Brazil is a dictatorial country.   The only dictator here is Getúlio Vargas.   Brazil is democratic and liberal. Do not confuse the president with Brazil."[22]

DESPS had agents on Lourival's tail just as they did on other members of the government and just about anyone else in politics. They reported back to their superiors at the Polícia Central that while Justice Minister Vicente Ráo was an alleged cocaine user, Fontes was notorious for appearing in public with his zipper down. Whether this was due to absent-mindedness or to attract feminine attention is unknown. Lourival lavishly spent over $2,000 a month on one of his mistresses. But there were several others, some of whom were apparently under the legal age. How young these females usually were, or if in fact his tastes bordered on pedophilia, could not be determined from the sources consulted. However, since Müller possessed such information on Lourival's interest in youthful women in his files, this alone suggests that Fontes' preferences may well have been in this twilight area.[23]

As Vargas' chief make-up man, Fontes' main job, especially following the formation of DIP, was to promote "the image of the dictator as the great benefactor of the working class."[24] Thus, out of the ashes of authoritarianism the phoenix of Comrade "Xuxu" (pronounced "Shoe-shoe") began to take wing.[25] Vargas was portrayed as the peerless administrator who had only the interests of the *povão* beating in his benevolent breast. From that day forward,

May 1st was not the date of solidarity with the international worker's movement, socialism, communism, or anything of the kind. In packed sports stadiums, May Day became the altar on which Getúlio was thanked for the care and nurturing he displayed for ordinary Brazilians. The pageantry was all faithfully recorded by DIP cameramen and shown as trailers in cinemas to those who wanted to relive the magic; as well as for those who wanted to get on with the feature film.[26] Still, Vargas was not entirely satisfied. Apparently he was interested in finding someone who could interpret his political whims with more acumen. By December 15, 1941, his feelings on the subject were said to be as follows: "In the absence of a genius–a Goebbels, for example–the person for the position is Lourival."[27]

DIP had its own group of thugs to implement the word of the dictator. They functioned independently when and where this was feasible.[28] On occasions when the assignment was too large, Lourival's operatives were assisted by the rest of Brazil's police forces. Probably the best example of the latter was in the application of the same laws that had done in the AIB to the 4,000,000 Italians in São Paulo and the 800,000 Brazilians of German extraction in the South. The Teuto-Brazilians especially had been open in their praise and bantam-like mimicking of the situation in the Fatherland. Among other things, Vargas' decree against domestic political groups was enlarged to include organizations with connections to foreign states. Moreover, a new ordinance required the thousands of German-language schools in Rio Grande do Sul and Santa Catarina to instruct their students entirely in Portuguese. This last statute, Decree Law No. 383 of April 18, 1938, marked the first open, major irritation in prewar relations between the two countries.[29]

PAJAMA-*PUTSCH*

The Integralists never really accepted their relegation to the pages of history. For months they tried to convince "Paschoal" (their own name[30] for Getúlio) to allow the AIB to function openly as a political or cultural entity. Vargas' refusal only served to intensify whatever schemes the AIB had for an uprising. With spies inside Salgado's movement, this planning could not be kept secret and DESPS was eventually alerted. Working against this is the assertion that since both Müller and Góis Monteiro may well have been passively involved, the degree to which Vargas was kept abreast of developments is uncertain. At a minimum DESPS knew by January 1938 that an attempt was going to take place sometime between the middle of the month and that year's Carnival. Arms were arriving for the AIB aboard Italian men-of-war on courtesy visits to Brazilian ports and shipped in crates supposedly containing Ford auto parts.

The Green rebellion was to start at the army installation in Quitaúna, in the São Paulo suburb of Osasco. To insure victory, *agents provocateurs* had been covertly dispatched to win over the barracks and local police stations. São Paulo was to rebel and, if necessary, secede from the union. In Rio, the *coup* was to count on the navy and a large number of officers who were members or AIB sympathizers.[31]   If successful, Eurico Gaspar Dutra would be arrested and Góis was to take his place as minister of war.   The entire incident would be passed off as the work of the Italians–since it was an open secret they were bedfellows with the Integralists–and the still muffled from the *paulista* Civil War Partido Republicano Paulista.

This São Paulo connection went deeper.   There were familial overtones. The wife of Antônio de Barros, one of the brothers of Ademar de Barros, an important PRP kingpin, was the first cousin of Joseph Goebbels.   That Ademar had been a student in Berlin, although before the advent of the Nazis, was one thing.   That his brother's wife worked actively at the German Consulate was quite another.   There were also several meetings at the São Paulo home of now ex-Minister of Justice Vicente Ráo.   Other suspicious rendezvous took place for several months.   Among those in attendance at these get-togethers was Carmela, the wife of Plínio Salgado; Leonor, the wife of Ademar de Barros; the wife of Ademar's brother; and the German council in São Paulo, Dr. Walter Molly.[32]

Funding for the budding overthrow came in part from the semilegal numbers racket based on animal symbols known as *jogo do bicho* ("The Game of the Animals").   Several controllers of *jogo* territories, called *banqueiros* (bankers), were known to have contributed funds.   As an example, one *banqueiro*, known only as "Fernandes," donated 20,000 *contos de réis* or slightly over $1,140 at the official rate of exchange in early January 1938.   Legitimate financial institutions, as well, either gave money or had it purloined.   Indicative here was the large amount of cash snatched off a detained Cuban by the police before it could reach AIB coffers.   The monies apprehended together with their origins were: 24:000$000 Caixa Economica Federal, 330:000$000 Casa Bancaria Borges, 70:000$000 Banco Comercial, and 50:000$000 from additional bank sources.   The German Transatlantic Bank likewise raised funds against stock in the Antarctica Brewing Company and put what it obtained at the disposal of the movement.[33]

More and more a recluse, and still in São Paulo, Plínio Salgado at first put the talk of a *coup* off, forever trying to win concessions from Getúlio.   But even Plínio had his limits.   When he finally concluded he could wait no longer, he chose Belmiro Valverde to turn the Integralists' belated dreams into a reality in the nation's capital.   Valverde was a man of action who wasted little time in assembling around him a group of associates determined to topple Paschoal's dictatorship and replace it with one of their own.

At about this point the AIB began using a secret code in their internal communications.   The cipher (on the following page) consisted of a set of hand-drawn symbols used together with regular and otherwise innocent Portuguese text.   The written words said one thing while the signs communicated a different idea or gave a direct order.   Unfortunately, two explanations accompanying the symbols were partially torn off with the passage of time and lost.   The meaning of the bottom two Portuguese translations given in italics in the right-hand column are unclear.[34]

A = Map of Ilha das Cobras

☆ = Diagram of the armament of the battleship São Paulo

⋊⋉ = Diagram of the armament of the battleship Minas Gerais

△ = Diagram of the armament of the cruisers

⋈ = Diagram of the armament of the mine sweepers

△ = Commit sabotage

△ = Commit sabotage

△ = Commit sabotage?

△ = Capture the telephone installations

◁ = Destroy whatever possible

◁ = Before repeating the agitation...[missing fragment]

◁ = Sabotage the weapons that...[missing fragment]

◁ = Shoot

◁ = Shoot the officers

◁ = Don't shoot

◁ = Enlisted men, soldiers and sailors

⟨∧⟩ = Surprise attack

⟨∨⟩ = Cut all telephone lines

⟨<⟩ = Capture the Central Telephone Station

⟨<>⟩ = Act together

∠ = *Para creado* [possible meaning: Give to]

∠ = *Agua Isolada* [possible meaning: Isolated water]

There followed a premature rebellion on March 10-11th, in which the attempted capture of a radio station and the simultaneous revolt by some AIB sailors were foiled. The government reacted with several hundred arrests, mainly in Guanabara and the surrounding state of Rio de Janeiro. They also seized AIB weapons[35] and materials, but closed only a single Integralist newspaper. A full two-thirds of the jailed Green Shirts in larger Rio were let go within a few days. Perhaps such light-handedness convinced the plotters that there was even more sympathy in government circles than they anticipated. There certainly was in the Federal District's Polícia Militar, where 123 officers of the law already were members of the AIB.[36] Buoyed by these developments, the conspirators were soon back at work perfecting a more intricate plan. The new blueprint called for 2,000 fascists in Rio de Janeiro, São Paulo, Minas Gerais, Bahia, and Rio Grande do Sul to seize control of a number of vital points, arrest key figures, and bring down the *Estado Novo* with a bang.

Still in charge of the details, Valverde selected a non-Integralist army officer, Lieutenant Severo Fournier,[37] to lead a team of diehards in the main assault on Guanabara Palace. Their goal was to capture or kill Getúlio Vargas. In what *carioca* wit would come to call the "pajama-*Putsch*," Fournier was promised 150 well-trained fighters. On the eve of battle, however, May 10, 1938,[38] a little over thirty showed up at the prearranged assembly point: Avenida Niemeyer 550.[39] Not only were they too few, several of the would-be revolutionaries had to be shown how to use their weapons. All wore naval uniforms similar to the palace guards, but with Σ-encrusted handkerchiefs around their necks. To work up courage they nervously gulped down shots of cheap cognac.

Owing to an undercover AIB member on sentry duty, Sergeant Luiz Gonzaga de Carvalho, when H-hour arrived at 1 A.M., the attackers gained control of the grounds around the palace. Vargas and his family were asleep when the shooting began. Together with his brother Benjamin, plus a few aides, Getúlio managed to hold off the *coup*-makers with small arms from the structure's windows and hallways. As this was going on, Fournier and his men overlooked cutting an important government telephone line. The president's daughter, Alzira, was thus free to repeatedly call for help over this single link to the outside. For the men who would depose a dictator, it was the error that proved to be their undoing.

Three calls were made to Filinto Müller and no less than one each to the Polícia Militar, the Polícia Especial, Copacabana Fort, Minister of Justice Francisco Campos, Minister of War Eurico Gaspar Dutra, Dutra's Chief of Staff Canrobert Pereira da Costa, as well as to army Chief of Staff Góis Monteiro. But all of the persons contacted, as if to suggest some kind of collusion, were either unable to respond or said that they had already dispatched forces to aid the president.

Delayed, Dutra ultimately arrived with a handful of soldiers and proceeded to scatter most of the Integralists before being chased off himself. Full government reinforcements did not appear until 9 A.M., some four hours after the fighting broke out. Coinciding with the action at Guanabara Palace, battles erupted across town at the Naval Ministry, out in Guanabara Bay, and at three local radio stations. The latter were broadcasting news of the struggle to the nation over the air, as well as to a prematurely overjoyed Plínio Salgado, listening in São Paulo. Not long after midmorning most of the bullets had been fired. The Integralists and their allies were soundly defeated due to cowardliness and bad planning.

Tomato Head chief Euzébio de Queiroz Filho was among those who finally got to Catete. He had two captives brought before him and inquired if either was a member of the Sigma assault team, there with the mission of killing Getúlio. Both men emotionally denied everything, going so far as to even accuse each other. Euzébio's patience wore thin. He abruptly told one of the prisoners, while handing him a revolver, "If you're innocent, shoot this other guy!" Observing the scene from a Guanabara Palace window, Alzira Vargas pleaded, "No! Please don't!" But it was too late. The Green Shirt who had the fortune of being given the weapon fired at close range, killing his brother-in-arms. Euzébio then screamed at the one left alive, "Get out of here!" The leader of the Polícia Especial let the man flee. Others did not have the luck of the draw. As many as nine attackers were shot dead on or near the palace grounds. Some may have been among those who were taken into custody and paraded before Vargas. Then marched toward the back of the Palace, they were executed by Benjamin and Euzébio for "trying to escape."[40]

Besides besieging the presidential mansion, the AIB planned to capture the Santos Dumont Airport, Barão de Mauá Railroad Station, Leopoldina Railroad Station, the Polícia Central, key telephone communication centers, and all telegraphic links into and out of the city. Diversionary fires were planned but only one took place. They were supposed to provide the cover for twenty-nine attacks on important government and military officials. Again, all but one never came to pass or failed entirely. The lone success was against Colonel Canrobert Pereira da Costa. Those assigned to deal with him, twenty men led by Antonio Fernandes, "arrested" the nightshirt-clad general and whisked him off into the early morning darkness in a car.

There was a simultaneous Integralist strike against the Central Naval Radio Station; but the invaders were talked into surrendering without bloodshed by the post's commander, Bemvindo Taques Horta. The Ministry of the Navy building was captured, lost, then retaken again before the assailants finally gave up. A group also set out from Praça XV in a launch to the warship *Bahia*. Along with the tender *Ceará*, both vessels went over to the AIB without resistance. The *Bahia* soon hoisted anchor and steamed around Guanabara Bay a few times waiting for further instructions. When news of the end of the revolt was radioed out to her, she surrendered. The *Ceará* sailed over to the Ilha do Boqueirão, also in Guanabara Bay, dispatched a squad of men and captured most of the island without incident. However, when the assaulting unit then tried to take the Armament Office on Boqueirão, a guard fired his rifle in their direction and the Green sailors meekly gave up.[41]

AFTERMATH

Following the pajama-*Putsch*, not only was Canrobert returned by his abductors, but both Müller and Góis submitted their resignations as things came under control. The ever-wily Vargas simply put the documents in his breast pocket and smiled one of his famous smiles.[42] Meanwhile, as many as 474 persons were picked up. The plotters were said to have been conspiring with the German Embassy; yet nothing was ever proven for sure or–put more succinctly–what really transpired was soon hushed up.[43] No one could, nevertheless, deny that the events of that May did not exacerbate an already irritated relationship between Rio de Janeiro and Berlin. They also contributed to an ambassadorial scuffle toward the end of the year, and played right into American hands.

That November, the U.S. Federal Bureau of Investigation was asked by Oswaldo Aranha to help set up a Brazilian secret service. The proposed body was to keep its undercover eyes on Nazi and Italian spies,[44] and also on Müller and his secret police. The Americans were not new to Brazil. They began in 1931 by assisting in Brazilian anticommunism efforts. But with the end of the decade, U.S. interests had shifted to the Axis powers.[45]

As for the rest of the AIB, in the capital many Green Shirts took refuge in the Italian, Portuguese, and other fascist embassies. Müller's police arrested 1,167 civilians and 437 members of the armed forces. Most of this second group was in the navy. The branch of service meant little to the police chief. By early June 1939, some 600 of these prisoners, mainly nonmilitary *cariocas*, had already been turned loose. This mild approach, moreover, was even more dramatic in other parts of the country. Unlike the endeavor to catch leftists, there was *no* comparable manhunt to grab the followers of Plínio Salgado.[46] Those who did stumble into police custody were nonetheless incarcerated together with communists, former members of the ANL, and common criminals, probably for lack of resources. How then to tell your friend from your foe? Green Shirts in detention for any length of time were apt to use a secret recognition signal between themselves and other Integralists. An upright hand with closed fist except for the index finger and thumb was the sign used when asking, "Are you an Integralist?" The raised index finger stood for God; the protruding thumb for Plínio Salgado. Either a verbal answer of *"Estou contigo"* ("I am with you") was given, or a hand sign in which all the fingers of a downwardly held open hand, except the thumb, were nervously twitched.[47]

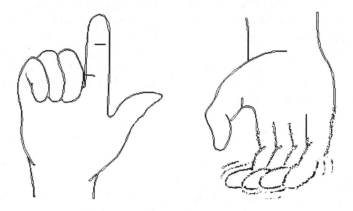

After a month in hiding, Fournier succeeded in making an ill-advised dash for the safety of the Italian Embassy. He ended up being traded to insistent Brazilian authorities for frozen Italian assets and sentenced to ten years in prison. At some point Severo contracted tuberculosis. When his TB became noticeable, care was curiously delayed for months as he suffered, locked in a cell with the usual bad hygiene. Following an operation for his disease, there were accusations that Müller tried to kill him by ordering a transfer too soon after the surgery. His father then asked Filinto to arrange for better treatment. The chief of police replied that the only thing he could do was to send the elder Fournier his son's body once he had passed away. But Severo did not die. Still sick, he too was released in the general amnesty decreed by Vargas in 1945.[48]

Valverde and a number of others also received stiff sentences. Yet many of the Integralist upper crust were ultimately allowed to go free as the pallid campaign against the Ação Integralísta Brasileira was by and large limited to the bottom half of the membership.

Gustavo Barroso was briefly held but not found to be guilty of anything and released. In his case, the Segurança judges evidently never heard of the crime of conspiracy.[49] Plínio Salgado, too, was taken into custody for a few days but declared innocent of any crime–by Filinto Müller–and allowed to leave the country just over thirteen months later.[50] Exiling himself to Salazar's Portugal, the *Chefe Nacional* lived off of the subscriptions to two AIB publications, and may have even been given a monthly grant by the Vargas administration until he returned home from Europe in 1945.[51]

While some Integralists were charged with offenses until the end of 1938, communists, socialists, and progressive idealists were tracked down for a further three years. In 1940, Felisberto Batista Teixeira sent his boss, Filinto Müller, a list of all the DESPS agents in Rio who had helped put down the specter of communism.[52] The roster was circulated strictly within government circles that September. The names of those agents are reprinted here for the first time (see Appendix, Table 2). They were aided by yet another new police detachment, the Quadro Móvel, or Mobile Squad. The latter functioned as an eavesdropping unit on selected mail, telephone calls, and conversations of all types. There were about thirty Quadro Móvel operatives. Members were formally assigned to another police or military unit. But each man really worked for Civis Müller, the nephew of the police chief. In essence, then, the Quadro Móvel was Filinto's private force. The group was thought to be so pervasive that they were referred to as "The Invisibles."

Denounced persons, those overheard making illegal remarks, or others already sought by the Quadro Móvel were added to those ushered into the horrors of the Central Police Station, which was reported to have gotten more ghastly with the start of the *Estado Novo*.[53] Along with the occasional Green Shirt, even children became a part of the screaming and torture. Some prisoners, both adults and probably more than one child, had their cases disposed of rapidly. They found themselves being loaded aboard a motorboat, taken out to sea, and fed to the sharks.[54]

With the increasing number of arrests, and since most of the convenient penal establishments were overcrowded, the government hurriedly made room for internees on Fernando de Noronha. Located 214 miles off the coast of Rio Grande do Norte, a penal colony had been built on the largest of Fernando de Noronha's islands in the middle of the seventeenth century. Charles Darwin visited the area for a few hours on February 20, 1832, while traveling south. Shortly after he departed, all of the trees, except those in the governor's backyard, were cut down to prevent the building of rafts on which prisoners might try to escape. The entire archipelago was later incorporated into the state of Pernambuco.

It was from the administration in Recife that Vargas took control of Fernando de Noronha near the end of 1937. The federal government needed a place to store individuals thought to be politically dangerous, and the distant island complex was felt to be perfect. In substitution, Agamenon Magalhães, the *interventor* in Pernambuco, received six thousand *conto de réis* (or $346,820.80) from Rio de Janeiro. The bulk of this money was supposed to go to help fight communism in his state by erecting another prison on the mainland.[55]

Construction became a part of the routine on Fernando de Noronha as well. The colony was enlarged through the creation of another so-called agricultural camp. To finish everything as soon as possible, the entire endeavor was placed under the *feitor*-like[56] direction of Vitório Caneppa. Caneppa used captives to complete the project. Two-hundred and eight men off the first prison ship to drop anchor made up a good part of his initial workforce. Although the inaugural delivery contained far more Integralists than leftists, no insurmountable problems were anticipated. The threat of the gun and the whip is a great mollifier; and right from the start, both groups were physically reminded that it was Caneppa who was in charge. On day one on the island, before going directly to work, everyone was forced to strip together and march nude 12.4 miles to the prison storehouse that dispatched numbered uniforms.

By March 1941, further shipments of both the detained and the sentenced brought the total number of politicals on the rock to about 350. Of these, 160 were Integralists and 190 were communists. In this same month there were 550 ordinary lawbreakers on Fernando de Noronha. Tuberculosis was rampant as were occasional outbreaks of beri-beri. Each of the three groups lived in separate bungalows; and in their spare hours, the two blocs of political prisoners organized classes attempting to win converts from both the other side and the common criminals. It was also a good way to keep up the faith. The reds were headed by Agildo Barata, who had led the 3rd Infantry Regiment in rebellion at Praia Vermelha during the failed *Intentona*.[57] Command among the blues was generally in disarray as the fascists were split into a number of subgroups, some of which collaborated with the authorities.

Assisting Caneppa were no less than two professional torturers. One was army Major Felisberto Batista Teixeira. The other was Alvaro Gurgel de Alencar Filho, who was placed in charge of the local *seção de explosivos*. Felisberto and Alvaro tormented prisoners in this compound with the usual bamboo slivers and steel pins of *adelfis*, the blowtorch, and a variation of the *bucha de mustarda*. Since the original idea worked so well on women, the two sadists had their men insert billy clubs covered in mustard into the anuses of male victims. Some prisoners even had the yellow, burning sauce dripped into their eyes.[58]

The atmosphere changed dramatically after Caneppa and Alencar Filho were dispatched to other assignments. The new administrator, Colonel Nestor Veríssimo da Fonseca, was a veteran of the *Coluna* Prestes and much more tolerant than his predecessor. Once he took over, prisoners were allowed the freedom of most of the island and permitted to lead their own lives.[59] They could even be sent money and supplies from the mainland. Albeit, the AIB prisoners received far more of these parcels either because they really had more mailed to them or because the gifts to the leftists were diverted. Back in Rio, one of the personalities who donated aid to the imprisoned Green Shirts was the chief of the Polícia Civil, Filinto Müller.[60]

Already in April 1939, Vargas gave the go-ahead to the formation of still another police apparatus. This newest unit functioned as the right arm of the

Serviço de Divulgação. It was called SIPS, or more formally the Serviço de Inquéritos Políticos Sociais (the Political and Social Investigation Service). SIPS' main job was to gather information on individuals that could be of interest to the regime.[61] It kept a particularly low profile; however, as Getúlio was beginning to inch closer to the government of Franklin D. Roosevelt.

AXIS OR ALLIES?

The latest round in the Americanization of Brazil began when Oswaldo Aranha, formerly Brazil's ambassador to Washington, was switched to head the Itamarati. By now an admirer of the American way of life, and popular himself in the United States, Aranha's new appointment was viewed with pleasure by FDR and his advisors. In the first weeks of 1939, the Americans thus requested that Oswaldo travel to Washington, DC to discuss economic, military, and political questions. German and Italian efforts on these topics in South America by the end of 1938 prompted Roosevelt's invitation.

Brazil had already purchased sizable amounts of German munitions in addition to three Italian submarines. In fact, it had been trading more and more with Germany in both the domestic and military areas for a number of years.[62] But this activity began turning sour in the latter half of the 1930s because it was a swap arrangement based on Brazilian raw materials for German manufactured goods. The Germans paid Brazil in "barter-*Marks*" that were nonconvertible. Imports coming from other countries had to be acquired with hard currency or gold. Many of these latter funds, in turn, were obtained on the world market from produce not sold to Germany. A snag in this tidy arrangement developed when world prices on the major goods Brazil was producing and using as trade, except cotton, began going down in value. Especially disastrous was the coffee situation. Over 60 million bags were burned by the government between 1932 and 1938 in an attempt to force a rise in international coffee prices. But the figures did not increase and cotton could not earn enough by itself to make up the difference.

Two of the more interested observers to this economic downswing were the army and navy. The Brazilian military was in the market for new arms and equipment because of the 1932-1933 Leticia conflict between Peru and Columbia. The Chaco War (1932-1935), which pitted Bolivia against Paraguay, added to their thirst for more modern means of destruction. Brazil's own forces were said to be badly supplied and in need of upgrading as early as the 1932 clash with the state of São Paulo. Not having the internal ability to produce much more than small arms, and at the urging of War Minister Dutra, Brazil arranged to buy its heavier military products from Germany. This was to be accomplished via the already established raw materials for barter-*Marks* agreement. The submarines were likewise bought and paid for with unprocessed produce. As the combat equipment began to reach Brazilian ports, however, the possibility of another European war was becoming disturbingly more apparent. Moreover, if a conflict broke out, one did not have to ponder the options to see that bellicose items for the Brazilian military might not make it across the South Atlantic. Foreign-bought weapons could be kept in the country of origin for internal use, confiscated by third parties, or damaged in transit. There consequently was the growing realization that what Brazil really needed was a steel mill so that it could make its own heavy armaments itself.

WASHINGTON CALLS

As Aranha sailed north out Guanabara Bay, both he and Getúlio felt they knew what the Americans were after. Vargas was also of the opinion that he could play both ends off against the middle. He thus instructed Aranha to string the Americans along as long as it would not injure his agreements with the Germans and Italians. Gegê then told each country's ambassador exactly what he thought they wanted to hear, continuing to negotiate separately with all sides, until just before the Battle of Britain.[63] It would be only the realization that the Germans could not deliver that would change his mind.

When the foreign minister arrived in the United States, FDR and Secretary of State Cordell Hull lost no time in getting him alone for private conversations. During these talks it was made clear to the Brazilian that his bargaining position would be improved should his country agree to cooperate militarily with the United States against the Axis governments. The Americans wanted to build air bases in Brazil's Northeastern corner and out on Fernando de Noronha. After cabling Vargas that the Roosevelt administration was promising to provide large amounts of U.S. military hardware and credits of up to $120 million, Aranha indicated that a deal could be made. As part of the package, it was also announced that the U.S. army's chief of staff, General George C. Marshall, would make an official visit to Brazil.[64]

Paper promises from the United States, coupled with Getúlio's continued efforts to milk both the American and German cows for weapons, lessened the impact of Aranha's Washington agreements. But undaunted, and right on schedule, Marshall arrived in Rio aboard the *USS Nashville* in May 1939. His counterpart, Góis Monteiro, was still unaffected by his likely connection to the pajama-*Putsch* one year earlier. Góis had moved himself into a position immediately behind Vargas. He was already one of the kingpins in the marketing of the Cohen Plan and an open admirer of Hitler's new Germany. *Der Führer* had personally invited Góis to the Fatherland to inspect German might at first hand and to lead a Nazi division during maneuvers. Later, the German leader had his ambassador to Brazil pin medals on General Monteiro.

Distrustful of the American officer's intentions, Góis reluctantly agreed to welcome Marshall and his party, and see to it that they were shown around the Brazilian military establishment. By the time the visit ended, Vargas was sufficiently impressed with the American to concede to a protocol visit by Góis to the United States. Monteiro would return with Marshall to the United States. It was a game of international poker; and this hand was won by the U.S. army's chief of staff when he pointed out that the military equipment Germany was sending to Brazil was far from the most modern available.

As the cruiser *USS Nashville* steamed away from Rio, the American team was already making plans to win Góis over. When they reached the high seas Marshall and his assistants could talk at will on the need for Brazil and the United States to come to some kind of military understanding. The United States wanted bases and Brazil wanted military parity with long-time adversary, Argentina. By the time the *Nashville* docked in Annapolis, Maryland, Góis was well on the road to accepting the idea of an inter-American solution to both sets of concerns. The icing on the cake was the red-carpet treatment Monteiro received in the United States. He met with FDR and key government officials, was shown military and industrial establishments, and taken on a two-month sightseeing tour, largely by air, from one coast to the other. The Brazilian army's chief of staff came very close to being swept off his feet. He sent effusive messages back to Getúlio on the industrial might, organizational capability, and military potential of his newfound suitor.

But Gegê would not yet accede to the North Americans. To stave off the army's anxiety over the possibility of an Argentine invasion, Getúlio blindly clung to the view that he could squeeze the best munitions deal from whichever side proved to be the strongest. Arguing against this on his return, Góis was able to talk Vargas into letting the United States construct several airfields in the Northeast to improve Brazil's defenses. Under joint control, these bases allowed the Brazilians to concentrate their forces in the South near Argentina. Along with Minister of War Dutra, Góis, whose trip to Germany was put off due to the start of World War II, was still among those officers who nonetheless thought that an Axis victory was a good likelihood.[65]

The Allies were aware of Eurico Gaspar Dutra's convictions. It was his frank opinion that a German triumph would only be a benefit for Brazil. So intense were Dutra's pro-Axis sentiments, that he and his wife had applauded the fall of France.[66] Furthermore, Dutra was not simply an admirer of the Nazi war machine as is commonly contended. In May 1940, he too received German battle ribbons from the Nazi ambassador to Brazil on orders from *Herr* Hitler.[67]

When he was a military cadet, Dutra was among those who revolted in 1904 against the government of Rodrigues "Big Daddy" Alves. But thirty-five years later Eurico was part of the administration and had mellowed out considerably. He is said to have had an unprepossessing personality and not too much intelligence.[68] In 1939 he signed the order closing the doors of the country's military colleges to Jews, non-Catholics, nonwhites, persons of working-class parentage, and to the sons of divorced or separated couples.[69] By 1941 the war minister felt he had so much power that he remarked, "I will resign only after the president also resigns."[70] Maybe, but he certainly came around in July 1942 once Brazilian ships began to be sunk by the Axis. This, however, was not necessarily true of his wife. That December, she was still plotting with those friendly to Axis causes and with those trying to regain control of the police.[71]

As for the Americans, the whole understanding with them rested on their willingness and ability to provide a good part of the agreed-upon military arsenal. Delaying, Roosevelt was more occupied with sending what supplies he could in secret to the British. America was officially neutral and unprepared to assist the Brazilians in anything really tangible. Realizing some or all of this, Vargas gave a speech aboard the battleship *Minas Gerais* on June 11, 1940, that could only be interrupted as pro-German. In part, his remarks were a banquet for the large number of Axis-friendly ears in the military. In his approximation with the United States, Getúlio had not yet gone beyond using veiled threats for those listening in Washington. He warned that he just might revise his position in favor of the Axis should the agreed-on American aid fail to materialize. After all, France would capitulate in just a few days. With this there would probably be an end to the war and a reopening of "European" (i.e., German) armament markets.

DESPS field operatives forwarded the reactions of several sections of the population to Xuxu's shipboard talk back to their superiors at the Polícia Central. The overwhelming opinion of educated persons was that it was "despotic," "smacked of nazism," or reminded them of something Salazar would say. Agent K-44 reported that the communists agreed. Getúlio's remarks were "totalitarian." But, as might be expected, the Integralists bubbled over with enthusiasm. In Germany too the reaction was euphoric. A Radio-Berlin commentary to the speech, monitored by DESPS' Social Section, announced that the Brazilian leader "was the first South American statesman to recognize the impotency of the system of democracy and the vigor of the Axis nations."[72]

In the Oval Office, FDR's response to these and other Brazilian moves was to have Marshall call a conference of all the army chiefs of staff in the Americas. Góis was thus off to Washington in October for a second whirl of the town, and more North American efforts to woo him come what may. But Góis was not the only Brazilian VIP being shown around. A negotiating team had preceded the general and was already ironing out the last details of a deal that would become one of the milestones of the Vargas administration. The United States agreed to a $20 million contract to start construction of a steel mill. This represented a great personal triumph for Getúlio Vargas. Some might even argue that it was his greatest victory. Work was soon started on the plant at Volta Redonda in the state of Rio de Janeiro.

SETTING THE HOOK

At the end of 1940, after protracted negotiations with the British, the White House was able to free the Brazilian merchant ship *Siqueira Campos*. The vessel had been transporting a cargo of Krupp munitions to Brazil when she was seized by the English. In addition, the Royal navy stopped a Brazilian ship off the Brazilian coast and removed from it several *Graf Spee* crew members. Britain's SIS believed other sailors from the scuttled pocket battleship were aboard the Brazilian steamer *Itapé*.[73] Aside from the U.S. intercession in the

Siqueira Campos case, and the airfields in the Northeast, concrete American help in the military field would occur only after Pearl Harbor. Following the Japanese attack, the United States poured $366 million in munitions into Brazil through the Lend-Lease Program. But even this large outlay of materials was preceded by several key events.

According to William Stephenson, Britain's counterintelligence mastermind during the war, one of the turning points prodding Getúlio into the Allies' camp came as the consequence of a letter forged by the English. The faked communication was supposed to have originated in late September 1941 in the Rome office of General Aurelio Liotta, president of LATI, Linee Aeree Transcontinentali Italiane (Italian Transcontinental Airlines). It was destined for LATI's regional manager in Brazil, Vicenzo Coppola; but copies were clandestinely leaked to people close to Vargas. The document convinced Getúlio that there was another plot in progress by the Italians, Germans, and Integralists. References were made to the "green gentleman" (Plínio Salgado), to Vargas as the "little fat man," that Berlin had concocted the plan, and that Brazil was a country of monkeys that "will dance for anyone who can pull the string!" Vargas' anger over the incident was sufficient to prod him into a reassessment of his relationships with all sides.[74]

The Third Foreign Minister's Conference in Rio de Janeiro in January 1942 was another of these side-switching milestones. It was a meeting held in the disinterested Brazilian capital, at U.S. insistence, that forced Vargas' hand. Because of the Argentina question and because of the war, the only practical place where Brazil could get major armaments was in the United States. Getúlio really had very little room to maneuver; especially since Aranha let it be known that he would resign and then tell the international community why, should his boss fail to take part. The U.S. delegate, Undersecretary of State Sumner Welles, was offering firm American commitments. Still, Vargas dragged his heels right up until the virtual last moment . . . finally giving in to make the bitter decision. It took effect on the evening of January 28th, just after the close of the conference. To get the long-promised military aid, Brazil, *quid pro quo*, broke diplomatic relations with the Axis powers.[75]

The aftermath of the rupture produced two governmental factions that vied for the president's ear. In an ensuing struggle by both groups over the holding of a pro-U.S. 4th of July parade, four notable personalities fell from power. The handling of the affair proved to be a golden opportunity for Getúlio to remove expendable members of his entourage. From the pro-Allies side, acting Justice Minister Vasco Leitão da Cunha and Justice Minister Francisco Campos were both fired. The latter had been on extended sick leave once becoming disenchanted with Vargas. From the pro-Axis bloc, there was DIP Director Lourival Fontes and Police Chief Filinto Müller. Each had their resignation put into effect on July 17, 1942. Vargas even agreed to Müller's being placed under house arrest for forty-eight hours.[76] Once his sentence was up, Filinto wasted little time in scurrying back to his office to destroy any incriminating or somehow compromising material. There was no doubt a great deal of such stuff, because he and his men burned up a small mountain of documents. The fire they produced was a much larger blaze than the one observed at the German Embassy, for the same reasons, following Brazil's rupture of relations between the two countries.[77]

Yet even before Müller–a man who always said that he was only obeying orders[78]–put a torch to his past, Nazi and Japanese spies were being arrested and in some cases tortured. Many ended up at a special concentration camp in the state of Pará at Tomé-Açu. Situated south of Belém on the Acará-Mirim River, thirty-seven inmates still imprisoned there by VE day were evidently not deported. The camp's administrator petitioned for their liberty from the state *interventor*; but at the same time admonished that they (1) be keep under constant police observation, (2) not be allowed to approach frontier areas nor come within 43½ miles of the coast, (3) not be permitted to live within two-thirds of a mile from naval or air bases, or artillery positions, and (4) be prohibited from traveling between municipalities without the permission of the political police. The other prisoners at the camp were to be kept "under strict police vigilance."[79]

This kind of scrutiny was not the case, however, for the Brazilian *Führer* sequestered across the Atlantic in Portugal. Believing there was another chance to depose Vargas,[80] toward the end of 1941 Plínio Salgado was providing German agents in Lisbon with information; although much of what he had was out of date. The initial approach was made by SD (Sicherheitsdienst or Security Service) officer, Erich Schröder. He in turn informed his superior SS Major-General Walter Schellenberg. It was not long thereafter that Adolf Nassenstein, an SD operative brought in especially from London, was acting as the contact between Salgado and Schellenberg. Plínio's cooperation was predicated on assurances that he would be the man in charge in Brazil following a Nazi conquest of Europe.[81] So sure was the *Chefe Nacional* of the outcome of the war that he instructed the AIB back in Rio to begin taking down license numbers of automobiles in the Federal District that openly displayed the "V" for victory decal of the Allies. Some of the guilty parties even had the audacity to use the national colors of Brazil, the red, white and blue of China, Free France, the United Kingdom, and the United States in their "V" signs. The vehicles' owners were to be taken care of later.[82] There may have been some truth in this because Salgado's movement outlived both the Nazis and the war. It even survived its founder.[83]

Vargas' ending of diplomatic ties with Germany resulted in a relocation of the Nazi's Brazilian operation center to Buenos Aires. In the Argentine capital the Germans and the AIB continued what must have been a fruitful relationship. One nexus started sometime after mid-1943 when SD agent Johannes Siegfried Becker established contact with exiled Integralists Jair Tavares and a "Doctor Caruso." Becker introduced the two to members of the pro-Axis Argentine General Staff. Soon a tentative deal was hammered out between the Integralists and Colonels Enrique González and Juan Perón with the following elements:

1. Argentina should broadcast pro-Axis propaganda in the Portuguese language to Brazil, by short wave.

2. The Argentine military attaché in Rio de Janeiro would be replaced by a more cooperative one, such as Lieutenant Colonel Lopez Muniz.

3. Establishment of good relations between the new military attaché and [Raimundo] Padilha.

4. Coded reports would be forwarded through diplomatic channels.

5. An Argentine civilian to be installed as secret agent in Rio de Janeiro, possibly under cover of the Argentine commercial mission there.

6. The German Propaganda Ministry should be advised that an effective means of undermining the esteem of the Vargas regime would be for the German radio to report that Italian submarines were responsible for the sinking of Brazilian merchant ships.[84]

Of course, it was the German navy and not the Italian that had torpedoed Brazilian ships in the South Atlantic. While some of the surviving crews were rescued by Nazi submarines, DIP did not want this mentioned in the press because Getúlio had already announced his decision. On August 22, 1942, war was declared against Germany and Italy.[85]

Three days later, on August 25th, DIP issued orders to all sections of the media not to mention anything about a secret German airfield that was "discovered" near Formosa in the state of Goiás. Several citizens of Axis origin were apprehended there and never heard from again. Was this landing strip a remnant from the administration's pro-Axis days? Was there another secret treaty in effect with the Nazis?[86] That the airport was uncovered when it was is certainly suspicious. Or, was it in fact part of larger Nazi plans for Brazil? The German airline Condor, as well as the Italian LATI, pioneered European air traffic to South America and were extremely active in the area, until having their possessions in Brazil confiscated after August 1942. Either of them could have chosen the spot. Formosa does have an airport just outside the city with a single runway. It is said to have been constructed in the 1940s by local industrialists. But it is too close to the urban area to have been the airstrip in question. Yet the point remains that the community continued to be nearly isolated in the early 1940s. There thus could well have been another field somewhere in the area.[87]

As to why the Germans would want an airport in the heart of Brazil–and assuming that it was clandestine–one of the most plausible answers would be to support another Integralist *coup* attempt. This could have been intended to be part of some operation with the German minorities in the South of the country; perhaps coordinated with pro-Axis elements in South America's Southern Cone. A document uncovered at the DOPS Archives in Rio de Janeiro provides the long-range goals of Berlin in this regard. Protectorates were to have been formed in Argentina, Chile, Uruguay, Paraguay, one-third of Bolivia, and in all parts of Brazil with a significant German population. The combined territory comprised nearly 4,039,000 square miles. Spanish was to be kept as the primary language in Chile and Argentina; but German would be taught in schools as the "second mother tongue." German was to replace Portuguese and Spanish in the South of Brazil, Paraguay, and Uruguay.[88]

When would it have all begun? An accounting still kept concealed by the Pentagon over half a century after the fact may hold the answer. The relevant dispatch, which the U.S. Embassy's Military Attaché Edwin Sibert sent to his superiors in Washington, DC in December 1940, elaborates as follows:

It is generally accepted here [in Rio de Janeiro] that the Nazis will use the Integralist Party as a framework and front in Brazil, if and when they decide to start an uprising. An officer in the Intelligence Section of the Brazilian General Staff, with whom I am in close contact, told me that they (the 2nd Section) have reason to believe that any Nazi-inspired outbreak will be coordinated in point of time with the Nazi invasion of England.[89]

We should not lose sight of historical reality by assuming that the Germans were the only power contemplating an invasion of Brazil. The Americans also had their own secret contingency plans. Getúlio's swinging back and forth between the Axis and Allies, before breaking diplomatic relations with the former, kept Washington worried. Had Brazil's leader maintained his country's neutrality, or had he openly aligned it with the fascists, the U.S. army did not want to be caught unprepared. The air bases in the Northeast were a strategic Allied necessity. The American military even drew up a last-ditch strategy, entitled "Operations Plan of Northeast Brazil Theater," should the diplomatic efforts fail. The scheme went through several alterations from the initial concept of November 1, 1941. If Vargas continued down the neutral road, or if he took the fascist fork, the Americans would simultaneously invade the cities of Natal, Belém, Recife, and Salvador with 100,000 men. They would then take São Luís, Fortaleza, and the Fernando de Noronha Islands. Natal was of course the prize, being the closest landfall in the Americas to North Africa. The political will was the difficult part because at some point Roosevelt would have had to decide that Brazilian neutrality was no longer an acceptable alternative. Naturally, had Vargas openly sided with the Axis, the Operations Plan of Northeast Brazil would have been much easier to justify.[90]

CONCESSIONS

From Müller's downfall until the last part of October 1945, Vargas would revamp the responsibilities of the Federal District's Polícia Civil, change its name, and shuffle its chiefs four separate times. It was all part of a design to stifle suspected antiregime maneuvering, be it from potential foreign enemies or domestic ones. A critical new maestro in Getúlio's first line of law and order consequently came to be the already-tainted Coriolano de Góis.[91] Coriolano had faithfully served in the police forces of Artur Bernardes, and was even chief of the Polícia Civil in the capital under Washington Luís. Acting in these capacities, de Góis dealt with many enemies of Catete during and after the 1922 and 1924 revolts.

Before accepting Vargas' offer to head the Federal District's newly created Federal Department of Public Security, previously the capital's Polícia Civil, de Góis had been the secretary of public security in the city of São Paulo. His leaving no doubt put a good number of *paulistanos* in a better frame of mind. On November 9, 1943, nearly eight months before taking up his new duties, he had a group of students, led by the law majors and some of the faculty at the University of São Paulo, tear gassed and machine-gunned in the streets.[92] During this carnage, Coriolano took orders by telephone from Vargas' younger brother Benjamin, who was safely up North in Rio de Janeiro. The students had marched in silence through the city center with handkerchiefs tied over their mouths as a protest against the lack of representative government. When they reached the Praça da Patriarca, there were two or three cries of "Viva à democrácia!" With this, the fire department, elements of the regular police force, and the local Polícia Especial, led by Major Anísio Miranda, moved into position blocking all exits from the square. Miranda then confronted the school's dean, Hélio Mota. The two had a run-in at the end of October when Mota grabbed a microphone at a student party and yelled the three forbidden words. This time, as Miranda approached, Mota was trying to convince the authorities that the meeting was over and all that anyone wanted to do was peacefully go home. The major would have none of it. He barked to his men, "Shoot him!"

In so doing, a nonviolent gathering was turned into a bloodbath as subelites blasted down or clubbed the bodies of unarmed, panicking academics. The number of dead and injured along with the newspaper coverage was hushed up by DIP censors. But such facts could not be kept quiet forever. A legislative commission, set up in 1947 to investigate criminal acts committed by the Vargas dictatorship, revealed that there were no less than two persons killed and twenty-five wounded, twenty-three of the latter through gunfire. None of the police under Miranda's command were among the victims. Heads did roll in the aftermath as Vargas was, nevertheless, forced to act over the prospects of an even larger reaction. The *paulista* secretaries of justice, education, and transport, together with Coriolano de Góis, were all dismissed.[93]

Concessions were one thing, Coriolano de Góis was another. De Góis' treatment of students in São Paulo earned him the moniker of "Coriolano Góistapo." Brazil's head of state evidently felt that this tough attitude only added to de Góis' résumé, and that he needed just such a man in the capital to lead the Federal Department of Public Security. Taking up his new post on July 4, 1944,[94] Coriolano wasted little time joining forces with the just-transferred Anísio Miranda, Labor and Justice Minister Alexandre Marcondes Machado Filho, and Benjamin Vargas, to intimidate Getúlio's political opponents. Their object "was to eliminate organized opposition in order to smooth the way for Getúlio to be reelected president, with a congress and a functioning constitution; he could then go to the [coming European] peace conference wrapped in an aura of democratic sanctity."[95]

But Vargas was languishing under the scrutiny of those wishing a return to democracy, and an economy inflated by World War II. The issue of more representative government had been growing as a spin-off effect all through Brazil's involvement with the hostilities in Europe. The Germans, Italians, and Japanese each ran dictatorships–and so did Getúlio, while fighting shoulder to shoulder with the Allies.

When Oswaldo Aranha renounced his post as foreign minister in August 1944, for becoming too interested in self-government, one of his recently hired assistants in Montevideo began to do some worrying. Army Chief of Staff Góis Monteiro had also quit the administration. His leaving was not based on any lack of democratic institutions but in Dutra's mediocre war policies. Now working for Aranha in Uruguay, Monteiro concluded that his new boss was the best diplomat Brazil had to negotiate for the much-needed American weapons. Moreover, since Oswaldo had resigned, the general felt that Brazil was threatened by Argentina, or soon would be, more so than ever before. In his opinion, the Argentines were preparing for a war of conquest. It was therefore crucial for Brazil's very existence that the vital U.S. military aid continue.

Traveling back to Rio at the request of Vargas, the former chief of staff spoke with the military commanders at several stops along the way. All were in agreement: the equipment from the United States must keep coming. This in turn could only be assured if America thought that Vargas would carry out his promises of a return to democratic elections. Getúlio was thus faced with an intricate dilemma. How could he satisfy his officers, the Americans, and himself all at the same time? After thinking it over, he came up with a bold plan. First, he gave way and allowed political parties to be formed. Luís Carlos Prestes and 562 other prisoners of conscience were freed. Elections were then set for December 1945 for president, and in March the following year for state governors and assemblies. The only question in everyone's mind, except Getúlio's, was would he really allow the transition to take place when he was not one of the candidates?

THE ECONOMY

The question of Brazil's finances was different. Sucked into the Allies' orbit, the country had become dependent on the war and the fortunes of its trading partners in it. As the United States and its associates began to purchase more of Brazil's commodities and strategic materials, large amounts of dollars accumulat-ed in Brazilian accounts in New York. Across the Atlantic as well, many pounds were being deposited in similar accounts in London. The semiindependent Banco do Brasil bought a good deal of these assets; paying for them at home with paper currency while Vargas put more banknotes into circulation, together with sundry government bonds, to cover the deficit. Getúlio then tried to solidify his position with the largely deceived common man in the cities.[96] In November 1943 he attempted this through decrees that gave pay increases ranging from 10 to 85 percent to urban labor or about one-third of the population. Poorer employees in the cities got the biggest raises.[97] The net result was a vast increase in the amount of money in circulation, inflation, and a rise in the cost of living. The annual-percentage increases[98] in this last all-important item were:

1941	1942	1943	1944	1945
10.9	22.9	37.8	65.1	81.8

Standing by watching was the exasperated Brazilian middle class. This group had lived a better life while Xuxu could repress the horde down below. Now, members of the middle class were afraid of a loss in the purchasing power they had come to enjoy. In their anxiety, a growing number from this key sector added their voices to those already calling for democratic elections. The combined roar was almost deafening.[99]

Yet Getúlio was determined to stay in office as either the elected write-in candidate, or via another usurpation of the democratic process. The popularity option was supposed to have been spontaneous. Part of it may well have been after Alexandre Marcondes and two of the Vargas brothers, Benjamin and Viriato, plus a few friends,[100] got it all organized. This of course was the *Queremos* ("We Want") Getúlio campaign that was officially launched in mid-1945.

The two declared presidential contestants, Gaspar Dutra and Eduardo Gomes, were both the heads of their branches of the armed forces: the army and the air force. The *queremistas* appealed to voters if only on the grounds of antimilitarism, continuity, and tacit enfranchisement.[101] But the *queremistas*' noisy demonstrations, the prospects of Getúlio's staying in power, and especially the thought of all those American arms staying in the United States, did not appeal to Góis Monteiro. The general had switched jobs again; this time taking over the minister of war slot from Dutra, who was obliged by law to step down while running for president. Probably as early as August, Monteiro began conspiring within the army to prevent Vargas from remaining in Catete.[102] To the new minister's surprise, however, he found that he did not have to scheme for very long.

Following several rallies in which the *queremistas* were gaining larger and larger audiences, and suspecting that they were planning a *coup d'état*, the Gomes people began to prepare their own counter-*coup*. The minister of war then got the *queremistas* to postpone a giant meeting scheduled for the 26th of October. It is quite possible that Vargas would have used this event to subvert the existing elections and continue in office. Meanwhile, other events collided into Getúlio's political hopes and behind-the-scene tactics. One of these was the planned move of Rio's mayor, Henrique Dodsworth, to the foreign minister's position. His spot was to be filled by João Alberto, who had been given Müller's old post. Taking over the command of the Federal District's Polícia Civil was the real bone of contention; because Getúlio had decided that his younger brother Benjamin was the man he wanted to head the force.[103]

NEPOTISM

Benjamin Vargas by this time in his life was often referred to by his nickname, "Bejo," and he was certainly a seedy character indeed. Bejo lived in the Guanabara Palace right along with Gegê where he was in charge of the Presidential Guards. According to Alzira Vargas, Bejo was "the most unruly and the most intimately linked" of all the Vargas brothers to her father.[104] He was well known around Rio not just because he was a Vargas; but as a man who invariably had a pistol with him at all times. Benjamin claimed he needed the weapon for protection against his many enemies, some of whom were certainly from Argentina.

In September 1933, Benjamin Vargas, accompanied by a group of relatives plus the usual hangers-on, got into a gun fight with Argentine boarder authorities. While this in itself was bad enough for the leader of the country's brother, two nephews were injured. Furious, Bejo crossed into Brazil and made straight for his family's hometown. Arriving in São Borja, he put together a group said to be composed of smugglers and misfits. The mishmash outfit then went back across the frontier and took possession of the village of Santo Tomé, Argentina. They killed several constables and proceeded to sack the town. This event so strained relations between the two countries that they nearly went to war. Getúlio finally calmed down the Argentine government with an indemnification of 60 million *cruzeiros*, or somewhere in the neighborhood of $5,068,600. The money apparently came from the Brazilian Coffee Institute.[105]

Four years later, in 1937, Bejo sent some of the family *peões* to murder Major Aureliano Coutinho, the head of a stud farm in a community neighboring São Borja. The act was carried out in the best Chicago gangland style with machine guns. Automatic weapons or handguns, it really did not matter to the youngest Vargas. In May 1938, along with nephew Serafim Vargas, Benjamin helped to shoot no less than seven Integralists who had surrendered during the unsuccessful storming of Guanabara Palace in the pajama-*Putsch*.[106]

Then there was the time that Bejo, watched over by four of his bodyguards, roughed up the director of the newspaper *O Globo*, Roberto Marinho, at the Hotel Quitandinha in Petrópolis. The cause of the problem was a notice in *O Globo* stating that a building in Copacabana was scheduled to be demolished.

Another victim was an attorney, William Monteiro de Barros, with whom Bejo got into an argument at the Urca Casino during the Carnival of 1942. The famous nighttime watering hole was the place for society to be seen in Getúlio's Rio de Janeiro. Thoroughly inebriated, and under the wing of a few associates, Benjamin Vargas would not let Barros off the hook when the lawyer walked out of the gambling hall. Chasing him in a car, Bejo crashed into a post. There was reported to have been the sound of gunfire. The next morning, the bullet-riddled body of a milkman was found at the scene. Later, and on another drunken rampage, Bejo went after the family of a friend of Barros with more of his *peões*. When the terrified family called the police, events were twisted around so that they were the ones who were arrested.

Benjamin was often the center of attention at the Urca Casino, where he could regularly be seen holding court, and where he never paid for losses at the roulette tables. It must have been a wonderful life for the president's little brother. It was not so much fun, on the other hand, for one individual at a fancy casino party who happened to make a few comments on seeing the drunk-again Bejo urinating in public. The ever-present *peões* stepped in and threw the unlucky guest out of the building. The man was fortunate not to have been killed.[107]

REMOVAL

Many of these and other escapades by Bejo were well known to the men in the upper ranks of the military. It was the opinion on the part of Góis Monteiro and the other officers that if and when Benjamin took office, Getúlio would be making his move. The military leaders may not have been too far off the mark. Vargas' secretary, Luiz Vergara, recalls in his memoirs the story that Bejo told several of his chums about how he was going to be the next chief of the capital's Department of Public Security. He had ordered 300 extra mattresses and beds for the Casa de Detenção to accommodate all the conspiring generals he intended to arrest after taking up his appointment.[108]

When Monteiro learned of Getúlio's intentions to really give his brother the job, it was the proverbial straw that broke the camel's back.[109] At first Góis thought of resigning a second time; but after being assured of the support of his colleagues, including Dutra, the minister of war acted. Deadly Fumes sent his chief of staff, Cordeiro de Farias, to tell Vargas that he was no longer the master of Brazil. Arriving at Catete, Cordeiro informed Vargas that the army had the situation under control and that they had decided that he must go. Allowed to mull over his options for fifteen minutes, one of the military's provisos included safe passage for himself and his family if he left without a struggle, Getúlio reluctantly complied.[110]

5

NO COMEBACKS

Vargas may have been gone but he would never be forgotten. In the voting that December, the *getulistas* returned him to office as both a federal congressman and senator. His slight preference for Dutra over Gomes resulted as well in a presidential victory for the former military leader. Getúlio took his seat in the Senate but never really took his new job seriously.

As the 1950 elections neared, he was back as the presidential candidate of his own PTB (Partido Trabalhista Brasileiro), or Brazilian Workers' Party. The PTB was specifically created to capture votes from the communists. It was a decisive move that helped turn Vargas' name into magic out on the campaign trail. One of the people who thought so, and who was running what would become an unsuccessful campaign for governor of his home state, was Filinto Müller. Along with his brother Júlio, who would likewise fail in his own bid for the Senate, Filinto got Getúlio to travel to Cuiabá and endorse the twin torturers.[1]

The election, which coincidentally enough was held on the twentieth anniversary of the start of the Revolution of 1930, was a substantial Vargas victory. Yet the old dictator's enemies were everywhere. Even before he took office his principal opponent, more and more, was turning out to be the irascible journalist Carlos Lacerda. Lacerda had been working at the *Correio da Manhã* but left in late April 1949 when a series of his acid-penned articles were stopped by the paper's owner, Paulo Bittencourt. At the urging of friends, and with generous bank loans and stock purchases by the public, Carlos opened his own paper, *Tribuna da Imprensa*, at the end of the same year.

As the 1950 elections approached, Lacerda was all over Vargas and even Vargas' wife Darcy. Once the couple again moved into Catete, Lacerda gave Gegê little breathing room. Charges by the journalist in *Tribuna da Imprensa*, in his public speeches, and over the radio seemed to occur with near daily frequency. No one in the Vargas camp was safe. Lacerda ran a tireless campaign, and three years later, in May 1953, he was still at it, insisting that the president was secretly behind a cover-up involving the Banco do Brasil. The charges were leveled over a succession of loans to the Wainer Group whose main property was *Última Hora*, the arch rival of *Tribuna da Imprensa*. *Última Hora's* editor, Samuel Wainer, had convinced Vargas that none of the major tabloids would support him in his 1950 presidential bid. If loans could be arranged, Wainer promised to give Getúlio a voice within forty-five days. The money came from three sources, among which was the Banco do Brasil, and Wainer purchased the old offices of *Diário Carioca*. The first issues of his pro-Vargas *Última Hora* soon hit the streets. Other loans were arranged to purchase new equipment, a radio station, and to underwrite various peripheral investments.

Largely due to Lacerda's probing, an official investigation was eventually launched to determine the origin of the seed money for Wainer's activities. The editor of *Última Hora* at first refused to divulge the sources, and spent fifteen days in jail for contempt as a result. He also appeared to transfer ownership of *Última Hora* to two trusted colleagues when Lacerda proved that Wainer was born in Bessarabia. The law then in effect prohibited foreigners from owning Brazilian newspapers.

Next came a new exposé in which Getúlio was denounced by the headlines of *Tribuna da Imprensa* for negotiating with Argentina's Juan Perón to form a triple alliance between themselves and the president of Chile, Carlos Ibáñez. This never-consummated ABC coalition (Argentina, Brazil, and Chile) was designed to counter American influence in South America.[2] As each fresh sensation came to the surface, Lacerda was one of the principals calling on Vargas to be impeached. Carlos wanted Getúlio's job. This is really what Carlos Frederico Werneck de Lacerda was all about. The public could take sides or ignore much of what was being said. But they could not overlook an additional feature that was perhaps more compelling than all of the oratory. What Brazilians were spending day after day to get by was starting to rise again.

Remembering the percentage increases in the cost of living for the war years only sharpened this concern. The augmentation in these crucial figures was one of the factors that contributed to Vargas' removal from office in 1945. By 1954, this telltale measure would once again jump to the same dangerous level during his term as the country's democratically elected president. Note that the percentage rate of increase in this data, given below by year, is actually somewhat less when Vargas was a dictator.[3]

1941	1942	1943	1944	1945		1951	1952	1953	1954
10.9	22.9	37.8	65.1	81.8		8.7	31.7	53.3	71.6

In the early 1950s, the difficulty with the economy continued to be a product of two key ingredients. The vast disparity of imports over exports that initially began after World War II was the chief worry. Next came failing revenues from coffee sold abroad. To these was added the claim by the PCB that friends of the economy minister, old-hand Oswaldo Aranha, were making fortunes out of speculating in coffee.[4]

ADVOCATE OF THE RANK AND FILE

Meanwhile, Xuxu was busy fine-tuning his "friend of the workingman" imagery. Once back in Catete, his first flings in this direction were cautious combinations of the old muscle tempered with demands that workers stay away from communism. A powerful case in point was the movement by civilian stevedores at the navy arsenal in Rio de Janeiro that came to a head in late August 1951. Their original demands resulted from a vote at union headquarters for wage increases of 10 to 80 percent and for more overtime pay. As the dockworkers discussed these issues, their leader, Hermes Alves de Oliveira, was picked up by DPS (Divisão de Polícia Política e Social, Division of Political and Social Police: the revamped Federal District political police[5]) and carried off to the Polícia Central. The thought police claimed that he was an undercover communist.

Hermes' arrest provoked telegrams of protest to Vargas, the navy minister, the director of the arsenal, and to the district judge. Banners and signs demanding Hermes' unconditional release went up immediately around the city. These same placards invited supporters to march with the stevedores in protest to Catete on September 21st. They would confront the president with their demands. When the throng arrived outside the presidential palace, however, Vargas would not see them. Instead, Lourival Fontes[6] sent the arsenal workers a telegram on Monday, the 24th, stating that Getúlio had time for them that very day at 3 P.M. Because this wire was unexpected, the dockworkers were already at their jobs, making it difficult for anyone to leave in order to go again to Catete. Nonetheless, a rally was quickly called and a number of workers eventually opted to attend the president's hastily called meeting. Deciding how to respond, of course, took time and all the delay caused the group to arrive at Catete late, at 5 P.M. Vargas was by then busy with other matters, or so he said, and Lourival penciled in another meeting for October 20th, nearly one month away.

Not long thereafter, Vargas had the director of the arsenal, Admiral Armando Belford, terminated because he declined to disassociate himself from the movement. The secretary of the stevedores local, Aloisio Cunha, was next taken to police headquarters for calling a general meeting of the dockworkers. This was followed with strong-arm tactics against three union leaders, two of whom were slapped around, while a third was discharged. Over the next few days everyone except Hermes Alves de Oliveira was released from police custody. Sympathy actions were called by laborers in other professions, and several of the dockworkers found themselves transferred. Then, at a union meeting on October 19th, the police moved in and grabbed everyone. The authorities claimed that the majority of those in attendance were communists or at the least leftists. Note that this mass arrest took place the day before the scheduled meeting with Vargas. The actual number of apprehended workers varies from fifty-six to eighty-six, depending on the sources examined.[7]

Whatever the actual figure, the detained were driven to the Polícia Central and crammed into a single sardine-can-like cell measuring 1 x 4 meters (about 3'3" x 13'2"). For twenty-four hours they were kept in this exhausting confine. At eleven o'clock the following morning some of the more important stevedores were let out. They were elbowed over to another part of the Central and forced to witness the beating of dockworker Epitacio José da Silva. The movement's leaders could take notice that they had been warned.

Finally, on October 23, 1951, Xuxu found a free moment for an audience with a commission from the stevedores. He patiently listened to their salary demands and charges of police brutality. At the conclusion of the meeting, Getúlio flashed the ever-ready smile and said that he would take immediate action to rectify the situation. For nearly two months nothing of consequence happened. As the public waited, there were charges that the navy had a torture chamber—which of course the commanding officers denied—at the naval facilities on nearby Ilha das Cobras. On December 23rd, DPS coincidentally reappeared back at the arsenal. This time they grilled workers to see who belonged to the union, and made all those present sign a document affirming that they were not communists.[8]

Rumors had been a part of the picture ever since Vargas said he was going to take action. When he finally did something, rural labor, or 60.4 percent of the working population, was still left out in the cold. They would continue to be dependent upon the salary dictates of their employers or landowners.[9] They would not be included in Getúlio's solution. But for some city wageearners, including the pesky stevedores, their salaries were raised by law as a 1951 Christmas present. The increase, however, was a mere 14 percent over the 1943 minimum wage. This was hardly enough and more strikes followed. There was a massive movement in São Paulo and others by the dockworkers in Belém, Santos and, again, those in Rio.

Vargas countered by bringing in PTB president João Goulart to assume the minister of labor position and to try to defuse the situation. Known as a friend of proletarian causes within the law, Goulart was chosen to maneuver Vargas back into the hearts of the workingman. Trouble was, Goulart did his job too well. The business sector, the military, and Oswaldo Aranha felt uncomfortable with the new minister. They were soon calling him not the minister of labor but the "minister of the laborers." Goulart ultimately lost his post when he began discussing a 100 percent inflation-fighting wage increase for the usual group of urban workers. The military led the charge when eighty-two colonels and lieutenant colonels signed a note of protest called the Manifesto dos Coronéis, or the "Declaration of the Colonels." Ignoring the long history of graft within the corps, the document thundered that through this and other policies the government was teetering dangerously close to state of moral corruption. Vargas was forced to give in to save himself. He accepted Goulart's resignation on the same day he was handed his copy of the Manifesto, February 22, 1954. That May, however, on the international day of labor, he put his ex-minister's proposals into effect. They did not stop inflation.[10]

OBSTACLES

A new scandal broke over Vargas' head ten days later when the police beat to death a reporter from the Rio daily *A Noite*. The journalist, Nestor Moreira, had gotten into a disagreement with a taxi driver over his fare and asked to be driven to the 2nd District Police Station in Copacabana to have the matter settled. While Moreira lay dying in the hospital, Justice Minister Tancredo Neves granted reporter Edmar Morél and a photographer permission to enter all of the civilian jails in the capital and see the conditions under which prisoners were housed and treated.[11] Tancredo should have remembered the way Getúlio and Filinto did things back in the 1930s and 1940s, because the story Morél brought out of the police catacombs showed that little had improved since the good old days.

Scattered across the city, eight-hundred prisoners were kept in the thirty-nine lockups visited by Morél.[12] Each jail was critiqued in some way. A few only needed a general cleaning; but many were so broken down that their toilets did not flush. In some there was no drinking water or the walls oozed with moisture. In others disease was rampant. Overcrowding was such that in many places inmates were forced to sleep nearly one on top of the other. Morél used words like "medieval," "abominable," and "worse than it is possible to imagine" to describe some of what he saw. The pictures that his photographer took proved him right.[13]

Morél's articles were appearing in *Última Hora*. As the stories churned out there were spin-off reports of police corruption, cruelty, and greed. They were not new either. Nor were they limited to adults. Morél had written in *Última Hora* back in 1951 about the SAM (Serviço de Assistência aos Menores, or euphemistically: the "Social Service for Minors") on Rua Clarimundo de Melo in the Rio suburb of Quintino Bocaiúva. Then one of the Brazilian chain of juvenile-detention centers, a fight had erupted among the residents there that August. The guards could not handle what was happening so the police were called in and ruthlessly put things back in order. Morél smelled a story and found one. His searing articles accused the jailers of beating, robbing, and even raping young inmates. At the time there were about 1,000 youngsters at the facility, ranging in age from three to eighteen. The main torturer was said to be a guard known only as "Lido." Someone called "Tatu" was the most perverse. Helping them were "Andrade," Irineu Werneck, and Paulo Ferreira.[14]

But it was the 1954 coverage on Nestor Moreira's murder that proved more embarrassing to the administration. The public became so interested in the affair that Moreira's burial

stopped Rio de Janeiro. Cinemas had a minute of silence. The funeral cortege left the *A Noite* building . . . at Praça Mauá and headed for the Brazilian Press Association in Castelo. From there, everyone walked to the São João Batista cemetery singing "Liberty, Liberty." Radio Globo broadcast the speeches given during the interment and among the authorities present was General Alcides Etchegóyen president of the Military Club.[15]

Vargas finally summoned Samuel Wainer to Catete and told him that his paper could "not have done better," if it was out to injure him.[16] Wainer returned to his office and Morél's *Última Hora* reportage was halted in midsentence. Edmar was soon out on the street, not reporting, but looking for a new employer.[17]

FINAL FALL

All of this was what brought Carlos Lacerda to an intentional boil. Subsequent to the Moreira incident, he came to be called "The Crow" for hovering over the event. The nickname was first used after the editorial cartoon of Lacerda lingering next to the body of Moreira in *Última Hora*, which began on May 25th. Journalist David Nasser would later make a pun of Lacerda's leftist past and insatiable lust for power, by counterpoising him against Luís Carlos Prestes. Prestes of course was known as "O Cavalheiro da Esperança," or "The Knight of Hope." Lacerda's more comprehensive title, according to Nasser, should thus be "O Corvo da Esperança," or "The Crow of Hope."[18]

The label was no laughing matter. Carlos Lacerda was a man who really would do just about anything to get to the top. It has been pointed out that after being taken prisoner in Bahia in 1937, he confessed his very soul to the police and provided them with a complete list of names and addresses of his former comrades in the Communist Youth Association. Several of these people were later picked up to become the victims of police violence. Lacerda was saved from any of this by the intercession of a known businessman who represented a number of North American firms. The entrepreneur managed to get Lacerda transferred to Rio and quickly released for lack of evidence. Carlos even wrote numerous articles for DIP later on praising the *Estado Novo*, for which he was paid by DIP's director Lourvial Fontes.[19]

That was then. Now, Carlos could smell victory. Lacerda's crusade against a beleaguered Gegê and the men around him twisted up into a fever pitch as 1954 wore on. By midyear, presumably Benjamin Vargas, for one, decided that he'd had enough. A solution to the badgering editor had to be found. It was decided that a warning would be administered first. A group of persuaders in police uniforms consequently appeared at Lacerda's apartment building and roughed him up. When this failed to subdue the Crow of Hope, a second team again tried to convince him with additional physical force. Once more, however, Lacerda would not give in. There were a number of what probably were assassination attempts, and at a minimum the final liquidation try was authorized by Bejo, or someone else. Through Gregório Fortunato, chief of the Presidential Guards, a killer was finally hired. In the morning hours of August 5th, Alcino João do Nascimento set out to do the job. The only hitch in the plan was that he murdered Lacerda's bodyguard, air force Major Rubens Vaz, wounded a passing patrolman, and merely shot the publisher in the leg.[20]

Fortunato had been involved with the Vargas' family most of his life. An imposing black *peão* on Getúlio's Itú *fazenda*, Bejo brought Gregório up from Rio Grande do Sul to look after his brother following the failed pajama-*Putsch* of May 1938. Gregório thrived at Catete. He became a virtual gatekeeper to the center of Brazilian power, and, of course, amassed wealth and influence along the way. He was ultimately tied to the plot because of the payoff money (new 500 *cruzeiro* bank notes), some of which was still in his quarters at the presidential compound. Taken in for questioning Fortunato implicated Bejo;[21] but insisted on Gegê's innocence. Even after being sentenced to twenty-five years imprisonment he maintained this story until the very end. In October 1963 he was murdered by a fellow prisoner, Feliciano Damas Emiliano.[22]

The storm that had been forming around Vargas now broke. There were again cries for his resignation together with police and air force investigations. The Crow outdid himself in the pages of *Tribuna da Imprensa* and on the radio. With the natural exception of *Última Hora*, all the media turned against Vargas as never before.[23] Near the peak of things the military led by the air force closed ranks and again called on Gegê to step aside. At seventy-two years of age, Getúlio must have known that this time there would be no comebacks.

Since 1930, all of his acts; all of his opinions; all of his excesses; all of his speeches; all of his attempts to mislead; all of his corruption and deals; all of his conspiracies; revolutions; agitations; strikes; riots and disorders . . . had as their single unalterable goal, the maintenance of himself in power at any cost.[24]

How then could this man who would be king accept a second humiliating fall from grace, and the chance, however slim, of some kind of criminal charge? He gave his answer to the ages when he fired a bullet through his heart in the early morning hours of Tuesday, August 24, 1954.[25]

Epilogue

Vargas' legacy would both benefit and brand his successors. The principal recipient would be his neighbor from São Borja and former minister of labor. Known since childhood as "Jango," João Belchoir Marques Goulart would reap the whirlwind. Jango too would become president. And not quite ten years after Gegê's suicide, Jango too would be deposed. Different from Getúlio, the military grabbed power outright in 1964. But similar to Vargas, the first leader of that *coup*, General Humberto de Alencar Castelo Branco, would not die of natural causes. A bleak dictatorship was what he and his fellow officers installed in the country. Years later a frank admirer of one of the two dead leaders, not both, contrasted each before the Federal Assembly. It might have been confusing, however, for his august listeners to tell just whom he favored. The commentary began with the observation that

one was a statesman, working for the present and for the future. The other was a blind man who put our country fifty years behind the times. One was a nationalist and intransigent defender of our sovereignty. The other was a reactionary who turned this land into a pasture for foreign business. One died gloriously, inscribing his name in the memory and gratitude of all Brazilians. The other died in obscurity, leaving a eulogy for his countrymen of pain, hate, and tears, as well as the conviction that never again would they be governed by individuals of a similar background.[1]

Out in the audience was a legislator who, like his earlier mentor, had returned to power. After he was fired in 1942, and all through Vargas' second administration, Filinto Müller never sat foot in Catete. In 1947, he was back as a federal senator from his home state, a position he was reelected to three times.[2] With the 1964 dictatorship, and the decree ending political parties, he helped to found the armed forces' rubber-stamp political apparatus A Aliança Renovadora

Nacional (the National Renovation Alliance) or ARENA. Asked personally by Castelo Branco to do so, Müller was only too happy to serve his new messiahs in uniform as ARENA president and head of the Senate. While acting in these dual capacities, Filinto decided to celebrate his birthday with a short vacation in France. He timed his trip to land in Paris on July 11, 1973, the morning of his birth seventy-three years earlier. But as VARIG flight 820 was on final approach into Orly Airport, a strange fire broke out in one of the craft's cargo bins. The pilot made an emergency landing in a field but it was too late. Müller was among those passengers overcome by fumes and then roasted alive still strapped to his seat.[3] Back in Brazil, when news of the appalling incident flashed across local TV screens, some of his old victims doubtlessly smiled at his fate.

Appendix

Table 1
Divisão de Polícia Política e Social (Division of Political and Social Police) Operatives in Rio de Janeiro on February 8, 1951 by Position, Name, and (when available) Badge Number

OFFICE OF
THE DIRECTOR
Secretary General
  Silva Jr., Manuel Fernandes da
Detective
  Vieira, Hicrólio *5*
Guarda Civil
  Galvão, Amadeu *1168*
Investigators
  Albuquerque, João Figueredo de *1263*
  Correa, Petronio Alves *1375*
  Costa, Amynthas Mouço da *1898*
  Jucá, João Galvão *1437*
  Marcílio, Lourenço Martins *251*
  Prates, João *764*
  Silva, Fausto Ignacio da *1952*
  Vieira, Cicero Soares *1989*
Servants
  Abreu, Antônio Moreira de
  Antonio, Raimundo
  Carvalho e Sá, Raimundo de
  Mocho, Abel Rodrigues
  Morais, Nelson de
  Pinto, Mario da Rocha

Santana, Norvaro Gomes de
Santos, Altamiro Gonçalves dos
Santos, Mario dos
Sena, Francisco Bernardino de

DEPARTMENT OF SOCIAL
SECURITY
Director
  Ferreira, Fredgard Martins
Deputy
  Ramos, Agenor Araujo
Detective
  Marques, Francisco *54*
Polícia Especial
  Serpa, Ademar *113*
Investigators
  Baltar, Alvaceli Coelho *988*
  Barros, Sebastião Pereira *1753*
  Bueno, Milton Silva *1702*
  Caldas, Helio de Azevedo Pereira *601*
  Cavalcanti, José Andrade *926*
  Domingues, Ildefonso *624*
  Farias, William de *2148*
  Lamha, José Sarto *1190*

Lisboa, Alexandrino 1906
Santos, José Ribamar Dias 1829
Serra, Raimundo Nenes 1756
Vassconcelos, Aylton 1762

REGISTRY
Chief Clerk
  Machado, Alberto
Clerk
  Lisboa, Roberto Brandão
Detective
  Silva, Durval Pereira da 120
Uniformity Official
  Pinto, Benjamin Lopes de Oliveira
Typists
  Raposo, Hekel de Miranda
  Tinoco, Nelarmino Teixeira
Identification
  Carvalho, José Fontes de
Investigators
  Mattar, Fahis 1212
  Santos, Feliciano da Silva 1940
  Silva, Marcilio Fernandes da 1807

DEPARTMENT OF POLITICAL SECURITY
Director
  Picoreli, José
Deputy
  Dias, Ataliba Pereira
Detective
  Barbosa, Luiz Rosa 85
Investigators
  Badre, Fauze 871
  D'Avila, Benjamim Monteiro 1998
  Lima, Olga Conceição Labeca Barbosa 959
  Santana, Helio Joaquim de 1570
  Silveira, Joaquim Antonio da 1956
  Soares, Mario José 1324
  Souza, Alcebiades da 1158
  Torres Jr., José Gonçalves 1104

INTELLIGENCE
Chief

Lahmeyer, Renato da Fonseca e Silva
Inspector of the Polícia Política
  Soares, Alberto Joaquim* (currently head of Sr/2)
Codes
  Faedrich, Roberto
Translations
  Braga, Eliza Pena Costa
Investigators
  Cavalcanti, José de Holanda 556
  Costa, Carlos Correa da 879
  Ferreira, Silvino Fernandes 1082
  Mello, Elizette Pereira de 2104
  Rodrigues, Jayme 2157
  Tolentino, Jose Gonçalves 1160

PUBLIC SERVICE SECTOR (Sr/1)
Chief
  Lucchetti, Geraldo
Detectives
  Castro, Edson Nobre de Almedia 390
  Costa, Danilo Rodrigues da 58
  Rigueira, Lourival 171
  Rodrigues, Paulo Guilherme da Fontoura 301
Bookkeeping
  Pinto, Onair
Investigators
  Alves, Ary Manoel 1389
  Araujo, Abdias Candido de 1674
  Camilo, William 982
  Castro, Francisco Theodoro de 1162
  Cavaleiro, José de Morais 979
  Cesarino, Pedro 204
  Coelho, Adelaide Mendonça Dias 1547
  D'Avila, Orsina de Moura 1625
  Fernandes, José dos Santos 2135
  Fonseca, Nathanael da 1642
  Lemos Filho, Anibal 259
  Mendes, Jorge 2181
  Oliveira, Armindo Ramos de 757
  Oliveira, Ayrton José de 2010
  Paixão Filho, Leonides Pinheiro da 374
  Pegorim, Jadyr Machado 2006
  Perdigão, Eduardo Ribas 1167

Ribeiro, Djalma Pinto 2025
Ribeiro, Hilda Neto 1726
Ribeiro, Ziney Lopes 805
Rico, Eduardo 2028
Siqueira, João de Deus 1963
Tavares, Dacio Torreão Mendes 289
Teixeira, Aloisio Pires 1888
Valle, José Carlos Niemeyer do 1315
Vasconcelos, Saulo Cesar de 1946
Viana, Nelson Segadas 221
Vinagre, Newton Maribondo 355
Vinagre, William Maribondo 1757

ARCHIVAL SECTOR (Sr/2)
Chief
Pavan, Osmar (on leave)
Detectives
Abreu e Silva, Otavio de 363
Almeida e Castro, Hilton Nobre de 229
Borges, Nelson 262
Identification
Almedia, Walter Soares de
Investigators
Albuquerque, João Otaviano de 1241
Alves, José Brandão 542
Carvalho, Nelson de Oliveira 993
Castro, Candido Monteiro de 552
Cerqueira, Heraldo de Oliveira 1231
Continho, Nelson 569
Gomes, Genildo Pereira 1601
Gomes, João dos Santos 348
Lopes, Jose Paulo da Silva 1372
Lopes, Lauro Raymundo 1211
Lopes, Luciano Vieira 884
Mandina, Luiz Alexandre 1200
Mclo, Anibal Jose de Souza 263
Pavan, João 617
Ramalho, Jose Renato 691
Ramos, Joaquim 666
Reis, Waldemar dos Santos 1704
Rizzo, Rubem 1641
Rocha, Gessio Jose Coelho da 910
Santos Filho, Luiz Ferreira dos 909
Silva, Antonio Alves da 1494
Silva, Mario Gomes da 463

TECHNICAL SECTOR (Sr/3)
Chief
Moliterno, Caio Bruno
Typist
Barão, Almir Teles
Statistical Assistant
Richter, Moyses
Radio Communications
Barbosa, Rui
Detectives
Carvalho, Luiz Gonzaga de 298
Nascimento, Jayme Aguiar de 271
Van Bugenhout, Francisco Back 252
Investigators
Almeida, Jacy Gomes de 686
Alvarez, Manoel Jose Vila 1318
Braga, Oswaldo 1260
Brito, Octavio Lopes 1481
Cardoso, José Duete 1149
Cardoso, Mario Valadão 1145
Couto, Luiz 934
Cursino Filho, Antonio 915
El-Bainy, Cyro Habib 711
Mandina, Ignacio 783
Marques, Zigomar Aurelio 808
Mata, Milton de Oliveira 1884
Medeiros, Hermenegildo Machado de
2125
Moulin, Fabio Lougon 1254
Nigro, José 398
Reis, Oscar dos Santos 905
Ribeiro, Marcelo Pinto 278
Silva, Alcedino Pedroso da 1034
Tavares, Raul 1083

CONTROL OF EXPLOSIVES,
ARMS, AND AMMUNITION
SECTOR (Sr/4)
Chief
Franco, Matheus de Olivcira
Archivist
Viana, Adelberto de Souza
Typist
Franco, Eulanda Areas
Artist

Ferreira, José Carvalho Damasceno
Detectives
  Cardoso, Pedro* 427
  Franco, Marcos Evangelista de Oliveira
    281
  Iatarola Neto, Francisco 141
  Oliveira, Bilac 329
  Oliveira, Oswaldo Portela de 418
Investigators
  Amorim, Lino Dias de 837
  Andrade, Severino Freire de 372
  Areas, João José de 1826
  Brito, Aureo Augusto Xavier de 332
  Brito, Joaquim Teixeira Soares de 429
  Campos, Albino 2016
  Caneco, José Soares 421
  Castro, João Francisco de* 729
  Cheis, Arnoldo 473
  Cohen, Aarão 1252
  Cosenza, Domingoes 68
  Costa, Mario Ferreira da 1834
  Delfino, João Candido 784
  Esteves, Maria Oldina Castro 843
  Faedrich, Mario Carlos 1693
  Fontes, Albino 445
  Fontes, Nei da Silva 1049
  França, Americo Romano 395
  Frutuoso, Laura Nunes 823
  Guedes, João Carlos 2052
  Leal, Fortunato Caetano 709
  Lins, Aylton Acioly 1364
  Marinho, Manoel de Souza 600
  Matos, Caetano Chagas 1843
  Nascimento Jose do 1045
  Neves, Hercilio 619
  Norton, Jayme Maia 1945
  Noury, Carlos Alberto da Cruz 1664
  Oliveira, Alice Volpi de 1556
  Oliveira, Oswaldo Francisco de 888
  Oliveira, Torquato Barreto de 638
  Prata, Jose Peres 1222
  Raymundo, Jose Egidio 1208
  Rocha, Severino João da 618
  Rocha, Tolentino Gonçalves da 117
  Santana, Jose Francisco 1517

  Sena, Eraldo Bernardino 621
  Silva, Edson Barroso 515
  Silva Filho, Firmino Soares da* 346
  Silva, Manoel Teixeira da 591
  Silva, Olivio Alves da 513
  Silva, Pedro Cipriano da 1967
  Souza, Adalberto Brasil de 1624
  Souza, Armando de 1795
  Souza, Humberto Brasil de 881
  Souza, Mario Pereira de* 121
  Souza, Orlando de 983
  Tomasi, Antonio 1735

        SECRET SECTOR (Sr/5)
Chief
  Silva, Arlindo Alves da
Detectives
  Menezes, Oton Eugenio de 330
  Rosa, Afonso da Gama 466
Investigators
  Braga, Jose Gomes 2056
  Campos, Deodato Rocha 2033
  Carmo, Jose Santana do 1640
  Cavalcanti Sobrinho, Jose 1973
  Coelho, Canor Simões 1374
  Duarte Sobrinho, Antonio 901
  Falcão e Frota, Francisco Anacleto 375
  Lima, Domar da Rocha 2089
  Marçal, Francisco 863
  Nazareth, Ubaldo Tinoco 921
  Oliveira, Jorge de 2185
  Pereira, João Macedo 350
  Pires, Gerardo de Magela de Oliveira
    452
  Santos, Fernando Batista dos 1117
  Sena, Joaquim Candido da Costa 918
  Silva, Gastão David Pereira da 284
  Soares, Manoel Albano 1677

      INVESTIGATIVE SERVICE
Chief
  Martins, Palaio Vidal (on leave)
Investigators
  Agnese, Humberto 163
  Bellot, Laerte da Silva 641

Berna Filho, João Ludovico Maria *632*

Bicudo, José Paes *870*

Cardozo Filho, Ezaul *557*

Carvalho, José Valmorim de *866*

Chagas, Joviano Cordeiro *512*

Corrêa, Roberto dos Santos *1332*

Costa, Marco Aurelio Bustamante *1057*

Cuiabano, Nobel *614*

Cursati, Antonio da Cunha de *1327*

Dias, Cesar Fernandes *420*

Freitas, Domingos de Souza *1239*

Leal, José Domingos *457*

Lucas, Arthur Geraldo Cony *507*

Mattos, Geraldo Santana *1622*

Mello e Silva, Alzisseth de *438*

Mendes, João Teixeira *1248*

Miranda, Edmundo *897*

Mundo, João Alfredo *1769*

Nacimento, Yedson Augusto do *1144*

Nogueira, Jacintho *2001*

Oliveira, José de *1323*

Oliveira, Nilo de *1028*

Pereira, Nestor Braga Martins *1309*

Piedade, José Manhães da *1857*

Pires, Luciano *912*

Rita, Luiz Varela de Santa *894*

Rocha, Jayme Dias da *723*

Rodrigues, Adriano *775*

Rosas, Alberto Gonçalves *661*

Salgado, Edil Botelho de Amaral *559*

Sampaio, Flavio Dantas *789*

Santo, Mauricio Pedro dos *2126*

Santos, Lamartine Quirino dos *458*

Santos, Walter dos *1932*

Severo, Octavio Fonseca *1485*

Silva, João Dufrayer Aleixo da *453*

Silveira, Ignacio Marques da *964*

Toledano, Guilherme *1321*

Vieira, Octavio Jardim *842*

INVESTIGATIVE SECTOR (St-3)

Chief

Mendes, Jair Leão

Investigators

Alencar, João Pereira de *576*

Amaral, Vicente Vieira do *1414*

Araujo, Antonio Baptista de* *286*

Barros, Daniel Sarmento de *1995*

Batalha, Geraldo Lodi *448*

Briggs, Guilherme *1874*

Campos, Francisco Oliveira *699*

Carneiro, Fernando de Azevedo *1460*

Castro, Heitor Francisco de *2067*

Colares, José *423*

Conceição Sobrinho, Antonio da *1882*

Costa, Euclydes Brito da *1591*

Coutinho, Lydio *603*

Cunha, Rubens Lopes da *1864*

Cunha, Suede Brasil da *1305*

D'Avila, Fernando Dantas *1953*

Dane, Alberto Messias *1275*

Gomes, Oswaldo Pereira *1471*

Gonçalez, Henrique *329*

Hervey, Eduardo *1416*

Leite, Ayrton Pinheiro *505*

Machado, Elpidio *1764*

Maciel, Laurindo *210*

Maiolino, Caetano *347*

Martins, Manoel *584*

Melucci, Newton de Souza *1244*

Neumann, Hermano Afonso* *270*

Rego, Aguinaldo Caheté *1217*

Reis, Sadoc Thales de Berredo *908*

Reis, Thales dos *1665*

Ribeiro, Luiz Gomes* *581*

Rodrigues, Paulo *1811*

Sá, José Alves de *1654*

Santos, Aloysio Aragão *902*

Santos, José dos *1469*

Santos, Sebastião da Costa *1896*

Scrivano, Francisco *1199*

Serzedello, Fernando Lima *132*

Silva, Dante Ribeiro da *1213*

Silva, Léo Corrêa da *903*

Silva, Octaviano Cardoso da *546*

Silva, Rosauro Fraga da *1836*

Souza, Alvaro Peixoto de* *295*

Souza, João Valente de *475*

Waknin, Simão *1553*

SPECIAL SERVICES SECTOR (St-4)
Chief
  Castro, José Francisco de*
Bookkeeping
  Lepore, Spartaco
Detectives
  Carvalho, Ubaldo Teixeira 340
  Chagas, Olimpio Francisco das 53
  Cornazani, Gaspare da Silva 149
  Passos Neto, José 253
Investigators
  Alexandria, Mario 1187
  Alvarez, Indalecio Villa 1175
  Amaral, Oswaldo Cardoso do 2098
  Andrade, Benevides de 1060
  Antonio, Abrahão José 1004
  Arruda, Decio Garcia Pinto de 877
  Assumpção, José Vicente de 2071
  Barbosa, Renato Paiva 1691
  Barrocas, Carlos Rodrigues* 293
  Barros, Dionisio Ignacio de 718
  Barros, Julio Nunes de 582
  Bessa, Fabio Fernandes 741
  Bittencourt Filho, Antonio Ildefonso
    758
  Bittencourt, João Soares 360
  Bommatis, Antonio Francisco 326
  Brigido, Lucio Aurelio 139
  Cabral, José Tomaz 1907
  Calazans, Geraldo de Castro 1824
  Carmo, José Baptista do 1338
  Carnaval, Salvador 1923
  Castro, Francisco de Souza 1353
  Coelho, Roberto 535
  Conceição, Faustino Jorge 1058
  Cony, Ernesto de Moraes 1210
  Costa, Anor Rodrigues da 1285
  Costa, Ayrton da 801
  Cumieira, Joaquim Teixeira 1453
  Cupertino, José 2177
  Dantas Filho, Humberto 418
  Dias, Miguel Gusmão 215
  Domingues, Rochael* 324
  Doria, Jorge da Fonseca 1133
  Ferreira, Werther 1655

Figueiredo, Abilio de Souza 1935
Figueiredo, Decio Valadares de 760
Fonseca, José Soares da 60
França, Waldyr Matos 2026
Freire, Edmundo José 1373
Freitas, Amilcar Warol de 1831
Freitas, Arnaldo Lopes de 1688
Furtado, Paulo Vieira 1806
Furtado, Romulo Barbosa 633
Gouvêa, Wellington Tassará de 1230
Groppo Filho, Umberto 889
Grosso, Carlos Basilio 1177
Guimarães, Gladstone Carneiro 876
Leal, Ede 530
Leitão, Nestor Francisco 1575
Lima, Manoel Barbosa 1782
Lisboa, Jorge 1731
Machado, Alvaro 1662
Machado, Arnobio 1493
Machado, Celio Corrêa 1220
Maciel, Transvalino Ferreira 1055
Magalhães, Alvaro de Oliveira 422
Marques, Edward Quadros 212
Mendes, Roberto Braga 1095
Miranda, João Cavalcanti de 1835
Nascimento, Jessé Torres do 298
Nascimento, Luiz 403
Oliveira, Gilberto Chaves de 634
Oliveira, Samuel Moraes de 731
Perdigão, Ademar Raimundo dos
  Passos 1754
Reis, Sylvio de Santana 479
Rocha, Joaquim Floriano Franco da
  351
Rocha, Sebastião Machado da 392
Rosa, Frederico da 2110
Sampaio, Odilon da Silva 650
Santos, Hamilton Ribeiro dos 1626
Sillos, Clodomiro Nogueira de 1943
Silva, Claudionor João da 1915
Silva, Claudionor Lourenço da 1878
Silva, Eduardo 1899
Silva Filho, Amaro da 1229
Silva, Horacio Francisco da 1919
Silva, Manoel Evangelista da 1867

Silva, Nelson Barros da *1487*
Silva, Orlando Caetano da* *209*
Silva, Raymundo Orestes da *1313*
Siqueira, Justiniano Antunes de *199*
Souza, Agenor Frota Correia de *1289*
Souza, Arlindo Castro de *506*
Souza, Francisco Solano de *586*
Souza, Henrique de *435*
Tavares Filho, José *1620*
Teixeira, Joaquim *1183*
Tetéo, José Correia *2084*
Vasconcelos, Ary de *1541*
Verçosa, Dhejar Vasconcelos *913*
Vilar, Pedro Celestino *223*

PRESIDENTIAL RESIDENCES
Investigators
Barros, Ermiro Pereira de *742*
Costa, Ernani Martins da *672*
Magdalena, Orestes *1287*
Nunes, Alcino Pinto *1264*
Silva, José Bispo da *1797*

INTERNAL CONTROL (St-6)
Chief
Rodrigues Filho, Manoel Antonio
Process Server
Pinheiro, Francisco da S. Alves
Administrative Assistant
Rubstein, Marta
Detective
Pace, Cleone *245*
Investigators
Almeida, Claudino José de *1195*
Almeida, Esichio Bernardo de *696*
Azambuja, Edú Jarbas Pedroso de *2059*

Bellar, Francisco Munhoz *468*
Bittencourt, Milton Pinto *1486*
Castro, Francisco de Paula Siqueira *1775*
Costa, Edgard de Andrade *2101*
Dutra, Gustavo *652*
Faria, Walter de Oliva *1846*
Ferreira, Antonio Paulo *1810*
Ferreira, Milton *1653*
Gomes, Paulo Teixeira *1277*
Gonçalves, Cristovam José *1093*
Guilarducci, Luiz de Albuquerque *1040*
Haddad, Elias *482*
Kronauer, Georges Lisboa *1125*
Leite, Antonio Lourenço Cavalcanti *1974*
Leite, Roberto da Silva *2042*
Lessa, Antonio Lopes *2153*
Martins, Paulo Afonso Vidal *975*
Mesquita, Amadeu de *825*
Nancife, Tufi *1615*
Oliveira, Darci da Rosa *1178*
Oliveira, Moisés Quintino *1111*
Prudente, José Alvaro *1760*
Rabelo, Leonidas Leite *923*
Redondo, Gilberto Olavo de Almeida Garcia *1090*
Rezende, Adelino *1512*
Ribeiro, Antonio de Souza *1462*
Ribero, Silvo Falcão *734*
Seiblitz, Adelberto Eugenio Lossio *2081*
Silva, Luciano Nogueira da *1506*
Simas, Fernando Campos de *1900*
Tossa, Ari *746*

Source: PPARJ, document "Relação de servidores lotados na divisão de Polícia Política e Social," [February 8, 1951], pp. 1-22, administração/pasta 1s.
*=also listed in Table 2.

Table 2
Rio de Janeiro DESPS Agents Recommended for Praise to Filinto Müller in September 1940 in the Effort to Suppress Communism by Felisberto Batista Teixeira

Alencar Filho, Alvaro Gurgel de
Alves, Julio
Andrade, Arnaldo Martins de
Araujo, Antonio Baptista de*
Assis, Frederico Ribeiro de
Barrocas, Carlos Rodrigues*
Caramurú, Manoel Pinto
Cardoso, Pedro*
Carino, Mario
Castro, João Francisco de*
Castro, José Francisco de*
Coelho, Cesar da Costa
Coelho, Waldyr Ribeiro
Costa, Afonso Rodrigues da
Costa, Climaco Saragoça Dias da
Domingues, Rochael*
Franchini, Amadeu
Leal, Lauro Maximo
Lima, Damasco Luiz de
Machado, Mario de Araujo
Mendonça, Ruy Ottoni
Naine, Luiz Galibe
Neumann, Hermano Afonso*
Neumann, Paulo Fiel**
Ovando, Oswaldo

Pinheiro Filho, Carlos Falcão
Pinheiro, Waldemar Octaciano
Reis, Ary Fonseca
Ribeiro, Carlos
Ribeiro, Cicero Gomes
Ribeiro, Luiz Gomes*
Rico, José Rodrigues
Roberto, José
Rocha, Monclair Martinho da
Sá, Geraldo Quadros de
Sandos, Santino dos
Santos, Adelson Araujo
Santos, Antonio Carlos Lima dos
Silva Filho, Firmino Soares da*
Silva, Orlando Caetano da*
Silva, Severino Monteiro da
Silveira, Lourenço Motta
Soares, Alberto Joaquim*
Souza, Alvaro Peixoto de*
Souza, Eustachio Telles de
Souza, Mario Pereira de*
Torres, Verissimo
Véras, Clodomir Collaço
Viana, Walter Segadas
Villanova, Cléto Clotario

Source: PPARJ, "Relatório apresentado ao Sr. Chefe de Polícia, Major Dr. Filinto Müller, pelo Delegado Especial de Segurança Política e Social, Capitão Felisberto Baptista Teixeira, e referente à campanha desenvolvida, sob sua orientação, para repressão às atividades do Partido Comunista no país," pp. 30, 32.
  *=also listed in Table 1
 **=of the Secret Service

Selected Glossary

adelfis – (from the botany term for a flower's stamen) A torture in which bamboo or steel pins were tapped under a victim's fingernail. Additional fingers were often targeted, as were toenails, and even the sensitive area between teeth and gums.

bucha de mostarda – "Mustard Plug" An instrument soaked in mustard that was inserted into the vaginas and/or anuses of female and/or male torture victims.

cabra – See *capanga, jagunço,* and *peão.*

capanga – A privately hired, armed bodyguard. *Capangas* were also sent to perform acts of terrorism by their employers, who were often large landowners. Sometimes the term is used synonymously with *cabra* (see below under *peão*) and *jagunço.*

carioca – A person from or something pertaining to the city of Rio de Janeiro.

Casa de Correção – House of Correction or prison.

Casa de Detenção – Literally "House of the Detained."

Catete – A small suburb in Rio de Janeiro where Catete Palace, one of the main presidential mansions, was located.

Central – The Central Police Station in Rio de Janeiro.

Chefe Nacional – The title used by Plínio Salgado, chief of the Integralists.

Comintern – Abbreviation of the Communist International, the organization that existed from 1919 to 1943 for the purpose of exporting Soviet-style revolutions.

coronel – Literally "colonel," the word was applied liberally to string-pulling, rural potentates up to the 1930s, as a sign of respect. The term does not necessarily mean that one served in the military.

fazenda – A large, usually rural, estate.

fazendeiro – The landholder of a large estate.

fichado – The process of having one's name recorded by the police, especially by the political police, who accumulated some 30,000 names of suspect individuals.

Força Pública – The Polícia Militar (see below) in some states.

gaúcho – A man from or something pertaining to the state of Rio Grande do Sul.

geladeira – The "ice box" or large common cell in a police station.

Gegê – A nickname for Getúlio Vargas.

Integralists – Brazil's fascists in the 1930s and beyond.

interventor – A state administrator with the role of governor during the first Vargas administrations (1930-1945) who was appointed by Getúlio and answerable directly to him. Some of these men functioned as a "super *coronel*."

Intentona Comunista – The ill-fated socialist uprising of November 23-27, 1935.

Itamarati – The Brazilian Foreign Ministry.

jagunço – An individual who did the killing for his bosses, who was retained to supervise the slaves on large estates in times of peace. *Jagunço* is often used interchangeably with *cabra* (see below under *peão*) and *capanga*.

jogo do bicho – The "Game of the Animals." A mainly working-class form of numbers gambling that is tacitly illegal.

mineiro – A man from or something pertaining to the state of Minas Gerais.

palmatória – A holed, wooden paddle, or ferule, used since colonial times to slap the palm of a hand.

Paschoal – The Integralists' nickname for Getúlio Vargas.

patrão – A protector and benefactor.

paulista – A person from or something pertaining to the state of São Paulo.

paulistano – A person from or something pertaining to the city of São Paulo.

peão – Often a strong farm hand or other able-bodied worker in Rio Grande do Sul who was occasionally pressed into service for his master as an assassin. A *peão* is referred to as a *cabra* in other parts of Brazil.

peões – Plural of *peão* (see above).

Polícia Central – The Central Police Station in Rio de Janeiro.

Polícia Civil – "Civilian Police." The main function of this plainclothes group was to carry out detective work. They were a separate entity from the Polícia Militar.

Polícia Militar – While their name came from the fact that they wore uniforms and lived together in barracks, these constables had nothing to do with the Brazilian armed forces nor the Polícia Civil. They were supposed to provide the services of a regular, uniformed police force protecting the civilian population.

Polícia Especial – "Special Police." An offensive police unit in selected metropolitan areas and especially Rio de Janeiro. Known in street vernacular as the "Tomato Heads," because of their khaki uniforms and red caps, they were generally not popular with the public.

povão – Common people in both rural and urban settings.

praça – A *plaza* or city square.

seção de explosivos – The "Explosives Section," or room specifically used for torture, within a detention facility.

Segurança – One of the shortened forms for the Tribunal de Segurança Nacional, or National Security Tribunal (TSN being the other abbreviation).

Beginning on September 11, 1936, the only function of the Segurança was to adjudicate political offenses against the Vargas regime. Using questionable judicial procedures, and after several small modifications, the court sat until just after the end of the first Vargas government in 1945. During its lifetime it judged 6,998 cases involving more than 10,000 persons, 4,099 of whom were found guilty.

sertanejo – At first, this word referred to peasants from the Northeast. Later, the term was loosely applied to all peasants.

sertão – The arid region in Brazil's Northeast.

sigma – The Greek letter "S," or Σ, commonly used as a symbol by the Integralists. In word form, Sigma was likewise employed as a synonym for their movement, the Ação Integralísta Brasileira.

subelites – Situational and transitory muscle providers, examples of which include the police, guards, and all types of bullies in the employ of some higher authority. Note that the Brazilian lower classes (including trustworthy nonwhites) were easily fitted into the fleeting roles of subelites.

tenentes – "Lieutenants." Often used in connection with *tenentismo* or the movement of idealistic lieutenants in the 1920s.

Tomato Heads – (see above under Polícia Especial).

Xuxu – A nickname for Getúlio Vargas which means "a proliferating Brazilian weed."

Notes

Preface

1. See the explanatory note at the start of the Bibliography.

2. Note on all numbered, unidentified sources: A few individuals were listed anonymously who chose not to have their names revealed. All of these persons feared physical harm, or that something negative would happen to their careers, should they be connected to the information they provided. In the small number of situations in which these sources were used, the unidentified informant was in a position to give an eyewitness' or an expert's accounting.

Introduction

1. *Cf.*: *Correio do Povo* (Porto Alegre), August 25, 1955, p. 16; August 25, 1957, p. 64; August 25, 1959, p. 16; *Folha da Tarde* (Porto Alegre), August 24, 1955, p. 9; *Correio da Manhã* (Rio de Janeiro), August 24, 1955, sec. 1, p. 3; and *Última Hora* (Rio de Janeiro), August 24, 1955, p. 1.

2. *Última Hora*, August 24, 1955, pp. 1-4.

3. *Tribuna da Imprensa* (Rio de Janeiro), August 24, 1955, p. 1. The larger article in this issue of *Tribuna da Imprensa* (p. 8) described, one more time, the rioting that besieged the newspaper's offices following Vargas' death. Understanding why the *Tribuna* was singled out can be found in chap. 5.

4. *Última Hora*, August 24, 1956, p. 4. This observation was made by Ruy Carneiro of the PSD (Partido Social Democrático), or Social Democratic Party. The party of rural landowners, the PSD was founded by Vargas in the 1940s.

5. *Ibid.* At the time the leader of the PSD party, Filinto Müller, so eulogized his former employer. For a preview of Müller, see above p. xvi.

6. *Tribuna da Imprensa*, August 24-25, 1957, p. 8. These remarks were included in the comments made by Fernando Ferrari (PTB-Rio Grande do Sul). For more on the Partido Trabalhista Brasileiro, see chap. 5.

7. *Última Hora*, August 24, 1955, p. 2. This statement was made by Luís Viana Filho, at the time a member of the PL (Partido Libertador), or Liberator Party.

8. *Jornal do Brasil* (Rio de Janeiro), August 24, 1966, p. 6. Martins Alonso added this note. Alonso was a former policeman and friend of Filinto Müller. *Jornal do Brasil* is one of the country's most respected independent tabloids.

9. *Ibid.*

10. *Última Hora*, August 24, 1964, p. 1.

11. *Jornal do Brasil*, August 24, 1987, sec. 1, p. 9. Such view was offered by Alexandre Demathey Camacho, Secretary of the State of Rio de Janeiro during the government of Moreira Franco.

12. *Última Hora*, August 24, 1966, p. 4.

13. Claudio de Lacerda [Paiva], *Uma crise de agosto: o atentado da rua Toneleros* (Rio de Janeiro: Nova Fronteira, 1994), p. 306.

14. *Cf.: Jornal do Brasil*, August 24, 1987, sec. 1, p. 9; and *Folha da Tarde*, August 25, 1954, p. 3. See also the blend of paternalism and contempt (the latter evident in the face of at least one bodyguard) in Photo 1.

15. For example, note the remark by Leonel Brizola in *Folha da Tarde*, August 25, 1982, p. 13.

16. *Última Hora*, August 24, 1966, p. 4.

Chapter 1. The Road to Power

1. *Cf.: Veja* (São Paulo), March 30, 1988, p. 25: Luthero Vargas, *Getúlio Vargas: a revolução inacabada* (Rio de Janeiro: Bloch, 1988), pp. 6-8; and Israel Beloch and Alzira Alves de Abreu (coords.), *Dicionário histórico-biográfico brasileiro, 1930-1983* (Rio de Janeiro: Forense-Universitária, 1984), p. 3436. Vargas changed his year of birth later to 1883 when he was trying to get into law school (see above p. 4 and below p. 130 n.24). Beloch and Abreu, *loc cit.*

2. These men are often confused with *cabras, jagunços,* and *capangas.* There were some subtle differences. Indigenous to Rio Grande do Sul, a *peão* (singular of *peões*), like the *cabra*, was usually a strong farmhand or other able-bodied worker who some-times was pressed into service for his boss as an assassin. In other parts of Brazil the *jagunço* did the killing for his master when called upon to do so. But "in times of peace they were retained to supervise the workers of the *fazendas.*" The *capanga*, however, was a privately hired armed killer who often performed acts of terrorism. *Cf.*: Gilberto Freyre, *The Masters and the Slaves: A Study in the Development of Brazilian Civilization*, Samuel Putnam (trans.), 2nd ed. (New York: Alfred Knopf, 1966), pp. 48n, 66n-67n; Francisco Julião, "The Practice and Preaching of Revolution," *Revolution in Brazil: Politics and Society in a Developing Nation*, Irving Horowitz (ed.) (New York: E.P. Dutton, 1964), p. 35n; Peter Singelmann, "Political Structure and Social Banditry in Northeastern Brazil," *Journal of Latin American Studies* [hereafter *JLAS*], vol. VII, no. 1, May 1975, p. 61; Jorge Amado, *The Violent Land*, Samuel Putnam (trans.), 4th ed. (New York: Avon, 1979), pp. 189, 220, 275-76; and Affonso Henriques, *Ascensão e queda de Getúlio Vargas: o maquiavélico* (Rio de Janeiro: Record, 1966), vol. I, p. 53. Keep in mind that this last author was the secretary of finance for the Aliança Nacional

Libertadora. Political Police Archives, Rio de Janeiro [hereafter PPARJ], document, "Aliança Nacional Libertadora, directorio municipal do Districto Federal, organisação interna dos nucleos," July 1, 1935, p. 4, comunismo/pasta 18. For more on the Aliança Nacional Libertadora, see above pp. 27-28 and chap. 3.

3. Henriques, *loc. cit.*

4. Manuel reached the rank of lieutenant colonel in the Paraguayan War. Beloch and Abreu, p. 3436. A common practice in the Brazilian army allowed him, as a colonel, to use the title of "general" after he retired.

5. *Cf.*: Henriques, p. 33; and Fernando Jorge, *Getúlio Vargas e o seu tempo: Um retrato com luz e sombra, 1883-1900* (São Paulo: T.A. Queiroz, 1985), p. 356. A picture of Protásio, Getúlio, Benjamin, and their father is presented in Photo 3.

6. *Cf.*: Jorge, pp. 423-24; and Henriques, *loc. cit.*

7. *Cf.*: Henriques, p. 53; Ciro Arno [Cícero Arpino Caldeira Brandt], *Memórias de um estudante,* 2nd ed., rev. (Rio de Janeiro: Gráfica Olímpica, 1952), p. 157; and Jorge, p. 191. See chapter XII of Jorge for the most comprehensive analysis of Getúlio's complicity in this affair.

8. *Cf.*: Jorge, pp. 438-41; Arno, *loc. cit*; Augusto de Lima Júnior, *Serões e vigílias: páginas avulsas* (Rio de Janeiro: Livros de Portugal, 1952), p. 36; and *Folha da Manhã* (São Paulo), January 15, 1930, p. 4. Augusto de Lima Júnior's account is slightly different than the one presented here. The *Folha da Manhã* was one of the three "Folhas" that in 1960 would become the *Folha de São Paulo.* Founded in January 1920 by Olival Costa and Pedro Cunha, *Folha da Manhã* aimed its circulation at small businessmen and the self-employed.

9. *Cf.*: Jorge, pp. 192, 438-42; and Arno, *loc. cit.*

10. *Manchete* (Rio de Janeiro), December 15, 1979, p. 46. The expression *carrasco sorridente* or "smiling hangman" was given to Getúlio by journalist David Nasser. *Ibid.*

11. Renato Jardim, *A adventura de outubro e a invasão de São Paulo* (São Paulo: Sociedade Impressora Paulista, 1932), p. 95. José Gomes de Pinheiro Machado was the man behind the throne in the national government of Hermes da Fonseca (1910-1914). Literally "colonel," the term *coronel* was applied to string-pulling, rural potentates up to the 1930s. The word was used as a sign of respect despite the fact that the recipient might have never have been a member of the military. See also above pp. 12, 79 and below p. 134 n.6.

12. Henry Koster, *Travels in Brazil* (London: Longman, 1816), p. 117.

13. Daniel Kidder, *Sketches of Residence and Travels in Brazil: Embracing Historical and Geographical Notices of the Empire and its Several Provinces* (Philadelphia: Sorin and Ball, London: Wiley and Putnam, 1845), vol. II, p. 102.

14. (Anonymous), *Brazil: Its History, People, Natural Productions, etc.* (London: Religious Tract Society, 1860), p. 201.

15. *Rio News* (Rio de Janeiro), January 24, 1884, p. 5.

16. This scene was nobly described fifty years later by the judge's son, a man on whom Getúlio would lavish a fond friendship in the years after the shooting. Jorge, pp. 191, 444.

17. Perhaps more than any other part of Brazil during the Republican period, the politicians of Rio Grande do Sul were influenced by positivism. The most important of

these early *gaúcho* leaders was Júlio de Castilhos. He created a positivist political approach that was passed on to Pinheiro Machado, Borges de Medeiros, Getúlio Vargas, and to a lesser degree, João Goulart. Tancredo Neves in Valentina da Rocha Lima (coord.), *Getúlio: uma história oral* (Rio de Janeiro: Record, 1986), pp. 47-48.

18. *Cf.*: Aureliano Leite, *Páginas de uma longa vida* (São Paulo: Martins, 1967), pp. 49-50, 50n; Jorge, pp. 190-91, 444-49; and Jardim, pp. 94-95. Henriques (p. 58) states that Lima's decision caused such a scandal that he was later transferred on orders of the state government. For the two Vargas birthdays, see above pp. 1, 128 n.1.

19. Jorge, pp. 457-58.

20. Mesquita became a hero in the Canudos messianic war (1896-1897), and later won temporary command of the government's forces in a second folk-religious conflict, the Contestado (1912-1916).

21. Jorge, p. 458. We will perhaps never know if this postponement from above had some connection to the slaying in Ouro Preto.

22. Vargas' daughter, Alzira, has written one of the only accounts of what happened. In her brief report, she tries to convince the reader that because of his solidarity with the revolting students, Getúlio asked to be expelled. This seems a dubious description. Since the overall effort of her book was to glamorize her father–the murder in Ouro Preto was completely twisted–her explanation of Rio Pardo seems likewise suspect. Alzira Vargas do Amaral Peixoto, *Getúlio Vargas: meu pai* (Porto Alegre: Globo, 1960), pp. 4-7. She does mention (p. 9), however, that at the law school he would eventually attend, he apparently had an itchy-trigger finger and began shooting just to break up a rally by student opponents.

23. Jordan Young, *The Brazilian Revolution of 1930 and the Aftermath* (New Brunswick: Rutgers University Press, 1967), pp. 32-33.

24. Young (p. 33) states that the near combat experience soured Getúlio on continuing his military career, and "his next move was to matriculate in the law school of Porto Alegre." Alzira Vargas do Amaral Peixoto (pp. 6-7), on the other hand, says that he had already begun to study law at the same school as an auditor before being shipped to the border area.

25. *Cf.*: Paul Frischauer, *Presidente Vargas: biografia*, Mário da Silva and Brutus Pedreira (trans.) (São Paulo: Nacional, 1943), p. 120; and Antonio Augusto Faria and Edgard Luiz de Barros, *Getúlio Vargas e sua época*, 2nd ed. (São Paulo: Global, 1983), pp. 17, 21.

26. *Cf.*: Young, p. 34; and Faria and Barros, p. 21.

27. See above pp. 2, 129 n.11.

28. Frischauer, pp. 64, 152-53. In his accounting of four murders attributable to Getúlio and or his brothers, Carlos Lacerda, then editor of the key anti-Vargas newspaper (see above pp. xv, 127 n.3), said that Torres "was receiving payments from the Vargas'." *Tribuna da Imprensa*, August 10, 1954, p. 2.

29. Frischauer, pp. 160-63. For the non-Vargas viewpoint, *cf.*: Henriques, vol. I, pp. 58-59; Jardim, pp. 95-96; and Jorge, pp. 192-93.

30. See above pp. 1-2, 129 nn.7-8.

31. *Cf.*: Jardim, p. 96; and *O Estado de São Paulo*, March 20, 1966, p. 85. There are several versions of just how this killing was completed. A summary can be found in

Jorge, pp. 192-93. *O Estado de São Paulo* was founded in 1875. For many years a paper of the elites, "*O Estadão*," as it is known, still retains a right-of-center flavor. As for *peão*, see above pp. 1, 128 n.2.

32. John W.F. Dulles, *Vargas of Brazil: A Political Biography* (Austin: University of Texas Press, 1967), p. 18.

33. Brazil, *Relatorio apresentado ao Dr. A.A. Borges de Medeiros, Presidente do Estado do Rio Grande do Sul pelo Engenheiro Ildefonso Soares Pinto, Secretario de Estado dos Negocios das Obras Publicas em 15 de agosto de 1923* (Porto Alegre: A Federação, 1923), p. 583. While the charges made in this *relatorio* are the only indications that the events took place, there is oblique confirmation in Alzira Vargas do Amaral Peixoto (p. 17). Carlos Lacerda also tried (*Tribuna da Imprensa*, August 10, 1954, p. 2) to pin the murder of Aureliano Coutinho on Getúlio. But see above p. 102.

34. Medeiros almost certainly lost the election. Getúlio, as chief of the commission reviewing the number of votes for each candidate, probably recounted the votes in Medeiros favor. Carlos Cortés, *Gaúcho Politics in Brazil: The Politics of Rio Grande do Sul, 1930-1964* (Albuquerque: University of New Mexico Press, 1974), p. 14.

35. *Cf.*: *Ibid.*, p. 15n; and Gilberto Freyre, *Order and Progress: Brazil from Monarchy to Republic*, Rod Horton (ed. and trans.) (New York: Alfred Knopf, 1970), p. 348. Note Cortés' observation (*loc. cit.*) that the *Chimango*, a vulture-like bird, is "a symbol of cowardliness in Gaúcho lore."

36. *Cf.*: Cortés, pp. 24-25; Faria and Barros, p. 23; and Paulo Brandi, *Vargas: da vida para a história*, 2nd ed., rev. (Rio de Janeiro: Zahar, 1985), p. 29.

37. *Cf.*: Dulles, p. 30; and Young, p. 35.

38. Young, pp. 35-37.

39. *Cf.*: *Ibid.*, pp. 37-38; Dulles, pp. 43-44; and Otávio Brandão in Lima, p. 255. In respect to Vargas' proletarian sympathies, which, such as they were, were limited to the urban proletariat, see above pp. 79, 100-101 and below pp. 167 n.9, 179 nn.96-97.

40. Young, p. 38.

41. The president had been given the title of Little Trepov years before by an anarchist-leaning newspaper (*A Voz do Trabalhador* [Rio de Janeiro], June 8, 1915, p. 3). The state's secretary of justice and public security from 1906 to 1912, Washington Luís was accused of being an economy-size Fyodor Fyodorovich Trepov, one of Tsarist Russia's most cruel St. Petersburg police chiefs. *Cf.*: Beloch and Abreu, p. 1952, and Pereira Reis Júnior, *Os presidentes do Brasil* (Rio de Janeiro: Divulbrás, 1975), p. 137.

42. This distrust stemmed not only from the well-known initial opposition of Antônio Carlos to the economic program of Washington Luís, but also to such things as the secret vote and woman's suffrage, which to the dismay of the president, Antônio Carlos had inaugurated in his state. Dulles, p. 44.

43. *Ibid.*, p. 49.

44. *Ibid.*, p. 50. Another author (Cortés, p. 19) states that Medeiros' true reason was that the recent civil war in his state had left him with too many enemies.

45. Dulles, p. 51.

46. *Cf.*: Cortés, p. 20; Young, p. 122n; *Enciclopédia Mirador Internacional* (São Paulo: Encyclopaedia Britannica do Brasil, 1975), pp. 3695-96; and John French, "Industrial Workers and the Birth of the Populist Republic in Brazil, 1945-1946," *Latin*

American Perspectives, vol. XVI, no. 4, Fall 1989, p. 7. One of Júlio Prestes campaign workers and long-time personal friends was Plínio Salgado. Salgado make his own mark on Brazil later in the decade (see above pp. 21-28 and chap. 4). Elmer Broxson, "Plinio Salgado and Brazilian Integralism, 1932-1938," unpublished PhD thesis, Department of History, Catholic University of America, 1972, p. 29.

47. Young, pp. 44-45.

48. *Cf.*: *Ibid.*, p. 52; Beloch and Abreu, pp. 2703-4; Ademar Vidal, *João Pessoa e a Revolução de 30* (Rio de Janeiro: Graal, 1978), pp. 248-52, 297-99; *A União* (João Pessoa), July 26, 1930, p. 6; Dulles, p. 64; Centro de Pesquisa e Documentação de História Contemporânea do Brasil [hereafter CPDOC], oral history, "José Joffily," 1977-1978, pp. 43-45, 48; Henriques, p. 120; *Parahyba mulher macho*, directed by Tizuka Yamasaki, 1983; and Joaquim Inojosa, *República de Princesa: José Pereira x João Pessoa-1930* (Rio de Janeiro: Civilização Brasileira, 1980), pp. 226-29. This book contains two unnumbered plates in Inojosa depicting the original and staged photographs of the jailhouse "suicides."

49. *Cf.*: CPDOC, "José Joffily, p. 46; Henriques, pp. 117-18; and John W.F. Dulles, *A faculdade de direito de São Paulo e a resistência anti-Vargas, 1938-1945*, Vanda Mena Barreto de Andrade (trans.) (São Paulo: Universidade de São Paulo, 1984), pp. 58-62, 65.

50. Henriques, pp. 118-20. The wife of Suassuna sent a letter to Vargas in which she claimed Juarez Távora (see above p. 11) had promised that her husband's assassin(s) would be punished. But, then Batista Luzardo (see above p. 12) stopped the resulting investigation into the murder. Luzardo was the one who tacked a criminal-political connection to João Suassuna's death. Henriques goes on to report that one of Getúlio's first acts after the success of hia revolution was to free Suassuna's killer. In Rita Suassuna's letter, she observed that the murderer was released on October 24, 1930, and promptly given a job as a police detective. The police, of course, denied everything. *Cf.*: Arquivo ·Nacional [hereafter AN]: letter, "Rita Vilaz Suassuna to Getúlio Vargas," February 18, 1931, Secretaria de Presidência da República: Polícia Civil do Distrito Federal/lata 527; letter, "Virgilio Barbosa to Joaquim Pedro Salgado Filho," March 21, 1931, Secretaria de Presidência da República: Polícia Civil do Distrito Federal/lata 527; and Henriques, p. 120.

51. *Cf.*: Jorge Amado, *A vida de Luís Carlos Prestes: o Cavaleiro da Esperança*, 4th ed. (São Paulo: Martins, 1945), p. 98; Boris Fausto, *A Revolução de 1930, historiografia e história*, 9th ed. (São Paulo: Brasiliense, 1983), p. 61; Dênis de Moraes and Francisco Viana, *Prestes: lutas e autocríticas*, 2nd ed. (Petrópolis: Vozes, 1982), p. 37; Young, p. 55; Stanley Hilton, *A Rebelião Vermelha* (Rio de Janeiro: Record, 1986), pp. 22-23; Beloch and Abreu, p. 2817; *Jornal do Commercio* (Rio de Janeiro), September 16-17, 1929, p. 13; *Folha de São Paulo*, September 30, 1987, p. A-4; and William Waack, *Camaradas: Nos arquivos de Moscou: a histórias secreta da revolução brasileira de 1935* (São Paulo: Companhia das Letras, 1993), pp. 28-29, 352n. Aristides Leal (CPDOC, oral history, "Aristides Leal," 1975, 1977, p. 53), adds that General Motors and General Electric provided Vargas with the original money. Note that the value of 800:000$000 was taken from business-oriented *Jornal do Commercio*, South America's third oldest newspaper. For what happened to a final $20,000, see above p. 37. That

Waack could have cited his sources more completely, but didn't, was due to the fact that the Comintern's Archives, largely located at the Российский Центр Хранения и Изучения Документов Новейшей Истории (Modern Russian History, Document Conservation and Research Center, hereafter РЦХИДНИ) in Moscow, and other sources used, were not fully open at the time of his study. Thanks to Luís Carlos Prestes' son, Yuri Ribeiro, a former long-time resident in Moscow, some doors were opened. Many times, however, it was made clear that if the source was acknowledged, the functionary providing the information would lose his or her job. Yuri Ribeiro, interview, Rio de Janeiro, November 11, 1994. Part of Waack's work is confirmed in the essay by Jürgen Mothes of the University of Leipzig ("Briefe aus Montevideo: Arthur Ewert und die Wandlung von Luis Carlos Prestes zum Kommunismus"). *Cf.*: William Waack: telephone interview, Rio de Janeiro/Berlin, May 29, 1994; and letter, June 4, 1994.

52. *Cf.*: United Kingdom, Public Records Office [hereafter UKPRO], document, "Brazil, Political 'Who's Who,'" November 26, 1940, p. 9, FO 371/24176; and John W.F. Dulles, *Brazilian Communism, 1935-1945: Repression during World Upheaval* (Austin: University of Texas Press, 1983), p. 2. While fighting the *Coluna* in Bahia, Góis "mobilized several *jagunços*, paid by *fazendeiros* in the region, to form 'tracker groups' to locate the major areas of the Column's movement." Beloch and Abreu, p. 2248. Born in Alagoas, Monteiro's family is said to have run "a bloody oligarchy that dominated the state for several decades." *Jornal do Brasil*, May 14, 1989, sec. 1, p. 9. Góis grew into a "fleshy drunkard" (Dulles, *Vargas of Brazil*, p. 99), a fact that did not go unnoticed by Colonel Edwin Sibert, the U.S. military attaché in Rio de Janeiro in April 1941. In a report back to Washington, Sibert commented as follows on the subject: "G-2 will remember that General Góes [Góis] drinks a lot at luncheons and dinners, he talks a lot even when he doesn't drink and more when he does, and is notoriously indiscreet and given to extravagant remarks." United States, National Archives [hereafter USNA], letter, "Sibert to G-2," April 25, 1941, no. 2693, p. 2, MID 2052-120/21.

53. *Cf.*: Beloch and Abreu, pp. 2939-41; and Young, pp. 53, 55-56.

Chapter 2. Head of the Provisional Government

1. Young, pp. 62-63.
2. Dulles, *Vargas of Brazil*, p. 68.
3. *Cf.*: *Ibid.*, pp. 72-73; and Young, pp. 65-68. Washington Luís and a number of his followers were sent packing to Europe, Argentina, and Uruguay. The leader of the Junta Pacificadora was General Augusto Tasso Fragoso. He had been the army's chief of staff until January 24, 1929. In this capacity, Fragoso "received much credit for the crushing of the revolt [of 1924] and the final pacification of the country. The opposition press also has censured him severely for some of the tactics employed." USNA, letter, "Baker to G-2," January 28, 1929, no. 854, p. 1, MID 2006-115. Fragoso's influence on the military of his day, and for generations to come, was considerable. He was an outspoken advocate of rearmament to face a growing hostility with Argentina, which had mushroomed since the Paraguayan War. It may well have been that Fragoso joined the Rio de Janeiro military plotters, and accepted the leading position among them, because

Washington Luís was unwilling to cooperate with his call for a military buildup. *Cf.*: Beloch and Abreu, pp. 1343, 1345; and Frank McCann, "The Brazilian General Staff and Brazil's Military Situation, 1900-1945," *Journal of Interamerican Studies and World Affairs* [hereafter *JISWA*], vol. XXV, no. 3, August 1983, pp. 307-8.

4. Aureliano Leite, *Memórias de um revolucionário: a Revolução de 1930: pródromos e consequências* (São Paulo: [no publisher given], 1931), p. 182.

5. *Cf.*: *Ibid.*; and Dulles, *Vargas of Brazil*, pp. 90-91. The Americans evidently had João Alberto pegged right. Accounts sent back to Washington branded him as a "successful opportunist." United States, Office of Strategic Services, Research and Analysis, document "Summary of Political Situation in Brazil (as of July, 1945)," August 2, 1945, 097.3/Z1092/no. 3329, appendix. One report has it that he once tried to join the Uruguayan Communist Party. Though he was rebuffed and told to join the organization in Brazil, he rapidly lost his leftist leanings as he became involved with Vargas. Later, in 1931, when he was made police chief in the Federal District, he gave his views as follows: "Communist? No! Catholic? Yes!" David Nasser, *Falta alguém em Nuremberg: torturas da polícia de Filinto Strubling Müller*, 4th ed. (Rio de Janeiro: O Cruzeiro, 1966), p. 13. João Alberto's new philosophy was already evident on being installed as *interventor* (see above, p. 12) in São Paulo. A little over three months after taking office Alberto arranged for a credit of 200:000$000 (then worth a little over $16,300) in Depression-scarce money, to be used in São Paulo to fight communism. He made one final flip in June 1935 when he wrote to Luís Carlos Prestes admitting that he'd chosen the wrong road in going with Vargas. *Cf.*: PPARJ, letter, "J[oão] Alberto to [Luís Carlos] Prestes," June 8, 1935, p. 2, comunismo/pasta 9; *Diario de Noticias* (Rio de Janeiro), March 3, 1931, p. 1; and March 4, 1931, p. 13. Founded in 1930, *Diario de Noticias* was a liberal paper opposed not only to the Old Republic, but soon to Vargas himself over the issue of returning the country to democracy.

6. It is of course incorrect to think that Vargas ended the institution of *coronelismo* by dispatching federal agents to many parts of the *sertão* in 1931 to demobilize the private armies of the main *coronéis*. Even though they were disarmed they were by no means destroyed. Many of these men ended up joining the new order. Whereas before they used their own resources to safeguard and promote their interests, now, as members of Getúlio's political apparatus or another political party, they aimed to secure their ends through allegiances to the state *interventor*. Rio de Janeiro approved of this arrangement in order to maintain order and promote area capitalism. As a result, *interventors* were often supported and patronized by many regional elites (former *coronéis*), frequently becoming a kind of "super *coronel*" in their respective state. *Cf.*: Eul-Soo Pang, "Agrarian Change in the Northeast," *Modern Brazil: Elites and Masses in Historical Perspective*, Michael Conniff and Frank McCann (eds.) (Lincoln: University of Nebraska Press, 1989), p. 131; and Mino Carta and Raimundo Rodrigues Pereira (directors), *Retrato do Brasil* (*da monarquia ao estado militar*) (São Paulo: Política Editora, 1984), vol. I, pp. 91-92.

7. *Cf.*: Karl Loewenstein, *Brazil under Vargas* (New York: Macmillan, 1944), p. 17; *Folha de São Paulo*, July 14, 1989, p. A-3; Cortés, *loc. cit.*; and Dulles, *Vargas of Brazil*, pp. 78-79. As early as February 20, 1931, Oswaldo Aranha, the incoming minister of justice, was touting the corporatism of Mussolini and wanting to create something of a

similar nature in Brazil. It was his view that the Brazilian people were not yet ready for democracy or universal suffrage owing to their lack of "civic education" (in this regard, see below p. 168 n.11). *A Noite* (Rio de Janeiro), February 20, 1931, p. 1. Founded in June 1911, *A Noite* was one of the leading journals opposed to Vargas before the Revolution of 1930 (but note also the future owners above on p. 48). That Vargas moved in a despotic direction should not have been a surprise. In 1955 one author, who was busy besmirching his name during the Vargas era (see above pp. 22-23, 88-89 and below pp. 139 n.62, 140 n.64, 173 n.49), pointed out that in twenty-six of the forty-eight years following the end of the monarchy (1889 until 1937), *all* heads of the Brazilian government, except Nilo Peçanha (who took over after the death in office of Afonso Pena to govern the country for a little over a year: June 14, 1909 to November 15, 1910), ruled at one time or another either as dictators or through states of siege or war. Gustavo Barroso, *Reflexões de um bóde* (Rio de Janeiro: Grafica Educadora, 1955), pp. 95-99.

8. *Cf.*: Brazil, *Collecção das leis da Republica dos Estados Unidos do Brazil de 1907* (Rio de Janeiro: Nacional, 1908), vol. I, p. 527, decree 6640, art. 9, sec. 3, no. 9; Eliana Rezende Furtado de Mendonça (director), *Os arquivos das polícias políticas: reflexos de nossa história contemporânea* (Rio de Janeiro: FAPERJ, 1994), pp. 12, 16; Arquivo Maurício de Lacerda, newspaper article, "*O Combate* [Rio de Janeiro]," February 2, 1928, n.p., Arquivo Edgard Leuenroth, roll 2/79; Beloch and Abreu, p. 1967; Michael Conniff, *Urban Politics in Brazil: The Rise of Populism, 1925-1945* (Pittsburgh: University of Pittsburgh Press, 1981), pp. 129, 138; and Hilton, p. 39.

9. *Cf.*: *Correio da Manhã*, January 20, 1931, p. 3; and *A Noite*, January 20, 1931, 2nd ed., p. 2. An interesting accounting of the Hunger March and its ramifications is also given in John W.F. Dulles, *Anarchists and Communists in Brazil, 1900-1935* (Austin: University of Texas Press, 1973), pp. 452-55.

10. *Correio da Manhã*, January 20, 1931, p. 3.

11. *Cf.*: *Ibid.*; *O Jornal* (Rio de Janeiro), January 20, 1931, p. 7; *A Noite*, January 20, 1931, 2nd ed., p. 2; and *Diario de Noticias*, January 20, 1931, p. 4. *O Jornal* was acquired by Assis Chateaubriand in 1919 and turned into his principal daily in Rio de Janeiro. The tabloid was at first in favor of the Revolution of 1930 but later generally against the Vargas dictatorship.

12. In view of the large numbers of arrests (*A Noite*, January 20, 1931, 2nd ed., p.2), and because of past policies and practices, it seems hard to believe that all of those picked up or arrested were soon released. See as well the statement by Polícia Civil Chief Luzardo in Mauricio de Lacerda, *Segunda Republica*, 2nd ed. (Rio de Janeiro: Freitas Bastos, 1931), p. 326.

13. Looking at the labor question in another way, "the 1931-32 federal budget allocated more money to the police department than to the labor ministry." Conniff, p. 97.

14. *Cf.*: Cortés, p. 30; and Arquivo Filinto Müller [hereafter AFM], biography, "Lindolfo Collor," 1937, CPDOC, pp. 1-3. The uncle of ex-President Fernando Collor de Mello, Lindolfo Collor likewise defrauded (AFM, "Lindolfo Collor," pp. 5-6) the governor of Minas Gerais–and presidential hopeful–Antônio Carlos out of money in connection with the installation of a phantom telegraph station during the days leading up to the election of 1930. This information comes from the private files of Filinto Müller. Müller was to become the police chief in the former Federal District. In this capacity, he

was occasionally referred to as the Heinrich Himmler of Brazil. Filinto kept a secret archive on 125 noteworthy personalities, including members of the government. These documents were often priceless sources of character information, sometimes based on fact, sometimes based on rumor, that were usually unknown to the general public of the day. Müller, no doubt Getúlio, and anyone else having access to these files, would have been in a position to use them, possibly for blackmail purposes, during and even after the Vargas era.

15. Cortés, *loc. cit.*

16. *Cf.*: Juarez Rubens Brandão Lopes, *Desenvolvimento e mundança social: formação da sociedade urbano no Brasil*, 3rd ed. (São Paulo: Nacional/MEC, 1976), pp. 13-14; and Brazil, Secretaria de Planejamento, *Anuário estatístico do Brasil, 1985* (Rio de Janeiro: IBGE, 1986), p. 121.

17. *Cf.*: Arquidiocese de São Paulo, *Brasil: nunca mais*, 6th ed. (Petrópolis: Vozes, 1985), pp. 125-26; and Beloch and Abreu, p. 1822. See above p. 108 and below 181 n.9.

18. Dinarco Reis, *A luta de classes no Brasil e o PCB* (São Paulo: Novo Rumos, 1982), vol. I, p. 28.

19. The chief of the Provisional Government is reported (Evaristo de Morais Filho in Lima, p. 255) to have viewed leftists as promoting the absolute slavery of the people. Nasser (p. 12) remarks that during the first years of Vargas' rule, the police began to take communism more and more seriously, and attempted by all means possible to keep them from even talking to workers outside of factories.

20. *Cf.*: *Correio da Manhã*, March 4, 1931, p. 1; *O Estado de São Paulo*, March 5, 1931, p. 1; *New York Times*, March 4, 1931, p. 21; and March 5, 1931, p. 10. Note that it was the Brazilian press that mentioned the "to help organize the fight against communism" role of the visiting policemen.

21. See in this regard the precedent on p. 35.

22. Dulles, *Anarchists and Communists*, pp. 476-77. See also below p. 167 n.9.

23. Michael Conniff, "The Tenentes in Power: A New Perspective on the Brazilian Revolution of 1930," *JLAS*, vol. X, no. 1, May 1978, pp. 64, 66.

24. Henriques, pp. 142-45. As an illustration, in October 1931, dissatisfied *tenentes* of several different political views revolted in Recife and Olinda. They chased the federal *interventor*, Carlos de Lima Cavalcanti, from the governor's palace. But they could not stand up against the onslaught of loyal forces that came to his aid. In the ensuing fight, between fifty and 100 rebels lost their lives. Dulles, *Anarchists and Communists*, pp. 487-88.

25. *Cf.*: Cortés, p. 31; and Frank McCann, "Origins of the 'New Professionalism' of the Brazilian Military," *JISWA*, vol. XXI, no. 4, November 1979, pp. 518-19.

26. *Cf.*: Beloch and Abreu, pp. 42, 1769-71; Henriques, p. 212; and Robert Levine, *The Vargas Regime: The Critical Years, 1934-1938* (New York, Columbia University Press, 1970), pp. 6, 8. Plínio Salgado, who would go on to become the Brazilian *Führer*, wrote the first manifesto of the Legion, but soon left, in part over the group's failure to implement the document. *Cf.*: Levine, p. 73; Dulles, *Vargas of Brazil*, pp. 122-23; and Broxson, pp. 34-35.

27. *Cf.*: Beloch and Abreu, p. 42; and Broxson, pp. 90-93. It is doubtful that João Alberto would have legalized these two groups without prior permission from Catete. On

the other hand, note the paradox to this question above on pp. 15, 134 n.5, 136 n.19. The Partido Comunista do Brasil, the original Moscow-oriented Brazilian Communist Party, changed its name in 1961 to the Partido Comunista Brasileiro.

28. John W.F. Rowe, "Studies in the Artificial Control of Raw Material Supplies: No. 3, Brazilian Coffee," *Royal Economic Society*, no. 34, February 1932, p. 86.

29. Young, p. 80.

30. John W.F. Rowe, *Primary Commodities in International Trade* (Cambridge: Cambridge University Press, 1965), pp. 134-35.

31. Leite, *Memórias de um revolucionário*, pp. 217-27.

32. Dulles, *Vargas of Brazil*, p. 91.

33. Beloch and Abreu, pp. 42-43, 2948-50.

34. *Ibid.*

35. On learning that Medeiros was against him, Getúlio is reported (Juraci Magalhães in Lima, p. 66) to have said, "How funny! I supported the dictatorship of old Borges for twenty-five years and never complained. Now he cries out because I've been a dictator for two years."

36. *Cf.*: Thomas Skidmore, *Politics in Brazil, 1930-1964: An Experiment in Democracy* (New York: Oxford University Press, 1967), pp. 15-16; and Dulles, *Vargas of Brazil*, pp. 94-101. The chants of "Death to Aranha!" should not have shocked Oswaldo, since "he was the biggest enemy of São Paulo in the Revolution of 1930." Henriques, p. 213.

37. *Cf.*: Claudio de Lacerda [Paiva], p. 16; Dulles: *Vargas of Brazil*, p. 103; *Brazilian Communism*, p. 7; Fernando Morais, *Olga*, 3rd ed. (São Paulo: Alfa-Omega, 1985), p. 134; *Jornal do Brasil*, November 1, 1987, sec. B/especial, p. 12; CPDOC, oral history, "Guilherme Figueiredo," 1977, p. 62; Brazil: *Coleção das leis da República dos Estados Unidos do Brasil de 1933: atos do Govêrno Provisório, janeiro a março* (Rio de Janeiro: Nacional, 1934), vol. I, p. 55, decree 22332, art. 2, sec. f, no. 4; Conselho Nacional de Estatística, *Anuário estatístico do Brasil, 1939-1940* (Rio de Janeiro: IBGE, 1941), p. 1277; Comissão Especial de Inquérito sôbre Atos Delituosos da Ditadura, "Depoimento do Luís Carlos Prestes," *Diario do Congresso Nacional*, September 20, 1947, pp. 5902, 5904; Tad Szulc, *Twilight of the Tyrants* (New York: Henry Holt, 1959), p. 82; and Nelson Werneck Sodré, *História militar do Brasil* (Rio de Janeiro: Civilização Brasileira, 1965), p. 278. Years later, when Euzébio became the president of the Metropolitan Federation of Boxing, the membership was now and again distracted by rumors of his continued sexual preferences. Robson Gracie, interview, Rio de Janeiro, August 6, 1991. A picture of Euzébio de Queiroz Filho is presented here as Photo 5. A photo of the Tomato Heads being transported into action–note the mounted Hotchkiss machine gun on the lead vehicle–is displayed in Photo 20.

38. Cortés, pp. 44-45. When the fighting broke out, it was rural, sporadic, disconnected, and easily stamped out. Many of the prominent *gaúcho* leaders escaped into exile in Uruguay or Argentina. Borges de Medeiros was not so fortunate. He was captured after running out of ammunition in a hopeless gunfight with loyalist forces at a remote ranch. His sentence was banishment to Pernambuco. *Ibid.*, pp. 47, 51. For more on Flôres da Cunha, see above pp. 33-34 and below p. 144 n.19.

39. Dulles, *Vargas of Brazil*, p. 111.

40. Faria and Barros, p. 32.

41. Skidmore. *Politics in Brazil*. p. 18.

42. Dulles. *Vargas of Brazil*. pp. 107. 116.

43. *Ibid.*, p. 119.

44. João Quartim. *Dictatorship and Armed Struggle in Brazil*. David Fernbach (trans.) (New York: Monthly Review. 1971). p. 24.

45. Stanley Hilton. *A guerra civil brasileira: história da Revolução Constitucionalista de 1932* (Rio de Janeiro: Nova Fronteira. 1982). p. 327.

46. AN. photograph. PH/FOT/5618. folder 1. This unnumbered snapshot shows detainees at the penal compound. See also the mention above of an earlier camp in Amapa on p. 35 and below at p. 145 n.23.

47. *Cf.*: USNA. letter. "Sackville to G-2." November 2. 1932. no. 1047. p. 1. MID 2657-K-86/16; Amado. *A vida de Luís Carlos Prestes*. p. 270; Gilson Ferreira de Souza. interview. Rio de Janeiro. March 21. 1989; John W.F. Dulles: letter. May 25. 1988; *Brazilian Communism*. p. 2; José Joffily: letter. February 17. 1989; and *Harry Berger* (Rio de Janeiro: Paz e Terra. 1986). pp. 47n. 144. For a Lloyd Brasileiro rendition of the *Pedro I*. see Joffily. *Harry Berger*. p. 144.

48. Gastão Goulart. *Verdades da Revolução Paulista* (São Paulo: [no publisher given. n.d.]). pp. 274-75. The only known photograph of Paula Pinto is reproduced here as Photo 13.

49. *Cf.*: Origenes Lessa. *Ilha Grande: do jornal de um prisioneiro de guerra* (São Paulo: Nacional. 1933). pp. 23-26. 47-48. 124-25; Leôncio Basbaum. *Uma vida em seis tempos: memórias* (São Paulo: Alfa-Omega. 1976). p. 131; and Thomé Amado. interview. Rio de Janeiro. October 9. 1994. The common criminals were sent to Ilha Grande to make room for the influx of São Paulo detainees entering Rio's jails and prisons. Commissioned in 1930. Caneppa was a former sergeant from Rio Grande do Sul who was accused of lacking the slightest human sentiment: a butcher who killed with hunger and cold. [Heron] Herondino Pereira Pinto. *Nos subterraneos do Estado Novo* (Rio de Janeiro: Germinal. 1950). p. 41. He was picked personally by Filinto Müller for the Ilha Grande job. By 1945. Caneppa could include on his résumé the following appointments: chief censor of the press (1932); director of the Ilha Grande correctional facility (1932-1937); warden of the Casa de Correção (1937-1945); director of the Fernando de Noronha penal colony (1942); head of a penal sanitarium (1945); warden of a woman's prison (1945). *Cf.*: Thomé Amado. interview. Rio de Janeiro. September 28. 1994; and Ronald Hilton (ed.). *Who's Who in Latin America*. 3rd ed.. rev. (Stanford: Stanford University Press. 1948). part VI. Brazil. p. 50. Caneppa is pictured here in Photo 8 in a photograph taken on August 25. 1945. Note also above pp. 54-55. 67-69. 89-90 and below p. 162 n.122. A relative of Francisco Chagas. Olimpio Francisco das Chegas. was active with the Rio political police at least until February 1951. By then. this group was called DPS (Divisão de Polícia Política e Social. Division of Political and Social Police). A list of DPS operatives in 1951 is given in the Appendix. Table 1. This accounting is from the only record in the PPARJ materials of every agent in the former capital. In respect to Chagas. "26." and Conrado Niemeyer. see below p. 145 n.23.

50. Pinto. pp. 45. 75.

51. *Cf.*: Goulart, pp. 278-79; and João Bonuma (cited in) [José Gabriel de] Lemos Britto, *Os systemas penitenciarios do Brasil* (Rio de Janeiro: Nacional, 1925), vol. II, p. 207.

52. Lessa, p. 70.

53. Goulart, p. 279.

54. *Cf.: Ibid.*, pp. 279-80; and Origenes Lessa, *Não ha de ser nada: notas de um reporter entre os "Voluntarios de Piratininga,"* 3rd ed. (São Paulo: Nacional, 1933), p. 163.

55. By October 22, 1932, depending on how one counts the prisoners repatriated to Santos, between 2,664 and 2,764 detainees had come home. *Cf.: O Estado de São Paulo,* October 16, 1932, p. 2; October 18, 1932, p. 1; October 19, 1932, p. 1; October 20, 1932, p. 1; and October 22, 1932, p. 1. Gastão Goulart (p. 280) talks about leaving his confine during "the last days of November 1931."

56. *O Estado de São Paulo,* October 25, 1932, p. 2.

57. *Cf.*: Agildo Barata, *Vida de um revolucionário: memórias* (Rio de Janeiro: Melso, 1962), pp. 209-10; and Hélio Silva, *1932, a Guerra Paulista: o cicio de Vargas* (Rio de Janeiro: Civilização Brasileira, 1967), vol. V, pp. 257-64. Barata (*loc. cit.*) states that 200 prisoners were deported to authoritarian Portugal on a single ship. This figure, however, is far from the total number, as other persons were taken for an unspecified period of time from local jails and placed aboard European-bound ships. For three examples, see *O Estado de São Paulo,* December 1, 1932, p. 1; December 3, 1932, p. 1; and December 7, 1932, p. 1.

58. Stanley Hilton, *A Rebelião Vermelha,* pp. 41-42.

59. Brazil, *Relatorio apresentado ao exmo Snr. Interventor Federal, Comandante Ary Parreiras pelo Chefe da Policia, Dr. Joubert Evangelista da Silva sobre a administração policial em 1933* (Nictheroy: Officinas Graphicas da Escola do Trabalho, 1934), p. 105.

60. Plinio Salgado, "Como eu vi a Italia," *Hierarchia,* no. 5, March-April 1932, p. 205.

61. Broxson, pp. 28, 42-55. Note that this was just after the conclusion of the Constitutionalist Civil War, which ended on October 2nd. Salgado evidently played no part in the 1932 conflict (*ibid.*, p. 46). As for the founding of Fascist parties, Plínio was not alone in the first days of October 1932. Sir Oswald Mosley, another admirer of Mussolini, formed the British Union of Fascists on October 1, 1932. One wonders if Salgado knew of this and was influenced by it? It is likewise interesting to observe that one of the members of the *paulista* study group, which called itself A Sociedade de Estudos Políticos, was Lourival Fontes (see above pp. 81-83). *Cf.*: Beloch and Abreu, p. 1309; and Margaret Todaro Williams, "Integralism and the Brazilian Catholic Church," *Hispanic American Historical Review* [hereafter *HAHR*], vol. LIV, no. 3, August 1974, p. 442.

62. *Cf.*: Robert Levine: "Brazil's Jews during the Vargas Era and After," *Luso-Brazilian Review* [hereafter *LBR*], vol. V, no. 1, June 1968, p. 51; *The Vargas Regime,* p. 89; and Beloch and Abreu, pp. 335-36. Code names used by Gustavo included: "Diva," "Demostenes," "Hilario," and "Lemos." Arquivo Público e Histórico do Município do Rio Claro [hereafter ARC], document, [Untitled List of Integralist Code Names for Miscellaneous Entities], n.d., p. 1.

63. *Cf.*: Arquivo Plínio Salgado [hereafter APS]: letter, "Marie Albuquerque to [Plínio Salgado]," July 21, 1939, Pi 39.07.21/2: letter. "Maurillo Mello to [Plínio Salgado]," August 1, 1939, p. 3, FPi 39.08.01/2; and PPARJ, document, (Antonio Emilio Romano to Affonso H. de Miranda Corrêa) "Relatorio sobre a 'Acção Integralista Brasileira.'" 1934, p. 3, integralismo/pasta 1.

64. In Portuguese: *A sinagoga paulista; Brasil, colônia de banqueiros; Comunismo, cristianismo e corporativismo; História secreta do Brasil; Judaísmo, maçonaria e comunismo; Integralismo e catolicismo; O integralismo de Norte a Sul;* "O kike-killer"; *O que o integralist deve saber; O quarto império;* and in Spanish: *Roosevelt es judio.*

65. *Cf.*: PPARJ, newspaper article, "*O Radical,*" August 30, 1942, p. 1, integralismo/pasta 4, cont. I; *Jornal do Brasil,* October 24, 1987, sec. 1, p. 11; and May 28, 1989, sec. B/especial, p. 5.

66. Consider as but one example the protest in official circles at the supposed large number of Jews "without professions or work, probably communists, that the government of Poland is expelling from that country." The commentary went on to identify Brazil as one of the prime destinations, despite Brazilian law, of these deported persons. AN, document, "Ministéro das Relações Exteriores: providências para impedir a entrada no Brasil de grande levas de israelitas expulsos dos seus paises de origem." 1937, p. 1, MJNI-1939, cx. 429. See also above pp. 79-80.

67. Maria Luiza Tucci Carneiro, *O anti-semitismo na era Vargas: fantasmas de uma geração, 1930-1945* (São Paulo: Brasiliense, 1988), p. 115. At one time Barroso went so far as to openly suggested that "concentration camps be established for 'Jewish communists.'" Levine, *The Vargas Regime,* p. 84.

68. For some of the others, the list includes Henry Ford and a host of local Brazilian "intellectuals," *cf.*: Carneiro, pp. 83-97, 373-90, *et passim*; and Levine, "Brazil's Jews during the Vargas Era and After," pp. 50-55, 50n-52n.

69. One of the better descriptions of these "sick-blooded" persons in Portuguese America and colonial Brazil is given in Maria Luiza Tucci Carneiro, *Preconceito racial: Portugal e Brasil-colônia,* 2nd ed. (São Paulo: Brasiliense, 1988), pp. 12, 19, 58-68, *et passim*.

70. *Cf.*: Nancy Leys Stepan, *"The Hour of Eugenics" Race, Gender, and Nation in Latin America* (Ithaca: Cornell University Press, 1991), pp. 47-54; and *Folha de São Paulo,* December 23, 1984, Folhetim, pp. 8-9.

71. PPARJ, photograph, "Fotografias integralistas," n.d., integralismo/pasta 9. See also the photographs in the Integralists' monthly magazine *Anauê!*. For example *cf.*: *Anauê!* (Rio de Janeiro), May 1936, pp. 15-18 [centerfold]; July 1936, p. 27; December 1937, pp. 1-65.

72. João Cândido, hero of the Naval Revolt of 1910, was one example. Edmar Morél, *A Revolta da Chibata* (Rio de Janeiro: Pongetti, 1959), p. 217.

73. *Cf.*: Levine: "Brazil's Jews during the Vargas Era and After," p. 50; and *The Vargas Regime,* pp. 84, 91. The Brazilian Catholic Church and the AIB were often close bedfellows. Both were after more social power, and both were determined to negate a proletarian (i.e., mixed-race) upheaval. Williams, pp. 434-35. Thus while

Sebastião Cardinal Leme, authoritative leader of the Church from 1928 until his death in 1942[,] . . . refused to align the Church to [the] AIB in a formal way, [numerous] members of the Church hierarchy felt no compunctions about cooperating with the movement on an individual basis. During the 1932-1937 period more than twenty bishops and archbishops issued statements supportive of Integralism. Williams, pp. 431, 443.

There were also many simple priests who became active members of the AIB. One of these cases, arguably the most notable, was the Archbishop of Recife, Hélder Pessoa Câmara. *Dom* Hélder, before going on to become one of Brazil's most active adherents of liberationist theology, was, when a modest *padre*, the national secretary-general of the organization. Williams, pp. 444-45. Father Hélder later claimed that his earlier Integralist affiliation was an error of his youth. Beloch and Abreu, p. 551.

74. Just what following the leadership principle meant can be seen in Article 5 of statutes of the movement: "It is prohibited, under penalty of automatic expulsion, for any Integralist to comment on any act of the *Chefe Nacional*, relative to the exercise of his office." PPARJ, document, "1° oficio de registro de titulos e documentos, estructuração do movimento integralista," titulo 2°, art. 5, integralismo/pasta 1.

75. PPARJ, newspaper article, "*A Offensiva*," [1936], p. 1, integralismo/pasta 1, cont. Note that the AIB did not break down the 46 percent who made up the category "Rural and urban workers."

76. Broxson, pp. 82-84.

77. PPARJ, letter, "Plinio Salgado to Getúlio Vargas," January 28, 1938, p. 9, integralismo/pasta 17.

78. PPARJ, newspaper article, "*Diario da Noite*," May 15, 1948, p. 1, integralismo/pasta 19.

79. Broxson, pp. 196-99, 196n-199n.

80. PPARJ, document, "Regulamento da 'Campanha do Ouro,'" December 30, 1936, pp. 1-3, integralismo/pasta 22.

81. PPARJ, document, "Coupons da campanha financeira 'Pelo Bem do Brasil, 1936-1937," integralismo/pasta 13. These 1$000 coupons could be pasted on letters and on the back of envelopes. One *milréi* was worth the same official amount for 1936 and 1937: 20¼¢. *Cf.*: *New York Times*, January 3, 1936, p. 32; and January 1, 1938, p. 27.

82. *Cf.*: Ricardo [Antônio] Silva Seitenfus, "Ideology and Diplomacy: Italian Fascism and Brazil, 1935-38," *HAHR*, vol. LXIV, no. 3, August 1984, pp. 515, 519; Levine, *The Vargas Regime*, pp. 94-96, appendix d; and Broxson, pp. 201-2, 201n-202n. The money was made available in monthly payments that began in late 1936. At first, Vargas was probably unaware of this Italian aid since for several months he had been negotiating with them to arrange for Brazilian commercial support of Italy's war against Ethiopia. *Cf.*: Broxson, *loc. cit.*; and Stanley Hilton, "Brazilian Diplomacy and the Washington-Rio de Janeiro 'Axis' during the World War II Era," *HAHR*, vol. LIX, no. 2, May 1979, pp. 203-4.

83. *Cf.*: Broxson, pp. 254-55, 255n; Levine, *The Vargas Regime*, pp. 96, 213n; and *Correio da Manhã*, September 11, 1937, p. 12. The original insinuations were made in *Correio da Manhã* (September 12, 1937, p. 4), which by this time in Vargas' dictatorship had once again come out as a voice of the opposition.

84. *Cf.*: Levine, *The Vargas Regime*, p. 96; and Loewenstein, pp. 156-66. In addition, see above pp. 35-36. A full-facial view of Müller is provided in Photo 6.

85. USNA, letter, "Sibert to A.C. of S., G-2," May 2, 1941, no. 2703, p. 2, MID 2657-K-128/5. For more information on the 5th column situation in Mato Grosso, *cf.*: PPARJ: document, "Atividades da 'quinta-coluna' no estado de Mato Grosso," n.d., pp. 1-5, alemão/pasta 17; and document, "O quinta colunismo," n.d., alemão/pasta 17.

86. *Cf.*: PPARJ, document, "Atividades particulares do atual interventor de Mato Grosso," n.d., alemão/pasta 17; and Beloch and Abreu, pp. 2347-48.

87. Brazil, Comissão Especial de Inquérito sôbre Atos Delituosos da Ditadura, "Depoimento do João Alves de Mota, "*Diario do Congresso Nacional,* August 28, 1947, p. 5206. See also above pp. 67-69, and below pp. 157 n.96, 179 n.100.

88. Beloch and Abreu, pp. 2342-43.

89. Brazil, "Depoimento do João Alves de Mota," *loc. cit.*

90. Upward of one-quarter of the entire officer corps was reported to have been Integralist members or sympathizers. *Cf.*: Levine, *The Vargas Regime,* pp. 90-91; Broxson, p. 197, 197n; and David Nasser, *A revolução dos covardes: diário decreto de Severo Fournier, reportagens políticas e ordens da censura do ditador* (Rio de Janeiro: O Cruzeiro, 1947), pp. 45-46. Among the top leaders of the army, one of the most noteworthy to identify with the AIB was Góis Monteiro. The

commander of the victorious rebels in 1930 and unquestionably the most influential army figure during the Vargas period, was a stern anti-Communist and great proponent of a disciplined, centralized regime. . . . In 1933 he hailed one of Salgado's books as a "notable work of collective psychology," praising it for its exposé of the "revolutionary confusionism" plaguing the country. . . . According to Salgado, it was Góes Monteiro who suggested to him the color of the Integralist uniform. . . . [Furthermore, in Góis' view of the world] there was a "very simple distinction" between Communism and Integralism. . . . The later was a "Brazilian" movement in pursuit of a "national" objective. Brazil was its "field of action" and "goal of its aspiration." . . . Stanley Hilton, "*Ação Integralist Brasileira*: Fascism in Brazil, 1932-1938," *LBR*, vol. IX, no. 2, Winter 1972, pp. 15-16. See also above pp. 83, 86-87 and below p. 172 n.42.

91. PPARJ, document, "Ação I. Brasileira," n.d., pp. 1-2, integralismo/pasta 1, cont.

92. PPARJ, document, "Companheiros não eleitores," n.d., pp. 1-2, integralismo/pasta 13.

93. *Cf.*: PPARJ: document, "Acção Integralista Brasileira, provincia da Guanabara, D.P.P.," by H.C. Moraes, January 17, 1936, integralismo/pasta 21; document, "S.R. boletim no. 644," September 6, 1944, p. iv, integralismo/pasta 4, cont. II; and photograph, "Desfile de pelotão da Brigada de Choque," n.d., integralismo/pasta 19.

94. Levine, *The Vargas Regime,* pp. 84, 210n. A copy of one of these dossiers is printed in Hélgio Trindade, *Integralismo: o fascismo brasileiro na década de 30* (São Paulo: Difusão Européia do Livro, 1974), plate between pp. 284-85.

95. PPARJ, newspaper article, "*O Jornal*," September 8, 1936, n.p., integralismo/pasta 4.

96. Lygia Prestes, interview, Rio de Janeiro, August 6, 1994. Lygia Prestes, Anita Leocadia Prestes (interview, Rio de Janeiro, August 6, 1994), and Alzira Vargas do Amaral Peixoto (*Jornal do Brasil,* May 8, 1988, sec. 1, p. 8) recount that people would paint chickens green and then let them loose on the street or at some function to display their contempt for Plínio and his followers.

97. PPARJ, newspaper article, "*Jornal do Povo*," October 9, 1934, p. 1, comunismo/livro preto, p. 38. For more on the Guarda Civil (civil guards), see above p. 36.

98. The Comintern existed from 1919 to 1943 for the sole purpose of exporting Soviet-style revolutions to other countries. The two main targets of Comintern efforts were Brazil and China.

99. *Cf.*: Waack, p. 19; Beloch and Abreu, p. 62; Dulles, *Anarchists and Communists*, p. 516; and Levine, *The Vargas Regime*, p. 61.

Chapter 3. "President"

1. *Cf.*: Dulles, *Anarchists and Communists*, p. 518, 518n; and Levine, *The Vargas Regime*, pp. 68, 207n-208n. Prestes reentered Brazil the month following the assembly. Lacerda had a problem with his reputation that was but a few months old. A synopsis is presented above on p. 33. Lacerda would, of course, go on to become one of Brazil's most controversial persons.

2. Beloch and Abreu, *loc. cit.*

3. *Cf.*: Armin Ludwig, *Brazil: A Handbook of Historical Statistics* (Boston: G.K. Hall, 1985), p. 335; *New York Times*, July 3, 1928, p. 29; July 2, 1929, p. 40; July 1, 1930, p. 44; July 1, 1931, p. 40; July 1, 1932, p. 31; July 1, 1933, p. 23; July 3, 1934, p. 33; and July 2, 1935, p. 38.

4. George Wythe, *Industry in Latin America* (New York: Columbia University Press, 1945), p. 154, 154n. These figures combine book and par value. For book value alone, see Carlos von Doellinger, "Política, política econômica e capital estrangeiro no Brasil: as décadas de 30, 40 e 50," *Revista Brasileira de Mercado de Capitais*, vol. III, no. 8, May/August 1977, p. 248.

5. Loewenstein, pp. 337-38.

6. See above pp. 14-15.

7. *Cf.*: Brazil: Ministerio da Agricultura, Industria e Commercio, *Synopse do censo da agricultura: superficie territorial, área e valor dos immoveis ruraes, categoria e nacionalidade dos proprietarios, systema de exploração, população pecuaria, producção agricola* (Rio de Janeiro: Directoria Geral de Estatística, 1922), pp. iii, 8; Instituto Brasileiro de Geografia e Estatística, *Censos econômicos: agrícola, industrial, comercial e dos serviços* (Rio de Janeiro: IBGE, 1950), p. 8; and Instituto Brasileiro de Geografia e Estatística, *Censo demográfico: população e habitação [, 1940]* (Rio de Janeiro: IBGE, 1950), Série Nacional, vol. II, p. 1. The percentage of owners is actually smaller since these figures were computed assuming that there was but one proprietor for each agricultural establishment. Government statistics for 1930 are not available.

8. Rural residency can be deduced from the data found on pp. 14 and 179 n.97

9. *Cf.*: Loewenstein, pp. 343-44; José Nilo Tavares, *Novembro de 1935: meio século depois*, Dario Canale, *et al.* (org.) (Petrópolis: Vozes, 1985), p. 48; *The New Republic* (Washington, D.C.) December 1, 1937, pp. 95-96, 95n; and Samuel Putnam, "Vargas Dictatorship in Brazil," *Science and Society*, vol. V, no. 2, Spring 1941, pp. 102-3. Putnam writes (p. 103) that workers on Henry Ford's 3,700,000-acre parcel of land, known as "Fordlandia," earned a top wage of twelve cents a day, which could only be spent in the company's store. Here too, women and children earned less as a rule, if at

all. Parenthetically, Integralists looked upon these kinds of things as quite natural and even desirable. Agricultural reform was clearly not a concept in the AIB's vocabulary. *Cf.: The New Republic*, December 1, 1937, p. 95; and Levine, "Brazil's Jews during the Vargas Era and After," p. 52.

10. Loewenstein, p. 340.

11. *Ibid.*

12. Edison Carneiro, "Situação do negro no Brasil," *Estudos afro-brasileiros: trabalhos apresentados ao 1° congresso afro-brasileiro reunido no Recife em 1934* (Rio de Janeiro: Ariel, 1935), vol. I, p. 239.

13. *Cf.:* Levine, *The Vargas Regime*, pp. 16-18, 198n; and Ernest Hambloch, *His Majesty the President of Brazil: A Study of Constitutional Brazil* (New York: E.P. Dutton, 1936), pp. 118-19.

14. United Nations, UNESCO, *Progress of Literacy in Various Countries: A Preliminary Statistical Study of Available Census Data since 1900* (Paris: UNESCO, 1953), p. 42.

15. *Cf.:* Henriques, p. 345; and Levine, *The Vargas Regime*, pp. 69, 79.

16. Levine, *The Vargas Regime*, pp. 72-73.

17. Women were not enfranchised until 1933. Vargas, however, found one excuse after another to keep them from voting during his entire first period in Catete. Females cast their initial ballots after he was deposed in 1945. For a United Nations' estimate of the proportion of males and females by race in 1940, who were illiterate and, *ipso facto*, excluded from voting, see above p. 32. Note that the percentages of black men in this category was 75.1 percent of the total number of black men in the population. The figures for black women was 83.0, brown men 66.3, and brown women 75.2 percent, respectively.

18. *Cf.:* PPARJ, document, "D.P.S. S.I.-S.F.P. no. 1240 ref.-prot.-1523/56," March 5, 1956, informações/pasta 16; and Thomé Amado: interviews, Rio de Janeiro, September 28, 1994; October 9, 1994. Thomé Amado was an eyewitness to this murder. The official version, complete with newspaper articles casting doubt on its creditability, can be found in PPARJ, file, "Tobias Warchavsky," prontuário 294. For more on Lacerda's character see chap. 5.

19. PPARJ, periodical article, "*O Preso Proletario*," November 1933, p. 3, comunismo/pasta 4b. Flôres would ally himself with the Nazis in Montevideo later in the decade. PPARJ, letter, "Pedro Aurelio de Góes Monteiro to Chefe de Polícia do Distrito Federal [Filinto Müller]," December 26, 1939, pp. 1-3, militar/pasta 1.

20. *Cf.:* PPARJ: periodical article, "*O Preso Proletario*," November 1933, p. 2; newspaper article, "*Diario de São Paulo*," January 17, 1930, p. 3, militar/pasta 1; newspaper article, "*O Tempo*," March 3, 1931, p. 1, militar/pasta 1; and Antônio Vieira, *Maria Zélia: mártires do monstruoso presídio: Augusto Pinto, João Varlota, Naurício Maciel Mendes e José Constâncio da Costa*, 2nd ed. (São Paulo: Cupolo, 1957), p. 48.

21. Hambloch, p. 121.

22. *Cf.:* Maria Luiza Tucci Carneiro, pp. 338-43; and, Conniff, *Urban Politics in Brazil*, pp. 138-39. For items pertaining to Filinto in this area of race and ethnic intolerance, see above pp. 45, 74-75 and below pp. 152 n.69, 165 n.155.

23. *Diario de Noticias*, March 3, 1935, p. 7. The article from which this quote is taken refers to the general atmosphere as well as to several individuals who disappeared while in police custody. The Bernardes reign of terror began almost as soon as he took office in 1922, but was particularly noticeable after 1924. Clevelandia was a government agricultural concentration camp in the territory of Amapa. The most pivotal victim thrown to his death from the upper floors of the Central Police Station while Bernardes was president was Conrado Niemeyer. This one case was likened by the press to the Dreyfuss affair for its negative impact on public confidence in the justice system. For the most complete accounting to date, see R.S. Rose, *Beyond the Pale of Pity: Key Episodes of Elite Violence in Brazil to 1930* (San Francisco: Austin and Winfield, 1998), pp. 175-80. The U.S. military attaché provided a concise summary of the event in his report back to Washington:

In July, 1925, a prominent merchant was arrested and taken . . . [in] for questioning under a charge of having supplied dynamite to political conspirators. The day following, it was announced that he had committed suicide by leaping from a fourth-story [second-story] window of . . . [the Central Police Station].

Unsatisfied with this version of the tragedy, as soon as martial law was lifted the family and friends of Conrado Borlido Niemeyer secured an investigation. . . .

The hearing was . . . open to the public and the press carried full reports of the proceedings. Convincing evidence was produced that the merchant, defending himself against the torture and beatings commonly employed to wring confessions from suspects, had been thrown from the window by two higher-up police authorities and two police agents. The chief culprit [Francisco Chagas] was later rewarded for his zeal by appointment as a civilian magistrate on the military court which conducts court-martials, and at the time of the investigation was enjoying a tour of Europe at the expense of the Ministry of War. This was out short [*sic*] and he was summoned home.

The results of the hearing reflect decided discredit on the past administration and have completely demoralized in public esteem the former chief of police, Marechal Fontoura. . . . The adroit questioning of the investigators proved . . . [him] to be anything but an accomplished liar and it finally developed that as head of the police department he was a mere figure head and that President Bernardes ran the police department directly from the executive mansion through the intermediary of General Santa Cruz, his military aide. *Cf.*: USNA, letter, "Barclay to G-2," May 21, 1927, no. 732, p. 5, MID 2052-112; and *O Globo* (Rio de Janeiro), May 9, 1927, p. 1.

For more on Francisco Chagas, see above pp. 20, 138 n.49. Likewise, note the case (above pp. 51-52 and below pp. 155 n.85, 156 n.88) nearly one year to the day after the above *Diario de Noticia* story. Finally, see above pp. 7-8 and below p. 156 n.87.

24. *Cf.*: Luís Carlos Prestes, interview, Rio de Janeiro, August 13, 1987; Morais, pp. 144-45; Amado, *A vida de Luís Carlos Prestes*, pp. 110-11, 110n; *Jornal do Commercio*, April 25, 1925, p. 10; *Manchete*, April 12, 1958, p. 75; January 22, 1977, p. 30; Beloch and Abreu, p. 2343; CPDOC, oral history, "Augusto do Amaral Peixoto," 1975, p. 284; and Brazil, *Coleção das leis da República dos Estados Unidos do Brasil de 1933*, vol. I, p. 57, decree 22332, art. 18. For more on the political police, see above pp. 12-13.

25. PPARJ, newspaper article, "*Novos Rumos*," January 24-30, 1964, p. 5, comunismo/ pasta 59. This same accounting was also broadcast on "Pingo Fogo," TV-Tupi, January 3, 1964.

26. For examples, see above pp. 25, 36, 45.

27. *Cf.*: Loewenstein, p. 162n; Nasser, *Falta alguém em Nuremberg*, pp. 32, 92-93; John W.F. Dulles, e-mail, July 27, 1999; CPDOC, oral history, "Alzira Vargas do Amaral Peixoto," 1979, p. 69; Elizabeth Cancelli, *O mundo da violência: a polícia da era Vargas*, 2nd ed. (Brasília: Editora Universidade de Brasília, 1994), pp. 59-60; Leslie Rout Jr. and John Bratzel, *The Shadow War: German Espionage and United States Counterespionage in Latin America during World War II* (Frederick, MD: University Publications of America, 1986), p. 113; *Status*, July 1986, pp. 36-45; PPARJ: document, "D.I.P.," D-31, January 7, 1940, p. 5, administração/pasta 13; document, "D.I.P.," D-31, January 21, 1940, pp. 5-6, administração/pasta 13; document, "D.I.P.," S-1, January 7, 1940, p. 8, administração/pasta 13; and document, "D.I.P.," [S-1], January 21, 1940, p. 8, administração/pasta 13. The $200,000-plus figure was averaged from three editions of the *Jornal do Commercio*: March 1, 1939, p. 9; July 1, 1939, p. 11; and November 1, 1939, p. 10. For more on the *Admiral Graf Spee* crew members, see above p. 94. For a picture of Müller and some of his admirers, see Photo 9.

28. Beloch and Abreu, p. 1744. In addition, see above pp. 41, 66 and below pp. 162 n.130, 162 n.132, 163 n.133.

29. Waack, pp. 41-47. See also above pp. 8, 132 n.51.

30. Waack, pp. 75-76.

31. *Cf.*: *Ibid.*, pp. 99-100; and Yuri Ribeiro, interview, Rio de Janeiro, December 16, 1994; and Waack, *loc.cit.*

32. As to how deep her knowledge of the issues she was fighting for went, Waack (p. 97) states that Olga had read some brochures by Marx, Engels, Lenin, and Stalin but was no theoretical expert. Morais (p. 49) says just the opposite.

33. *Cf.*: Morais, pp. 49-62, 88; Waack, pp. 95, 99; Beloch and Abreu, pp. 2817-18; Luís Carlos Prestes, letter, November 19, 1987; PPARJ, file, "Maria Prestes, Olga Benario," prontuário 1675, pp. 7, 7a; and Cecil Borer: interviews, Rio de Janeiro, May 13, 1998; May 28, 1998.

34. Elise Berger's maiden name was Saborowski; hence her nickname. *Cf.*: Joffily, *Harry Berger*, p. 21; and Maria Werneck, *Sala 4: primeira prisão política feminina* (Rio de Janeiro: CESAC, 1988), p. 21. Her U.S. passport was in issued to a real American, Machla Lenczycki. USNA, microfilm, "Gibson to Secretary of State," December 28, 1935, M1472/8.

35. *Cf.*: Superior Tribunal Militar [hereafter STM], deposition, "Depoimento de Rodolpho Ghioldi," February 11, 1936, apelação 4899, série a, vol. II, p. 348; PPARJ: file, "Rodolfo Ghioldi," prontuário 5878, n.p.; and newspaper article, *A Offensiva*, March 21, 1936, p. 1 [in: PPARJ, file "Carmen Alfaza (*sic*) Ghioldi," prontuário 21409, n.p.].

36. *Cf.*: РЦХИДНИ, telegram, фонд 495, опись 184, дело 60, лист 70; USNA, microfilm, "Gibson to Secretary of State," January 15, 1936, M1472/8; PPARJ, file, "Arthur Ernst Ewert ou Harry Berger," prontuário 1721, p. 17; Rudolf de Graaf, letter, June 30, 1994; Ernst Krüger, interview, Rio de Janeiro, October 17, 1994; Morais, pp. 67-68; Werneck, p. 69; Stanley Hilton, *A Rebeliao Vermelha*, pp. 53, 196n; *New Masses*

(Washington D.C.), March 24, 1936, p. 15; Marly de Almeida Gomes Vianna, "Revolucionários de 1935: sonho e realidade," PhD thesis, Faculdade de Filosofia, Letras e Ciências Humanas, Universidade de São Paulo, 1990, vol. I, p. xxii; and Waack, pp. 83, 90-92, 105-7, 154-56, 173-74, 206, 265, 269, 311, 365n, 381. Various authors have misspelled Marcus Jungmann's name as "Marcos Youbman" or some version thereof. Waack consistently spells Barron's last name with one "r." The correct spelling is Barron. Harold E. Barron, interview, Hayward, CA, January 15, 1994. Harold Barron is Victor's brother. Their adopted father was Clifton Barron. PPARJ, file, "Victor Allen Barron," prontuário 1447, p. 1. Some of the aliases used by the inner circle of radicals were: **Victor Allen Barron**: James Martin and "Raymond." **Olga Benário**: Ana Braum de Revidor, Eva Krüger, Frida Leuschner, Frieda Wolff Behrend [or Behrendt], Maria Meirelles, Maria Prestes, Maria Bergner Vilar, Maria Bergner Prestes, Olga Sinek, Olga Vilar, Olga Meirelles, Olga Gutmann Benario, Olga Benário Prestes, Olga Berger, Yvonne Vilar, and "Zarkovich." **Johann de Graaf**: "August," Franz Guber, "Iedko," "Jonny," "Matern," "Pedro," "Professor," "Richard," Richard M. Walter, and "Walter." **Arthur Ewert**: "Albert," Arthur Korner, Arthur Braun, "Bento," "Blom," "Castro," Georg Keller, Geu Pilnick, Harry Berger, "Negro," and Ulrich Dach. **Elise Ewert**: Annie Bancourt, "Braun," "Clara," "Josef," Machla Berger, Machla Leczycki, and "Sabo." **Rodolfo Ghioldi**: "Altobelli," "Índio" ("Indian"), Luciano Busteros, Luciano Busteros Orobengos, Juan Oliviera, and "Quiroga." **Helena Krüger**: Helena Gruber (in addition to the names given in the text). **Amelto Locatelli**: "Bruno," Ezio Adolphe Hala, Jean Savell, and "Walter." **Luís Carlos Prestes**: "A," Almeida Castro, "Antônio," Antônio Almeida, Ary Bhering de Ribeiro Pontes, "Fernandes," "Fernando," "G," "Ga," "Garoto" (or "Boy"), "Léa," "Léo," Luís Carlos Fernandes, "Maria," Pontes Ribeiro, and "S." **Pavel Stuchevski**: Christos Thomas Sacarney, Grec Christos Thomas Sacarmey, "E," "Eça," "Eme," "L," Leon Jules Vallée, and "René." *Cf.*: PPARJ: file, "Luiz Carlos Prestes," prontuário 22251, n.p.; "Maria Prestes, Olga Benario," anotações diversas, p. 1; "Arthur Ernst Ewert ou Harry Berger," p. 7; file, "Auguste Elise Ewert," prontuário 21237, p. 16; "Rodolfo Ghioldi," informação 4261-s/4; РЦХИДНИ: telegram, фонд 495, опись 184, дело 6, лист 9; file, "Де Граф," фонд 495, опись 205, дело 6385, лист 35; STM: document, "Copias authenticas referentes ao accusado Luiz Carlos Prestes," n.d., apelação 4899, série a, vol. II, p. 375; document, "Leon Jules Vallée," May 7, 1937, apelação 4899, série a, vol. VI, p. 1280; Vianna: vol. I, pp. xx-xxiv; *Revolucionários de 35: sonho e realidade* (São Paulo: Companhia das Letras, 1992), pp. 12-14; Waack, pp. 373-80; and Morais, pp. 131, 133, 308-9. Additional code names, some of which the police never identified, are given in AN, letter, "Eurico Bellens Porto to chefatura de policia," May 4, 1936, Tribunal de Segurança Nacional [hereafter TSN] processo 1381, vol. II/312. For more on Antônio Bonfim aliases, see below p. 148 n39.

37. PPARJ, file, "Franz Gruber ou Jonny de Graaf," prontuário 33989, pp. 21-27. There are no less than six schools of thought as to just whom Johnny, and perhaps Helena, worked for if anyone. The first position (*cf.*: Morais, p. 113, unnumbered plate between pp. 170-71: "Brazilian Embassy, London, no. 1556, January 17, 1940"; Aspásia Camargo, *et al.*, *O golpe silencioso: as origens da república corporativa* [Rio de Janeiro: Rio Fundo, 1989], p. 54; Robert Moss, *Carnival of Spies* [New York: Simon and Schuster, 1987], *passim*; Michael Smith, *Foley: The Spy who Saved 10,000 Jews*

[London: Hodder and Stoughton, 1999], pp. 51-63; Stanley Hilton, *A Rebelião Vermelha*, pp. 65-66; and Dulles, *Brazilian Communism*, p. 6) holds that Johnny worked solely for British Intelligence, who in turn retransmitted material to Müller. Camargo, however, does not mention Helena and shortens Johnny's cover to "Paul Gruber." Dulles qualifies Hilton's thesis by indicating that Gruber "cooperated with the Rio police," which could mean that he did so directly. Vianna (*Revolucionários de 35*, p. 351n) agrees that Gruber was a working for the English; the only question in her mind is when he started to do so: before or after the events of November 1935? A second opinion (*cf.*: Leôncio Basbaum, *História sincera da República: de 1930 a 1960*, 4th ed. [São Paulo: Alfa-Omega, 1976], vol. III, pp. 80-81; and Levine, *The Vargas Regime*, pp. 121, 218n-219n) maintains that Gruber, a former member of the German Communist Party, was employed by the Gestapo, and after arriving in Brazil collaborated immediately with the Brazilian government and with Müller. The third hypothesis (Tavares, p. 73) combines the above two, and contends that he worked for the British, the Germans, and the Brazilians. Fourth, there are the assertions that de Graaf had large amounts of money in his possession when he was arrested (Carlos Lacerda, *Depoimento* [Rio de Janeiro: Nova Fronteira, 1977], p. 53n), that he received about $40,000 from American sources (Morais, unnumbered plates between pp. 170-71: "U.S. Embassy, Rio de Janeiro, no. 2206, December 12, 1939"), and that even the FBI was involved in some of the above events (Basbaum, *História sincera da República*, p. 77). Fifth, there is the conclusion by Paulo Sérgio Pinheiro (*Estratégias da ilusão: a revolução mundial e o Brasil, 1922-1935* [São Paulo: Companhia das Letras, 1991], pp. 306-7) that de Graaf was not a double agent. Finally, the view that Johnny was not a double agent is expanded by Waack (pp. 144-46, 258, 277, 299, 307-8, 326, 366n, 368n) to include his wife. In Waack's view the couple were not working for anyone but Moscow.

38. Cecil Borer: interviews, Rio de Janeiro, May 13, 1998, May 28, 1998. Borer was uncertain if these agents were Americans or English since the contact with the authorities was through a police colleague. See above in this regard, p. 50 and below p. 154 n.82. If the agents were in fact English, observe the obvious candidate(s) above on pp. 38-39, 42.

39. *Cf.*: Waack, pp. 119-41; Levine, *The Vargas Regime*, p. 100; Henriques, pp. 356-57; and Dulles, *Anarchists and Communists*, pp. 530-31. One of the convincers back in the USSR was perhaps not all that inept. Antônio Bonfim was one of the key people present. Bonfim also used the alias of Adalberto de Andrade Fernandes. Dulles, *Anarchists and Communists, loc cit.* He was known to his leftist colleagues by the code names "Américo," "Miranda," "Queiroz," and "Tavares." Miranda was the most common. Vianna, "Revolucionários de 1935," vol. I, pp. xx, xxii-xxiv.

40. *A Manhã* (Rio de Janeiro), July 6, 1935, p. 1. *A Manhã* was the voice of the ANL.

41. *Ibid.*, p. 2.

42. *Ibid.*

43. *Ibid.*

44. *Ibid.*

45. See also above pp. 36, 66 and below pp. 162 n.130, 162 n.132, 163 n.133. Prestes stated in a letter to Miguel Costa that October that "the pretext employed by the government wasn't the July 5th manifesto; but a secret document put together by the

[Secret] Intelligence Service and manipulated by Ráo and Müller." PPARJ, letter, "[Luís Carlos Prestes] to Miguel Costa," October 10, 1935, comunismo/pasta 9.

46. *Cf.*: Henriques, pp. 357-59, 367-68; and Levine, *The Vargas Regime*, p. 101.

47. Dulles, *Vargas of Brazil*, p. 148.

48. *Cf.*: Arquivo Histórico do Itamarati: document, "Regis de Oliveira to Oswaldo Aranha," December 20, 1939, no. 477; telegram, "Souza Leão to Itamarati," January 9, 1940; and РЦХИДНИ, telegram, "Commission Politique to Куда, Rio de Janeiro," July 31, 1935, фонд 495, опись 184, дело 54, листов 17-18.

49. *Cf.*: João Mederios Filho: *Meu depoimento* (Natal: Oficial, 1937), pp. 47-48; *82 horas de subversão: Intentona Comunista de 1935 no Rio Grande do Norte* (Natal: [no publisher given], 1980), pp. 48-49, 187-91; and Basbaum, *História sincera da República*, pp. 81-82. Waack (p. 217) suggests that Vargas may well have started things in the Northeast by way of a "provocation."

50. *Cf.*: Dulles, *Vargas of Brazil*, pp. 148-49; Beloch and Abreu, p. 2307; Tavares, pp. 72-73; *Leia*, November 1985, p. 21; *Veja*, September 18, 1991, p. 67; and Vianna, "Revolucionários de 1935," vol. II, pp. 439-40.

51. *Cf.*: Light, personnel file, "Alfred Hutt," folio 2643, p. 1; PPARJ: document, "Intelligence Service," "Serviço secréto inglês," December 17, 1940, p. 1, inglês/pasta 3; "Franz Gruber ou Jonny de Graaf," pp. 24-25; and Gordon Scott, interview, Victoria, January 8, 1996.

52. PPARJ, catalogue, "Álbum do Delegacia Especial de Seguança Politica e Social," 1940, n.p., Rio Grande do Norte. Although things were put down in short order, Sodré (p. 256) points out that the government's troops were insufficient in Pernambuco and Rio Grande do Norte, and had to be helped out to a large degree by the forces of local *fazendeiros*. Loyalists also managed to swing some artillery into action along with a number of aircraft that flew over the insurgent's positions dropping bombs. PPARJ, document, "A revolução communista no Brasil e os commentarios da 'internacional communista," n.d., comunismo/pasta 9.

53. One of the most riveting hour-by-hour accounts of the revolt in Rio de Janeiro from the vantage point of the insurgents is contained in Waack (pp. 204-39).

54. *Cf.*: Faria and Barros, p. 38; Beloch and Abreu, p. 2932; Brandi, p. 102; and Dulles, *Vargas of Brazil*, pp. 150, 152.

55. Defined as situational and transitory muscle providers, examples include the police, guards, bodyguards, and all types of bullies in the employ of some higher authority. Note that the Brazilian lower classes (including trustworthy nonwhites) were and are easily fitted into the fleeting roles of subelites.

56. As one illustration, anyone in another country who signed and mailed Vargas a preprinted postcard demanding the release of the November 1935 revolutionaries had their names placed on the huge DESPS' list of the politically suspect.

57. These committees were the brainchild of Vicente Ráo. Correia was reputed to be extremely zealous in carrying out his duties. He often ignored the rights of the innocent in order to apprehend rebel suspects. *Cf.*: Beloch and Abreu, pp. 934, 2889; and Stanley Hilton, *A Rebelião Vermelha*, p. 98. The second commission to fight communism was set up on October 7, 1937. Its proposals got lost in the events taking place one month later, the *Estado Novo*, and were never enacted. They would have included the establish-

ment of forced-labor agricultural colonies and concentration camps for reeducating civilians and families from their communist ways (see also above pp. 20, 25-26, 67-69 and below p. 163 n.137). Beloch and Abreu, p. 851. As far back as the era of Artur Bernardes, and perhaps even dating from the administration of Epitácio Pessoa (*O Jornal*, January 3, 1928, p. 6), succeeding administrations used concentration camps to stifle political opponents (for the Bernardes connection, see above pp. 35, 145 n.23). In practice, however, all kinds of persons, including common criminals, women, and children were sent to such places.

58. PPARJ, miscellaneous documents, "Comissão Nacional de Repressão ao Comunismo," 1936, administração/ pasta 14.

59. Tavares, p. 47. A report by the U.S. military intelligence community (United States, War Department, "Survey of the Rio de Janeiro Region of Brazil," paper prepared under the direction of the chief of staff by the Military Intelligence Service, General Staff, August 6, 1942, vol. I, p. 143) published the month after Müller's dismissal, indicated that "the police force is considered the weakest element in the public service. Its members, untrained and underpaid, are notorious for their low morale and their proclivity to solicit and accept bribes. . . . Any attempt to cut down on their perquisites merely causes them to resign." In addition to being corrupt, when he was at his peak the individuals working for Müller could be ruthless, so much so, one journalist wrote (*Manchete*, December 15, 1979, p. 46), that "no police force exceeded those of Vargas, not even the ones of Himmler." According to another commentary (*The New Republic*, February 9, 1938, p. 11), these attributes meant that "in Brazil no one has any security. A simple telephone denunciation . . . may be enough to cause an arrest in the middle of the night. . . . [And] anyone who is arrested, if he has no great influence and is thought to be dangerous, may be killed."

60. *Cf.*: *International Press Correspondence*, May 16, 1936, p. 632; and PPARJ, document, "Ao povo e ás classes armadas do Brasil," November 27, 1936, comunismo/pasta 20. Occasional killings went on for months. Tactics were used that would be made egregious in the 1960s and 1970s by *paulistano* death-squad leader Sérgio Fleury (*cf.*: *Jornal do Brasil*, October 24, 1973, sec. 1, p. 30; and *Isto É* [São Paulo], March 1, 1978, p. 7). Victims were told that they were to be eliminated then, some time later, taken from their cells and shot full of holes in the hills. Arms of different caliber were the murder weapons. The police habitually blamed the communists for these executions (see above pp. 33, 57 and below p. 158 n.102). The above passage from the *International Press Correspondence*, a news summary and commentary put out by the Comintern, was written by Richard Freeman, who was the secretary to two upper-class English women, Christine Hastings and Mariam Cameron Campbell. Lady Hastings was already a well-known leftist if only through the portrait of her painted by Frida Kahlo in 1931. The husbands of both women were members of the House of Commons. The trio traveled to Rio in the hopes of gathering enough material to write a book. Once arriving, Hastings and Campbell declared at dockside that the accusations of torture being used against political prisoners–particularly foreign political prisoners–cried out to be investigated. The trio was met at their hotel by Müller and a group of policemen. Filinto suspected that Moscow was behind the visit. He thus had the three detained. Later, at the intercession of the English ambassador, they were freed

but then reconfined and told in no uncertain terms to be on the next boat out of the country. During the ordeal, Freeman was held in jail together with a number of recently apprehended and tortured political prisoners. Morais, p. 166. His harrowing story is written off by Hilton (*A Rebelião Vermelha*, pp. 144-48) as a mere propaganda effort in a Soviet attempt to win freedom for Prestes, Ewert, and the rest of their colleagues. Pictures of the little group leaving Brazil on the liner *Arlanza* can be found in *O Imparcial*, March 10, 1938, p. 2. Returning home, Lord Hastings filed a letter to the editors of *The Manchester Guardian* (March 27, 1936, p. 22), which in part caused an arrogant denial from José Joaquim Muniz de Aragão, Brazil's ambassador to the Court of St. James (*The Times* [London], July 7, 1936, p. 12). There followed rebuttals from Lord Hastings (*The Times*, July 10, 1936, p. 12), together with one from Harry Berger's sister, Minna Ewert (*The Times*, July 18, 1936, p. 8). This was but part of what prompted the Brazilian ambassador to inform his superiors that he had received "innumerable letters from members of Parliament and other important persons insisting in the rumors that our police were mistreating a certain Arthur Ewert, ex-member of the Reichstag, and his wife." Morais, *loc. cit.*

61. Morais, p. 175. Morais took this citation from the police statement issued through Müller's office on March 25, 1936. That the chief probably understated his statistics is apparent from his overstatement of the truth when concluding his remarks. "*All* of the persons arrested were duly heard by the Federal Judge under terms of Article 175, paragraph 3, of the Federal Constitution." USNA, microfilm, "Gibson to Secretary of State," March 25, 1936, M1472/8 (italics added). Prestes observed that the large number of military personnel among the insurgents resulted from the fact that it was easier to recruit within the armed forces than at the factory in those days. Luís Carlos Prestes, interview, Rio de Janeiro, August 13, 1987. Data by Vianna ("Revolucionários de 1935," vol. II, pp. 489, 543, 620-21) puts Prestes' statement into perspective. The three major centers of the uprising had the following percentages of workers and military among the rebels:

	Workers	Military[a]
Natal	27.0	45.0
Recife	25.0	52.5
Rio de Janeiro	9.0	65.0
a=includes police		

62. Levine (*The Vargas Regime*, p. 130) remarks as follows: "The domestic communist press claimed that 20,000 Brazilians had been imprisoned . . . [while] the French communist journal, *L'Humanité*, offered the figure of 17,000. In October 1937, the New York *Times* [sic] claimed that Filinto Müller had acknowledged 7,000 arrests by federal authorities, not counting those carried out on state and local levels." To these accounts, one reporter (Pinto, p. 62) who was actually imprisoned himself, and therefore able to see and hear things from the inside out, puts the total number of apprehensions at more than 35,000 by the end of 1936. The figure of 30,000 was given in a letter by leftists archived in Moscow. РЦХИДНИ, general file, "Бразилия," letter, "Frederic to Fernando Morales," December 4, 1936, фонд 495, опись 29, дело 98, лист 18.

63. *New York Times*, September 16, 1936, p. 14. To give added impact to the this article, the news dispatch sent from Rio de Janeiro stated that the leader of Caldeirão, Zé Lourenço, practiced polygamy.

64. A religiously active lay person who has made vows of chastity, and who has no profession. *Beatos* or *beatas* (male or female versions) live off of charity. Xavier de Oliveira, *Beatos e cangaceiros* (Rio de Janeiro: Revista dos Tribunais, 1920), p. 39.

65. *Cf.*: João Oliveira, interview, Juazeiro do Norte, May 11, 1993; Fátima Menezes, interview, Juazeiro do Norte, May 12, 1993; Generosa Alencar, interview, Juazeiro do Norte, May 13, 1993; Daniel Walker Almeida Marques, interview, Juazeiro do Norte, May 13, 1993; Rui Facó: *Cangaceiros e fanáticos: gênese e lutas* (Rio de Janeiro: Civilização Brasileira, 1963), pp. 200-210; *Cangaceiros e fanáticos: gênese e lutas*, 2nd ed. (Rio de Janeiro: Civilização Brasileira, 1965), pp. 200-212; and Abelardo Montenegro, *História do fanatismo religioso no Ceará* (n.p.: Fortaleza, 1959), pp. 59-65. Note the pictures of some of the people from Caldeirão facing pages 129 and 144 in Montenegro. The fact that they appear to be sufficiently fed, with more than rags on their backs, suggests that the communal organization at Caldeirão worked. Another source puts the number of killed at 150 *sertanejos*. The dead were said to have left sixty orphans. PPARJ, newspaper article, *"Grade,"* August 4, 1938, p. 2, comunismo/pasta 4. *Grade* was an ornate, handwritten newspaper was put out by the by the Orgão dos Nacional Libertadores presos na Casa de Detenção, or the Organ of the ANL Prisoners in the Casa de Detenção. The paper appears to have been edited by Eduardo Ribeiro Xavier. Someone from the political police in Rio wrote his name on the front page of every edition.

66. Levine, *The Vargas Regime*, pp. 130, 221n.

67. *Cf.*: *Ibid.*, p. 221n; Maria Luiza Tucci Carneiro, p. 461; and Amado, *A vida de Luís Carlos Prestes*, p. 271. Although there are several spellings of his middle name (Strümbling, Strubing, and Strübbling have all been cited. [*Cf.*: Morais, p. 312, Beloch and Abreu, p. 2342; and CPDOC, "Alzira Vargas do Amaral Peixoto," *loc. cit.*]), Müller never used it. Alzira Vargas do Amaral Peixoto suggests (*loc. cit.*) that perhaps this was because it was of Jewish origin. If such were the case, Filinto surely had a problem rationalizing himself to his behavior in respect to Jews. The chief of police was one of several key advisors close to Vargas who hated Jews. Besides the other ways he displayed this, in February 1938 he sent a memorandum to another anti-Semite, Minister of Justice Francisco Campos. The purpose of the communication was to inform Campos of the fact that Jews, some of whom Müller thought to be communists, were fleeing Central Europe and illegally entering Brazil. After Jews, Filinto felt that Brazil was receiving too many "Japanese, Chinese, and the trash of the white race." According to the chief, the solution was to repatriate "the parasites as well as the extremists among us." Maria Luiza Tucci Carneiro, pp. 148, 338-43, 420.

68. *Cf.*: Light, "Alfred Hutt," *loc. cit.*; and PPARJ, "Franz Gruber ou Jonny de Graaf," pp. 24-25. For the police go-between, see above p. 50 and below p. 154 n.82.

69. *Cf.*: PPARJ, "Franz Gruber ou Jonny de Graaf," p. 21; Waack, pp. 252-53; and Morais, p. 108.

70. Brazil's political police worked intermittently with the sister organizations of several different countries ever since being created in 1907. Waldecy Catharina

Magalhães Pederia, interview, Niterói, October 26, 1994. The important point, however, is to what degree they worked with any given one of them at any given time.

71. *Cf.*: Abguar Bastos, *Prestes e a revolução social*, 2nd ed. (São Paulo: HUCITEC, 1986), p. 289; Cancelli, pp. 88-91; Morais, pp. 110, 117-19, 126-27; Nasser, *Falta alguém em Nuremberg*, pp. 115-19; Putnam, p. 101; Stanley Hilton: *Brazil and the Soviet Challenge, 1917-1947* (Austin: University of Texas Press, 1991), pp. 118-20; e-mail, April 6, 2000; William Waack, telephone interview, Rio de Janeiro/Berlin, May 29, 1994; Ricardo Antônio Silva Seitenfus, *O Brasil de Getúlio Vargas e a formação dos blocos, 1930-1942: o processo do envolvimento brasileiro na II Guerra Mundial* (São Paulo: Nacional, 1985), pp. 86-90, 86n-90n; Paulo Duarte, *Prisão, exílio, luta . . .* (Rio de Janeiro: Zelio Valverde, 1946), p. 51; and Beloch and Abreu, p. 2344. Some of this material is reported erroneously by Beloch and Abreu (*loc. cit.*). For more on Muniz de Aragão, see above p. 150 n.60. For the American link, see above pp. 15, 39, 87, 136 n.20, 148 n.38. Miranda Corrêia and Francisco Julien can be seen in Photo 11.

72. Busy working at his desk, Emílio Romano is presented here in Photo 10. Romano later denied that "Harry Berger had suffered any kind of torture or moral abuse by components of the Polícia Especial." PPARJ, "Arthur Ernst Ewert ou Harry Berger," p. 39. See above in this regard pp. 72-73 and below p. 164 nn.148-50. For more on Emílio Romano, see above p. 59 and below p. 159 n.113.

73. *Cf.*: USNA, document, "Communist Activities in Brazil," March 19, 1936, p. 1, MID 2657-K-70/28; Morais, pp. 118-19, 122-29, 137; PPARJ: "Auguste Elise Ewert," p. 9; periodical article, "*Revista Proletaria*," August 1938, p. 6, comunismo/pasta 4e; Waack, *Camaradas*, pp. 252-61; Thomé Amado, interview, Rio de Janeiro, August 21, 1994; Amado, *A vida de Luís Carlos Prestes*, pp. 266-67; *Jornal do Brasil*, November 1, 1987, sec. B/especial, p. 9; July 24, 1988, sec. 1, p. 8; *The Times*, July 18, 1936, p. 8; Henriques, pp. 400-401; Levine, *The Vargas Regime*, p. 127; Nasser: *Falta alguém em Nuremberg*, pp. 72-73; *A revolução dos covardes*, p. 157; and Werneck, p. 69.

74. *A Noite*, January 7, 1936, final ed., p. 2.

75. *Cf.*: *O Globo*, January 6, 1936, p. 1; and January 7, 1936, p. 1. Formally under the control of Roberto Marinho since 1931, *O Globo* was often a staunch supporter of Vargas' policies. For more on Marinho, see above p. 102.

76. PPARJ, "Arthur Ernst Ewert ou Harry Berger," p. 1. Arthur's father died in Potsdam in 1917. His mother, Emilie Ewert, nee Markward or Marquard, passed away in Berlin in 1926. Ulrich [no first name given]. [Stiftung Archiv der Parteien und Massenorganisationen der DDR im Bundesarchiv], letter, October 31, 1996.

77. See above pp. 60, 90, for more on the "Mustard Plug."

78. *Cf.*: РЦХИДНИ, telegram, "René [Stuchevski] to [Moscow]," December 28, 1935, фонд 495, опись 184, дело 6, лист 35; Cecil Borer, interview, Rio de Janeiro, May 13, 1998; R.S. Rose and Gordon Scott, "Johnny," prepublication manuscript, p. 248; AN: document, "Sentença," TSN processo 1381, vol. III/478; document, "Tribunal de Segurança Nacional," TSN processo 1381/1940, cx. 10565, vol. II/278, 285-86; document, "Promptuario No. 42," TSN processo 1381, vol. I/42; letter, "Antonio Maciel Bomfim to Luiz Copelo Calonio," April 19, 1940, TSN processo 1381, vol. I/apelação 639/22-24; STM, document, "Pelo accusado: Leon Jules Vallée," April 15, 1937, apelação 4899, série a, vol. IV, p. 940 [reverse side]; PPARJ: "Ao povo e ás classes

armadas do Brasil"; letter, "Seraphim Braga, chefe da S-2 to chefe da S/4," June 10, 1938, p. 2, administração/pasta 17; Beloch and Abreu, p. 935; Dulles, *Brazilian Communism*, p. 9; Waack, *Camaradas*, pp. 283, 286-87; Morais, pp. 133, 137-39; Tavares, p. 73; and Carlos Lacerda, pp. 45-46, 52n. Basbaum (*Uma vida em seis tempos*, pp. 138-39) surmised back in 1932 that Bonfim was a police spy when he arrived on Ilha Grande as a prisoner. Prestes came to feel that Bonfim helped his 1936 captors only on learning that Elza Fernandes had been executed (see above p. 75 and below p. 165 n.159). For more on Serafim Braga (he is pictured in Photos 7 and 11), see above pp. 58-59. Elza Fernandes went by the alias of "Garota" (or "Girl"). Her first name was really Elvira, but her second and last names have various spellings: Capello Colon, Copello Calonio, Cupello Calonio, Cupelo Calonio, Cupelo Coloni, and Cupelo Colônio. *Cf.*: РЦХИДНИ, telegram, фонд 495, опись 17, дело 157, лист 2; AN: "Sentença," vol. III/353; "Tribunal de Segurança Nacional," cx. 10565, vol. II/278; deposition, "Antonio Maciel Bomfim," TSN processo 1381, vol. II/353; PPARJ, letter, "Hugo Auler to Capitão Dr. Delegado Especial de Segurança Política e Social," May 27, 1940, no. 94, p. 1, comunismo/pasta 13; and Morais, p. 120.

79. There is some confusion as to the dates on which Ghioldi and his wife were apprehended and arrested. Morais (p. 132) says they were seized in the dawn of January 23, 1936. Waack (p. 286) places the capture in the A.M. hours of Monday, January 21st, a date which he obtained from the Comintern materials at РЦХИДНИ in Moscow. Police procedure (see above p. 52 and below p. 155 n.85) was such that suspects were placed in custody before being charged. Thus, the date of January 25th mentioned in Dulles (*Brazilian Communism*, p. 9) as well as in Ghioldi's DESPS file (PPARJ: "Rodolfo Ghioldi," n.p.; and "Carmen Alfaza Ghioldi," n.p.) is probably the day on which the pair were formally indicted. As the date in Morais is based on an interview of Ghioldi by Fernando Morais in Buenos Aires before Ghioldi's death (*Jornal do Brasil*, October 13, 1985, sec. B/especial, p. 12.), it is deemed to be the most reliable accounting and is the date used here, pending additional research.

80. *Cf.*: PPARJ, "Carmen Alfaza Ghioldi," pp. 3[b]-4[a], Dulles, *Brazilian Communism*, pp. 9-10; Cecil Borer, interview, Rio de Janeiro, May 13, 1998; Anita Leocadia Prestes, interview, Rio de Janeiro, August 6, 1994; Luís Carlos Prestes, interview, Rio de Janeiro, August 13, 1987; Lygia Prestes, interview, Rio de Janeiro, August 6, 1994; Jacob Gorender, telephone interview, Rio de Janeiro/São Paulo, July 12, 1993; Fernando Morais: telephone interview, Rio de Janeiro/São Paulo, July 1, 1993; *Olga*, pp. 132-33, 137-39, 189-90; Vianna, "Revolucionários de 1935," vol. II, pp. 664-68; Waack, *Camaradas*, pp. 281-82, 285, 290; *Jornal do Brasil*, October 13, 1985, sec. B/especial, p. 12; Beloch and Abreu, p. 1461; and Brazil, Policia Civil do Districto Federal, *A insurreição de 27 de novembro: relatorio do Delegado Eurico Bellens Porto* (Rio de Janeiro: Nacional, 1936), p. 52. The revelation that Ghioldi was not tortured was related by him to Fernando Morais in Buenos Aires in 1985. *Jornal do Brasil*, October 13, 1985, sec. B/especial, p. 12.

81. Waack, *Camaradas*, pp. 285, 287-88.

82. *Cf.*: PPARJ, document, "Inteligence [*sic*] Service," S.S.I. boletim no. 14, January 15, 1941, p. vi, inglês/pasta 3; and Cecil Borer, interview, Rio de Janeiro, May 28, 1998.

Julien was also the contact with the Americans. Cecil Borer, interview, Rio de Janeiro, May 28, 1998.

83. *Cf.*: РЦХИДНИ, telegram, фонд 495, опись 184, дело 4, лист 30; Waack, *Camaradas*, pp. 176, 180, 262, 265, 269. 281-82, 286-90, 297-99; Brazil, Policia Civil do Districto Federal, *A Insurreição de 27 de Novembro*, p. 50; Morais, *Olga*, p. 133; Dulles, *Brazilian Communism*, pp. 10, 15-16; and Beloch and Abreu, p. 3430.

84. Morais, *Olga*, pp. 134-36, 163-65. See also the comments in the CPUSA's, *Daily Worker* (New York), May 13, 1936, pp. 2, 6.

85. *Cf.*: PPARJ: document, "Ao povo brasileiro," [1936?], p. 1, comunismo/pasta 17; "Victor Allen Barron," n.p.; *O Estado de São Paulo*, March 6, 1936, p. 1; Henriques, p. 404; and Amado, *A vida de Luís Carlos Prestes*, p. 269. The political police file lists Barron's date of arrest as February 22, 1936. If this was some kind of misprint or done for some other reason is not known. It was police practice, however, to take suspects in for questioning without charging them. In this regard see also above pp. 52, 154 n.79. If this is what happened to Barron, he would have been in custody for twenty-six days before formally being indicted. Nasser (*Falta alguém em Nuremberg*, p. 50) claims that insulin injections–designed to produce hypoglycemia, and sociability–killed the American. Luís Carlos Prestes (interview, Rio de Janeiro, August 13, 1987) stated that Barron did not appear to be in good health when he entered the country. He evidently had severe stomach problems that were not connected to a change of cultures. Harold Edward Barron, Victor's brother, mentioned that he had heard that Victor had consumption (usually tuberculosis) before he left New York, although he could not be sure. Curiously, however, stomach problems run in the family. Victor, Harold, and their mother Edna Hill all had or have stomach ailments apparently of varying intensities. Harold Barron, interview, Hayward, CA, January 15, 1994. A third accounting (Waack, *Camaradas*, p. 300) asserts that Victor had tuberculosis and syphilis when he landed in Rio. The shots were not insulin but alcohol; and they were injected into Barron's tongue. This, however, seems a very difficult kind of torture to administer. If alcohol was used, his mouth was probably forced open and it was poured in. A letter in the Barron file from an American attorney in Rio at the time agrees with this last supposition. PPARJ, file, "Victor Allen Barron," letter, "Joseph Brodsky to (unknown)," n.d., pp. 2-3. According to an assistant at the autopsy who was friendly with the PCB, Barron's stomach contained large amounts of alcohol; and there were signs that the police tried to wash it out at the last moment. Amado (*A vida de Luís Carlos Prestes, loc. cit.*) adds another twist by writing that the police eventually became frustrated with the efforts of the physician and ended up beating Barron to death. Check as well, Fernando Morais' remarks (*Olga*, pp. 154, 162-63) on the coroner's evaluation and journalistic assessment of the cause of Barron's death, combined with the fact that the large number of accompanying hematomas could not have been sustained in the fall (see above p. 52 and below p. 156 n.88). *Cf.*: *Jornal do Brasil*, March 14, 1987, sec. Cidade, p. 5; July 19, 1987, sec. B/especial, p. 8; Moraes and Viana, p. 64; and Sodré, p. 262n.

86. *Cf.*: PPARJ, document, "Situação do movimento revolucionario no Brasil," May 23, 1936, p. 13, administração/pasta 1h; and Waack, *Camaradas, loc. cit.* The comments by Waack about *paulistano* papers mentioning the "suicide" of Jungmann came from the remarks of Honório de Freitas Guimarães, secretary of the Central Committee of the

PCB, after having returned to Moscow. Evidently, someone in the party had seen an article in a now-defunct São Paulo newspaper. William Waack, telephone interview, Rio de Janeiro/Berlin, May 29, 1994.

87. "Lulu" Barbosa was a relative of former president Nilo Peçanha. He was accused of being involved in a plot to kill Artur Bernardes at the urging of Peçanha. Lulu was probably the first prisoner thrown to his death from the Central Police Station. Maurício de Lacerda, *História de uma covardia* (Rio de Janeiro: Nova Fronteira, 1980), pp. 185-90. For more on Conrado Niemeyer see above p. 145 n.23. Observations on Aloisio Rodrigues de Souza can be found in PPARJ, document, "A policia de Felinto Muller prende e assassina trabalhadores maritimos," March 1939, comunismo/pasta 16; and Thomé Amado, interview, Rio de Janeiro, October 9, 1994. The sole reference to Salomão Zelcer's "suicide" at the Polícia Central is in *Diario de Noticias*, July 10, 1936, p. 7. See also above p. 54 and below n.88.

88. *Cf.*: PPARJ, "Victor Allen Barron," p. 2; Morais, *Olga*, pp. 153-54, 161; Waack, *Camaradas*, pp. 290, 300; and *Diario Carioca* (Rio de Janeiro), March 6, 1936, p. 2. Until 1938, *Diario Carioca* was in opposition to the government. Together with a Polícia Civil architect, this author physically measured the distance of the second floor to the inside courtyard. Two different photos of Barron's body from the shoulders on up were published in *A Noite* (March 5, 1936, edição 14 horas, n.p. [back page]) and *Diario de Noticias* (March 6, 1936, p. 1). A copy of the notification of death telegram sent by the U.S. Department of State to Victor Barron's mother, which she had to pay for (Morais, *Olga*, p. 162), is located in the unnumbered plates in Morais, *Olga*. The *Daily Worker* (May 13, 1936, p. 6), reported that Barron's body was not shipped back to his mother, but "destroyed in quick lime." What Edna Hill did receive was the brunt of the guilt-by-genetics press. Although she never was a communist, she was accused of being one. Years before, there was an effort made to convert her other son, Harold, to the red cause. A beautiful female agent was dispatched to California to try to persuade him; but he would have none of it and refused. Harold Barron, interview, Hayward, CA, January 15, 1994.

89. PPARJ, "Rodolfo Ghioldi, pp. 4[a], 42-43. Without ever having seen the political police file on Ghioldi, Prestes ultimately came to the conclusion that in fact it was the Argentine who turned him in. Luís Carlos Prestes, interview, Rio de Janeiro, August 13, 1987. A final fact weighs heavily against Ghioldi. Along with Antônio Bonfim, another person who could not keep quiet, the Ghioldis received two of the lightest sentences of the movement's captured inner core. See above in this regard p. 72.

90. Cecil Borer: interviews, Rio de Janeiro, May 13, 1998; May 28, 1998. André Trifino Correia had been with Prestes in Rio Grande do Sul when the latter led his men to Foz do Iguaçu and formed the *Coluna* Prestes. He remained a faithful Prestes confidant through the years. Astrojildo Pereira Duarte Silva was one of the PCB's founding members in 1922. By 1935 he was going through a difficult period with the party, but would resolve his differences in the 1940s. Beloch and Abreu, pp. 942-43, 2676-79. For more on Graciliano Ramos, see above pp. 62, 67-68 and below p. 161 n.120.

91. *Cf.*: Luís Carlos Prestes, interview, Rio de Janeiro, August 13, 1987; Thomé Amado: interviews, Rio de Janeiro, September 28, 1994; October 9, 1994; Morais, *Olga*, pp. 128-29, 133-34, 150-52; Nasser, *Falta alguém em Nuremberg*, p. 76; and *O Imparcial* (Rio de Janeiro), March 6, 1936, p. 1. Major William Sackville, the U.S.

military attaché at the time, informed Washington that Olga was "in the fourth month of gestation." USNA, letter, "Sackville to G-2," May 21, 1936, no. 1651, p. 2, MID 2651-K-70/38.

92. The English later attempted to suppress any mention by their diplomats of the connection Light had to the Brazilian authorities in the attempted revolution. UKPRO, telegram, "Foreign Office to Sir H[ugh] Gurney," January 10, 1936, no. 4, FO 371/19766, pp. 16-17.

93. *Cf.*: USNA, microfilm, "Gibson to Secretary of State," July 10, 1936, M1472/8; Thomé Amado: interviews, Rio de Janeiro, September 28, 1994; October 9, 1994; *Correio da Manhã*, March 6, 1936, p. 14; July 9, 1936, p. 3; July 10, 1936, p. 3; *O Imparcial*, July 9, 1936, pp. 1, 12; July 10, 1936, p. 1; *Jornal do Brasil*, July 9, 1936, p. 11; Stanley Hilton, *A rebelião vermelha*, pp. 104, 201; and Morais, *Olga*, p. 194. The story behind the newspaper articles on the Galvão-Ernani affair was furnished by Thomé Amado. Amado was being held by the Polícia Especial at the time and learned what really took place from his guards.

94. For the *Estado Novo*, see chap. 4.

95. *Cf.*: Brazil, Comissão Especial de Inquérito sôbre Atos Delituosos da Ditadura, "Depoimento do Luís Carlos Prestes," pp. 5902-3, 5905; PPARJ, letter, "H[eráclito]. F[ontoura]. Sobral Pinto to A[lexander]. Marcondes Filho," June 1, 1943, pp. 2-3, comunismo/pasta 8; John W.F. Dulles, e-mail, July 27, 1999; Cancelli, p. 190; Morais, *Olga*, p. 203; and Nasser, *Falta alguém em Nuremberg*, p. 38. For more on Caneppa see above pp. 20-21, 67-69, 90, 138 n.49 and below pp. 161 n.116, 162 n.122.

96. *Correio da Manhã*, May 12, 1936, p. 3. U.S. military attaché Sackville wrote to his superiors at the War Department that on May 9th, Vargas had given another less publicized talk while traveling home; this one to a gathering of workers in the Rio suburb of Benfica. Getúlio mentioned that the dangerous agitators could be removed to "remote agricultural colonies, where healthful labor involving actual delving in the soil may be hoped to bring these misguided citizens back to an understanding of the realities of life and clear from their brains the phantastic [*sic*] notions implanted by the foreign doctrines to which they had given ear." Major Sackville then concluded by observing that "whether confinement in distant farm colonies is a definitely adopted measure or merely a suggestion offered to observe the reaction of public opinion remains to be seen. The slight comment that followed the President's speech, on the part of the press, held the proposal to be excellent." USNA, "Sackville to G-2," May 21, 1936, p. 1. See also above pp. 25-26, 67-69 and below p. 179 n.100.

97. *Correio da Manhã*, June 7, 1936, p. 2. This note was published in several newspapers.

98. Basbaum, *História sincera da República*, p. 82. During this period, Vargas was personally given a letter outlining in detail the tortures inflicted on prisoners. The communication was signed by former detainees who had gone through "the process." All were professionals: professors, physicians, naval officers, journalists, lawyers, and the like. The only reaction from Getúlio was one of his renowned grins. Brazil, Comissão Especial de Inquérito sôbre Atos Delituosos da Ditadura, "Depoimento do Carlos Marighella," *Diario do Congresso Nacional*, August 28, 1947, p. 5204.

99. Sodré, pp. 260-61.

100. *Cf.*: Vianna, "Revolucionários de 1935," vol. II, pp. 534-35; Dulles, *Brazilian Communism*, pp. 34, 67-69; Beloch and Abreu, pp. 387-88, 2919; (Anonymous), *Quem é que no Brasil: biografias contemporâneas* (São Paulo: Sociedade Brasileira de Espansão Comercial, 1955), vol. IV, p. 365; Morais, *Olga*, p. 106; Nasser, *Falta alguém em Nuremberg*, pp. 19-21; PPARJ: booklet, "*Eu, Gregório Bezerra, acuso!*" (n.p.: n.p., 1967), p. 7, comunismo/pasta 82; "Situação do movimento revolucionario no Brasil," *loc. cit.*; document, "Histórico das atividades políticas dos parlamentares comunistas," n.d., p. 7, comunismo/pasta 23; and UKPRO, document, "Political Situation in Pernambuco," December 17, 1935, FO 371/19766, pp. 11-12. The unnamed author of this last dispatch was told that in addition to the men there were 150 arrested women, a figure which he did not believe. Nasser equated (*Falta alguém em Nuremberg*, p. 61) Frederico Mindelo Carneiro Monteiro (here Photo 17) and police Assistant Etelvino Lins (here Photo 18), the latter would be the successor to Malvino Reis Neto (here Photo 19), as being the *pernambucano* equivalents of Filinto Müller. Frederico ultimately became the head of the political police in Pernambuco. He would continue his career as, among other things, chief of the military commission making purchases from the U.S. army. AN, *Correio da Manhã* Photo Collection, "Frederico Mindelo," unnumbered bibliographic document. Etelvino Lins had more ability. After his tour of duty as the secretary for public security in Pernambuco, he was made the state's *interventor*, then its federal senator, then governor. *Correio da Manhã*, November 20, 1954, sec. 1, p. 3. Homicide charges against Lins and Frederico Mindelo in the José Lourenço Bezerra murder were suspended with the start of the *Estado Novo* (see chap. 4). Beloch and Abreu, pp. 387-88. Chico Pinote, a nickname that means "Chico Jump," would be brought back into service in Recife as a torturer following the overthrow of João Goulart in 1964. At that time he would make up one part of the abhorrent "Quartet of Death."

101. See above pp. 43, 150 nn.59-60.

102. *Cf.*: РЦХИДНИ, general file, "Бразилия," letter, "Raul to Brandão," August 29, 1936, фонд 495, опись 29, дело 98, листов 15a-b; Brazil: Comissão Especial de Inquérito sôbre Atos Delituosos da Ditadura, "Depoimento do Carlos Marighella," pp. 5203-4; and "Depoimento do Abel Chermont," *Diario do Congresso Nacional*, September 20, 1947, pp. 5900-5901. Part of Marighela's testimony was based on a letter from João Mangabeira. Mangabeira and Abel Chermont were two of five federal lawmakers arrested in the legislature in March 1936. The police accused the group of acting as a lobby in the service of Luís Carlos Prestes. For Tobias Warchavski, see above pp. 33, 144 n.18. Some prisoners died from the torture they received and then had their bodies taken to the Chinese View where they were shot, *ex post facto*. See as example the cases of army Captain José Augusto de Medeiros and infantryman Abguardo Martins, recounted in the Senate by Abel Chermont. Both men actually died from effects of the "Chinese Torture" (see above p. 61). *Cf.*: PPARJ: "Auguste Elise Ewert," *loc. cit.*; document, "Abaixo as provocações da policia assassina de Getulio, Vicente Ráo, Felinto Muller e Miranda Correia," n.d., comunismo/pasta 17; document, "A policia de Felinto Muller prende e assassina trabalhadores maritimos"; *O Imparcial* (Rio de Janeiro), March 4, 1936, pp. 3, 11; Brandi, p. 102; Beloch and Abreu, p. 2063; and Dulles, *Brazilian Communism*, pp. 82-83.

103. Brazil, Comissão Especial de Inquérito sôbre Atos Delituosos da Ditadura, "Depoimento do Carlos Marighella," p. 5204.

104. *Cf.*: Nasser, *Falta alguém em Nuremberg*, pp. 25-26; Marcelo Guarany, *O pequeno ditador* (Rio de Janeiro: Moderna, 1947), p. 44; Sodré, p. 283n; Dulles, *Brazilian Communism*, pp. 43-44; and Thomé Amado: interviews, Rio de Janeiro, September 28, 1994; October 9, 1994. For more on Mattos, see above p. 60 and below n.113.

105. For the TSN, see above p. 66 and below pp. 162 n.130, 162 n.132, 163 n.133.

106. Brazil, Comissão Especial de Inquérito sôbre Atos Delituosos da Ditadura, "Depoimento do Francisco de Oliveira Melo," *Diario do Congresso Nacional*, October 23, 1947, p. 7244. Lúcio Martins Meira would rise to be one of Getúlio's assistants in military matters during the second Vargas government. His star continued to ascend and during the presidency of Juscelino Kubitschek it reached ministerial rank. Beloch and Abreu, p. 2175.

107. PPARJ, periodical article, "*Ancora*," April 1935, pp. 2-3, comunismo/pasta 4.

108. Taking the official rate of exchange on March 1st, July 1st, and November 1st each year, starting with November 1935 and ending with November 1942, fifty *milréis*, in U.S. currency, was worth a high of $4.41 and a low of $2.89. *Cf.*: *Jornal do Commercio*, various issues, November 1, 1935 to November 2-4, 1942.

109. *Cf.*: *A Classe Operaria*, October 26, 1939, p. 2; Jose Luiz Del Roio, telephone interview, Rio de Janeiro/São Paulo, July 31, 1994; and Vladimir Sacchetta: telephone interview, Rio de Janeiro/São Paulo, July 31, 1994; interview, São Paulo, August 17, 1994. One should take care in accepting the validity of all names on every *A Classe Operaria* inventory. It was common practice to label those deviating from the party line once they had been expelled. The above edition of *A Classe Operaria*, as example, states that Hetor Ferreira da Silva and his mother were Trotskyite informants. Actually, Hetor's real name was Hetor Ferreira Lima; and he was not a Trotskyite nor an informer. He had fallen out of favor with the party and because of this was so branded. Vladimir Sacchetta, interview, São Paulo, August 17, 1994.

110. Cecil Borer, interview, Rio de Janeiro, May 28, 1998. Borer believed that Adalto Alves dos Santos moved to the United States where, under a different name, he began working for the U.S. Central Intelligence Agency. He was said to have continued in his new role for many years. For more on the *Quadro Movel*, see above p. 89.

111. *Cf.*: PPARJ, deposition, "Testemunha do Cleobulo Azambuja," [December 1939], comunismo/pasta 21; Brazil, Comissão Especial de Inquérito sôbre Atos Delituosos da Ditadura, "Depoimento do Carlos Marighella," p. 5203; Dulles, *Brazilian Communism*, p. 4; Werneck, p. 19; and Nasser, *Falta alguém em Nuremberg*, pp. 94-95, 97-98.

112. Eliana Rezende Furtado de Mendonça (director), *DOPS: a lógica de desconfiança* (Rio de Janeiro: Arquivo Público do Estado do Rio de Janeiro, 1993), p. 11.

113. Felisberto Batista Teixeira (here, Photo 12) was ultimately to become the chief of police in the old Federal District. In 1947 a police investigation was started to determine how the newspaper *O Mundo* got copies of the police identity photos of Cecil Borer. They are reproduced here as Photo 14. Clodomir Collaço Véras is shown in Photo 15. Emílio Romano was later fired for extortion and placed in the same cell where Prestes had been kept at the Casa de Correção. He also spent a year in isolation but began to show signs of a mental collapse after only three weeks. He had refused to help Sobral

Pinto when the semiofficial lawyer for Prestes asked him to get Prestes' isolation lifted. At the time, Romano said "There's nothing I can do." Once Romano got out of the Correção, Getúlio rewarded him with a job as one of his "special guards." In the last years of his life Romano suffered from bouts of extreme paranoia. *Cf.*: PPARJ: miscellaneous documents, "Sindicancia para apurar como o jornal *O Mundo* obteve fotografias idênticas do prontuário de Cecil Borer," 1947, administração/pasta 1e; "H[eráclito]. F[ontoura]. Sobral Pinto to A[lexander]. Marcondes Filho," pp. 3-4; Nasser, *Falta alguém em Nuremberg*, p. 63; and Thomé Amado, interview, Rio de Janeiro, September 28, 1994. Assuming that "Tira" Vasconcelos was a DPS agent (see Appendix, Table 1), and that he remained with that unit until 1951, his full name was either Ary de Vasconcelos, Dhejar Vasconcelos Verçosa, or Saulo Cesar de Vasconcelos. Making the same supposition about Mattos, he may have been Geraldo Santana Mattos. The mysterious Mattos committed suicide after the military took power in 1964. Thomé Amado, interview, Rio de Janeiro, September 28, 1994.

114. *Cf.*: Noé Gertel, interview, São Paulo, August 17, 1994; Lygia Prestes, interview, Rio de Janeiro, August 6, 1994; Solomão Malina, interview, São Paulo, July 28, 1994; Cecil Borer, interview, Rio de Janeiro, May 28, 1998; Jose Luiz Del Roio, telephone interview, Rio de Janeiro/São Paulo, July 31, 1994; Thomé Amado: interviews, Rio de Janeiro, August 21, 1994; September 28, 1994; PPARJ: booklet, "Relatório apresentado ao Sr. Chefe de Polícia, Major Dr. Filinto Müller, pelo Delegado Especial de Segurança Política e Social, Capitão Felisberto Baptista Teixeira, e referente à campanha desenvolvida, sob sua orientação, para repressão às atividades do Partido Comunista no país," September 1940, p. 30, comunismo/pasta 13; "A policia de Felinto Muller prende e assassina trabalhadores maritimos"; letter, "[Felisberto] Baptista Teixeira to Dr. Major Chefe da Polícia [Filinto Müller]," June 17, 1941, p. 30, comunismo/pasta 13; letter, "O Comité Regional do Rio do Partido Comunista do Brasil (S.I.C.) to anonymous," April 2, 1940, pp. 1-2, comunismo/pasta 27; letter, "Joaquim Marcelino Nepomuceno to Comité Nacional do Partido Comunista do Brasil," September 17, 1945, p. 4, comunismo/pasta 2c; AN, telegram "Family of Clodomir Colaço Veras to Getulio Vargas," [1942], Secretaria da Presidência da República: Polícia Civil do Distrito Federal/lata 527; Sodré, *loc. cit.*; Werneck, p. 19; Nasser, *Falta alguém em Nuremberg*, pp. 38, 53-56, 59, 61-64, 109; Brazil: Comissão Especial de Inquérito sôbre Atos Delituosos da Ditadura, "Depoimento do Olindo Semeraro," *Diario do Congresso Nacional*, July 23, 1947, p. 3882; "Depoimento do David Nasser," *Diario do Congresso Nacional*, August 8, 1947, p. 4438; "Depoimento do José Alexandre dos Santos," *Diario do Congresso Nacional*, September 9, 1947, pp. 5506-7; "Depoimento do João Massena Melo," *Diario do Congresso Nacional*, September 9, 1947, p. 5509; "Depoimento do João Basilio dos Santos," *Diario do Congresso Nacional*, September 25, 1947, p. 6043; and "Depoimento do Carlos Marighella," pp. 5203-4. Marighela ("Depoimento do Carlos Marighella," p. 5204) and Sodré (*loc. cit.*) call the process of using the *máscara de couro*, the torture *americana*, not to be confused, on their part (?), with the *cadeira americana*.

115. *Cf.*: PPARJ: newspaper article, "*Centelha*," September 23, 1933, pp. 2, 4, comunismo/pasta 4; "*O Preso Proletario*," November 1933, p. 3; Brazil: Comissão Especial de Inquérito sôbre Atos Delituosos da Ditadura, "Depoimento do Paulo Franklin de Souza Elejalde," *Diario do Congresso Nacional*, May 27, 1947, pp. 2005-6;

"Depoimento do Samuel Lopes Pereira," *Diario do Congresso Nacional*, May 28, 1947, pp. 2057-59; "Depoimento do Bernardino de Oliveira Carvalho," *Diario do Congresso Nacional*, June 7, 1947, pp. 2370-72; "Acareação entre os depoentes," *Diario do Congresso Nacional*, June 19, 1947, pp. 2774-77; "Depoimento do Belmiro Valverde," *Diario do Congresso Nacional*, May 27, 1947, p. 2004; and *Diretrizes* (Rio de Janeiro), April 18, 1947, pp. 1, 2, 5. *Diretrizes* was first published as a monthly in 1938 by Samuel Wainer. In 1941 he transformed it into a weekly, in part, with the help of a monthly grant of 30:000$000 (a little more than $1,800) from the American Embassy. The periodical aimed "at producing a democracy similar to that in the United States." *Cf.*: PPARJ, document, "S-1, boletim no. 88," April 12-13, 1941, p. xxi, comunismo/pasta 4d; and *New York Times*, April 12, 1941, p. 27.

116. The male, common criminals were sent to the Dois Rios Correctional Colony on Ilha Grande. *Cf.*: Henriques, pp. 419, 435; and AFM, telegram, "Caneppa to Müller," November 8, 1937, CPDOC/FM 33.03.23 chp/ad, I-87. See also the 1932 precedent above at p. 138 n.49, and the description of the man in charge on the island, Vitório Caneppa (*Estatistica carceraria do Distrito Federal* [Rio de Janeiro: Franco-Brasileira, 1939], p. 12), when referring to incorrigible prisoners at the Casa de Correção.

117. *Cf.*: PPARJ: newspaper article, "*A Classe Operaria*," February 16, 1937, p. 2, comunismo/pasta 17; letter, "Antonio Mendes Napoleão *et al.*, to Magalhães de Almeida *et al.*," [1936?], comunismo/pasta 20; letter, "José Reynaldo Serra Costa *et al.*, to Magalhães de Almeida *et al.*," [1936?], comunismo/pasta 20; CPDOC, "José Joffily," p. 66; and Pinto, pp. 28-31, 79. Pinto (p. 79) puts the number of women at the Detenção at about thirty on some unspecified date in 1937.

118. *Cf.*: PPARJ, "*O Preso Proletario*," November 1933, *loc. cit.*; and Elizabeth Cancelli, "O poder da polícia e o mundo da prisão na era Vargas (1930-1945)," prepublication manuscript, p. 14. According to the prisoners and the prison authorities, even pederasty was very frequent. Cancelli, "O poder da polícia e o mundo da prisão na era Vargas," *loc.cit.*

119. *Cf.*: Cancelli, "O poder da polícia e o mundo da prisão na era Vargas," p. 8; and PPARJ, "*A Classe Operaria*," February 16, 1937, p. 4; and Henriques (p. 433) states that forty prisoners were crammed together in his smaller 13'1½" x 13'1½" cell. Cancelli ("O poder da polícia e o mundo da prisão na era Vargas," pp. 5, 8) comments that in December 1935 the Detenção held 1,480 inmates in an environment designed for a maximum of 450.

120. Graciliano Ramos, *Memórias do cárcere*, 21st ed. (Rio de Janeiro: Record, 1986), vol. I, p. 198. Ramos (see also above pp. 67-68) was picked up in Alagoas on March 14, 1936, accused by an Integralist of being a communist (he was not at the time, but he joined the party years later), and for conspiring in the 1935 November uprising. He was imprisoned without trial for ten months, and released on January 13, 1937. *Cf.*: PPARJ, document "Dirigentes da 'Organização Brasileira de Defesa da Paz e da Cultura,'" March 15, 1949, comunismo/pasta 38; and Amado, *A vida de Luís Carlos Prestes*, p. 272.

121. *Cf.*: PPARJ: document, "Prestes, está em greve de fome," March 1941, comunismo/pasta 20; "*A Classe Operaria*," February 16, 1937, p. 2; "*O Preso Proletario*," November 1933, *loc. cit.*; Ramos, pp. 196, 207-8; Pinto, pp. 26-30; Bastos, p.292; and Henriques, pp. 419, 433-34.

122. *Cf.*: Brazil: Comissão Especial de Inquérito sôbre Atos Delituosos da Ditadura, "Depoimento do Iguatemi Ramos da Silva," *Diario do Congresso Nacional*, September 9, 1947, p. 5509; "Depoimento do Belmiro Valverde," p. 2003; Cancelli: "O poder da polícia e o mundo da prisão na era Vargas." p. 3; *O mundo da violência*, p. 189; and Britto, pp. 177-200. In respect to Alencar Filho's previous post, see above p. 90. Things got particularly rough when Vitório Caneppa (see above pp. 20-21, 54-55, 67-69, 89-90, 138 n.49) was transferred from Dois Rios to be the Correção's warden. Nasser (*Falta alguém em Nuremberg*, p. 38) informs us that on assuming his new responsibilities in 1937, this Integralist and "personal friend of Getúlio Vargas . . . having received specific orders from Catete, practiced the most inhuman acts [imaginable]." Indeed he did. "Caneppa, Prestes had said, tried to bring to the Casa de Correção the methods used on Ilha Grande . . . and therefore 'violence after violence' became the rule." Dulles, *Brazilian Communism*, p. 109.

123. Dulles, *Brazilian Communism*, p. 2. See also above p. 20 and below n.127.

124. PPARJ, document, "[untitled]," Paraizo, August 25, 1936, Machado, p. 1, comunismo/pasta 20. A photograph Egas Botelho is reproduced here as Photo 16. A photograph of the entire corps of political police in the city of São Paulo in 1937 can be seen as Photo 21.

125. Vieira (pp. 150-51, 158) spells this individual's last name as Schiavo.

126. *Cf.*: *Ibid.*, pp. 79-81, 97-98, 104, 116-17, 122, 135-37, 148-51, 158-59; PPARJ, document, "[untitled]," Paraizo, August 25, 1936, *loc. cit.*; Machado, pp. 2-4; Cancelli, "O poder da polícia e o mundo da prisão na era Vargas," pp. 13-14; and Dulles, *Brazilian Communism*, pp. 22-64.

127. *Cf.*: Dulles, *Brazilian Communism*, pp. 63-67; Vieira, pp. 168, 171, 173-75, 192, 204-7; Bastos, pp. 292-93; and Paulo Duarte, *Memórias: apagada e vil mediocridade* (São Paulo: HUCITEC, 1977), pp. 146-55. Escapees were consistently dealt with severely. On the *Pedro I* (see above p. 63), those who succeeded in fleeing only to be recaptured had their backs brutally lacerated with a rawhide knout or whip called a *chicote*. Ramos, vol. I, p. 250.

128. *Cf.*: PPARJ, document, "A todos os nucleos e a todos os alliancistas," [late 1935 or early 1936], p. 8, comunismo/pasta 20; and Dulles, *Brazilian Communism*, p. 70.

129. See above p. 36, 41 and below nn.130, 132, p. 162 n.133.

130. *Cf.*: Henriques, p. 414; Werneck, p. 98; and Reynaldo Pompeu de Campos, *Repressão judicial no Estado Novo: esquerda e direita no banco dos réus* (Rio de Janeiro: Achiamé, 1982), p. 53. The court sat, after several streamlining modifications (as example, see below n.132), until just after the end of the first Vargas regime in 1945. During its lifetime, the tribunal judged 6,998 cases involving more than 10,000 persons, 4,099 of whom were found guilty.

131. Loewenstein, p. 212.

132. *Cf.*: *Ibid.*, pp. 218-19; Campos, pp. 134, 150-52; and Levine, *The Vargas Regime*, p. 129. This change to hurry things up resulted from the failed Integralist Revolt of May 11, 1938 (see below, chap. 4). There was no time limitation on the answering of allegations or the testimony of witnesses before May 16th. This was because formal charges and the replies to those indictments were conducted in the first instance in writing. Campos, pp. 133-34.

133. Levine, *The Vargas Regime*, pp. 129-30. Luís Carlos Prestes was the main individual processed by the *Segurança*. As concerns the sentences, Nasser (*Falta algém em Nuremberg*, p. 57) observes that [Clodomir] Véras (see above p. 59) stated that "the sentences leave police headquarters already written. All the Tribunal does is ratify them." For the rich, however, decisions against them were always reduced or absolved. Bribery of the judges by the upper classes took place as well. Nasser, *Falta algém em Nuremberg*, pp. 57-59.

134. Pinto, p. 35.

135. Caneppa, p. 10.

136. *Cf.*: Pinto, pp. 37, 40; and Thomé Amado, interview, Rio de Janeiro, August 21, 1994. From December 2, 1936 to June 13, 1937, a period just over six months, Thomé Amado was incarcerated on Ilha Grande. Thomé Amado, interview, Rio de Janeiro, August 21, 1994.

137. Brazil, Comissão Especial de Inquérito sôbre Atos Delituosos da Ditadura, "Depoimento do Abel Chermont," p. 5901. Pinto (p. 39) relates that in 1936, his barrack had 400 political prisoners and 300 common criminals.

138. *Cf.*: Thomé Amado, interview, Rio de Janeiro, August 21, 1994; AFM, telegram, "Sardinha to Müller," October 5, 1937, CPDOC/FM 33.03.23 chp/ad, I; Amado, *A vida de Luís Carlos Prestes*, p. 272n; Nasser, *Falta alguém em Nuremberg*, pp. 40-44; Pinto, pp. 39-45, 64; Ramos, p. 38; and Brazil, "Depoimento de João Alves de Mota," *loc. cit.* Sardinha was at Ilha Grande as early as 1932 when the warden was Marcillio de Souza Maior. PPARJ, "*O Preso Proletario*," November 1933, p. 4. Pinto (p. 43) mentions that another medical functionary, Orlando Dotto (it is not known if Dotto was a physician), was present on Ilha Grande in 1936. A second source (AFM, telegram, "Dotto to Müller," October 21, 1937, CPDOC/FM 33.03.23 chp/ad, I-93) shows that Dotto, nevertheless, was there through most of 1937.

139. *Cf.*: PPARJ: document, "Documentação em torno de melhoramentos internos sugeridos á DESPS, 1943, administração/pasta 1; and periodical article, "*Diretrizes*," April 16, 1942, p. 16, comunismo/pasta 4d. In addition, see above pp. 25-26, 157 n.96 and below p. 179 n.100.

140. *Cf.*: Amado, *A vida de Luís Carlos Prestes*, p. 271; Cancelli, "O poder da polícia e o mundo da prisão na era Vargas," pp. 4, 20-25; and Nasser, *Falta alguém em Nuremberg*, pp. 26-27, 36-37, 54. Nasser goes on (p. 27) to assert that without the economic support of their husbands, some families broke up, becoming vagabonds and the wives prostitutes. In the "or worse" category, many persons were no doubt aware that the police simply picked up people, murdered them, and then dumped their bodies on some desolate road or somewhere else as a warning. See as example Sodré, *loc. cit.*

141. *Cf.*: O *Estado de São Paulo*, August 29, 1993, especial/p. 6; and Waack, *Camaradas*, pp. 282, 301-2, 307-14, 317-18, 342.

142. *Cf.*: Waack, *Camaradas*, pp. 273-77, 282-83, 286, 318, 342; and Yuri Ribeiro, interview, Rio de Janeiro, November 20, 1994.

143. An inhabitant or thing of Buenos Aires.

144. *Cf.*: Waack, *Camaradas*, pp. 318-19, 325-29, 342; and PPARJ, "Franz Gruber ou Jonny de Graaf," pp. 17, 47.

145. *Cf.*: Dulles, *Brazilian Communism*, pp. 9, 46, 79; Beloch and Abreu, p. 406; and Morais, *Olga*, p. 296.

146. *Cf.*: Argentina, Registro del Estado Civil y Capacidade de las Personas, Departamento Central Defunciones [Buenos Aires], affidavit, "Registro Civil [for Rodolfo José Ghioldi]," tomo 2L, numero 1022, año 1985; and PPARJ, "Rodolfo Ghioldi," pp. 44-46. For more on Fernando de Noronha, see above pp. 89-90.

147. *Cf.*: PPARJ, "Rodolfo Ghioldi," p. 43; Felix Barata Lopez, letter, November 13, 1996; Susana O.F. de Ghioldi, letter, January 7, 1997; and Americo Ghioldi, interview, Buenos Aires, June 5, 1998.

148. Pinto found Berger's condition so appalling that he petitioned the chief judge at the TSN, Raul Machado, for an improvement based on the law prohibiting cruelty to animals. He included with his remarks a clipping from the newspaper *A Noite* that he said inspired him. It was a story of a man in Paraná who was given a seventeen-day jail sentence and fined 520$000 (or $31.90) for beating his horse to death. *Cf.*: [Heráclito Fontoura] Sobral Pinto, *Por que defendo os comunistas* (Belo Horizonte: Comunicação, 1979), pp. 73-82; *A Noite*, January 29, 1937, pp. 3-4; and STM, letter, "Heraclito Fontoura Sobral Pinto to Raul Machado," January 15, 1937, apelação 4899, série a, vol. II, pp. 251-53. Dulles (*Brazilian Communism*, p. 73) adds that Machado passed Sobral Pinto's request on to Müller and "no action was taken."

149. STM, letter, "Euzebio de Queiroz Filho to Raul Machado," January 25, 1937, apelação 4899, série a, vol. II, p. 254. Euzébio blamed Berger's condition on the fact, according to the police, that he frequently went on hunger strikes.

150. *Cf.*: PPARJ: "Arthur Ernst Ewert ou Harry Berger," pp. 58, 69, 77; document, "Decreto-lei no. 7474, de 18 abril de 1945 [with attached card 'dossier: anistia, anistiados']," geral/pasta 3; letter, "João Alberto Lins de Barros to Agamenon Magalhães," April 20, 1945, geral/pasta 3; letter, "Victorio Caneppa to Sr. Ministro Chefe de Polícia do Depart. Federal de Segurança Pública," April 23, 1945, copy of ofício 199; geral/pasta 3; Germany, Kreisverwaltung Eberswalde, affidavit, "Auszug aus dem Todesregister," September 9, 1993; and Beloch and Abreu, pp. 363-64; Dulles, *Brazilian Communism*, pp. 79, 84, 109; Joffily, *Harry Berger*, pp. 93-94, 116; Nasser: *Falta alguém em Nuremberg*, pp. 72, 74; *A revolução dos covardes*, p. 158. A copy of the psychiatric evaluation of Berger, made on April 11, 1938, itself a rather sick report, is available in Joffily, *Harry Berger*, pp. 174-85. Photographs of Rio's Polícia Especial headquarters, as well as a number of interesting observations, are also in Joffily, *Harry Berger*, pp. 102-3, 146-47. The Tomato Heads did not have a corner on under-the-stairs torture. There was also a similar arrangement over at the Polícia Central. Brazil, Comissão Especial de Inquérito sôbre Atos Delituosos da Ditadura, "Depoimento do Iguatemi Ramos da Silva," p. 5508. Following the 1964 military takeover, placing political detainees in cells under staircases would be used again at other lock ups in the Rio de Janeiro area.

151. *Cf.*: PPARJ: telegram, "Embaixada do Brasil em Berlim ao Ministerio das Relações Exteriores," April 19-20, 1937, p. 37 [file "Arthur Ernst Ewert ou Harry Berger"]; "Maria Prestes, Olga Benario," p. 3; Dulles, *Brazilian Communism*, p. 211; Morais, *Olga*, pp. 266-68; Beloch and Abreu, p. 363; Joffily, *Harry Berger*, p. 92; Amado, *A vida de Luís Carlos Prestes*, p. 268; Waack, *Camaradas*, p. 341; and Levine, *The Vargas Regime*, p. 220n.

152. *Cf.*: PPARJ: "*Eu, Gregório Bezerra, acuso!*," p. 8; "Histórico das atividades políticas dos parlamentares comunistas," pp. 7-8; and Beloch and Abreu, p. 388.

153. *Cf.*: Luís Carlos Prestes, interview, Rio de Janeiro, August 13, 1987; and Werneck, p. 69. See also above pp. 35-36. For an example of the Jew-baiting in the press, see *O Imparcial*, May 20, 1936, p. 1. Frota Aguiar, an ex-aid to Filinto Müller, attempted years later to remove any blame from his old boss and, in fact, charge Prestes for Olga's expulsion. Supposedly based on the gossip of João Alberto, this curious effort to sanitize his former mentor can be found in the Letters to the Editor section of *O Globo* (February 18, 1989, sec. 1, p. 4). Prestes never dignified Aguiar with a reply. Frota can be seen among the well-wishers in Photo 9.

154. *Cf.*: Morais, *Olga*, pp. 187-88; and Seitenfus, *O Brasil de Getúlio Vargas*, p. 87. A plan to deport 900 Jews to Germany in 1937 was shelved by Oswaldo Aranha (see above pp. 79-80 and below p. 168 n.11) owing to the adverse international reaction it might have caused. Maria Luiza Tucci Carneiro, pp. 265-66.

155. *Cf.*: *Manchete*, January 22, 1977, p. 34; and Stanley Hilton, "Brazilian Diplomacy and the Washington-Rio de Janeiro 'Axis' during the World War II Era," p. 204.

156. USNA, "Sackville to G-2," May 21, 1936, p. 2.

157. *Manchete*, December 15, 1979, p. 47.

158. *Cf.*: Seitenfus, *O Brasil de Getúlio Vargas, loc. cit*; Morais, *Olga*, pp. 152, 206, 217, 259-93, 312; Dulles, *Brazilian Communism*, p. 31; and Nasser, *Falta alguém em Nuremberg*, pp. 77-78.

159. José Homem Correia de Sá, interview, Rio de Janeiro, August 20, 1994. See above p. 153 n.78. Waack (*Camaradas*, p. 297) states that Moscow "put things in this order: the suggestion was Stuchevski's, the order was Prestes', and the execution was carried out by the [local] party leadership."

160. To break down just the writers from the United States, there were fifty-three letters or postcards by individual senders, one communication from the Portland (Oregon) Progressive Educational Club, one letter unsigned by the 100 members of the Ethical Culture Society, a letter from the Commission to Obtain the Freedom of Luís Carlos Prestes, and seven other anonymous dispatches. In each case, the author or the organization had their name underlined with a red or blue pencil. A specific DESPS folder was then begun on that person or group. The total number of writers, without the 100 from the Ethical Culture Society, was eighty-seven. PPARJ, miscellaneous letters, [various dates], comunismo/pasta 8.

161. Even though it was legal, this did not mean that the political police stopped accumulating every scrap of information possible from informants within the PCB during this period. *Cf.*: PPARJ: miscellaneous documents, "Documentos constantes dos arquivos do PCB," [various dates], comunismo/pastas 2; 2a; 2b; 2c; 2f; 2g; 2h; 2i; 2j; 2l; 2m; 2n; and 2p.

162. As but one example, anyone who sent a telegram to Prestes while he was a senator, even if it was only to wish him a happy birthday, had their names registered for future reference by DESPS agents. The political police had someone at the telegraph office who sent them copies of any wires they desired. *Cf.*: PPARJ: telegram, "Eliezer Menezes *et al.*, to Luís Carlos Prestes," January 3, 1948, comunismo/pasta 24; telegram, "Arlindo Souza to Luís Carlos Prestes," January 3, 1948, comunismo/pasta 24; telegram,

"Deosdedith Mendes Rocha to Luís Carlos Prestes," January 4, 1948, comunismo/pasta 24; and telegram, "Maria Augusta de Brito to Luís Carlos Prestes," January 4, 1948, comunismo/pasta 24. There were an additional three telegrams without dates in pasta 24 that might rightly be included here.

163. *Cf.*: Dulles: *Vargas of Brazil*, p. 154; *Brazilian Communism*, pp. 79, 162, 213; Beloch and Abreu, pp. 2824-25; and *Jornal do Brasil*, March 8, 1990, sec. 1, pp. 1, 14.

Chapter 4. *Estado Novo*

1. *Cf.*: Stanley Hilton, *A Rebelião Vermelha*, pp. 171-89; and Levine, *The Vargas Regime*, p. 50. The term *Estado Novo* was lifted from the tyrannical Salazar administration in Portugal.

2. *Cf.*: Seitenfus, *O Brasil de Getúlio Vargas*, p. 142; Morais, *Olga*, pp. 242-43; and Dulles, *Vargas of Brazil*, p. 166. In Dulles' view, Getúlio obviously knew that 1,200 army officers, out of 4,000 then on active duty, were Integralists or Integralist sympathizers. The navy, although smaller in manpower, was noted for having about half of its officer corps in the AIB camp. A strong fascist-style administration would not have been distasteful to many of the rest of the military elite. Nevertheless, in order to gain the green light for his *coup d' état* from the army, Vargas had to stop payment on the foreign debt and give the money to the army. Stanley Hilton, "Military Influence on Brazilian Economic Policy, 1930-1945: A Different View," *HAHR*, vol. LIII, no. 1, February 1973, p. 89, 89n. Concerning the seriousness of a communist grab at power, Seitenfus (*O Brasil de Getúlio Vargas*, p. 143) points out that after the widespread hounding of leftists following November 1935, the Communist Party practically ceased to exist. The man behind the Cohen Plan would later come to be credited with another memorable event. Once becoming a general, Olímpio Mourão would lead the first column of troops south from Juiz de Fora in the overthrow of João Goulart in 1964.

3. *Cf.*: Conniff, *Urban Politics in Brazil*, pp. 139-40; Levine, *The Vargas Regime*, pp. 150-51, 167; Dulles, *Vargas of Brazil*, pp. 176-77; and USNA, letter, "Mitchell to G-2," May 18, 1938, no. 2097, MID 2271-K-43/7. Regarding capital punishment, the American military attaché in Rio in 1938, Major Lawrence Mitchell, continued with his dispatch (USNA, letter, "Mitchell to G-2," May 18, 1938, *loc. cit.*) to his superiors in Washington. Translating from the amended new constitution, after the events of May 10, 1938 (see above pp. 83-87), he stated that article 122 of paragraph thirteen had been changed to include (f), (g), (h), and (i) below. The earlier version encompassed only the offenses listed in (a) through (e). Note the deceptive opening sentence as well as the arbitrary nature of the document:

There shall not be perpetual bodily punishments. The penalties established or aggravated in the new law shall not be retroactive. In addition to the cases treated in the military legislation for time of war, the death penalty shall be applied to the following crimes:

(a) To attempt to bring the territory of the nation or a part of it under the sovereignty of a foreign state;

(b) To attempt, with the aid or financial support of a foreign state or organization of international character, to damage the unity of the nation, seeking to dismember the territory subject to its sovereignty;

(c) To attempt by means of an armed movement, the dismembering of the national territory when repression of such movement requires operations of war;

(d) To attempt, with the aid or financial support of a foreign state or organization of international character, a change in the political or social order established by the constitution;

(e) To attempt to subvert by violent means the political and social order for the establishment of a dictatorship by a social class;

(f) Armed insurrection against the powers of the state, even though the arms be hidden;

(g) Practicing acts intended to provoke civil war, if this follows as the result of such acts;

(h) To attack the security of the state, committing devastation, sacking, arson, depredations, or any other act to implant terror;

(i) To make an attempt against the life, security or liberty of the president of the republic;

(j) Homicide when committed for a trivial motive or with extreme ferocity.

4. Dulles, *Anarchists and Communists*, pp. 459-60.

5. *The New Republic*, February 9, 1938, p. 11.

6. Robert Levine, "Elite Intervention in Urban Popular Culture in Modern Brazil," *LBR*, vol. XXI, no. 2, Winter 1984, pp. 9-17.

7. *Cf.*: Brazil, Polícia Civil do Distrito Federal, *Policia politica preventiva: programa organisação e realisações* (Rio de Janeiro: Serviço de Inqueritos Politicos Sociais, 1939), pp. 10-11; Epitácio Torres, *A polícia: uma perspectiva histórica* (Porto Alegre: Bels, 1977), pp. 68-69; and Carlos Steven Bakota, "Getúlio Vargas and the Estado Novo: An Inquiry into Ideology and Opportunism," *Latin American Research Review* (hereafter *LARR*), vol. XIV, no. 1, 1979, p. 207.

8. *Cf.*: Bakota, *loc. cit.*; and Brazil, *Constituição dos Estados Unidos do Brasil: leis constitucionais nr. 1 e 2* (Rio de Janeiro: Nacional, 1938), p. 46. As if to mark Getúlio's new position, note the AIB's final code name for Filinto Müller below p. 170 n30.

9. *Cf.*: Roberto Gambini, *O duplo jogo de Getúlio Vargas: influência americana e alemã no Estado Novo* (São Paulo: Símbolo, 1977), pp. 71-72; and Nasser, *Falta alguém em Nuremberg*, pp. 95-96. Michael Hall and Paulo Sérgio Pinheiro ("The Control and Policing of the Working Class in Brazil," paper presented to the Conference on the History of Law, Labor and Crime, University of Warwick, September 15-18, 1983, p. 16), very interestingly point out that

even before the Estado Novo, physical violence against the independent labor movement intensified. The leading figures of the regime made it clear that the new labor legislation in no way precluded police action against unacceptable mobilizations of the working class. Repression of militants soon became quite violent and aggressive. In 1934, for example, the United States military attaché, after describing the demolition of a union headquarters by the police, remarked that it was "a typical example of police excess. There was no justification for it, but there will be no redress."

The press accounts of the period make clear that the extent of violence against resistance to the official legislation scarcely differed in scale from that practiced before 1930. There were no effective limits to police activities: workers were assassinated, meetings broken up, union headquarters invaded, workers imprisoned and beaten. After the attempted Communist putsch of 1935, kidnapping and torture were institutionalized. Vigilance over workers and militants became even more complete at this period than it had been in the 1920s, . . . [since DESPS] carried out minute investigations of the political views and ideological characteristics of *whole towns* (italics added). See also above pp. 14-15, 136 n.19.

10. Ruth Landes, *The City of Women* (New York: Macmillian, 1947), p. 5.

11. *Cf*.: PPARJ, document, "S.I.-Sr/2," no. 9473, ref.-prot.-11236/53, August 13, 1953, p. 3, comunismo/pasta 39; Maria Luiza Tucci Carneiro, pp. 158-80, 184-88, 201-2, 208, 213, 266-71, 273, 277-78, 280-85, 288, 325, 331, 336-37, 348, 524, 543-49; Bakota, p. 209; Thomas Skidmore, "Race and Class in Brazil: Historical Perspectives, *LBR*, vol. XX, no. 1, Summer 1983, pp. 106-7; *Folha de São Paulo*, November 11, 1987, p. A-4; *Veja*, November 4, 1987, pp. 111-12; Affonso Henriques, *Ascensão e queda de Getúlio Vargas: o Estado Nôvo* (Rio de Janeiro: Record, 1966), vol. II, pp. 43-44; Jeff Lesser, "Are African-Americans African or American?: Brazilian Immigration Policy in the 1920s," prepublication manuscript, p. 17; and Jeff Lesser, telephone interview, Fresno/New London, November 29, 1990. See Lesser's review of Maria Luiza Tucci Carneiro's *O antissemitismo na era Vargas* in the *JLAS*, vol. XXI, no. 3, October 1989, pp. 613-15; and his comments in *Senhor*, April 4, 1988, pp. 61-64. Aranha usually kept his prejudices within government circles so that Vargas could hedge his bets with both the Allies and the Axis. But he slipped occasionally and let his true (class-based) feelings be known to outsiders. As concerns blacks, this *faux pas* occurred once when American anthropologist Ruth Landes visited Brazil to do research on African religions. Passing through Rio while on her way to Bahia, she met Oswaldo in his office after he had become foreign minister. He told her then that "since you are going to study Negroes, I must tell you that our political backwardness, which made this dictatorship necessary, is due entirely to our Negro blood. Unfortunately. So we are trying to breed the blood out, making one nation of all the people, 'whitening the Brazilian race.'" Landes, p. 6. Perhaps Aranha thought Landes would not mind him speaking this way, seeing as she came from a country where *apartheid* was called "separate but equal." What Oswaldo really wanted for Brazil was more white Christian immigration, especially from the Scandinavian countries and other places in Europe with a high percentage of blue-eyed blonds. Maria Luiza Tucci Carneiro, p. 212. The American government, years later, had the following excerpt in their file on Aranha: "he is a brilliant, charming, and exceedingly vain man of mercurial temperament whose long political and diplomatic career has been characterized by opportunism entirely unaffected by considerations of principle." United States, Department of State [hereafter USDS], document, "Intelligence Report No. 8002: Nationalism in Brazil," July 24, 1959, AW-02/552/no. 8002/c.1, p. 72.

12. See, for example, the remarks by Seitenfus ("Ideology and Diplomacy," p. 527) that Italy and Germany thought Brazil might soon join with them by signing the anti-Comintern pact.

13. Dulles, *Vargas of Brazil*, p. 178. Getúlio may have put out the order to start cracking down on the AIB even before his November 10th speech. As early as October 8th, there were two separate reports of the police arresting AIB members in different parts of Paraná. In one case violence was used; in the other the arrested Green Shirts were held incommunicado. *Cf*.: APS: telegram, "Carvalho e Fernandes Campos to Plinio Salgado," October 8, 1937, Pi 37.10.08/5; and telegram, "Ramos Angelo Fraxino to Plinio Salgado," October 8, 1937, Pi 37.10.08/7.

14. John Gunther, "This is Vargas," *Current History and Forum*, June 1941, p. 15. This hypocorism was in use at least by December 1937. PPARJ, newspaper article, "*16 de Julho*," December 1, 1937, p. 1, comunismo/pasta 4. The reason behind the name Gegê for Vargas is obscure. One translation defines the word as a black African brought to Brazil during the days of slavery.

15. *Cf.*: PPARJ: document, "K-55 'Cadernos da Hora Presente,'" February 8, 1940, integralismo/pasta 8; letter, "Waldemar Pereira Cotta to general public," September 13, 1941, integralismo/pasta 7; document, "S-1, boletim no. 17," January 20, 1941, p. x-xiii, integralismo/pasta 3; document, "S-1, boletim no. 39," February 14, 1941, p. xii, integralismo/pasta 3; document, "S-1, boletim no. 49," February 26, 1941, p. x, integralismo/pasta 3; document "S-1, boletim no. 101," April 29, 1941, pp. xi-xii, integralismo/pasta 3; document, "S-1, boletim no. 167," July 15, 1941, p. xi, integralismo/pasta 3; document, "S-1, boletim no. 184," August 4, 1941, pp. xii, xviii, integralismo/pasta 3; document, "S-1, boletim no. 187," August 7, 1942, pp. xi, integralismo/pasta 3; document, "S-1, boletim no. 223," September 18, 1942, pp. xii, integralismo/pasta 3; document, "S-1, boletim no. 229," September 25, 1942, pp. xv, integralismo/pasta 3; document, "S-1, boletim no. 238" September 30, 1940, p. xiii, integralismo/pasta 3; document, "S.S.I boletim no. 13," January 14, 1941, pp. vi-vii, integralismo/pasta 3; miscellaneous documents, "Associação dos Amigos de São José," n.d., integralismo/pasta 10; miscellaneous documents, "Centro Espírita Nossa Senhora do Carmo," n.d., integralismo/pasta 10; miscellaneous documents, "Clube Hipico de Vila Guilherme," n.d., integralismo/pasta 10; miscellaneous documents, "Curso Tuiutí," n.d., integralismo/pasta 10; miscellaneous documents, "Distinta Atlético Clube," n.d., integralismo/pasta 10; miscellaneous documents, "Empresa Metreleco," n.d., integralismo/pasta 10; miscellaneous documents, "Excelsior Sociedade Anônima," n.d., integralismo/pasta 10; miscellaneous documents, "*Revista Brasil Mineral*," n.d., integralismo/pasta 10; miscellaneous documents, "Sociedade Dramatica Particular Filhos de Talma," n.d., integralismo/pasta 10; and miscellaneous photographs, "[untitled]," integralismo/pasta 9.

16. *Cf.*: Morais, *Olga*, p. 144; and CPDOC, oral history, "Paulo Pinheiro Chagas," 1977, p. 71. In respect to the creation of the *polaca*, the British assert that "Campos drew up and presented on Vargas' invitation, three Fascist-type Constitutions for him to choose from within a period of ten days–a typical example of his intellectual capacity and superficilaity [*sic*]." UKPRO, "Brazil, Political 'Who's Who,'" *loc. cit.*

17. CPDOC, "Augusto do Amaral Peixoto," p. 120.

18. AFM, biography, "Francisco da Silva Campos," 1937, CPDOC, p. 7.

19. See above p. 139 n.61.

20. *Cf.*: PPARJ: document, [untitled, but commencing:] "Senhor capitão, Devolvo a V.S. devidamente informada, a inclusa relação dos funcionários do D.I.P.," n.d., p. 3, administração/pasta 13; document, "D-15, *A Tarde*," August 6, 1940, geral/pasta 1; Duarte, *Prisão, exílio, luta . . .* , p. 208; and Beloch and Abreu, pp. 1076-77, 1310. The official rate of exchange on 10:000$000 was $606.06. *Jornal do Commercio*, July 8-9, 1940, p. 7.

21. Claudio de Lacerda [Paiva], p. 36.

22. PPARJ, document, "Confidential," November 23, 1940, p. 2, administração/pasta 13.

23. *Cf.*: *Ibid.*, p. 1; DIP, document, "S-1, boletim no. 234," October 11-12, 1941, p. xx [PPARJ, administração/pasta 13]; *Jornal do Commercio*, October 13-14, 1941, p. 9; AFM: biography, "Vicente Ráo," n.d., CPDOC, p. 2; and biography, "Lourival Fontes," 1941, CPDOC, pp. 2-4.

24. Hall and Pinheiro, p. 18.

25. Along with Gegê, Xuxu is said to have been another name given to Getúlio by the people. The word is an adulteration of "chuchu," a type of "proliferating Brazilian Weed." Gunther, *loc. cit.* A chuchu plant (gen. *Sechium edule*) is known in English as a chayote.

26. Hall and Pinheiro, *loc.cit.*

27. AFM, "Lourival Fontes," p. 4. The English were already convinced that Fontes was "a second Goebbels." UKPRO, "Brazil, Political 'Who's Who,'" p. 11.

28. *Cf.*: Anonymous-1: interviews, Rio de Janeiro, October 5, 1992; and October 6, 1992.

29. *Cf.*: Seitenfus, "Ideology and Diplomacy," p. 528, 528n; and Dulles, *Vargas of Brazil*, p. 180. The statute prohibiting schools from teaching in languages other than Portuguese was apparently not enforced against the Italian schools. Frank McCann, *The Brazilian-American Alliance, 1937-1945* (Princeton: Princeton University Press, 1973), p. 90.

30. PPARJ, document, "S-1, boletim no. 227," September 23, 1941, pp. xiii-xiv, integralismo/pasta 9. An orthographic change in the 1930s spelling of Paschoal now renders it as Pascal. It is translated as anything dealing with Easter or Passover. Note the oblique AIB bond between Vargas and things Jewish. Paschoal will be cited in the original. The Integralists, moreover, had nicknames for everybody and everything. As examples, some of the people or items of importance to this text are listed below. Where applicable a translation is provided in parentheses:

Alberto, João: "Herminio"

Aranha, Oswaldo: "Martinho," "Mendonça," "Arminda"

Army: "Torres," "Comadre Tonica" ("Tonic Godmother"), "Cia. Metalurgica" ("Metal Company")

Barata, Agildo: "Toledo"

Brazilian government: "Delegado" ("policeman"), "-cidio," (when used as a suffix "-death")

Chief of the Communist Revolution: "Trajano" ("Trojan")

Comintern: "Guido," "Ibarra," "Pardal da Cunha" ("Cunha Sparrow"), "*Dona* Ramires"

Communist cells: "Coleções de selos" ("Stamp Collections")

Communist cells in the army: "Pamfilio" ("Chrysanthemum" or "To Goad")

Constitution of November 10, 1937: "Rubião" ("Large Ruby")

Diario Carioca: "Nolasco"

Diretrizes: "Edgard"

DOPS: "Higino"

Dutra, Eurico Gaspar: "Lira," "Nicota," "Rosita," "Venancio," "Salustiana," "Francisco Lopes"

England: "Gamaliel," "Zulmira"

Fontes, Lourival: "Barradas"

Italy: "Homero"

Itamarati: "Umbelina"

Luzardo, Batista: "Leitão" ("Big Pig")

Monteiro, Góis: "Juvelino," "Olavo," "Risoleta," "José Cardoso"

Müller, Filinto: "David," "Ezequiel," "Sinhazinha" ("Little Miss" A sympathetic form of speech previously used to address the daughter of one's *coronel*.)

Police: "Deolinda"

Post and telegraph: "Temistocles"

Press campaign against integralism: "O dieta vegetariana" ("The Vegetarian Diet")

Prestes, Luís Carlos: "Humberto," "Ivo," "*Dona* Izabel Regueira"

Prison: "Casa da Lucinda" ("House of Lucinda")

Ráo, Vicente: "Justino"

Supreme Military Tribunal: "Amaral"

Teixeira, Felisberto Batista: "Nicolino"

Vargas, Benjamin: "Belarmino"

Cf.: ARC, [Untitled List of Integralist Code Names for Miscellaneous Entities], n.d., pp. 1-3.

31. For more on the Góis Monteiro-officer-Integralist link, plus an estimate of AIB size in the military, see above p. 142 n.90. For a second calculation of Sigma's strength in the armed forces, see above p. 166 n.2.

32. Molly was described as

one of the most dangerous of individuals owing to his "kinship" with Göring in addition to the fact that he was one of Ribbentrop's agents. This put him in a situation of being more of a figure than the German ambassador himself. Dr. Molly regularly held meetings among elements of nazism-fascism at his residence at Rua Morro Verde 15 [in Pacaembu]. Confidentially, Mussolini told us that on various occasions even Brazilian personalities went to these encounters. PPARJ, document, "L/1-R/2," July 23, 1941, p. 2, alemão/pasta 1.

33. Cf.: Jornal do Commercio, January 5, 1938, p. 11; PPARJ: document, "MM/4.557-18-2-42," February 18, 1942, p. 6 [7], alemão/pasta 15; and "Relatorio," [January 1938], pp. 1-3, comunismo/pasta 22. Note that this last item was/is incorrectly filed in these archives. It should be stored along with the bundles on integralismo.

34. PPARJ, document, "Integralismo, sinais convencionais (correspondencia)," n.d., integralismo/pasta 4.

35. Following the events later in the year, in May, there are only two further reports by DESPS/DOPS agents warning headquarters in Rio that they had uncovered more arms caches. Both cases were uncovered in 1941 in other states (São Paulo and Espírito Santo). There is no comment on what action was taken. Cf.: PPARJ: document, "S.R. boletim no. 506," March 3, 1941, p. vii, integralismo/pasta 4, cont. II; and document, "Atividades integralistas no. 6° batalhão de caçadores da Força Publica," [archived October 20, 1941], pp. 1-4, integralismo/ pasta 4, cont. II.

36. PPARJ, document, "Relação dos officiaes e praças da policia militar que fazem parte da extintax[sic]–A.B.I.[sic]," May 16, 1938, administração/pasta 15. The Polícia Militar component was made up of 1 colonel, 3 majors, 11 captains, 11 first lieutenants, 10 second lieutenants, 21 sergeants, 9 corporals, 2 privates 1st class, 49 police soldiers, 1 official (unspecified), 1 civilian electrician, 1 motorist, 1 male nurse, 1 member of the band, and 1 trainee. See also below pp. 176 n.80, 178 n.92.

37. Cf.: Beloch and Abreu, pp. 1339, 2934-35, 3058; Dulles, Vargas of Brazil, pp. 182-83; a nd Seitenfus, O Brasil de Getúlio Vargas, p. 196. Fournier has been described by Figueiredo (CPDOC, "Guilherme Figueiredo," 1977, p. 63) as a "stupid scoundrel, completely nuts, inconsistent in political philosophy, and rabidly against Getúlio."

38. The Plínio Salgado Archives in Rio Claro contain but a single innocuous letter for the entire month of May 1938. This may well have been the result of an act of cleansing by Carmela Salgado, or others, who spent several years organizing Plínio's documents before they were opened to the public. Rio Claro was chosen as the place to house the would-be dictator's papers because it was the first city in Brazil to go AIB. Monitor Integralista (Rio de Janeiro), May 1-15, 1934, p. 1. A good paulista, Plínio wanted his memorial left in his home state. There are still numerous sympathizers living in the area.

39. Cf.: PPARJ: document, "O assalto ao Palácio Guanabara 11-5-1938," by [illegible], July 2, 1938, p. 2, integralismo/pasta 5; and catalogue, "Álbum do Delegacia Especial de Segurança Politica e Social," Distrito Federal, loc. cit.; Dulles (Vargas of Brazil, p. 184) says there were forty-five while Beloch and Abreu (p. 2936), and Nasser (A revolução dos covardes, p. 100) put the number at only thirty. The actual figure was probably between thirty-two and thirty-four. Alzira Vargas do Amaral Peixoto (Jornal do Brasil, July 28, 1991, sec. 1, p. 14) later stated that the attackers she saw were all beardless adolescents. Fournier had taken the plan of attack to a prison hospital where one of the earlier plotters, and 1932 Civil War opposition officer, Euclydes Figueiredo, was being

detained. The father of one of Brazil's future military dictators, Figueiredo fine-tuned the strategy. Beloch and Abreu, p. 1273.

40. *Cf.*: Beloch and Abreu, p. 2936; Brandi, p. 130; Alzira Vargas do Amaral Peixoto, *Getúlio Vargas: meu pai*, pp. 187-94; *Jornal do Brasil*, July 28, 1991, sec. 1, p. 14; Levine, *The Vargas Regime*, p. 164; Dulles, *Vargas of Brazil*, pp. 184-86; Seitenfus, *O Brasil de Getúlio Vargas*, pp. 196-97, 197n; PPARJ: "O assalto ao Palácio Guanabara 11-5-1938," pp. 2-3, 7, 12-13; catalogue, "Álbum do Delegacia Especial de Segurança Politica e Social," *loc. cit.*; USNA, microfilm, "Caffery to Secretary of State," May 12, 1938, M1472/8; Hélio Silva, *1938, terrorismo em campo verde* (Rio de Janeiro: Civilização Brasileira, 1971), pp. 234-44; and Robson Gracie, interview, Rio de Janeiro, August 6, 1991. Euzébio de Queiroz Filho recounted his activities after the AIB attack to Robson Gracie. The number of AIB dead is listed at between seven and nine. There was no one injured nor any losses on the government side. Hélio Silva, *1938, terrorismo em campo verde, loc. cit.*

41. *Cf.*: PPARJ: document, "Relatório movimento integralista 11 de maio de [1]938," by Alberto Tornaghi, July 16, 1938, pp. 5, 7, 9-10, 13-17, 19-24, 26-31, 33, integralismo/pasta 5; catalogue "Álbum do Delegacia Especial de Segurança Politica e Social," *loc. cit.*; document, [untitled declaration of Euzébio de Queiroz Filho], 735-41, pp. 1-4, integralismo/pasta 5; and document, "Delegado Dr. Bradão Filho: copia do relatorio referente ao processo que apurou o movimento revolutionario na marinha," July 1938, pp. 1-19, integralismo/pasta 5. *Jornal do Brasil* (May 4, 1988, sec. 1, p. 4) states that about twenty fascists lost their lives in the fighting throughout the city. For a report of the aborted AIB plans up in Paraíba, see PPARJ, document, "54 [by hand]," 656, May 20, 1938, integralismo/pasta 5, cont.

42. One American diplomat noted two months later that since Vargas had not acted on these resignations, this indicated a complicity on the part of the police. USNA, microfilm, "Woodward to Buttler, Duggan, and Wells," July 11, 1938, M1472/8. See as well the references in Alzira Vargas do Amaral Peixoto (*Getúlio Vargas: meu pai*, pp. 198-99), Seitenfus ("Ideology and Diplomacy," p. 530n), and Augusto do Amaral Peixoto (CPDOC, "Augusto do Amaral Peixoto," p. 295) for commentary that lends weight to a conspiracy thesis. For what happened to Müller's resignation, see above pp. 95-96.

43. *Cf.*: PPARJ: document, "Relação dos individuos presos por esta secção, 11 a 31 de maio último, com uma sintese do historico e a situação em que se encontram," June 10, 1938, pp. 1-81, integralismo/pasta 9; and letter, "321, S/2 to chefe da S/4," June 22, 1938, integralismo/pasta 9. Another DESPS report places the number of arrested at only 455. PPARJ, document, "Delegacia Especial de Segurança Politica e Social secção," June 10, 1938, pp. 1-81, administração/pasta 17. A patrol of anti-Vargas fighters near the presidential palace led by Friedrich Kempter, one of the principal Nazi spies in South America, was reportedly discovered by government troops on the very night of the AIB offensive, May 10-11, 1938. Two pictures of Kempter appear among the unnumbered plates between pp. 246-47 in Rout and Bratzel. Fournier is supposed to have purchased arms for the attack from the German firms he represented in Brazil (Seitenfus, *O Brasil de Getúlio Vargas*, pp. 201, 204). Beloch and Abreu (*loc. cit.*) add that Gustavo Barroso contacted the German news agency, Transocean, with the same objective. Finally, Levine (*The Vargas Regime*, p. 164) remarks that "one of the captured rebels confessed that the Banco Germânico had aided the plot . . . [and] as a result, several of the bank's officers were held." In regard to the German Transatlantic Bank's connection to the overall intrigue, see above p. 84. For another governmental measure that grew out of the events of May 10, 1938, see above p. 166 n.3.

44. The PCB sent a letter to Vargas three years later in which it claimed that the activity of Nazi 5th columnists had become so extensive that even Francisco Campos quipped

about it to friends. The minister stated that "at the desired hour, Hitler can conquer Brazil by telephone." PPARJ, letter, "[PCB] Carta aberta ao Sr. Getulio Vargas," September 8, 1941, p. 4, comunismo/pasta 20.

45. For the American police contribution in 1931, see above pp. 15, 136 n.20. See also above pp 39, 148 n.38, 154 n.82. Müller had always had his own informants (see, as examples, above pp. 58, 89). And, Filinto kept his eyes on no less than 125 important individuals of his day (see above p. 135 n.14). The chief even had his boys shadow Aranha when Oswaldo was foreign minister. The U.S. military attaché Edwin Sibert commented on this state of affairs in May 1941. His communiqué back to Washington noted that Aranha

was in a bookstore a few days ago in the presence of a friend of mine. It seems that Mr. Aranha had purchased a few books and started out of the store. Near the entrance he whirled and seized a man by his coat collar, shook his fist in his face and told him to go back and tell his blankety-blank boss that he would not have his spies following him anymore. USNA, letter, "Sibert to A.C. of S., G-2," May 10, 1941, no. 2714, p. 1, MID 2657-K-128/6.

46. Cf.: Rout and Bratzel, pp. 113-14; Levine, *The Vargas Regime*, p. 56; and Dulles, *Vargas of Brazil*, p. 189. Note that different figures have been presented by other authors. For example, Levine (*The Vargas Regime*, p. 164) puts the total number of arrests at 1,500, one-third of whom were enlisted men. Beloch and Abreu (*loc. cit.*) agree with Levine but make no mention of the military portion. And Edgar Carone (*O Estado Novo, 1937-1945* [São Paulo: Difusão Européia do Livro, 1976], p. 200), places the data for the city and state of Rio de Janeiro much lower, at 600 arrests with over 400 being released in the days following the attempted takeover. But here, too, the military aspect is not mentioned. Dulles' statistics were based on a communication of the then U.S. Ambassador Jefferson Caffery. In respect to the uneven pursuit of leftists over fascist, note the comment by Filinto in November 1939 that while they were watching the Integralists, the communists were the only ones being imprisoned. AFM, telegram, "Filinto Müller to Riograndino da Costa e Silva," November 12, 1939, CPDOC/FM 33.02.21/ dip/ad.

47. PPARJ, document, "[untitled manuscript from agent] K. 47," [archived June 6, 1940], pp. 1-2, integralismo/ pasta 4b.

48. Cf.: PPARJ, letter, "Odylio Denys to Exmᵒ Snr. Dr. Delegado Especial de Segurança Politica e Social," April 20, 1945, geral/pasta 3; Brazil, Comissão Especial de Inquérito sôbre Atos Delituosos da Ditadura, "Depoimento do David Nasser," *loc. cit.*; Beloch and Abreu, p. 1340; and Hélio Silva, *1938*, p. 211.

49. For one of Barroso's conspiracies, see above p. 172 n.43. A Green Shirt later stated that Gustavo's brief visit with the authorities was anything but comfortable. According to this witness, Barroso was thrown into a cell that was originally built to hold but twenty prisoners. There were some 200 apprehended persons in the same confine. Forty-eight hours later, he was moved to another, more comfortable, cell. Brazil, Comissão Especial de Inquérito sôbre Atos Delituosos da Ditadura, "Depoimento do Olindo Semeraro," *loc. cit.* Minister of War Eurico Gaspar Dutra was probably the one who interceded. He told Barroso that he would send an army escort to defend him, and that he wanted the press to cease their campaign against Integralists and recognize that they are in fact true patriots. APS, telegram, "[Unsigned] to [Plínio Salgado]," [September 10, 1938], Pi 38.09.10/1. This same telegram also notes that some AIB leaders, Rio Chief Raimundo Padilha among them, received the kid-glove treatment.

50. If the astonishment of his followers at his sudden liberation can be taken as an indication of his guilt, Plínio was decidedly involved with the planning of the pajama-

Putsch. As examples of their surprise *cf*.: APS: letter, "Thompson to Chefe [Plínio Salgado]," March 2, 1939, Pi 39.03.02/5; telegram, "Dorval Santos to Plinio Salgado," March 12, 1939, Pi 39.03.12/1; telegram, "Mario Matos to Plinio Salgado," March 11, 1939, Pi 39.03.11/1; telegram, "Mayrink to Plinio Salgado," February 28, 1939, Pi 39.02.28/8; telegram, "Pedro Rodrigues to Plinio Salgado," March 7, 1939, Pi 39.03.07/1; and telegram, "Reinaldo Veloso Jose Antunes to Plinio Salgado," March 11, 1939, Pi 39.03.11/3.

51. *Cf*.: PPARJ: document, "Introito," June 15, 1954, pp. 1-2, integralismo/pasta 21; "K-55 'Cadernos da hora presente," integralismo/pasta 8; Dulles, *Vargas of Brazil*, pp. 182, 191; and Carone, p. 208. The two publications were *Cadernos da hora presente* and V*ida de Jesus*.

52. For more on what some of these individuals did in their fight against communism, as well as for additional comments on Felisberto Batista Teixeira, see above pp. 59-60, 90, 159 n.113 and below n.58.

53. *Cf*.: Cecil Borer: interviews, Rio de Janeiro, May 28, 1998; May 29, 1998; *Diario Carioca*, June 28, 1963, p. 6; Sodré, pp. 278-79, 278n-280n; and *Jornal do Brasil*, March 11, 1987, sec. Cidade, p. 1. A picture of Civis Müller can be seen in Photo 9.

54. *Cf*.: Sodré, p. 283n; Beloch and Abreu, pp. 1340, 2936; *Veja*, July 17, 1974, p. 28; Gregório Bezerra in Lima, p. 140; Brazil: Comissão Especial de Inquérito sôbre Atos Delituosos da Ditadura, "Depoimento do Olindo Semeraro," *loc. cit*.; and "Depoimento do Carlos Marighella," p. 5204. Nasser (*Falta alguém em Nuremberg*, p. 59) discounts that Integralists were tortured, adding that only communists and other persons on the left, or those sympathizing with them, were really roughed up, never members of the AIB. As concerns feeding prisoners to the sharks (*Veja*, July 17, 1974, p. 28), the author of this observation mistakenly attributes these murders to "Filinto Müller and his Polícia Especial." Müller was never in charge of the Tomato Heads. See also above pp. 18, 137 n.37.

55. *Cf*.: AN: document, 571, December 28, 1937, Secretária da Presidência da República, 14.15/lata 99; document, 5315, March 3, 1938, Secretária da Presidência da República, 14.15/lata 99, p. 2; *Jornal do Commercio*, December 29, 1937, p. 13; March 4, 1938, p. 8; and Brazil, Conselho Nacional de Desenvolvimento Científico e Technológico, *Boletim do Museu Paraense Emílio Goeldi* (Belem: Instituto Nacional de Pesquisas da Amazônia, Zoologica, no. 118, October 13, 1982), pp. 2-3.

56. A *feitor* was an overseer from the days of Brazilian slavery.

57. See chap. 3.

58. *Cf*.: Brazil, Comissão Especial de Inquérito sôbre Atos Delituosos da Ditadura, "Depoimento do Iguatemi Ramos da Silva," *loc. cit*.; PPARJ: document, "Em Fernando de Noronha," [archived October 19, 1940], pp. 36-37, administração/pasta 16; letter, "Aos camaradas do B.B. do P.C. dos Estados Unidos," n.d., comunismo/pasta 20; letter, "Sub-chefe de grupo da P.E and detetive da classe I to Exmo Sr. Dr. Major Chefe da Policia [Filinto Müller]," March 7, 1941, pp. 1, 4, administração/pasta 16; periodical article, "*Solidariedade*," September 1939, pp. 17-18, comunismo/pasta 4e; *Jornal do Brasil*, March 14, 1987, sec. Cidade, p. 5; and Dulles, *Brazilian Communism*, p. 148. For the *seção de explosivos* see above p. 63. For the *adelfis* and *bucha de mustarda*, see above p. 60. As if these things never took place and were not taking place, in 1941 Felisberto confidently wrote his superior, Filinto Müller, an embellished thirty-one page letter. At one point in his commentary, he observed that "we grasp the feeling of justice and serenity that you have transmitted to your subordinates, creating an energetic and combative mentality; but never permitting any excess no matter how deliberate the crime." PPARJ, "[Felisberto] Baptista Teixeira to Dr. Major Chefe da Polícia [Filinto Müller]," p. 28.

59. *Cf.*: Dulles, *Brazilian Communism*, pp. 148-49, 186-87; and Nasser, *Falta alguém em Nuremberg*, p. 45. For Caneppa and Alencar Filho's new duties, see above pp. 54-55, 59, 63, 162 n.122.

60. Nasser, *Falta alguém em Nuremberg*, p. 50.

61. *Cf.*: Torres, p. 69; Levine, *The Vargas Regime*, p. 231n; and Brazil, Polícia Civil do Distrito Federal, *Policia politica preventiva*, pp. 11-15. For the Serviço de Divulgação, see above pp. 78-79.

62. In March 1938, the Brazilian army ordered $55 million in artillery pieces plus accessories from the Krupp concern. Vargas was also planning to spend $100 million on German weapons over a five-year period. McCann, *The Brazilian-American Alliance*, p. 111.

63. *Cf.*: Stanley Hilton: "Brazilian Diplomacy and the Washington-Rio de Janeiro 'Axis' during the World War II Era," pp. 205-10; and "The Armed Forces and Industrialists in Modern Brazil: The Drive for Military Autonomy, 1889-1954," *HAHR*, vol. LXII, no. 4, November 1982, p. 647. For examples of the way Vargas dealt in secret with the Germans, *cf.*: Henriques, vol. II, pp. 288-92; and Seitenfus, *O Brasil de Getúlio Vargas*, pp. 324-36. As for the Americans, while talks with them were going on, a postcard began to circulate in Brazil which may have been an attempt to prod the U.S. government into supplying military aid. The postcard depicted three oval portraits. On the left was Mussolini; in the center, Hitler; and on the right, Vargas. Henriques, vol. II, pp. 296-97.

64. *Cf.*: Beloch and Abreu, pp. 2233-34; Dulles, *Vargas of Brazil*, pp. 201-4; Stanley Hilton, "Military Influence on Brazilian Economic Policy," pp. 73-94; Frank McCann, "The Brazilian Army and the Problem of Mission, 1930-1964," *JLAS*, vol. XII, no. 1, May 1980, p. 117; and John Wirth, *The Politics of Brazilian Development, 1930-1954* (Stanford: Stanford University Press, 1970), pp. 9-12.

65. *Cf.*: Duarte, *Prisão, exílio, luta . . . , loc. cit.*; Levine, *The Vargas Regime*, p. 156; Stanley Hilton, *A Rebelião Vermelha*, pp. 171-75; Dulles, *Vargas of Brazil*, pp. 145, 196, 204-5; Beloch and Abreu, pp. 1134, 2255; Lourival Coutinho, *O General Góes depõe* (Rio de Janeiro: Coelho Branco, 1955), pp. 360-65; *Jornal do Brasil*, January 26, 1985, sec. B, p. 8; McCann, *The Brazilian-American Alliance*, pp. 260n-261n; and Seitenfus, *O Brasil de Getúlio Vargas*, pp. 389n-390n. American agents in Brazil analyzed the international-political preferences of the army and civilian sectors of the population as the following: "Most reports indicate that the army officers are overwhelmingly pro-Nazi, the non-commissioned officers are more evenly divided, and sentiment among the privates, like the sentiment outside the army, is pro-United States." USDS, document, "The Relation of Brazil to the Defense of the Northeast" [probably 1941], 097.3/Z1092/no. 142, p. 3.

66. *Cf.*: PPARJ, document, "Politica externa britanica com o Brasil," July 11, 1940 [by hand], p. 2, inglês/pasta 3; and McCann, *The Brazilian-American Alliance*, p. 256.

67. *Cf.*: McCann, *The Brazilian-American Alliance, loc. cit.*; and Duarte, *Prisão, exílio, luta . . . , loc. cit.*

68. *Cf.*: Freyre, *Order and Progress*, p. 348; *Jornal do Brasil*, August 30, 1987, sec. 1, p. 4; and USNA, letter, "Sibert to A.C. of S., G-2," May 17, 1941, no. 2727, p. 1, MID 2657-K-128/7.

69. *Cf.*: Sodré, p. 282; and José Murilo de Carvalho (*Jornal do Brasil*, May 21, 1988, sec. 1, p. 11.

70. PPARJ, document, "Inteligence [sic] Service," S-1. boletim no. 229, September 25, 1941, p. xii, inglês/pasta 3.

71. McCann, *The Brazilian-American Alliance*, pp. 256, 280, 301. One of the conspirators was the then ex-chief of the Polícia Civil, Filinto Müller. See below n.76.

72. *Cf.*: William Stevenson, *A Man Called Intrepid: The Secret War* (New York: Ballantine, 1976), pp. 166-70; and PPARJ, document, "Discurso presidencial de 11 de junho," June 1940, pp. 30-32, 40-41, 44-46, administração/pasta 11.

73. *Cf.*: USDS, "The Relation of Brazil to the Defense of the Northeast," pp. 4-5; Beloch and Abreu, pp. 1134, 2255-56; Dulles, *Vargas of Brazil*, 205-41, 226; and PPARJ, document, "Politica externa britanica com o Brasil," p. 4. For more on the *Graf Spee*'s crew members, and an interesting tie in with Filinto Müller, see chap. 3, nn. 26-27.

74. Stevenson, pp. 293-96. Stephenson claimed (p. 295) that this was the major episode that moved Vargas "under the Anglo-American umbrella."

75. Stanley Hilton, "Brazilian Diplomacy and the Washington-Rio de Janeiro 'Axis' during the World War II Era," pp. 218-22, 221n, 230; and McCann, *The Brazilian-American Alliance*, pp. 256-57.

76. Seitenfus, *O Brasil de Getúlio Vargas*, pp. 415-18. Filinto's offer to quit his post had been tendered way back in 1938. In this respect, see above pp. 83-87, 95-96, 172 n.42.

77. Nasser, *Falta alguém em Nuremberg*, p. 29. That which did not go up in smoke eventually became the property of Müller's two daughters, Maria Luíza Müller de Almeida and Rita Julia Lastra Müller. They or someone else removed many other no doubt interesting items from the material finally donated to the CPDOC Archives at the Fundação Getúlio Vargas in Rio de Janeiro. Anonymous-5, interview, Rio de Janeiro, July 5, 1990. At the insistence of the two daughters, even this delimited material was not opened to the public until 1990.

78. *O Estado de São Paulo*, August 19, 1979, p. 11. A congressional commission was later empowered to investigate crimes committed by the police during the Vargas dictatorship. All accusations against Müller came to naught. Beloch and Abreu, p. 2345. A small part of the testimony presented to the commission is, nevertheless, recounted here in items citing the "Comissão Especial de Inquérito sôbre Atos Delituosos da Ditadura."

79. PPARJ, letter, "Alexandre Zacarias de Assumpção to interventôr federal," July 20, 1945, pp. 1-3, administração/pasta 5. The thirty-seven prisoners fell into three apparent groups: (1) twenty-eight Germans or Austrians, (2) six Japanese, and (3) three Brazilian and German/Austrians. There were no Italians. Note that no less than one Nazi accused Müller (Rout and Bratzel, p. 192) of being one of his torturers. This was an exception because Müller rarely got involved in the dirty work himself.

80. See the report by political police agents in 1940 and 1941 that 1,000 men were ready to support any armed movement that Plínio desired; that there were plans by conspiring members of the AIB to go to the Northeast to foment revolution; and that elements within the fire department affirmed that they were ready for the next Integralist insurrection. The number of AIB members in the Federal District's Polícia Militar, however, was down from 123 in May 1938 to forty-three by 1941 (see above pp. 85, 171 n.36). Note also the comments (above, pp. 97-98 and below p. 178 n.87) about the secret Nazi airfield near Formosa in Goiás. *Cf.*: PPARJ: document, "Boletim reservado S-1, conspiração integralista," March 11, 1940, pp. 1-2, integralismo/pasta 6; document, "S-1, boletim no. 173," July 22, 1941, p. xv, integralismo/pasta 6; document, "S.S.I, boletim no. 192," July 26, 1941, pp. i-ii, integralismo/pasta 6; and document, "Relação dos integralistas da policia militar do Distrito Federal." [1941], administração/ pasta 15.

81. Stanley Hilton, *Hitler's Secret War in South America, 1939-1945: German Military Espionage and Allied Counterespionage in Brazil* (Baton Rouge: Louisiana State University Press, 1981), pp. 272-74. Schellenberg later tried to take credit for the first contact with Salgado. He evidently used the pseudonym "Rolf L. Larson" when reporting the details of the story to Brazilian authorities after Vargas left power. *Cf.*: PPARJ, letter, "Rolf L. Larson to [Chief of Police]," June 18, 1946, p. l, integralismo/pasta 4, cont. I; and Rout and Bratzel, p. 360

82. *Cf.*: PPARJ: document, "Integralismo, S.1, boletim no. 119," p. xiii, May 20, 1942, integralismo/pasta 4, cont. I; and miscellaneous documents, "Campanha do 'V'," n.d., inglês/pasta 2. This last report includes examples of "V" lapel pins and "V" advertisements from the newspapers.

83. Although Plínio Salgado went to his reward of natural causes in 1975, the AIB never died out. As late as September 1942, they were letting off bombs at newspaper stands they did not like, and placing explosive devices in the trash on Avenida Rio Branco or on trams that ran throughout the former capital. In the ensuing decades they surfaced now and again to rattle sabers at nonbelievers. In October 1987, fifty surviving members held a beer-hall-type reunion at a restaurant in the Cinelândia section of downtown Rio de Janeiro. At this gathering, the public was informed that it could keep abreast of Integralist opinions and campaigns through the party newspaper, *O Jornal da Comarca.* One of the coming events, it was revealed, was a national convention on January 22nd of the following year, Salgado's birthday. Recognition was likewise offered for the support given at different times by some of Brazil's political elite and/or their relatives. The list of names included ex-dictator Emílio Médici and his wife; the parents of ex-dictator João Figueiredo; the wife of then President-elect Tancredo Neves; the parents of former Vice President Aureliano Chaves; then current leader of the Partido de Frente Liberal, Marco Maciel, who would become Brazil's vice president in 1995; ex-Justice Minister Alfredo Buzaid; then Planning Minister Aníbal Teixeira; Congressman Cunha Bueno; two federal audit office officials, Ivan Luz and Alberto Holefmann; along with former AIB theorist, and at the time University of São Paulo academician, Miguel Reale. A photograph of this Sigma get together, complete with fascist salutes, and no doubt shouts of *Anauê!*, were part of the press coverage. Claiming to have 4,000 members, and now calling themselves the PAI (Partido da Ação Integralista) or Integralist Action Party, the patriots in green were at it again on May 1, 1988, in the center of São Paulo. Aided by three other far-right groups and a bunch of skinheads, the never-say-die Integralists tried to disrupt a Labor Day rally at which Luís Carlos Prestes was scheduled to speak. Twelve of the fascists were arrested but soon released. It was later announced that the PAI faithful would defend in the streets the candidate they proposed to offer the nation for president in the general elections scheduled for 1989. Two months later, on April 20, 1989, the centennial of Adolf Hitler's birth, the new PAI *Führer*, Anésio de Lara Campos, ominously told stiff-armed celebrators at the Praça de Sé in São Paulo that he doubted the reports of the Nazis having killed all those Jews during World War II. *Cf.*: PPARJ: newspaper article, "*Meio-Dia*," September 3, 1942, n.p., integralismo/pasta 4, cont. I; newspaper article, "*Diário da Noite*," September 7, 1942, n.p., integralismo/pasta 4, cont. I; newspaper article, "*Vanguarda*," September 4, 1942, n.p., integralismo/pasta 4, cont. I; *Folha de São Paulo*, May 2, 1988, p. A-27; April 21, 1989, p. A-10; *Jornal do Brasil*, October 8, 1987, sec. 1, pp. 1, 6; May 3, 1988, sec. 1, p. 2; and February 8, 1989, sec. 1, p. 2.

84. *Cf.*: PPARJ: "Rolf L. Larson to [Chief of Police]," pp. 1-2, integralismo/pasta 4, cont. I; letter, "MCPG to [Chief of Police]," cópia DPO/125/600.(41)/1946/anexo único, May 27, 1946, integralismo/pasta 4, cont. I; and Rout and Bratzel, p. 378.

85. *Cf.*: Departamento de Imprensa e Propaganda [hereafter DIP], document, "S-1, boletim no. 220," September 15, 1942, pp. xiii-xiv [PPARJ, administração/pasta 13]; Dulles, *Vargas of Brazil*, pp. 289-90; McCann, *Brazilian American Alliance*, p. 298; and Rout and Bratzel, pp. 190-93, 208.

86. DIP, document, "S-1, boletim no. 202," August 25, 1942, p. xii [PPARJ, administração/pasta 13]. For the other accords with the Germans, see above pp. 45-46, 175 n.62. But also see above p. 152 n.70. Nearly all DIP records were destroyed by the end of the Vargas era. Some of what's left, mainly a few newspaper clippings, were saved when the old presidential palace became the Museu da República. A handful of DIP orders are among the mountain of items at the archives of the political police in Rio de Janeiro. Confirmation of the entire Formosa affair might well be available in the circumspect vaults of the Itamarati. Rarely penetrated by outsiders, the Itamarati's Archives were partially opened by President Fernando Collor de Mello before he was impeached in 1993. A number of items, at least thirty years old, are now available to researchers. Secret accords with the Germans before and during World War II, however, are among those materials still being withheld.

87. A trip to Formosa in May 1994 failed to sustain the existence of this mysterious airstrip. A discussion with Formosa's police scribe from 1942 likewise provided little evidence that any Axis citizens were arrested. Prisoners, on the other hand, are an easily transportable commodity, particularly when the military gets involved. Formosa was surrounded at the time by hundreds of miles of scrub forests where a landing field and supplies would have been simple to conceal, especially if they had been on the property of a pro-German landowner. *Cf.*: José das Moças Júnior, interview, Formosa, May 4, 1994; Clovis Muniz: interview, Formosa, May 4, 1994; telephone interview, Rio de Janeiro/Formosa, May 16, 1994; and Severino Penachio, telephone interview, Rio de Janeiro/Formosa, May 22, 1994.

88. PPARJ, document, "Plano de sublevação nazista na América do Sul," p. 1, alemão/pasta 1.

89. USNA, document, "Integralista' Organization," December 16, 1940, pp. 3-4, MID 2657-K-70/74. See also above pp. 96, 176 n.80. Note that it took years of battling under the Freedom of Information Act to get this one segment of the above document released.

90. *Isto É*, May 26, 1993, pp. 52-55.

91. McCann, *The Brazilian American Alliance*, p. 334. Coriolano de Góis (pictured together with Vargas in Photo 2) was preceded by Colonel Alcides Gonçalves Etchegoyen and Lieutenant Colonel Nélson de Melo. He was followed by João Alberto who had been Getúlio's second chief of the Federal District's Polícia Civil. Beloch and Abreu, p. 1472. See also above p. 17.

92. An apparent contact at the Gabinete de Investigações wrote Luís Carlos Prestes some seventeen months later, alleging that there were still many Integralists or Integralist sympathizers within *paulistano* security apparatus. The tipster affirmed that the percentages of these individuals within selected departments were as follows: Office of the Secretary of Public Security: ninety percent, Gabinete de Investigações: nearly 50 percent, Guarda Civil: 60 percent, Força Pública: about 50 percent, and among state authorities: some 60 percent. PPARJ, letter, "João Arruda Campos to Luiz Carlos Prestes," June 15, 1945, comunismo/pasta 2b. See also above pp. 85, 171 n.36, 176 n.80.

93. *Cf.*: *Time*, August 28, 1944, p. 39; Beloch and Abreu, pp. 1471-72; Conniff, *Urban Politics in Brazil*, p. 170; Roland Hall Sharp, *South America Uncensored* (New York: Longmans, Green, 1945), pp. 3-5; Dulles, *A faculdade de direito de São Paulo e a resistência anti-Vargas*, pp. 278-79; and Brazil, Comissão Especial de Inquérito sôbre Atos Delituosos da Ditadura, "Relatório dos acontecimentos de novembro de 1943 em São Paulo (culminando com o acontecimento de 9 de novembro). Eviado ao Deputado Plínio

Barreto pelo Centro Acadêmico xi de agôsto," *Diario do Congresso Nacional*, September 27, 1947, pp. 6141-44. Among the many indelible observations made to the commission was the following by the Centro Acadêmico XI de agôsto:

Everything was done with the precision of Nazi organizations. The downtown area was isolated. Ambulances and police vehicles were requisitioned. The former to transport the injured and dead, the latter to apprehend those who had not been wounded. Mounted police lined the city whose center, painted red with blood, could only be washed with the help of the fire department and the use of brushes. Brazil, "Relatório dos acontecimentos de novembro de 1943 em São Paulo (culminando com o acontecimento de 9 de novembro), p. 6143.

94. *Cf*.: Cancelli, *O mundo da violência*, pp. 40n, 41; and *Correio da Manhã*, July 5, 1944, p. 2. Sharp (p. 8) adds the final touch by noting that once he was put in charge of the Federal Department of Public Security, Coriolano de Góis, who "was on trial in São Paulo for his part in the student massacre, . . . promptly quashed his own trial."

95. McCann, *The Brazilian-American Alliance*, p. 334.

96. For a glimpse at some of Vargas' much touted, but in reality window-dressing, social legislation, see Conniff, *Urban Politics in Brazil*, pp. 163-70. John French (p. 10) points out as well that

most of the measures hailed by Vargas in 1945 as the "workers' code of economic emancipation," including the eight-hour day, had been suspended as part of the wartime industrial production drive. Thus despite Getúlio's claims, it is clear that the material existence of the majority of [urban] workers had not been markedly improved by government action during the war years.

97. The percentage of persons living in urban settings is presented above on p. 14. The estimate of city dwellers for November of 1943 was just under one-third (33.2 percent) of the population.

98. *Cf*.: McCann, *The Brazilian-American Alliance*, pp. 322-25; Dulles, *Vargas of Brazil*, pp. 246-48, 253-65; Frederic Ganzert, *Brazil*, Lawrence Hill (ed.) (Berkeley: University of California Press, 1947), p. 319; and Oliver Ónody, *A inflação brasileira, 1820-1958* (Rio de Janeiro: [no publisher given], 1960), p. 25.

99. Bakota, pp. 207-8.

100. Corrupt financing of the *queremistas* by cotton magnate Hugo Borghi resulted in the "Scandal of the Cotton" in 1946. Borghi, besides all his wheelings and dealings for Getúlio, acquired at one time a *fazenda* in Goiás where the workers were kept in debt peonage after he took over. "These sad people, virtual slaves, were housed and fed like pigs; their salaries withheld to prevent escape. They even had their mail seized and censured." Affonso Henriques, *Ascensão e queda de Getúlio Vargas: declínio e morte* (Rio de Janeiro: Record, 1966), vol. III, p. 35. See also above pp. 23-26, 67-69, 157 n.96.

101. *Cf*.: McCann, *The Brazilian-American Alliance*, p. 465; and French, pp. 6-9. French (p. 7) shows how Getúlio manipulated the literacy requirement to enlist support in the coming election. This was done by momentarily giving the vote, owing to his position as president, to numerous illiterate urban workers.

The largest number of ex-officio voters came through factory payroll enrollments. The appropriate company official was required to submit a list of employees to an electoral judge, who returned the required electoral identification cards for distribution within the factory. Since the lists submitted did not have the signature of the applicant, many illiterate urban workers thus escaped disenfranchisement despite the law's literacy provisions.

102. Luiz Vergara, *Fui secretário de Getúlio Vargas: memórias dos anos de 1926-1954* (Porto Alegre: Globo, 1960), pp. 199-200. No less than on one other occasion, that time in 1934, Góis attempted to get a *coup* going against Vargas. CPDOC, oral history, "Odilon Batista," 1978, p. 36.

103. *Cf.*: McCann, *The Brazilian-American Alliance*, pp. 468-82; and Dulles, *Vargas of Brazil*, pp. 267-71.

104. Jorge, p. 123. *Bejo* is also erroneously spelled "*Beijo*" by some authors. *Bejo* does not translate as anything in Portuguese. *Beijo*, however, means "kiss." The origin of this error may be in the inability of Brazilians to pronounce their language correctly. Nelson Werneck Sodré, interview, Rio de Janeiro, August 8, 1991. But there could also be a perpetuation of this misinterpretation due of the paradoxical message behind the mistake. Benjamin Vargas is, nonetheless, pictured to the extreme right in Photo 3.

105. *Cf.*: Henriques: vol. II, pp. 106-10; vol. III, p. 328; Richard Bourne, *Getulio Vargas of Brazil, 1883-1954: Sphinx of the Pampas* (London: Charles Knight, 1974), p. 98; *Jornal do Commercio*, September 30, 1933, p. 13; October 30-31, 1933, p. 14; November 30, 1933, p. 14; and December 31, 1933, p. 20. It is assumed that Vargas would have dealt with his matter by the end of 1933. The conversion rate is thus the average taken from the last day of each month, September to December 1933. Henriques contends (vol. III, *loc. cit.*) that the purchasing power of the *cruzeiro* was far greater in Argentina at the time than the above amount suggests.

106. *Cf.*: Jorge, pp. 193-94, 204; Bourne, *loc. cit.*; and Nasser, *A revolução dos covardes*, pp. 134-35. Bejo merrily recounted the details of this last crime to a group of confidants at Rio's horse track, the Jockey Club, sometime later. Nasser, *A revolução dos covardes*, p. 135. The number of summary executions could actually have been as high as nine. In this respect, see above pp. 86, 172 n.40.

107. *Cf.*: Nélson de Melo in Lima, p. 221; Jorge, p. 203; and Henriques, vol. III, pp. 327-28. Henriques (vol. III, pp. 328-29) lists several additional adventures in Bejo's life after 1945 in which he threatened, beat, or wounded people.

108. Vergara, pp. 175-76.

109. *Cf.*: Augusto do Amaral Peixoto in Lima, pp. 157-58; Cordeiro de Farias, in Lima, p. 219; Nero Moura, in Lima, p. 219; Nélson de Mello, in Lima, p. 221; Beloch and Abreu, p. 3436; Coutinho, pp. 442-47; and Dulles, *Vargas of Brazil*, pp. 271-72. Taken in 1942, a photograph of Góis standing behind Vargas, and perhaps staring at him, can be seen in Photo 4.

110. Dulles, *Vargss of Brazil*, p. 274.

Chapter 5. No Comebacks

1. *Cf.*: *Tribuna da Imprensa*, September 12, 1950, p. 1; and Beloch and Abreu, pp. 2345, 2347-48. See also above pp. 25-26.

2. *Cf.*: Claudio de Lacerda [Paiva], pp. 41-44, 48, 60; John W.F. Dulles: *Carlos Lacerda, Brazilian Crusader, Volume I: The Years 1914-1960* (Austin: University of Texas Press, 1991), pp. 105-46; and *Vargas of Brazil*, pp. 281, 298-99, 317.

3. Ónody, *loc. cit.*

4. *Imprensa Popular* (Rio de Janeiro), August 5, 1954, p. 1. Aranha was shuffled into the Minister of Economy job on June 16, 1953. Beloch and Abreu, p. 186.

5. Eliana Rezende Furtado de Mendonça (director), *Os arquivos das polícias políticas: reflexos de nossa história contemporânea* (Rio de Janeiro: Fundação de Amparo à Pesquisa do Estado do Rio de Janeiro, 1994), p. 44.

6. See above pp. 81-83.

7. The lowest figure of fifty-six can be found in PPARJ, newspaper article, "*Última Hora*," October 24, 1951, n.p., administração/pasta 9; then comes fifty-eight in newspaper article, "*A Noticia*," October 25, 1951, n.p., administração/pasta 9. The total number apprehend next jumps to eighty-two in PPARJ: newspaper article, "*O Popular*," October 22, 1951, n.p., administração/pasta 9; newspaper article, "*O Jornal*," October 20, 1951, n.p., administração/pasta 9; and newspaper article, "*Diario Carioca*," October 20, 1951, n.p., administração/pasta 9. The higher statistic of eighty-six is reported in PPARJ: newspaper article, "*Imprensa Popular*," October 21, 1951, n.p., administração/pasta 9; and newspaper article, "*Gazeta de Noticias*," October 28, 1951, n.p., administração/pasta 9.

8. *Cf.*: PPARJ: newspaper article, "*Imprensa Popular*," August 24, 1951, n.p., administração/pasta 9; newspaper article, "*Imprensa Popular*," August 29, 1951, n.p., administração/pasta 9; newspaper article, "*Imprensa Popular*," September 14, 1951, n.p., administração/pasta 9; newspaper article, "*Imprensa Popular*," September 19, 1951, n.p., administração/pasta 9; newspaper article, "*Imprensa Popular*," September 20, 1951, n.p., administração/pasta 9; newspaper article, "*Imprensa Popular*," September 22, 1951, n.p., administração/pasta 9; newspaper article, "*Imprensa Popular*," September 25, 1951, n.p., administração/pasta 9; newspaper article, "*Imprensa Popular*," September 26, 1951, n.p., administração/pasta 9; newspaper article, "*Imprensa Popular*," September 28, 1951, n.p., administração/pasta 9; newspaper article, "*Imprensa Popular*," October 3, 1951, n.p., administração/pasta 9; newspaper article, "*Imprensa Popular*," October 5, 1951, n.p., administração/pasta 9; newspaper article, "*Imprensa Popular*," October 6, 1951, n.p., administração/pasta 9; newspaper article, "*Imprensa Popular*," October 7, 1951, n.p., administração/pasta 9; newspaper article, "*Imprensa Popular*," October 18, 1951, n.p., administração/pasta 9; newspaper article, "*Imprensa Popular*," October 21, 1951, n.p., administração/pasta 9; newspaper article, "*Imprensa Popular*," October 23, 1951, n.p., administração/pasta 9; newspaper article, "*Imprensa Popular*," December 23, 1951, n.p., administração/pasta 9; newspaper article, "*O Popular*," September 28, 1951, n.p., administração/pasta 9; newspaper article, "*O Popular*," October 22, 1951, n.p., administração/pasta 9; newspaper article, "*O Popular*," November 20, 1951, n.p., administração/pasta 9; newspaper article, "*Diario Carioca*," October 28, 1951, n.p., administração/pasta 9; newspaper article, "*A Manhã*," October 20, 1951, n.p., administração/pasta 9; newspaper article, "*Diario do Rio*," October 20, 1951, n.p., administração/pasta 9; newspaper article, "*Diario de Noticias*," October 20, 1951, n.p., administração/pasta 9; newspaper article, "*Diario da Noite*," October 20, 1951, n.p., administração/pasta 9; newspaper article, "*A Noite*," October 20, 1951, n.p., administração/pasta 9; and newspaper article, "*A Folha Carioca*," October 27, 1951, n.p., administração/pasta 9.

9. The events just outside Porecatú in the state of Paraná are a good example. In 1951, between 15,000 and 20,000 rural workers became involved in a dispute with proprietors and the Polícia Militar over lands that they occupied and worked. The owners wanted the workers removed. A clash resulted in which the police defended the interests of the landlords, and ended up terrorizing the agricultural laborers and their families. A number of peasants appealed directly to Vargas, but there is no evidence that he ever replied. *Cf.*:

PPARJ: document, "Relatorio do inquerito relativo aos acontecimentos de Porecatú," June 2, 1951, pp. 1-9, comunismo/pasta 2; newspaper article, "*Diario Trabalhista,*" November 14, 1951, pp. 1, 4, comunismo/pasta 2; newspaper article, "*O Globo,*" September 20, 1951, n.p., comunismo/pasta 2; newspaper article, "*O Mundo,*" August 15, 1951, n.p., comunismo/pasta 2; and newspaper article, "*Imprensa Popular,*" August 12, 1951, n.p., comunismo/ pasta 2. See also above pp. 14-15.

10. *Cf.*: Robert Levine, "Elite Perceptions of the *Povo,*" *Modern Brazil: Elites and Masses in Historical Perspective,* Conniff and McCann (eds.), p. 222; Talarico in Lima, p. 186; Dulles, *Vargas of Brazil,* pp. 307, 315-17; Beloch and Abreu, pp. 1505-7, 2071; and Shawn Smallman, "Shady Business: Corruption in the Brazilian Army before 1954," *LARR,* vol. XXXII, no. 3, 1997, pp. 56-57.

11. *Cf.*: *Última Hora,* May 13, 1954, p. 6; and Carlos Lacerda *et al., Reportagens que abalaram o Brasil* (Rio de Janeiro: Bloch, 1973), p. 155.

12. Tancredo Neves said that there were an additional 10,000 persons already adjudged guilty in the capital who were not incarcerated due to a lack of space. *Jornal do Brasil,* February 20, 1988, sec. Cidade, p. 4.

13. *Última Hora,* May 22, 1954, p. 3. Two of the photographs are reproduced here as Photos 22 and 23.

14. *Cf.*: PPARJ: newspaper article, "*Última Hora,*" August 13, 1951, n.p., administração/pasta 22; newspaper article, "*Última Hora,*" August 14, 1951, n.p., administração/ pasta 22; and newspaper article, "*Última Hora,*" August 15, 1951, n.p., administração/ pasta 22. Note that an Antonio Paulo Ferreira is listed among the investigators of the Internal Control, or St-6, unit of the Political Police in Rio de Janeiro given in Table 1 of the Appendix.

15. Claudio de Lacerda [Paiva], p. 119.

16. Carlos Lacerda *et al., Reportagens que abalaram o Brasil, loc. cit.*

17. *Ibid.*

18. *Última Hora,* May 25, 1954, p. 3.

19. *Cf.*: David Nasser, *A face cruel e outras histórias desagradáveis* (Rio de Janeiro: O Cruzeiro, 1961), pp. 119-22; Epitácio Caó, *Carreirista da traição,* 2nd ed., rev. (n.p.: Gernasa, 1964), pp. 12-14; and Beloch and Abreu, p. 1719. For more on Lacerda's left-of-center youth, see above pp. 29, 33, 144 n.18.

20. *Cf.*: *O Globo,* August 5, 1989, sec. 1, p. 4; *Veja,* April 4, 1973, p. 25; Beloch and Abreu, *loc. cit.*; Dulles, *Vargas of Brazil,* pp. 318-19; and Jarbas Passarinho, *Na planície,* 2nd ed. (Belém: CEJUP, 1991), p. 18. For the hard-to-believe story of Alcino João do Nascimento, see his *Mataram o presidente: memórias do pistoleiro que mudou a história do Brasil,* Palmério Dória de Vasconcelos *et al.* (eds.) (São Paulo: Alfa-Omega, 1978), pp. 44, 50-51. Note that this book was published after Nascimento got out of prison on April 9, 1975. For his part in the attempt to kill Lacerda, plus his assorted other crimes that night, Alcino was condemned to thirty-three years. He served twenty-one years and eight months. Beloch and Abreu, p. 51.

21. Nothing was ever done to Benjamin Vargas. He lived out his life working for the old federal district as a public functionary before retiring to die of a heart attack on March 26, 1973. His last years were devoted to his one hobby: the study of Napoleon

Bonaparte. *Cf.*: Beloch and Abreu, p. 3436; and *Jornal do Brasil*, March 27, 1973, sec. 1, pp. 1, 15.

22. *Cf.*: Carlos Lacerda, *Depoimento*, p. 138; Claudio de Lacerda [Paiva], pp. 211-21, 292; and Beloch and Abreu, pp. 1337-38.

23. Nelson Werneck Sodré, interview, Rio de Janeiro, August 8, 1991.

24. Henriques, vol. III, p. 369.

25. This appears to have been the fifth and fatal time Vargas seriously contemplated suicide over the prospects of not obtaining or in losing power. The other occasions were in the event of failure of the Revolution of 1930; on the eventuality of defeat in the Consitituionalist Civil War of 1932; during the thick of fighting at Guanabara Palace in the 1938 pajama-*Putsch*; and on being forced from office in 1945. *Jornal do Brasil*, August 24, 1994, sec. 1, pp. 8-9, 11.

Epilogue

1. These observations were made by Federal Assemblyman Hélio Navarro of the emerging Movimento Democrático Brasileiro (Brazilian Democratic Movement) in 1967. For his effort the military put Navarro's name on the list of persons dangerous to the new regime. On December 30, 1968, his mandate and political rights were canceled for ten years via their AI-5 (Ato Institucional No. 5, or Institutional Act No. 5). *Cf.*: *Última Hora*, August 24, 1967, p. 4; and Beloch and Abreu, p. 2369.

2. Filinto, it will be recalled (see above p. 105), lost his 1950 bid for governor of Mato Grosso.

3. *Cf.*: Beloch and Abreu, pp. 2345-46; *Jornal do Brasil*, July 12, 1973, sec. 1, pp. 1, 4-5; and *Correio da Manhã*, July 12, 1973, p. 6.

Bibliography

Much of the foundation for this work came from the Rio de Janeiro archives of the political police, known colloquially and collectively as the Departamento de Ordem Política e Social (DOPS). Since 1988, when it was turned over to the state government, this material has been housed at the Arquivo Público do Estado do Rio de Janeiro (APERJ), first at their facility in Niterói and then at two different locations in Rio de Janeiro itself. It should be pointed out, however, that the numbering systems used by the many variations of these police over the years was found to be inconsistent. For this reason, items from this source are cited by headline, date (when given), identifying topic, plus *pasta* (or folder) number in which each can be located.

Moreover, once the archive was moved to Rio, it was divided into documents from the Delegacia Especial de Segurança Política e Social (DESPS) and objects from DOPS. A third division is in the planning stages. Because these changes are beyond the scope of this project, and since every object can be located by the above system, the generic acronym PPARJ (for Political Police Archives, Rio de Janeiro) is used in this volume, before each entry, to signify *all* political police materials housed at APERJ.

In respect to the rest of the references, the names of authors, titles of works, places of publication, and publishers appear exactly as they appeared at the time of publication. Orthographic reforms between Portugal and Brazil have resulted in slightly different spellings of some Portuguese words in the text. All archival items, unless specifically noted, are from Brazil.

ARCHIVES

Argentina, Registro del Estado Civil y Capacidade de las Personas, Departamento Central Defunciones [Buenos Aires], affidavit, "Registro Civil [for Rodolfo José Ghioldi]," tomo 2L, numero 1022, año 1985.

Arquivo Filinto Müller [AFM], biography, "Francisco da Silva Campos," 1937, CPDOC.
____, biography, "Lindolfo Collor," 1937, CPDOC.
____, biography, "Lourival Fontes," 1941, CPDOC.
____, biography, "Vicente Ráo," n.d., CPDOC.
____, letter, "Israel Souto to Herbert Moses," August 12, 1933, CPDOC/FM 33.02.21/
     dip/ad (used in captions to Photos).
____, telegram, "Caneppa to Müller," November 8, 1937, CPDOC/FM 33.03.23 chp/ad,
     I-87.
____, telegram, "Dotto to Müller," October 21, 1937, CPDOC/FM 33.03.23 chp/ad, I-93.
____, telegram, "Filinto Müller to Riograndino da Costa e Silva," November 12, 1939,
     CPDOC/FM 33.02.21/dip/ad.
____, telegram, "Sardinha to Müller," October 5, 1937, CPDOC/FM 33.03.23 chp/ad, I.
Arquivo Histórico do Itamarati, document, "Regis de Oliveira to Oswaldo Aranha,"
     December 20, 1939, no. 477.
____, telegram, "Souza Leão to Itamarati," January 9, 1940.
Arquivo Maurício de Lacerda, newspaper article, "O Combate [Rio de Janeiro],"
     February 2, 1928, n.p., Arquivo Edgard Leuenroth, roll 2/79.
Arquivo Nacional [AN], Correio da Manhã Photo Collection, "Frederico Mindelo,"
     unnumbered bibliographic document.
____, deposition, "Antonio Maciel Bomfim," TSN processo 1381, vol. II.
____, document, 571, December 28, 1937, Secretária da Presidência da República,
     14.15/lata 99.
____, document, 5315, March 3, 1938, Secretária da Presidência da República, 14.15/lata
     99.
____, document, "Ministéro das Relações Exteriores: providências para impedir a entrada
     no Brasil de grande levas de israelitas expulsos dos seus paises de origem," 1937,
     MJNI-1939, cx. 429.
____, document, "Promptuario No. 42," TSN processo 1381, vol. I.
____, document, "Sentença," TSN processo 1381, vol. III.
____, document, "Tribunal de Segurança Nacional," TSN processo 1381/1940, cx. 10565,
     vol. II.
____, letter, "Antonio Maciel Bomfim to Luiz Copelo Calonio," April 19, 1940, TSN
     processo 1381, vol. I.
____, letter, "Eurico Bellens Porto to chefatura de policia," May 4, 1936, TSN processo
     1381, vol. II.
____, letter, "Rita Vilaz Suassuna to Getúlio Vargas," February 18, 1931, Secretaria de
     Presidência da República: Polícia Civil do Distrito Federal/lata 527.
____, letter, "Virgilio Barbosa to Joaquim Pedro Salgado Filho," March 21, 1931,
     Secretaria de Presidência da República: Polícia Civil do Distrito Federal/lata 527.
____, photograph, PH/FOT/5618, folder 1.
____, telegram, "Family of Clodomir Colaço Veras to Getulio Vargas," [1942], Secretaria
     da Presidência da República: Polícia Civil do Distrito Federal/lata 527.
Arquivo Plínio Salgado [APS], letter, "Thompson to Chefe [Plínio Salgado]," March 2,
     1939, Pi 39.03.02/5.
____, letter, "Marie Albuquerque to [Plínio Salgado]," July 21, 1939, Pi 39.07.21/2.

____, letter, "Maurillo Mello to [Plínio Salgado]," August 1, 1939, FPi 39.08.01/2.

____, telegram, "Carvalho e Fernandes Campos to Plinio Salgado," October 8, 1937, Pi 37.10.08/5.

____, telegram, "Dorval Santos to Plinio Salgado," March 12, 1939, Pi 39.03.12/1.

____, telegram, "Mario Matos to Plinio Salgado," March 11, 1939, Pi 39.03.11/1.

____, telegram, "Mayrink to Plinio Salgado," February 28, 1939, Pi 39.02.28/8.

____, telegram, "Pedro Rodrigues to Plinio Salgado," March 7, 1939, Pi 39.03.071.

____, telegram, "Ramos Angelo Fraxino to Plinio Salgado," October 8, 1937, Pi 37.10.08/7.

____, telegram, "Reinaldo Veloso Jose Antunes to Plinio Salgado," March 11, 1939, Pi 39.03.11/3.

____, telegram, "[Unsigned] to [Plínio Salgado]," [September 10, 1938], Pi 38.09.10/1.

Arquivo Público e Histórico do Município do Rio Claro [ARC], document, [Untitled List of Integralist Code Names for Miscellaneous Entities], n.d.

Centro de Pesquisa e Documentação de História Contemporânea do Brasil [CPDOC], oral history, "Alzira Vargas do Amaral Peixoto," 1979.

____, oral history, "Aristides Leal," 1975, 1977.

____, oral history, "Augusto do Amaral Peixoto," 1975.

____, oral history, "Guilherme Figueiredo," 1977.

____, oral history, "José Joffily," 1977-1978.

____, oral history, "Odilon Batista," 1978.

____, oral history, "Paulo Pinheiro Chagas," 1977.

Departamento de Imprensa e Propaganda [DIP], document, "S-1, boletim no. 202," August 25, 1942 [PPARJ, administração/pasta 13].

____, document, "S-1, boletim no. 220," September 15, 1942, [PPARJ, administração/ pasta 13].

____, document, "S-1, boletim no. 234," October 11-12, 1941, [PPARJ, administração/ pasta 13].

Germany, Kreisverwaltung Eberswalde, affidavit, "Auszug aus dem Todesregister," September 9, 1993.

Light, personnel file, "Alfred Hutt," folio 2643.

Political Police Archives, Rio de Janeiro [PPARJ], booklet, "*Eu, Gregório Bezerra, acuso!*" n.p.: n.p., 1967, comunismo/ pasta 82.

____, booklet, "Relatório apresentado ao Sr. Chefe de Polícia, Major Dr. Filinto Müller, pelo Delegado Especial de Segurança Política e Social, Capitão Felisberto Baptista Teixeira, e referente à campanha desenvolvida, sob sua orientação, para repressão às atividades do Partido Comunista no país," September 1940, comunismo/pasta 13.

____, catalogue, "Álbum do Delegacia Especial de Segurança Politica e Social," 1940.

____, deposition, "Testemunha do Cleobulo Azambuja," [December 1939], comunismo/ pasta 21.

____, document, "Abaixo as provocações da policia assassina de Getulio, Vicente Ráo, Felinto Muller e Miranda Correia," n.d., comunismo/pasta 17.

____, document, "Ação I. Brasileira," n.d., integralismo/pasta 1, cont.

____, document, "Acção Integralista Brasileira, provincia da Guanabara, D.P.P.," by H.C. Moraes, January 17, 1936, integralismo/pasta 21.

____, document, "Alliança Nacional Libertadora, directorio municipal do Districto Federal, organisação interna dos nucleos," July 1, 1935, comunismo/pasta 18.

____, document, (Antonio Emilio Romano to Affonso H. de Miranda Corrêa) "Relatorio sobre a 'Acção Integralista Brasileira,'" 1934, integralismo/pasta 1.

____, document, "Ao povo brasileiro," [1936?], comunismo/pasta 17.

____, document, "Ao povo e ás classes armadas do Brasil," November 27, 1936, comunismo/pasta 20.

____, document, "A policia de Felinto Muller prende e assassina trabalhadores maritimos," March 1939, comunismo/pasta 16.

____, document, "A revolução communista no Brasil e os commentarios da 'internacional communista," n.d., comunismo/pasta 9.

____, document, "Atividades da 'quinta-coluna' no estado de Mato Grosso," n.d., alemão/pasta 17.

____, document, "Atividades integralistas no. 6° batalhão de caçadores da Força Publica," [archived October 20, 1941], integralismo/pasta 4, cont. II.

____, document, "Atividades particulares do atual interventor de Mato Grosso," n.d., alemão/pasta 17.

____, document, "A todos os nucleos e a todos os alliancistas," [late 1935 or early 1936], comunismo/pasta 20.

____, document, "Boletim reservado S-1, conspiração integralista," March 11, 1940, integralismo/pasta 6.

____, document, "Companheiros não eleitores," n.d., integralismo/pasta 13.

____, document, "Confidential," November 23, 1940, administração/pasta 13.

____, document, "Coupons da campanha financeira 'Pelo Bem do Brasil, 1936-1937," integralismo/pasta 13.

____, document, "Decreto-lei no. 7474, de 18 abril de 1945 [with attached card 'dossier: anistia, anistiados']," geral/pasta 3.

____, document, "Delegacia Especial de Segurança Politica e Social secção," June 10, 1938, administração/pasta 17.

____, document, "Delegado Dr. Bradão Filho: copia do relatorio referente ao processo que apurou o movimento revolutionario na marinha," July 1938, integralismo/pasta 5.

____, document, "D-15, *A Tarde*," August 6, 1940, geral/pasta 1.

____, document, "D.I.P.," D-31, January 7, 1940, administração/pasta 13.

____, document, "D.I.P.," D-31, January 21, 1940, administração/pasta 13.

____, document, "D.I.P.," S-1, January 7, 1940, administração/pasta 13.

____, document, "D.I.P.," [S-1], January 21, 1940, administração/pasta 13.

____, document, "Dirigentes da 'Organização Brasileira de Defesa da Paz e da Cultura,'" March 15, 1949, comunismo/pasta 38.

____, document, "Discurso presidencial de 11 de junho," June 1940, administração/pasta 11.

____, document, "Documentação em torno de melhoramentos internos sugeridos á DESPS [Delegacia Especial de Segurança Política e Social], 1943, administração/pasta 1.

____, document, "D.P.S. S.I.-S.F.P. no. 1240 ref.-prot.-1523/56," March 5, 1956, informações/pasta 16.

____, document, "Em Fernando de Noronha," [archived October 19, 1940], administração /pasta 16.

____, document, "54 [by hand]," 656, May 20, 1938, integralismo/pasta 5, cont.

____, document, "1° oficio de registro de titulos e documentos, estructuração do movimento integralista," titulo 2°, art. 5, integralismo/pasta 1.

____, document, "Histórico das atividades políticas dos parlamentares comunistas," n.d., comunismo/pasta 23.

____, document, "Integralismo, sinais convencionais (correspondencia)," n.d., integralismo/pasta 4.

____, document, "Integralismo, S.1, boletim no. 119," May 20, 1942, integralismo/pasta 4, cont. I.

____, document, "Intelligence Service," "Serviço secréto inglês," December 17, 1940, inglês/pasta 3.

____, document, "Inteligence [sic] Service," S-1. boletim no. 229, September 25, 1941, inglês/pasta 3.

____, document, "Inteligence [sic] Service," S.S.I. boletim no. 14, January 15, 1941, inglês/pasta 3.

____, document, "Introito," June 15, 1954, integralismo/pasta 21.

____, document, "K-55 'Cadernos da hora presente.'" February 8, 1940, integralismo/pasta 8.

____, document, "L/1-R/2," July 23, 1941, alemão/pasta 1.

____, document, "MM/4.557-18-2-42," February 18, 1942, alemão/pasta 15.

____, document, "O assalto ao Palácio Guanabara 11-5-1938," by [illegible], July 2, 1938, integralismo/pasta 5.

____, document, "O quinta colunismo," n.d., alemão/pasta 17.

____, document, "Plano de sublevação nazista na América do Sul," alemão/pasta 1.

____, document, "Politica externa britanica com o Brasil," July 11, 1940 [by hand], inglês/pasta 3.

____, document, "Prestes, está em greve de fome," March 1941, comunismo/pasta 20.

____, document, "Regulamento da 'Campanha do Ouro,'" December 30, 1936, integralismo/pasta 22.

____, document, "Relação de servidores lotados na divisão de Polícia Política e Social," [February 8, 1951], administração/pasta 1s.

____, document, "Relação dos individuos presos por esta secção, 11 a 31 de maio último, com uma sintese do historico e a situação em que se encontram," June 10, 1938, integralismo/pasta 9.

____, document, "Relação dos integralistas da policia militar do Distrito Federal," [1941], administração/pasta 15.

____, document, "Relação dos officiaes e praças da policia militar que fazem parte da extintax[sic]–A.B.I.[sic]," May 16, 1938, administração/pasta 15.

_____, document, "Relatorio," [January 1938], comunismo/pasta 22.

_____, document, "Relatorio do inquerito relativo aos acontecimentos de Porecatú," June 2, 1951, comunismo/pasta 2.

_____, document, "Relatório movimento integralista 11 de maio de [1]938," by Alberto Tornaghi, July 16, 1938, integralismo/pasta 5.

_____, document, "S.I.-Sr/2," no. 9473, ref.-prot.-11236/53, August 13, 1953, comunismo/ pasta 39.

_____, document, "Situação do movimento revolucionario no Brasil," May 23, 1936, administração/pasta 1h.

_____, document, "S-1, boletim no. 17," January 20, 1941, integralismo/pasta 3.

_____, document, "S-1, boletim no. 39," February 14, 1941, integralismo/pasta 3.

_____, document, "S-1, boletim no. 49," February 26, 1941, integralismo/pasta 3.

_____, document, "S-1, boletim no. 88," April 12-13, 1941, comunismo/pasta 4d.

_____, document, "S-1, boletim no. 101," April 29, 1941, integralismo/pasta 3.

_____, document, "S-1, boletim no. 167," July 15, 1941, integralismo/pasta 3.

_____, document, "S-1, boletim no. 173," July 22, 1941, integralismo/pasta 6.

_____, document, "S-1, boletim no. 184," August 4, 1941, integralismo/pasta 3.

_____, document, "S-1, boletim no. 187," August 7, 1942, integralismo/pasta 3.

_____, document, "S-1, boletim no. 223," September 18, 1942, integralismo/pasta 3.

_____, document, "S-1, boletim no. 227," September 23, 1941, integralismo/pasta 9.

_____, document, "S-1, boletim no. 229," September 25, 1942, integralismo/pasta 3.

_____, document, "S-1, boletim no. 238" September 30, 1940, integralismo/pasta 3.

_____, document, "S.R. boletim no. 506," March 3, 1941, integralismo/pasta 4, cont. II.

_____, document, "S.R. boletim no. 644," September 6, 1944, integralismo/pasta 4, cont. II.

_____, document, "S.S.I boletim no. 13," January 14, 1941, integralismo/pasta 3.

_____, document, "S.S.I, boletim no. 192," July 26, 1941, integralismo/pasta 6.

_____, document, "[untitled]," Paraizo, August 25, 1936, Machado, comunismo/pasta 20.

_____, document, [untitled, but commencing:] "Senhor capitão, Devolvo a V.S. devidamente informada, a inclusa relação dos funcionários do D.I.P.," n.d., administração/ pasta 13.

_____, document, [untitled declaration of Euzébio de Queiroz Filho], 735-741, integralismo/ pasta 5.

_____, document, "[untitled manuscript from agent] K. 47," [archived June 6, 1940], integralismo/pasta 4b.

_____, file, "Alphonsine Vallée," prontuário 21343.

_____, file, "Arthur Ernst Ewert ou Harry Berger," prontuário 1721.

_____, file, "Auguste Elise Ewert," prontuário 21237.

_____, file, "Carmen Alfaza [sic] Ghioldi," prontuário 21409.

_____, file, "Franz Gruber ou Jonny de Graaf," prontuário 33989.

_____, file, "Leon Jules Valée[sic]," prontuário 14957.

_____, file, "Leon Jules Vallée," prontuário 14957/envelope.

_____, file, "Luiz Carlos Prestes," prontuário 22251.

_____, file, "Maria Prestes, Olga Benario," prontuário 1675.

_____, file, "Rodolfo Ghioldi," prontuário 5878.

____, file, "Tobias Warchavsky," prontuário 294.

____, file, "Victor Allen Barron," prontuário 1447

____, letter, "Alexandre Zacarias de Assumpção to interventôr federal," July 20, 1945, administração/pasta 5.

____, letter, "Antonio Mendes Napoleão et al., to Magalhães de Almeida et al.," [1936?], comunismo/pasta 20.

____, letter, "Aos camaradas do B.B. do P.C. dos Estados Unidos," n.d., comunismo/pasta 20.

____, letter, "[Felisberto] Baptista Teixeira to Dr. Major Chefe da Polícia [Filinto Müller]," June 17, 1941, comunismo/pasta 13.

____, letter, "H[eráclito]. F[ontoura]. Sobral Pinto to A[lexander]. Marcondes Filho," June 1, 1943, comunismo/pasta 8.

____, letter, "Hugo Auler to Capitão Dr. Delegado Especial de Segurança Política e Social," May 27, 1940, no. 94, comunismo/pasta 13.

____, letter, "João Alberto Lins de Barros to Agamenon Magalhães," April 20, 1945, geral/pasta 3.

____, letter, "João Arruda Campos to Luiz Carlos Prestes," June 15, 1945, comunismo/pasta 2b.

____, letter, "Joaquim Marcelino Nepomuceno to Comité Nacional do Partido Comunista do Brasil," September 17, 1945, comunismo/pasta 2c.

____, letter, "José Reynaldo Serra Costa et al., to Magalhães de Almeida et al.," [1936?], comunismo/pasta 20.

____, letter, "Joseph Brodsky to [unknown]," n.d., [file "Victor Allen Barron"].

____, letter, "[Luís Carlos Prestes] to Miguel Costa," October 10, 1935, comunismo/pasta 9.

____, letter, "MCPG to [Chief of Police]," cópia DPO/125/600.(41)/1946/anexo único, May 27, 1946, integralismo/pasta 4, cont. I.

____, letter, "O Comité Regional do Rio do Partido Comunista do Brasil (S.I.C.) to anonymous," April 2, 1940, comunismo/pasta 27.

____, letter, "Odylio Denys to Exmº Snr. Dr. Delegado Especial de Segurança Política e Social," April 20, 1945, geral/pasta 3.

____, letter, "[PCB] Carta aberta ao Sr. Getulio Vargas," September 8, 1941, comunismo/pasta 20.

____, letter, "Pedro Aurelio de Góes Monteiro to Chefe de Polícia do Distrito Federal [Filinto Müller]," December 26, 1939, militar/pasta 1.

____, letter, "Plinio Salgado to Getúlio Vargas," January 28, 1938, integralismo/pasta 17.

____, letter, "Rolf L. Larson to [Chief of Police]," June 18, 1946, integralismo/pasta 4, cont. I.

____, letter, "Seraphim Braga, chefe da S-2 to chefe da S/4," June 10, 1938, administração/pasta 17.

____, letter, "Sub-chefe de grupo da P.E and detetive da classe I to Exmº Sr. Dr. Major Chefe da Policia [Filinto Müller]," March 7, 1941, administração/pasta 16.

____, letter, "321, S/2 to chefe da S/4," June 22, 1938, integralismo/pasta 9.

____, letter, "Victorio Caneppa to Sr. Ministro Chefe de Polícia do Depart. Federal de Segurança Pública," April 23, 1945, copy of oficio 199, geral/pasta 3.

____, letter, "J[oão]. Alberto to [Luís Carlos] Prestes," June 8, 1935, comunismo/pasta 9.

____, letter, "Waldemar Pereira Cotta to general public," September 13, 1941, integralismo/pasta 7.

____, miscellaneous documents, "Associação dos Amigos de São José," n.d., integralismo/pasta 10.

____, miscellaneous documents, "Campanha do 'V," n.d., inglês/pasta 2.

____, miscellaneous documents, "Centro Espírita Nossa Senhora do Carmo," n.d., integralismo/pasta 10.

____, miscellaneous documents, "Clube Hipico de Vila Guilherme," n.d., integralismo/pasta 10.

____, miscellaneous documents, "Comissão Nacional de Repressão ao Comunismo," 1936, administração/pasta 14.

____, miscellaneous documents, "Curso Tuiutí," n.d., integralismo/pasta 10.

____, miscellaneous documents, "Distinta Atlético Clube," n.d., integralismo/pasta 10.

____, miscellaneous documents, "Documentos constantes dos arquivos do PCB," [various dates], comunismo/pastas 2; 2a; 2b; 2c; 2f; 2g; 2h; 2i; 2j; 2l; 2m; 2n; and 2p.

____, miscellaneous documents, "Empresa Metreleco," n.d., integralismo/pasta 10.

____, miscellaneous documents, "Excelsior Sociedade Anônima," n.d., integralismo/pasta 10.

____, miscellaneous documents, "*Revista Brasil Mineral*," n.d., integralismo/pasta 10.

____, miscellaneous documents, "Sindicancia para apurar como o jornal *O Mundo* obteve fotografias idênticas do prontuário de Cecil Borer," 1947, administração/pasta 1e.

____, miscellaneous documents, "Sociedade Dramatica Particular Filhos de Talma," n.d., integralismo/pasta 10.

____, miscellaneous letters, [various dates], comunismo/pasta 8.

____, miscellaneous photographs, "[untitled]," integralismo/pasta 9.

____, newspaper article, "*A Classe Operaria*," February 16, 1937, comunismo/pasta 17.

____, newspaper article, "*A Folha Carioca*," October 27, 1951, administração/pasta 9.

____, newspaper article, "*A Manhã*," October 20, 1951, administração/pasta 9.

____, newspaper article, "*A Noite*," October 20, 1951, administração/pasta 9.

____, newspaper article, "*A Noticia*," October 25, 1951, administração/pasta 9.

____, newspaper article, "*Centelha*," September 23, 1933, comunismo/pasta 4.

____, newspaper article, "*16 de Julho*," December 1, 1937, comunismo/pasta 4.

____, newspaper article, "*Diario Carioca*," October 28, 1951, administração/pasta 9.

____, newspaper article, "*Diario de Noticias*," October 20, 1951, administração/pasta 9.

____, newspaper article, "*Diario de São Paulo*," January 17, 1930, militar/pasta 1.

____, newspaper article, "*Diario do Rio*," October 20, 1951, administração/pasta 9.

____, newspaper article, "*Diario Trabalhista*," November 14, 1951, comunismo/pasta 2.

____, newspaper article, "*Gazeta de Noticias*," October 28, 1951, administração/pasta 9.

____, newspaper article, "*Grade*," August 4, 1938, comunismo/pasta 4.

____, newspaper article, "*Jornal do Povo*," October 9, 1934, comunismo/livro preto.

____, newspaper article, "*Meio-Dia*," September 3, 1942, integralismo/pasta 4, cont. I.

____, newspaper article, "*Novos Rumos*," January 24-30, 1964, comunismo/pasta 59.

____, newspaper article, "*O Globo*," September 20, 1951, comunismo/pasta 2.

____, newspaper article, "*O Mundo*," August 15, 1951, comunismo/pasta 2.

_____, newspaper article, "*O Radical*," August 30, 1942, integralismo/pasta 4, cont. I.

_____, newspaper article, "*O Tempo*," March 3, 1931, militar/pasta 1.

_____, newspaper articles: "*A Offensiva*," [1936], integralismo/pasta 1, cont.; March 21, 1936, p. 1, file, "Carmen Alfaza Ghioldi," prontuário 21409, n.p.

_____, newspaper articles, "*Diário da Noite*," September 7, 1942, integralismo/pasta 4, cont. I.; May 15, 1948, integralismo/pasta 19; October 20, 1951, administração/pasta 9.

_____, newspaper articles, "*Imprensa Popular*," August 12, 1951, comunismo/pasta 2; August 24, 1951, administração/pasta 9; August 29, 1951, administração/pasta 9; September 14, 1951, administração/pasta 9; September 19, 1951, administração/pasta 9; September 20, 1951, administração/pasta 9; September 22, 1951, administração/pasta 9; September 25, 1951, administração/pasta 9; September 26, 1951, administração/pasta 9; September 28, 1951, administração/pasta 9; October 3, 1951, administração/pasta 9; October 5, 1951, administração/pasta 9; October 6, 1951, administração/pasta 9; October 7, 1951, administração/pasta 9; October 18, 1951, administração/pasta 9; October 21, 1951, administração/pasta 9; October 23, 1951, administração/pasta 9; December 23, 1951, administração/ pasta 9.

_____, newspaper articles, "*O Jornal*," September 8, 1936, integralismo/pasta 4; October 20, 1951, administração/pasta 9.

_____, newspaper articles, "*O Popular*," September 28, 1951, administração/pasta 9; October 22, 1951, administração/pasta 9; November 20, 1951, administração/ pasta 9.

_____, newspaper articles, "*Última Hora*," August 13, 1951, administração/pasta 22; August 14, 1951, administração/pasta 22; August 15, 1951, administração/pasta 22; October 24, 1951, administração/pasta 9.

_____, newspaper article, "*Vanguarda*," September 4, 1942, integralismo/pasta 4, cont. I.

_____, periodical article, "*Ancora*," April 1935, comunismo/pasta 4.

_____, periodical article, "*Diretrizes*," April 16, 1942, comunismo/pasta 4d.

_____, periodical article, "*O Preso Proletario*," November 1933, comunismo/pasta 4b.

_____, periodical article, "*Revista Proletaria*," August 1938, comunismo/pasta 4e.

_____, periodical article, "*Solidariedade*," September 1939, comunismo/pasta 4e.

_____, photograph, "Desfile de pelotão da Brigada de Choque," n.d., integralismo/pasta 19.

_____, photograph, "Fotografias integralistas," n.d., integralismo/pasta 9.

_____, telegram, "Arlindo Souza to Luís Carlos Prestes," January 3, 1948, comunismo/pasta 24.

_____, telegram, "Deosdedith Mendes Rocha to Luís Carlos Prestes," January 4, 1948, comunismo/pasta 24.

_____, telegram, "Eliezer Menezes *et al.*, to Luís Carlos Prestes," January 3, 1948, comunismo/pasta 24.

_____, telegram, "Embaixada do Brasil em Berlim ao Ministerio das Relações Exteriores," April 19-20, 1937, [file "Arthur Ernst Ewert ou Harry Berger"].

_____, telegram, "Maria Augusta de Brito to Luís Carlos Prestes," January 4, 1948, comunismo/pasta 24.

Russia, Российский Центр Хранения и Изучения Документов Новейщей Истории [РЦХИДНИ], file, "Де Граф," фонд 495, опись 205, дело 6385, лист 35.

____, general file, "Бразилия," letter, "Frederic to Fernando Morales," December 4, 1936, фонд 495, опись 29, дело 98, лист 18.

____, general file, "Бразилия," letter, "Raul to Brandão," August 29, 1936, фонд 495, опись 29, дело 98, листов 15a-b.

____, telegram, "Commission Politique to Куда, Rio de Janeiro," July 31, 1935, фонд 495, опись 184, дело 54, листов 17-18.

____, telegram, "René [Stuchevski] to [Moscow]," December 28, 1935, фонд 495, опись 184, дело 6, лист 35.

____, telegram, фонд 495, опись 17, дело 157, лист 2.

____, telegram, фонд 495, опись 184, дело 4, лист 30.

____, telegram, фонд 495, опись 184, дело 6, лист 9.

____, telegram, фонд 495, опись 184, дело 60, лист 70.

Superior Tribunal Militar [STM], deposition, "Depoimento de Rodolpho Ghioldi," February 11, 1936, apelação 4899, série a, vol. II.

____, document, "Copias authenticas referentes ao accusado Luiz Carlos Prestes," n.d., apelação 4899, série a, vol. II.

____, document, "Leon Jules Vallée," May 7, 1937, apelação 4899, série a, vol. VI.

____, document, "Pelo accusado: Leon Jules Vallée," April 15, 1937, apelação 4899, série a, vol. IV.

____, letter, "Euzebio de Queiroz Filho to Raul Machado," January 25, 1937, apelação 4899, série a, vol. II.

____, letter, "Heraclito Fontoura Sobral Pinto to Raul Machado," January 15, 1937, apelação 4899, série a, vol. II.

United Kingdom, Public Records Office [UKPRO], document, "Brazil, Political 'Who's Who,'" November 26, 1940, FO 371/24176.

____, document, "Political Situation in Pernambuco," December 17, 1935, FO 371/19766.

____, telegram, "Foreign Office to Sir H[ugh] Gurney," January 10, 1936, no. 4, FO 371/19766.

United States, Department of State [USDS], document, "Intelligence Report No. 8002: Nationalism in Brazil," July 24, 1959, AW-02/552/no. 8002/c.1.

____, Department of State, document, "The Relation of Brazil to the Defense of the Northeast" [probably 1941], 097.3/Z1092/no. 142.

____, National Archives [USNA], document, "Communist Activities in Brazil," March 19, 1936, MID 2657-K-70/28.

____, National Archives, document, "Integralista' Organization," December 16, 1940, MID 2657-K-70/74.

____, National Archives, letter, "Baker to G-2," January 28, 1929, no. 854, MID 2006-115.

____, National Archives, letter, "Barclay to G-2," May 21, 1927, no. 732, MID 2052-112.

____, National Archives, letter, "Mitchell to G-2," May 18, 1938, no. 2097, MID 2271-K-43/7.

____, National Archives, letter, "Sackville to G-2," May 21, 1936, no. 1651, MID 2651-K-70/38.

____, National Archives, letter, "Sackville to G-2," November 2, 1932, no. 1047, MID 2657-K-86/16.

____, National Archives, letter, "Sibert to A.C. of S., G-2," May 2, 1941, no. 2703, MID 2657-K-128/5.

____, National Archives, letter, "Sibert to A.C. of S., G-2," May 10, 1941, no. 2714, MID 2657-K-128/6.

____, National Archives, letter, "Sibert to A.C. of S., G-2," May 17, 1941, no. 2727, MID 2657-K-128/7.

____, National Archives, letter, "Sibert to G-2," April 25, 1941, no. 2693, MID 2052-120/21.

____, National Archives, microfilm, "Caffery to Secretary of State," May 12, 1938, M1472/8.

____, National Archives, microfilm, "Gibson to Secretary of State," January 15, 1936, M1472/8.

____, National Archives, microfilm, "Gibson to Secretary of State," March 25, 1936, M1472/8.

____, National Archives, microfilm, "Gibson to Secretary of State," July 10, 1936, M1472/8.

____, National Archives, microfilm, "Gibson to Secretary of State," December 28, 1935, M1472/8.

____, National Archives, microfilm, "Woodward to Buttler, Duggan, and Wells," July 11, 1938, M1472/8.

____, Office of Strategic Services, Research and Analysis, document, "Summary of Political Situation in Brazil (as of July, 1945)," August 2, 1945, 097.3/Z1092/no. 3329.

BOOKS, JOURNAL ARTICLES, MANUSCRIPTS, AND DISSERTATIONS

Amado, Jorge, *A vida de Luís Carlos Prestes: o Cavaleiro da Esperança*, 4th ed. São Paulo: Martins, 1945.

____, *The Violent Land*, Samuel Putnam (trans.) 4th ed. New York: Avon, 1979.

(Anonymous), *Brazil: Its History, People, Natural Productions, etc.* London: Religious Tract Society, 1860.

(Anonymous), *Quem é que no Brasil: biografias contemporâneas.* São Paulo: Sociedade Brasileira de Espansão Comercial, 1955, vol. IV.

Arno, Ciro [Cícero Arpino Caldeira Brandt], *Memórias de um estudante*, 2nd ed., rev. Rio de Janeiro: Gráfica Olímpica, 1952.

Arquidiocese de São Paulo, *Brasil: nunca mais*, 6th ed. Petrópolis: Vozes, 1985.

Bakota, Carlos Steven, "Getúlio Vargas and the Estado Novo: An Inquiry into Ideology and Opportunism," *Latin American Research Review*, vol. XIV, no. 1, 1979.

Barata, Agildo, *Vida de um revolucionário: memórias.* Rio de Janeiro: Melso, 1962.

Barroso, Gustavo, *Reflexões de um bóde.* Rio de Janeiro: Grafica Educadora, 1955.

Basbaum, Leôncio, *História sincera da República: de 1930 a 1960*, 4th ed. São Paulo: Alfa-Omega, 1976, vol. III.

_____, *Uma vida em seis tempos: memórias*. São Paulo: Alfa-Omega, 1976.

Bastos, Abguar, *Prestes e a revolução social*, 2nd ed. São Paulo: HUCITEC, 1986.

Beloch, Israel and Alzira Alves de Abreu (coords.), *Dicionário histórico-biográfico brasileiro, 1930-1983*. Rio de Janeiro: Forense-Universitária, 1984.

Bourne, Richard, *Getulio Vargas of Brazil, 1883-1954: Sphinx of the Pampas*. London: Charles Knight, 1974.

Brandi, Paulo, *Vargas: da vida para a história*, 2nd ed., rev. Rio de Janeiro: Zahar, 1985.

Britto, [José Gabriel de] Lemos, *Os systemas penitenciarios do Brasil*. Rio de Janeiro: Nacional, 1925, vol. II.

Broxson, Elmer, "Plinio Salgado and Brazilian Integralism, 1932-1938," unpublished PhD thesis, Department of History, Catholic University of America, 1972.

Camargo, Aspásia *et al.*, *O golpe silencioso: as origens da república corporativa*. Rio de Janeiro: Rio Fundo, 1989.

Campos, Reynaldo Pompeu de, *Repressão judicial no Estado Novo: esquerda e direita no banco dos réus*. Rio de Janeiro: Achiamé, 1982.

Cancelli, Elizabeth, *O mundo da violência: a polícia da era Vargas*, 2nd ed. Brasília: Editora Universidade de Brasília, 1994.

_____, "O poder da polícia e o mundo da prisão na era Vargas (1930-1945)," prepublication manuscript.

Caneppa, Vitório, *Estatistica carceraria do Distrito Federal*. Rio de Janeiro: Franco-Brasileira, 1939.

Caó, Epitácio, *Carreirista da traição*, 2nd ed., rev. n.p.: Gernasa, 1964.

Carneiro, Edison, "Situação do negro no Brasil," *Estudos afro-brasileiros: trabalhos apresentados ao 1° congresso afro-brasileiro reunido no Recife em 1934*. Rio de Janeiro: Ariel, 1935, vol. I.

Carneiro, Maria Luiza Tucci, *O anti-semitismo na era Vargas: fantasmas de uma geração, 1930-1945*. São Paulo: Brasiliense, 1988.

_____, *Preconceito racial: Portugal e Brasil-colônia*, 2nd ed. São Paulo: Brasiliense, 1988.

Carone, Edgard, *O Estado Novo, 1937-1945*. São Paulo: Difusão Européia do Livro, 1976.

Carta, Mino and Raimundo Rodrigues Pereira (directors), *Retrato do Brasil (da monarquia ao estado militar)*. São Paulo: Política Editora, 1984, vol. I.

Conniff, Michael, "The Tenentes in Power: A New Perspective on the Brazilian Revolution of 1930," *Journal of Latin American Studies*, vol. X, no. 1, May 1978.

_____, *Urban Politics in Brazil: The Rise of Populism, 1925-1945*. Pittsburgh: University of Pittsburgh Press, 1981.

Cortés, Carlos, *Gaúcho Politics in Brazil: The Politics of Rio Grande do Sul, 1930-1964*. Albuquerque: University of New Mexico Press, 1974.

Coutinho, Lourival, *O General Góes depõe*. Rio de Janeiro: Coelho Branco, 1955.

Duarte, Paulo, *Memórias: apagada e vil mediocridade*. São Paulo: HUCITEC, 1977.

_____, *Prisão, exílio, luta . . . .* Rio de Janeiro: Zelio Valverde, 1946.

Dulles, John W.F., *A faculdade de direito de São Paulo e a resistência anti-Vargas, 1938-1945*, Vanda Mena Barreto de Andrade (trans.). São Paulo: Universidade de São Paulo, 1984.

____, *Anarchists and Communists in Brazil, 1900-1935*. Austin: University of Texas Press, 1973.

____, *Brazilian Communism, 1935-1945: Repression during World Upheaval*. Austin: University of Texas Press, 1983.

____, *Carlos Lacerda, Brazilian Crusader, Volume I: The Years 1914-1960*. Austin: University of Texas Press, 1991.

____, *Vargas of Brazil: A Political Biography*. Austin: University of Texas Press, 1967.

Enciclopédia Mirador Internacional. São Paulo: Encyclopaedia Britannica do Brasil, 1975.

Facó, Rui, *Cangaceiros e fanáticos: gênese e lutas*. Rio de Janeiro: Civilização Brasileira, 1963.

____, *Cangaceiros e fanáticos: gênese e lutas*, 2nd ed. Rio de Janeiro: Civilização Brasileira, 1965.

Faria, Antonio Augusto and Edgard Luiz de Barros, *Getúlio Vargas e sua época*, 2nd ed. São Paulo: Global, 1983.

Fausto, Boris, *A Revolução de 1930, historiografia e história*, 9th ed. São Paulo: Brasiliense, 1983.

French, John, "Industrial Workers and the Birth of the Populist Republic in Brazil, 1945-1946," *Latin American Perspectives*, vol. XVI, no. 4, Fall 1989.

Freyre, Gilberto, *Order and Progress: Brazil from Monarchy to Republic*, Rod Horton (ed. and trans.). New York: Alfred Knopf, 1970.

____, *The Masters and the Slaves: A Study in the Development of Brazilian Civilization*, Samuel Putnam (trans.), 2nd ed. New York: Alfred Knopf, 1966.

Frischauer, Paul, *Presidente Vargas: biografia*, Mário da Silva and Brutus Pedreira (trans.). São Paulo: Nacional, 1943.

Gambini, Roberto, *O duplo jogo de Getúlio Vargas: influência americana e alemã no Estado Novo*. São Paulo: Símbolo, 1977.

Ganzert, Frederic, *Brazil*, Lawrence Hill (ed.). Berkeley: University of California Press, 1947.

Goulart, Gastão, *Verdades da Revolução Paulista*. São Paulo: [no publisher given, n.d.].

Guarany, Marcelo, *O pequeno ditador*. Rio de Janeiro: Moderna, 1947.

Gunther, John, "This is Vargas," *Current History and Forum*, June 1941.

Hall, Michael and Paulo Sérgio Pinheiro, "The Control and Policing of the Working Class in Brazil," paper presented to the Conference on the History of Law, Labor and Crime, University of Warwick, September 15-18, 1983.

Hambloch, Ernest, *His Majesty the President of Brazil: A Study of Constitutional Brazil*. New York: E.P. Dutton, 1936.

Henriques, Affonso, *Ascensão e queda de Getúlio Vargas: o maquiavélico*. Rio de Janeiro: Record, 1966, vol. I.

____, *Ascensão e queda de Getúlio Vargas: o Estado Nôvo*. Rio de Janeiro: Record, 1966, vol. II.

_____, *Ascensão e queda de Getúlio Vargas: declínio e morte*. Rio de Janeiro: Record, 1966, vol. III.

Hilton, Ronald (ed.), *Who's Who in Latin America*, 3rd ed., rev. Stanford: Stanford University Press, 1948, part VI, Brazil.

Hilton, Stanley, "*Ação Integralist Brasileira*: Fascism in Brazil, 1932-1938," *Luso-Brazilian Review*, vol. IX, no. 2, Winter 1972.

_____, *A guerra civil brasileira: história da Revolução Constitucionalista de 1932*. Rio de Janeiro: Nova Fronteira, 1982.

_____, *A Rebelião Vermelha*. Rio de Janeiro: Record, 1986.

_____, *Brazil and the Soviet Challenge, 1917-1947*. Austin: University of Texas Press, 1991.

_____, "Brazilian Diplomacy and the Washington-Rio de Janeiro 'Axis' during the World War II Era," *Hispanic American Historical Review*, vol. LIX, no. 2, May 1979.

_____, *Hitler's Secret War in South America, 1939-1945: German Military Espionage and Allied Counterespionage in Brazil*. Baton Rouge: Louisiana State University Press, 1981.

_____, "Military Influence on Brazilian Economic Policy, 1930-1945: A Different View," *Hispanic American Historical Review*, vol. LIII, no. 1, February 1973.

_____, "The Armed Forces and Industrialists in Modern Brazil: The Drive for Military Autonomy, 1889-1954," *Hispanic American Historical Review*, vol. LXII, no. 4, November 1982.

Inojosa, Joaquim, *República de Princesa: José Pereira x João Pessoa-1930*. Rio de Janeiro: Civilização Brasileira, 1980.

Jardim, Renato, *A adventura de outubro e a invasão de São Paulo*. São Paulo: Sociedade Impressora Paulista, 1932.

Joffily, José, *Harry Berger*. Rio de Janeiro: Paz e Terra, 1986.

Jorge, Fernando, *Getúlio Vargas e o seu tempo: um retrato com luz e sombra, 1883-1900*. São Paulo: T.A. Queiroz, 1985.

Julião, Francisco, "The Practice and Preaching of Revolution," *Revolution in Brazil: Politics and Society in a Developing Nation*, Irving Horowitz (ed.). New York: E.P. Dutton, 1964.

Kidder, Daniel, *Sketches of Residence and Travels in Brazil: Embracing Historical and Geographical Notices of the Empire and its Several Provinces*. Philadelphia: Sorin and Ball, London: Wiley and Putnam, 1845, vol. II.

Koster, Henry, *Travels in Brazil*. London: Longman, 1816.

Lacerda, Carlos, *Depoimento*. Rio de Janeiro: Nova Fronteira, 1977.

_____ et al., *Reportagens que abalaram o Brasil*. Rio de Janeiro: Bloch, 1973.

Lacerda, Maurício de, *História de uma covardia*. Rio de Janeiro: Nova Fronteira, 1980.

_____, *Segunda Republica*, 2nd ed. Rio de Janeiro: Freitas Bastos, 1931.

Landes, Ruth, *The City of Women*. New York: Macmillian, 1947.

Leite, Aureliano, *Memórias de um revolucionário: a Revolução de 1930: pródromos e conseqüências*. São Paulo: [no publisher given], 1931.

_____, *Páginas de uma longa vida*. São Paulo: Martins, 1967.

Lessa, Origenes, *Ilha Grande: do jornal de um prisioneiro de guerra*. São Paulo: Nacional, 1933.

____, *Não ha de ser nada: notas de um reporter entre os "Voluntarios de Piratininga,"* 3rd ed. São Paulo: Nacional, 1933.

Lesser, Jeff, "Are African-Americans African or American?: Brazilian Immigration Policy in the 1920s," prepublication manuscript.

____, Book review of Carneiro's *O antissemitismo na era Vargas* in *Journal of Latin American Studies*, vol. XXI, no. 3, October 1989.

____, Book review of Carneiro's *O antissemitismo na era Vargas* in *Senhor*, April 4, 1988.

Levine, Robert, "Brazil's Jews during the Vargas Era and After," *Luso-Brazilian Review*, vol. V, no. 1, June 1968.

____, "Elite Intervention in Urban Popular Culture in Modern Brazil," *Luso-Brazilian Review*, vol. XXI, no. 2, Winter 1984.

____, "Elite Perceptions of the *Povo*," *Modern Brazil: Elites and Masses in Historical Perspective*, Michael Conniff and Frank McCann (eds.). Lincoln: University of Nebraska Press, 1989.

____, *The Vargas Regime: The Critical Years, 1934-1938*. New York, Columbia University Press, 1970.

Lima, Valentina da Rocha (coord.), *Getúlio: uma história oral*. Rio de Janeiro: Record, 1986.

Lima Júnior, Augusto de, *Serões e vigílias: páginas avulsas*. Rio de Janeiro: Livros de Portugal, 1952.

Loewenstein, Karl, *Brazil under Vargas*. New York: Macmillan, 1944.

Lopes, Juarez Rubens Brandão, *Desenvolvimento e mundança social: formação da sociedade urbano no Brasil*, 3rd ed. São Paulo: Nacional/MEC, 1976.

Ludwig, Armin, *Brazil: A Handbook of Historical Statistics*. Boston: G.K. Hall, 1985.

McCann, Frank, "Origins of the 'New Professionalism' of the Brazilian Military," *Journal of Interamerican Studies and World Affairs*, vol. XXI, no. 4, November 1979.

____, *The Brazilian-American Alliance, 1937-1945*. Princeton: Princeton University Press, 1973.

____, "The Brazilian Army and the Problem of Mission, 1930-1964," *Journal of Latin American Studies*, vol. XII, no. 1, May 1980.

____, "The Brazilian General Staff and Brazil's Military Situation, 1900-1945," *Journal of Interamerican Studies and World Affairs*, vol. XXV, no. 3, August 1983.

Mederios Filho, João, *82 horas de subversão: Intentona Comunista de 1935 no Rio Grande do Norte*. Natal: [no publisher given], 1980.

____, *Meu depoimento*. Natal: Oficial, 1937.

Mendonça, Eliana Rezende Furtado de (director), *DOPS: a lógica de desconfiança*. Rio de Janeiro: Arquivo Público do Estado do Rio de Janeiro, 1993.

____, *Os arquivos das polícias políticas: reflexos de nossa história contemporânea*. Rio de Janeiro: Fundação de Amparo à Pesquisa do Estado do Rio de Janeiro, 1994.

Montenegro, Abelardo, *História do fanatismo religioso no Ceará*. n.p.: Fortaleza, 1959.

Moraes, Dênis de and Francisco Viana, *Prestes: lutas e autocríticas*, 2nd ed. Petrópolis: Vozes, 1982.

Morais, Fernando, *Olga*, 3rd ed. São Paulo: Alfa-Omega, 1985.

Morél, Edmar, *A Revolta da Chiabta*. Rio de Janeiro: Pongetti, 1959.

Moss, Robert, *Carnival of Spies*. New York: Simon and Schuster, 1987.

Nascimento, Alcino João do, *Mataram o presidente: memórias do pistoleiro que mudou a história do Brasil*, Palmério Dória de Vasconcelos *et al.* (eds.). São Paulo: Alfa-Omega, 1978.

Nasser, David, *A face cruel e outras histórias desagradáveis*. Rio de Janeiro: O Cruzeiro, 1961.

____, *A revolução dos covardes: diário decreto de Severo Fournier, reportagens políticas e ordens da censura do ditador*. Rio de Janeiro: O Cruzeiro, 1947.

____, *Falta alguém em Nuremberg: torturas da polícia de Filinto Strubling Müller*, 4th ed. Rio de Janeiro: O Cruzeiro, 1966.

Oliveira, Xavier de, *Beatos e cangaceiros*. Rio de Janeiro: Revista dos Tribunais, 1920.

Onody, Oliver, *A inflação brasileira, 1820-1958*. Rio de Janeiro: [no publisher given], 1960.

[Paiva], Claudio de Lacerda, *Uma crise de agosto: o atentado da rua Toneleros*. Rio de Janeiro: Nova Fronteira, 1994.

Pang, Eul-Soo, "Agrarian Change in the Northeast," *Modern Brazil: Elites and Masses in Historical Perspective*, Michael Conniff and Frank McCann (eds.). Lincoln: University of Nebraska Press, 1989.

Passarinho, Jarbas, *Na planície*, 2nd ed. Belém: CEJUP, 1991.

Peixoto, Alzira Vargas do Amaral, *Getúlio Vargas: meu pai*. Porto Alegre: Globo, 1960.

Pinheiro, Paulo Sérgio, *Estratégias da ilusão: a revolução mundial e o Brasil, 1922-1935*. São Paulo: Companhia das Letras, 1991.

Pinto, [Heron] Herondino Pereira, *Nos subterraneos do Estado Novo*. Rio de Janeiro: Germinal, 1950.

Pinto, Sobral, [Heráclito Fontoura,] *Por que defendo os comunistas*. Belo Horizonte: Comunicação, 1979.

Putnam, Samuel, "Vargas Dictatorship in Brazil," *Science and Society*, vol. V, no. 2, Spring 1941.

Quartim, João, *Dictatorship and Armed Struggle in Brazil*, David Fernbach (trans.). New York: Monthly Review, 1971.

Ramos, Graciliano, *Memórias do cárcere*, 21st ed. Rio de Janeiro: Record, 1986, vol. I.

Reis, Dinarco, *A luta de classes no Brasil e o PCB*. São Paulo: Novo Rumos, 1982, vol. I.

Reis Júnior, Pereira, *Os presidentes do Brasil*. Rio de Janeiro: Divulbrás, 1975.

Rose, R.S., *Beyond the Pale of Pity: Key Episodes of Elite Violence in Brazil to 1930*. San Francisco: Austin and Winfield, 1998.

Rose, R.S. and Gordon Scott, "Johnny," prepublication manuscript.

Rout Jr., Leslie, and John Bratzel, *The Shadow War: German Espionage and United States Counterespionage in Latin America during World War II*. Frederick, MD: University Publications of America, 1986.

Rowe, John W.F., *Primary Commodities in International Trade*. Cambridge: Cambridge University Press, 1965.

Salgado, Plinio, "Como eu vi a Italia," *Hierarchia*, no. 5, March-April 1932.

Seitenfus, Ricardo [Antônio] Silva, "Ideology and Diplomacy: Italian Fascism and Brazil, 1935-38," *Hispanic American Historical Review*, vol. LXIV, no. 3, August 1984.

____, *O Brasil de Getúlio Vargas e a formação dos blocos, 1930-1942: o processo do envolvimento brasileiro na II Guerra Mundial*. São Paulo: Nacional, 1985.

Sharp, Roland Hall, *South America Uncensored*. New York: Longmans, Green, 1945.

Silva, Hélio, *1932, a Guerra Paulista: o cicio de Vargas*. Rio de Janeiro: Civilização Brasileira, 1967, vol. V.

____, *1938, terrorismo em campo verde*. Rio de Janeiro: Civilização Brasileira, 1971.

Singelmann, Peter, "Political Structure and Social Banditry in Northeastern Brazil," *Journal of Latin American Studies*, vol. VII, no. 1, May 1975.

Skidmore, Thomas, *Politics in Brazil, 1930-1964: An Experiment in Democracy*. New York: Oxford University Press, 1967.

____, "Race and Class in Brazil: Historical Perspectives, *Luso-Brazilian Review*, vol. XX, no. 1, Summer 1983.

Smallman, Shawn, "Shady Business: Corruption in the Brazilian Army before 1954," *Latin American Research Review*, vol. XXXII, no. 3, 1997.

Smith, Michael, *Foley: The Spy who Saved 10,000 Jews*. London: Hodder and Stoughton, 1999.

Sodré, Nelson Werneck, *História militar do Brasil*. Rio de Janeiro: Civilização Brasileira, 1965.

Stepan, Nancy Leys, *"The Hour of Eugenics" Race, Gender, and Nation in Latin America*. Ithaca: Cornell University Press, 1991.

Stevenson, William, *A Man Called Intrepid: The Secret War*. New York: Ballantine, 1976.

Szulc, Tad, *Twilight of the Tyrants*. New York: Henry Holt, 1959.

Tavares, José Nilo, *Novembro de 1935: meio século depois*, Dario Canale *et al.* (org.). Petrópolis: Vozes, 1985.

Torres, Epitácio, *A polícia: uma perspectiva histórica*. Porto Alegre: Bels, 1977.

Trindade, Hélgio, *Integralismo: o fascismo brasileiro na década de 30*. São Paulo: Difusão Européia do Livro, 1974.

Vargas, Luthero, *Getúlio Vargas: a revolução inacabada*. Rio de Janeiro: Bloch, 1988.

Vergara, Luiz, *Fui secretário de Getúlio Vargas: memórias dos anos de 1926-1954*. Porto Alegre: Globo, 1960.

Vianna, Marly de Almeida Gomes, "Revolucionários de 1935: sonho e realidade," PhD thesis, Faculdade de Filosofia, Letras e Ciências Humanas, Universidade de São Paulo, 1990, vols. I and II.

____, *Revolucionários de 35: sonho e realidade*. São Paulo: Companhia das Letras, 1992.

Vidal, Ademar, *João Pessoa e a Revolução de 30*. Rio de Janeiro: Graal, 1978.

Vieira, Antônio, *Maria Zélia: mártires do monstruoso presídio: Augusto Pinto, João Varlota, Naurício Maciel Mendes e José Constâncio da Costa*, 2nd ed. São Paulo: Cupolo, 1957.

von Doellinger, Carlos, "Política, política econômica e capital estrangeiro no Brasil: as décadas de 30, 40 e 50," *Revista Brasileira de Mercado de Capitais*, vol. III, no. 8, May/August 1977.

Waack, William, *Camaradas: Nos arquivos de Moscou: a história secreta da revolução brasileira de 1935*. São Paulo: Companhia das Letras, 1993.

Werneck, Maria, *Sala 4: primeira prisão política feminina*. Rio de Janeiro: CESAC, 1988.

Williams, Margaret Todaro, "Integralism and the Brazilian Catholic Church," *Hispanic American Historical Review*, vol. LIV, no. 3, August 1974.

Wirth, John, *The Politics of Brazilian Development, 1930-1954*. Stanford: Stanford University Press, 1970.

Wythe, George, *Industry in Latin America*. New York: Columbia University Press, 1945.

Young, Jordan, *The Brazilian Revolution of 1930 and the Aftermath*. New Brunswick: Rutgers University Press, 1967.

FILMS AND TELEVISION PROGRAMS

Parahyba mulher macho, directed by Tizuka Yamasaki, 1983.

"Pinga Fogo," TV-Tupi, January 3, 1964.

GOVERNMENT AND OFFICIAL PUBLICATIONS

Brazil, *Coleção das leis da República dos Estados Unidos do Brasil de 1933: atos do Govêrno Provisório, janeiro a março*. Rio de Janeiro: Nacional, 1934, vol. I.

____, *Collecção das leis da Republica dos Estados Unidos do Brazil de 1907*. Rio de Janeiro: Nacional, 1908, vol. I.

____, Comissão Especial de Inquérito sôbre Atos Delituosos da Ditadura, "Acareação entre os depoentes," *Diario do Congresso Nacional*, June 19, 1947.

____, Comissão Especial de Inquérito sôbre Atos Delituosos da Ditadura, "Depoimento do Abel Chermont," *Diario do Congresso Nacional*, September 20, 1947.

____, Comissão Especial de Inquérito sôbre Atos Delituosos da Ditadura, "Depoimento do Belmiro Valverde," *Diario do Congresso Nacional*, May 27, 1947.

____, Comissão Especial de Inquérito sôbre Atos Delituosos da Ditadura, "Depoimento do Bernardino de Oliveira Carvalho," *Diario do Congresso Nacional*, June 7, 1947.

____, Comissão Especial de Inquérito sôbre Atos Delituosos da Ditadura, "Depoimento do Carlos Marighella," *Diario do Congresso Nacional*, August 28, 1947.

____, Comissão Especial de Inquérito sôbre Atos Delituosos da Ditadura, "Depoimento do David Nasser," *Diario do Congresso Nacional*, August 8, 1947.

____, Comissão Especial de Inquérito sôbre Atos Delituosos da Ditadura, "Depoimento do Francisco de Oliveira Melo," *Diario do Congresso Nacional*, October 23, 1947.

____, Comissão Especial de Inquérito sôbre Atos Delituosos da Ditadura, "Depoimento do Iguatemi Ramos da Silva," *Diario do Congresso Nacional*, September 9, 1947.

____, Comissão Especial de Inquérito sôbre Atos Delituosos da Ditadura, "Depoimento de João Alves de Mota," *Diario do Congresso Nacional*, August 28, 1947.

____, Comissão Especial de Inquérito sôbre Atos Delituosos da Ditadura, "Depoimento do João Basilio dos Santos," *Diario do Congresso Nacional*, September 25, 1947.

____, Comissão Especial de Inquérito sôbre Atos Delituosos da Ditadura, "Depoimento do João Massena Melo," *Diario do Congresso Nacional*, September 9, 1947.

____, Comissão Especial de Inquérito sôbre Atos Delituosos da Ditadura, "Depoimento do José Alexandre dos Santos," *Diario do Congresso Nacional*, September 9, 1947.

____, Comissão Especial de Inquérito sôbre Atos Delituosos da Ditadura, "Depoimento do Luís Carlos Prestes," *Diario do Congresso Nacional*, September 20, 1947.

____, Comissão Especial de Inquérito sôbre Atos Delituosos da Ditadura, "Depoimento do Olindo Semeraro," *Diario do Congresso Nacional*, July 23, 1947.

____, Comissão Especial de Inquérito sôbre Atos Delituosos da Ditadura, "Depoimento do Paulo Franklin de Souza Elejalde," *Diario do Congresso Nacional*, May 27, 1947.

____, Comissão Especial de Inquérito sôbre Atos Delituosos da Ditadura, "Depoimento do Samuel Lopes Pereira," *Diario do Congresso Nacional*, May 28, 1947.

____, Comissão Especial de Inquérito sôbre Atos Delituosos da Ditadura, "Relatório dos acontecimentos de novembro de 1943 em São Paulo (culminando com o acontecimento de 9 de novembro). Eviado ao Deputado Plínio Barreto pelo Centro Acadêmico xi de agôsto," *Diario do Congresso Nacional*, September 27, 1947.

____, Conselho Nacional de Desenvolvimento Científico e Technológico, *Boletim do Museu Paraense Emílio Goeldi*. Belem: Instituto Nacional de Pesquisas da Amazônia, Zoologica, no. 18, October 13, 1982.

____, Conselho Nacional de Estatística, *Anuário estatístico do Brasil, 1939-1940*. Rio de Janeiro: IBGE, 1941.

____, *Constituição dos Estados Unidos do Brasil: leis constitucionais nr. 1 e 2*. Rio de Janeiro: Nacional, 1938.

____, Instituto Brasileiro de Geografia e Estatística, *Censo demográfico: população e habitação* [, *1940*]. Rio de Janeiro: IBGE, 1950, Série Nacional, vol. II.

____, Instituto Brasileiro de Geografia e Estatística, *Censos econômicos: agrícola, industrial, comercial e dos serviços*. Rio de Janeiro: IBGE, 1950.

____, Ministerio da Agricultura, Industria e Commerico, *Synopse do censo da agricultura: superfície territorial, área e valor dos immoveis ruraes, categoria e nacionalidade dos proprietarios, systema de exploração, população pecuaria, producção agricola*. Rio de Janeiro: Directoria Geral de Estatistica, 1922.

____, Policia Civil do Districto Federal, *A insurreição de 27 de novembro: relatorio do Delegado Eurico Bellens Porto*. Rio de Janeiro: Nacional, 1936.

____, Polícia Civil do Distrito Federal, *Policia politica preventiva: programa organisação e realisações*. Rio de Janeiro: Serviço de Inqueritos Politicos Sociais, 1939.

____, *Relatorio apresentado ao Dr. A.A. Borges de Medeiros, Presidente do Estado do Rio Grande do Sul pelo Engenheiro Ildefonso Soares Pinto, Secretario de Estado dos Negocios das Obras Publicas em 15 de agosto de 1923*. Porto Alegre: A Federação, 1923.

____, *Relatorio apresentado ao exmo Snr. Interventor Federal, Comandante Ary Parreiras pelo Chefe da Policia, Dr. Joubert Evangelista da Silva sobre a administração policial em 1933.* Nictheroy: Officinas Graphicas da Escola do Trabalho, 1934.

____, Secretaria de Planejamento, *Anuário estatístico do Brasil, 1985.* Rio de Janeiro: IBGE, 1986.

United Nations, UNESCO, *Progress of Literacy in Various Countries: A Preliminary Statistical Study of Available Census Data since 1900.* Paris: UNESCO, 1953.

United States, War Department, "Survey of the Rio de Janeiro Region of Brazil," paper prepared under the direction of the chief of staff by the Military Intelligence Service, General Staff, August 6, 1942, vol. I.

INTERVIEWS

Alencar, Generosa, interview, Juazeiro do Norte, May 13, 1993.

Amado, Thomé: interviews, Rio de Janeiro, August 21, 1994; September 28, 1994; and October 9, 1994.

Anonymous-1: interviews, Rio de Janeiro, October 5, 1992; and October 6, 1992.

Anonymous-5, interview, Rio de Janeiro, July 5, 1990.

Barron, Harold, interview, Hayward, CA, January 15, 1994.

Borer, Cecil: interviews, Rio de Janeiro, May 13, 1998; May 28, 1998; and May 29, 1998.

Del Roio, Jose Luiz, telephone interview, Rio de Janeiro/São Paulo, July 31, 1994.

Gertel, Noé, interview, São Paulo, August 17, 1994.

Ghioldi, Americo, interview, Buenos Aires, June 5, 1998.

Gorender, Jacob, telephone interview, Rio de Janeiro/São Paulo, July 12, 1993.

Gracie, Robson, interview, Rio de Janeiro, August 6, 1991.

Krüger, Ernst, interview, Rio de Janeiro, October 17, 1994.

Lesser, Jeff, telephone interview, Fresno/New London, November 29, 1990.

Malina, Solomão, interview, São Paulo, July 28, 1994.

Marques, Daniel Walker Almeida, interview, Juazeiro do Norte, May 13, 1993.

Menezes, Fátima, interview, Juazeiro do Norte, May 12, 1993.

Moças Júnior, José das, interview, Formosa, May 4, 1994.

Morais, Fernando, telephone interview, Rio de Janeiro/São Paulo, July 1, 1993.

Muniz, Clovis: interview, Formosa, May 4, 1994; and telephone interview, Rio de Janeiro/Formosa, May 16, 1994.

Oliveira, João, interview, Juazeiro do Norte, May 11, 1993.

Pederia, Waldecy Catharina Magalhães, interview, Niterói, October 26, 1994.

Penachio, Severino, telephone interview, Rio de Janeiro/Formosa, May 22, 1994.

Prestes, Anita Leocadia, interview, Rio de Janeiro, August 6, 1994.

Prestes, Luís Carlos, interview, Rio de Janeiro, August 13, 1987.

Prestes, Lygia, interview, Rio de Janeiro, August 6, 1994.

Ribeiro, Yuri: interviews, Rio de Janeiro, November 11, 1994; November 20, 1994; and December 16, 1994.

Sacchetta, Vladimir: telephone interview, Rio de Janeiro/São Paulo, July 31, 1994; and interview, São Paulo, August 17, 1994.

Sá, José Homem Correia de, interview, Rio de Janeiro, August 20, 1994.

Scott, Gordon, interview, Victoria, January 8, 1996.
Sodré, Nelson Werneck, interview, Rio de Janeiro, August 8, 1991.
Souza, Gilson Ferreira de, interview, Rio de Janeiro, March 21, 1989.
Waack, William, telephone interview, Rio de Janeiro/Berlin, May 29, 1994.

LETTERS AND E-MAIL

De Graaf, Rudolf, letter, June 30, 1994.
Dulles, John W.F., letter, May 25, 1988.
____, e-mail, July 27, 1999.
Ghioldi, Susana O.F. de, letter, January 7, 1997.
Hilton, Stanley, e-mail, April 6, 2000.
Joffily, José, letter, February 17, 1989.
Lopez, Felix Barata, letter, November 13, 1996.
Prestes, Luís Carlos, letter, November 19, 1987.
Ulrich [no first name given], [Stiftung Archiv der Parteien und Massenorganisationen der
        DDR im Bundesarchiv], letter, October 31, 1996.
Waack, William, letter, June 4, 1994.

NEWSPAPERS AND PERIODICALS

A Classe Operaria (Rio de Janeiro), 1937-1939.
A Manhã (Rio de Janeiro), 1935-1951.
Anauê! (Rio de Janeiro), 1936-1937.
Ancora (Rio de Janeiro), 1935.
A Folha Carioca (Rio de Janeiro), 1951.
A Noite (Rio de Janeiro), 1931-1937.
A Noticia (Rio de Janeiro), 1951.
A Offensiva (Rio de Janeiro), 1936.
Arquivos Brasileiros de Higiene Mental (Rio de Janeiro), 1931-1934.
A União (João Pessoa), 1930.
A Voz do Trabalhador (Rio de Janeiro), 1915.
Centelha (Campos), 1933.
Correio da Manhã (Rio de Janeiro), 1931-1973.
Correio do Povo (Porto Alegre), 1955-1959.
Daily Worker (New York), 1936.
Diario Carioca (Rio de Janeiro), 1936-1963.
Diario da Noite (Rio de Janeiro), 1942-1951.
Diario de Noticias (Rio de Janeiro), 1931-1951.
Diario de São Paulo, 1930.
Diario do Rio (Rio de Janeiro), 1951.
Diario Trabalhista (Rio de Janeiro), 1951.
Diretrizes (Rio de Janeiro), 1942-1947.
Folha da Manhã (São Paulo), 1930.
Folha da Tarde (Porto Alegre), 1954-1982.

Folha de São Paulo, 1984-1989.

Gazeta de Noticias (Rio de Janeiro), 1951.

Grade (Rio de Janeiro), 1938.

Imprensa Popular (Rio de Janeiro), 1951-1954.

International Press Correspondence (London), 1936.

Isto É (São Paulo), 1993.

Jornal do Brasil (Rio de Janeiro), 1966-1994.

Jornal do Commercio (Rio de Janeiro), 1927-1942.

Jornal do Povo (Rio de Janeiro), 1934.

Leia (São Paulo), 1985.

Manchete (Rio de Janeiro), 1958-1979.

Meio-Dia (Rio de Janeiro), 1942.

Monitor Integralista (Rio de Janeiro), 1934.

New Masses (Washington, D.C.), 1936.

New York Times, 1928-1941.

Novos Rumos (Rio de Janeiro), 1964.

O Estado de São Paulo, 1931-1993.

O Globo (Rio de Janeiro), 1927-1989.

O Imparcial (Rio de Janeiro), 1936.

O Jornal (Rio de Janeiro), 1928-1968.

O Mundo (Rio de Janeiro), 1951.

O Popular (Rio de Janeiro), 1951.

O Preso Proletario (Rio de Janeiro), 1933.

O Radical (Rio de Janeiro), 1942.

O Tempo (Rio de Janeiro), 1931.

Revista Proletaria (Rio de Janeiro), 1938.

Rio News (Rio de Janeiro), 1884.

Senhor (São Paulo), 1988.

16 de Julho (Rio de Janeiro), 1937.

Solidariedade (Rio de Janeiro), 1939.

Status (São Paulo), 1986.

The Manchester Guardian, 1936.

The New Republic (Washington, D.C.), 1937-1938.

The Times (London), 1936.

Time (New York), 1944.

Tribuna da Imprensa (Rio de Janeiro), 1954-1955.

Última Hora (Rio de Janeiro), 1951-1967.

Vanguarda (Rio de Janeiro), 1942.

Veja (Rio de Janeiro), 1973-1991.

Index

3rd of October Club. *See tenentes*
4ª Delegacia Auxiliar, 12
"26." *See* Costa Lima, Manoel da

"Abóbora." *See* Xavier, Eduardo
  Ribeiro
Abreu, Antenor de Santa Cruz Pereira,
  145 n.23
Ação Integralísta Brasileira, 54, 56, 74,
  77, 89-90, 102, 161 n.120, 162 n.
  122, 162 n.132, 167 n.8, 171 n.31,
  171 n.38, 177 n.83, 178 n.92; AIB
  nicknames, 170 n.30; agricultural
  reform, 143 n.9; arms caches, 171
  n.35; Belmiro Valverde, 84-85, 88;
  Brazilian Catholic Church, 24, 140
  n.73; broken up, 80-81, 168 n.13;
  correspondence with other fascist
  entities, 25; deal between Argentine General Staff and German
  intelligence, 96-97; Eurico Gaspar
  Dutra, 173 n.49; files on enemies,
  26, 142 n.94; founded, 22; funding,
  24-25, 84, 141 nn.81-82; Góis
  Monteiro, 83, 86-87, 142 n.90, 172
  n.42; "Green Chickens," 27, 142
  n.94; imprisoned members recognition signs, 88; Integralist National
  Council, 26; Italians, 22, 25, 84;
  leftists, 26-27, 42; March 1938 pre-
  rebellion, 85; membership: arrests
  of, 85, 174 n.54; size claims of,
  requirements for, 23-24, 26, 140
  nn.71-72, 141 n.75, 166 n.2, 176
  n.80; Nazis, 22-26; Pajama-*Putsch*,
  83-87, 172 nn.40-41, 173 n.46;
  plots to kill members of the navy,
  26; plots to kill students and state
  representatives, 26-27; publications, 24-25, 57; recruitment within
  military and police, 26, 57-58, 142
  n.90, 166 n.2, 171 n.36; secret
  code, 84-85; Severo Fournier, 85-
  86, 88, 171 n.37, 171 n.39, 172
  n.43; social programs, 25; uniform,
  salute, and symbols, 24-25, 26. *See
  also* Partido da Ação Integralista
  and Salgado, Plínio
adelfis, 61, 90
Admiral Graf Spee, 36, 94
agricultural labor. *See* rural labor
Aguiar, Frota, 165 n.153
Alberto, João. *See* Barros, João Alberto
  Lins de

About the Author

R. S. ROSE is an independent researcher. He has published on induced abortion in the Republic of Ireland, racism and ethnic discrimination in the Swedish job market, and elite violence in Brazil. He can be reached at: rsrose@altavista.net

ISBN 0-313-31358-x

EAN

HARDCOVER BAR CODE